WESTMINSTER
The Art, Architecture and Archaeology of the Royal Abbey and Palace

General Editor Helen Lunnon

WESTMINSTER
II. The Art, Architecture and Archaeology of the Royal Palace

Edited by
Warwick Rodwell *and* Tim Tatton-Brown

The British Archaeological Association
Conference Transactions XXXIX, Part II

The Association is very grateful to the Palace of Westminster
for a generous grant towards the cost of publishing this volume.

Cover illustration: 'The First Day of Term':
Westminster Hall, 1758, coloured line engraving by H.-F. Gravelot
Palace of Westminster Collection, WOA 673

ISBN Hardback 978-1-910887-27-1
ISBN Paperback 978-1-910887-26-4

Parts I and II
ISBN Hardback 978-1-910887-29-5
ISBN Paperback 978-1-910887-28-8

© The British Archaeological Association 2015. All rights reserved. No part of this publication may be reproduced, stored in a retrieval system or transmitted in any form or by any means (electronic, mechanical, photocopying, recording or otherwise) without the written permission of the copyright holders.

Photocopying For users in the UK, the Copyright Licensing Agency, cla@cla.co.uk, is mandated to give permission to make copies. For Australia, please see www.copyright.com.au or www.copyright.org.au for more information. For North America and the rest of the world, permission is granted by the copyright holder for libraries and others registered with the Copyright Clearance Center (CCC), www.copyright.com.

Disclaimer Statements in the volume reflect the views of the authors, and not necessarily those of the Association, editors or publisher.

Product or corporate names may be trademarks or registered trademarks, and are used only for identification and explanation without intent to infringe.

LONDON AND NEW YORK

PUBLISHED FOR THE BRITISH ARCHAEOLOGICAL ASSOCIATION

Published 2017 by Routledge
2 Park Square, Milton Park, Abingdon, Oxon OX14 4RN
711 Third Avenue, New York, NY 10017, USA

Routledge is an imprint of the Taylor & Francis Group, an informa business

Contents

	PAGE
List of Abbreviations	vi
Preface	vii
An Introduction to the Topography of the Medieval Palace of Westminster JOHN CROOK	1
Romanesque Westminster Hall and its Roof ROLAND B. HARRIS and DANIEL MILES with an appendix by THOMAS HILL	22
The Great Hall at Caen and its Affinities with Westminster EDWARD IMPEY	72
Henry III's Palace at Westminster VIRGINIA JANSEN	89
St Stephen's Chapel, Westminster JOHN GOODALL	111
Late-14th-Century Reconstruction of Westminster Hall JULIAN MUNBY	120
Parliaments, MPs and the Buildings of Westminster in the Middle Ages DAVID HARRISON	133
A Monument to St Edward the Confessor: Henry III's Great Chamber at Westminster and its Paintings CHRISTOPHER WILSON	152
'The New Tower at the End of the King's Garden': The Jewel Tower and the Royal Treasure JEREMY ASHBEE with an appendix by PAUL EVERSON	187
The Topography of the Old Palace of Westminster, 1510–1834 MARK COLLINS	206
The New Palace of Westminster STEVEN BRINDLE	257

List of Abbreviations

Antiq. J.	*Antiquaries Journal*
Archaeol. J.	*Archaeological Journal*
Art Bull.	*Art Bulletin*
AS	All Souls College, Oxford
BAA Trans.	*British Archaeological Association Transactions*
BL	British Library, London
BM	British Museum, London
CCR	*Calendar of the Close Rolls*
CLR	*Calendar of the Liberate Rolls*
CPR	*Calendar of the Patent Rolls*
CR	*Close Rolls*
JBAA	*Journal of the British Archaeological Association*
L&P	J. S. Brewer, J. Gairdner and R. H. Brodie ed., *Letters and Papers, Foreign and Domestic, of the Reign of Henry VIII*, 21 vols (London 1862–1910 and 1920–32)
LMA	London Metropolitan Archive
MoLAS	Museum of London Archaeology Service
MPW	Medieval Palace of Westminster (images forming part of the 'Medieval Palace of Westminster Research Project' funded by the Arts and Humanities Research Board, currently held by John Crook)
PR	*Patent Rolls*
RCHME	Royal Commission on the Historical Monuments of England
SAL	Society of Antiquaries of London
TLAMAS	*Transactions of the London and Middlesex Archaeological Society*
TNA	The National Archives, Kew
VCH	Victoria County History
WAM	Westminster Abbey Muniments
WCA	Westminster City Archives
WS	Wren Society
WSA	Westminster School Archives

Editors' Preface

THE summer conference of 2013 took place between Saturday 20 and Wednesday 24 July in London, the theme being the *Architecture and Archaeology of the Royal Abbey and Palace of Westminster*. Although the Association based its 1984 conference on the City of London, it had not been to Westminster since 1902. The Lord Mayor of Westminster was President at that time, and in his inaugural address he mused on the fact that it had taken the Association fifty-nine years to bring its annual congress to Westminster, but expressed great satisfaction that it had finally done so in the year of the coronation of King Edward VII (*JBAA*, ns, 9 (1903), 2).

After an interval of a further 111 years, holding the Association's 2013 conference at Westminster was equally felicitous, falling as it did just six weeks after Her Majesty The Queen had celebrated the diamond jubilee of her coronation in the Abbey in 1953. The conference was jointly hosted by the Dean and Chapter of Westminster, Westminster School, and the Palace of Westminster. Unlike the 1902 congress, when delegates went on excursions around London and the home counties, the 2013 conference was firmly focused on the Abbey and Palace, but also included Westminster School, which was established within the monastic precinct and adopted many of its buildings.

The conference was over-subscribed, necessitating a ballot for places. In all, 192 delegates attended, the highest number recorded in the history of the Association. Twelve scholarships were awarded to students covering the full costs of the conference, and five scholarships that allowed students to attend lectures but not the site visits. In total, twenty-five papers were read in Westminster School Hall (formerly the monastic dormitory).

In the late afternoon of Saturday the conference enjoyed its first visit to the Abbey, when the chapter-house, Undercroft Museum and Pyx Chamber were open. On Sunday and Monday delegates split into groups to visit parts of the Abbey not normally accessible to the public, including the triforium (where the Abbey's new museum and gallery is to be established), the Shrine of Edward the Confessor, the Cosmati pavement in the sanctuary, the Coronation Chair, the chapter-house crypt, St Faith's Chapel, the Islip Chapel, the Library, Jerusalem Chamber and College Hall. There were also extensive tours of Westminster School and the surviving monastic precincts. Tuesday afternoon took the conference to St Margaret's Church and the Palace of Westminster, where on-site presentations were made.

The President's reception was held in the east walk of the great cloister, while the Association was also honoured with receptions and dinners in the Abbey cellarium, College Garden, College Hall and the Members' Dining Room in the Palace of Westminster, for which we offer grateful thanks to the Dean and Chapter of Westminster, Westminster School, the House of Commons and English Heritage. The reception in College Garden, which followed a visit to the Jewel Tower, marked the launch of a new 'red guide' to the Tower, and we are grateful to English Heritage, and to Simon Thurley, Edward Impey and the guidebook's author, Jeremy Ashbee, for honouring the conference with its launch. Holding the conference dinner in the 14th-century College Hall was an enormous privilege granted by the Dean, the Very Reverend Dr John Hall, who attended in person and gave a very warm and entertaining speech of welcome. Lindy Grant, the President, was in attendance throughout the conference, introducing proceedings and offering eloquent thanks to our various hosts.

Preface

The Association wishes to record its deep gratitude to all those who assisted in the organization and smooth running of the conference, in the first place, for granting permission for privileged access to, and use of, buildings which are not normally available to visiting groups: the Dean and Chapter of Westminster; Dr Stephen Spurr, Headmaster of Westminster School; and Chris Silcock, School Bursar. Similarly, we would like to thank David Harrison and Mark Collins, who facilitated access to areas in the Palace of Westminster. Organizing an event such as this for a large number of delegates, in the heart of London, at the height of the tourist season, presented unprecedented challenges for the Association, not least on account of the level of security in force in all three of the hosting institutions. Any number of things could have gone wrong, but two years of careful planning, patient negotiation and enormous goodwill from all concerned paid off, and everything ran like clockwork.

The Association is most grateful to the lecturers for sharing the fruits of their researches, and would also like to thank most warmly the on-site speakers and guides, without whom the visits would have been much the poorer. Collectively, the volume of new information and fresh insights that they presented is truly impressive. We are additionally grateful to everyone for responding to a tight production schedule for these *Transactions*. Nearly all the speakers have contributed to the present volume, to which have been added a further three papers arising from on-site presentations by Steven Brindle (the New Palace), Martin Henig (the Roman sarcophagus) and Eddie Smith (the Westminster School buildings). A fourth paper kindly offered by Paul Binski and Emily Guerry has also been included.

For help in setting up the complex visits to the Abbey, and for assisting more generally, the Association would like to record its deep gratitude to Ptolemy Dean, Surveyor of the Fabric; Tony Trowles, Librarian and Head of the Collection; Matthew Payne, Keeper of the Muniments; Diane Gibbs, Museum Coordinator; Vanessa Simeoni, Head Conservator; and Marie Louise Sauerberg, Painting Conservator. All made site presentations. Many other members of staff at Westminster Abbey also helped in various ways, both in planning the conference and in its day-to-day running. Particular mention must be made of Sir Stephen Lamport KCVO, Receiver General; Lorraine Rossdale, Head of Event Management; Alex Anderson, Head Marshal; and Martin Castledine, Dean's Verger; and their respective teams. The volunteers responsible for keeping delegates refreshed with teas, coffees and lunches did sterling work, and the conference would have seized up without Jenny Freeman, Susan Rigg and Robert Tatton-Brown. Gareth Hughes also rendered valuable administrative assistance on site.

Ultimately, there are many individuals without whose assistance the conference would not have run smoothly, but the Association wishes to offer particular thanks to Kate Davey, conference organizer, and Abigail Wheatley, conference secretary, for making this such a successful event. They had to weather an exceptionally challenging conference, both in terms of coping with the varying wishes and needs of the greatest number of delegates the Association has ever accommodated at a conference, and the logistics of orchestrating visits to so many places — some of them very restricted — in three complexes of buildings that lie at the heart of Britain's royal and ecclesiastical life, and its seat of government. We are profoundly in their debt.

Finally, the magnitude of the papers resulting from the conference rendered publication in a single volume impracticable, and it was decided that in this instance the Transactions should be divided into two parts. The papers relating to Westminster Abbey are contained in Part I, and those relating to the Palace of Westminster in Part II.

Preface

In order to make it possible for each part to stand alone, this preface and the two plans accompanying Tim Tatton-Brown's introductory paper on the topography of Westminster are included in both.

The editors are enormously grateful for the help they have received in bringing this complex work to publication: Joseph Spooner painstakingly copy-edited the whole manuscript, John Osborn and Fred Uhde kindly defrayed the cost of preparing several line drawings, John McNeill made a wealth of valuable comments and suggestions, and Linda Fisher undertook the exacting task of laying out and setting up the volume for printing with great efficiency and patience.

Warwick Rodwell and Tim Tatton-Brown
Conference Convenors

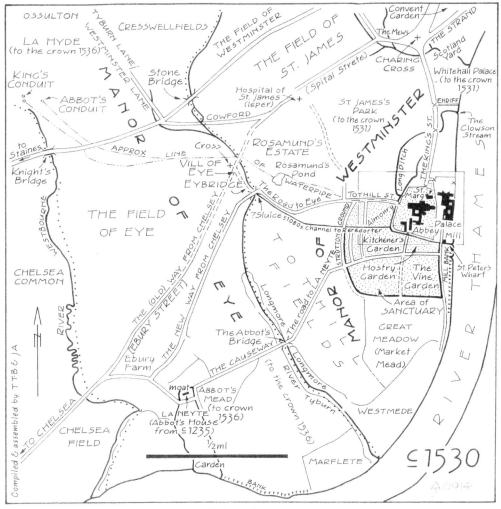

PLAN A. Reconstructed plan of the Westminster area in *c.* 1530
Jill Atherton

Preface

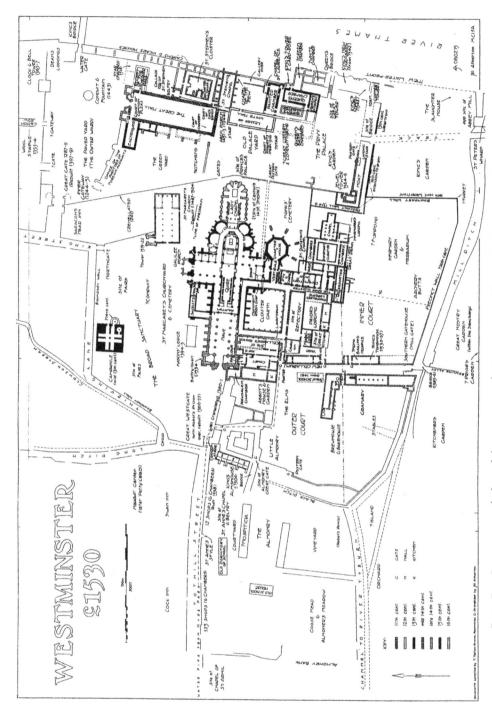

PLAN B. Reconstructed plan of the precincts of Westminster Abbey and Westminster Palace in *c.* 1530
Jill Atherton

An Introduction to the Topography of the Medieval Palace of Westminster

JOHN CROOK

The main purpose of this paper is to provide an overview of the architecture of the medieval Palace. Other contributors to this volume have written more extensively on specific buildings, and I have accorded correspondingly briefer treatment to these. I also consider the dating of certain elements of the medieval complex, drawing on the investigations of the Medieval Palace of Westminster Research Project.[1]

THE devastating fire of 16–17 October 1834 is usually regarded as the abrupt demise of one of the most important medieval architectural complexes in England.[2] That is a simplification, and is not entirely accurate, for by 1834 the amount of medieval survival was already limited, as is evident from the plans drawn immediately after the fire by Robert Billings (Collins, Fig. 14, 226) and, a few months later, by Charles Richardson (Fig. 1),[3] both of whom depicted in black the medieval work that was still standing before the conflagration: it comprised but a small proportion of the entire complex.[4]

The destruction of the medieval Palace had indeed begun in the 16th century, when, twenty years or so after a fire in 1512, much of the Privy Palace at the south end of the site was demolished, providing some 3,000 cartloads of building materials for Henry VIII's Palace of Whitehall.[5] St Stephen's Chapel, the debating chamber of the Commons since 1548, had lost its clerestory elevations under Christopher Wren in 1692, and in 1800 James Wyatt's attempt at gaining a few more square feet of seating to accommodate the new Irish MPs had resulted in the destruction of important mid-14th-century wall-paintings. The medieval origins of the chamber were unrecognizable from within. Other buildings had also been demolished only a few years before the fire, ironically at a time of increasing antiquarian interest. The upper storey of the 14th-century bell-tower of St Stephen's Cloister had been removed in 1805 or just before, when the lower parts were adapted to house a grand entrance stair to the Speaker's House. In 1808, three bays of a long range of building on the east side of New Palace Yard, ultimately dating from 1507 if not earlier,[6] had been taken down; one further bay was demolished in 1822. In 1823, the former Queen's Chamber and Queen's Chapel at its south end (later wrongly called the Prince's Chamber), built in 1237–38 for Eleanor of Provence, had been razed when the Lords moved into the Lesser Hall, formerly the Court of Requests. The same year had witnessed the demolition of the Court of the Exchequer, on the west side of the Great Hall, an Elizabethan building of 1569–70 that retained elements of Henry III's work on the south and east sides.[7] Much of the Receipt of the Exchequer on the other side of the hall had also been demolished or greatly modified by then.[8]

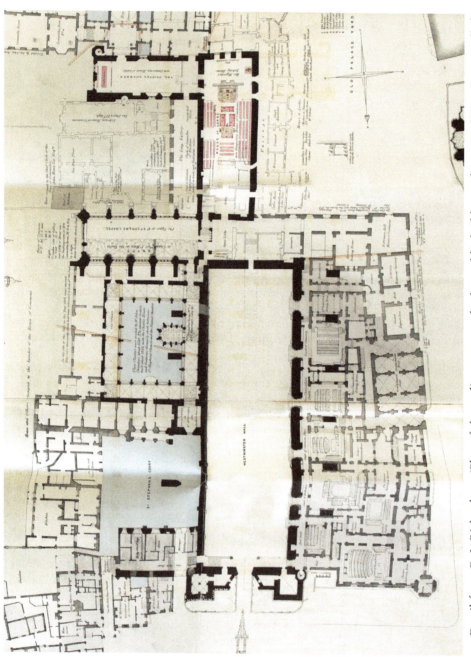

Fig. 1. Detail from C. J. Richardson, 'Plan of the parliamentary and other public buildings adjacent to Westminster Hall, from a survey made with the intention of supplying the necessary information for the proper consideration of the proposed new buildings', August 1835 (MPW 409)

Topography of the Medieval Palace

Thus, several important elements of the medieval Palace had been destroyed before the conflagration. It is by no means sure that the medieval shell of St Stephen's Chapel would have survived even if there had been no fire, for the radical MP Joseph Hume was at that very time campaigning vigorously for the Commons to be rehoused, and the knock-on effect would have been considerable.

Conversely, the fire had the effect of bringing to view several medieval buildings by burning away subsequent accretions (notably Wyatt's regrettable frontage to New Palace Yard), and the medieval fabric had proved surprisingly resilient. The Lesser Hall and the Painted Chamber were indeed sufficiently intact for Sir Robert Smirke to refurbish them as the temporary House of Commons and House of Lords respectively. The buildings (together with the burnt-out shell of St Stephen's Chapel) would undoubtedly have been retained had the fire occurred in recent times, but by 1835 the momentum for a clean sweep of all medieval fabric was too strong, and everything was cleared away as the new buildings went up, the Lesser Hall being demolished in 1851.

Before 1800, graphical evidence for the Palace is limited. The earliest extant views show the precincts from the river. One of a pair of anonymous views of c. 1530 attributed to Lucas Cornelisz de Kock (Collins, Fig. 1, 207),[9] and Wyngaerde's slightly later panorama,[10] provide tantalizing hints as to the then extant buildings of the Privy Palace (actually labelled 'The Kinges palace' by Wyngaerde), and also show St Stephen's Chapel before the loss of the clerestory. Extant maps and plans are of later date, well after the destruction of the southern part of the Privy Palace. The 'Agas' map of the end of the 16th century is of limited interpretive value;[11] of greater cartographic merit are William Morgan's map of c. 1682 and, five years later, a plan of the Palace published in Sandford's *Coronation of James II*, illustrating the processional route for that event.[12] This clearly shows the main division of the Palace into an outer court, 'New Palace Yard'; an intermediate area often called the Green Yard; and the site of the old Privy Palace, 'Old Palace Yard'. This tripartite layout is still vaguely discernible today, though the Green Yard is now the regrettable racetrack of St Margaret's Street, separating Westminster Abbey from the Palace.

By the early 19th century, there is abundant graphical evidence for the layout of the Palace, and this provided the raw material for the Medieval Palace of Westminster Research Project (MPW).[13] The project seeks to study the lost Palace by means of the rich archive of graphical material left by cartographers, architects, antiquaries, and artists before the final demise of the Palace in 1834, and to use that material in conjunction with documentary sources and archaeology in order to reconstruct the medieval layout as accurately as possible. The project has made use, for example, of the possibilities opened up by drawing and rectification software, allowing perspective views to be converted into orthogonal elevations. An early priority was to catalogue and evaluate the available sources, and the MPW database currently holds around 1,700 items. At the same time, work began on the creation of an accurate base plan of the medieval Palace. That this was possible was due to the survey undertaken in the very year of the fire by Thomas Chawner and Henry Rhodes.[14] Ironically, the survey was commissioned in order to inform the proposals being urged by Joseph Hume to rehouse the Commons. It includes plans of the Palace on all levels, and a section — the latter being of especial value, as it allows levels to be determined, there being no spot heights on the plans. Less accurate, but full of useful historical detail, is the extraordinary plan by William Capon, compiled over a thirty-year period from 1793 and thus including many of the buildings that were lost in the early years of the

19th century.[15] These, and other surveys, may be superimposed on the accurate modern survey of the Palace undertaken for the Parliamentary Works Directorate in August 1991 by Plowman Craven. It must, however, be recognized that the location of many elements of the Palace, and particularly the Privy Palace (which was demolished in the early 16th century, so predating any significant graphical evidence), will only ever be schematic. Lucas Cornelisz de Kock's view stands alone to taunt the researcher.

To date, the Project has made full assessments of two of the most important buildings of the medieval Palace. The Great Hall ('Westminster Hall') is discussed in detail elsewhere in these proceedings by Roland Harris and Daniel Miles.[16] The Lesser Hall was a free-standing building, south of the Great Hall and off-set slightly eastwards. As already noted, it had housed the Lords from 1801 until 1834, and a few months after the fire (which actually started in its basement) was still capable of being put into sufficiently good order to serve as the House of Commons for a further sixteen years while Barry and Pugin's new Houses of Parliament were under construction immediately to the east.

THE LESSER HALL

BEFORE 1834, the medieval origins of the Lesser Hall were not at all apparent either internally or externally, though three Romanesque windows were briefly exposed at the south end *c.* 1800 before being covered up again. The appearance of the building had been drastically changed in 1722–25 when the floor level was raised over a brick undercroft and the upper walls heightened with the addition of Diocletian windows. The fire of 1834 removed the later accretions, and this was particularly dramatic internally, where Romanesque wall arcading and further windows, hidden for many centuries, were revealed (Fig. 2). Frederick Mackenzie seems to have been the only artist to record this important detail.[17] Also visible was the head of a 13th-century doorway in the south-east corner, half-embedded below the raised 1720s floor, and this doorway was also revealed in the adjacent Painted Chamber after a similarly raised floor there had burnt away. Rectification of Mackenzie's engraving produced a viable internal elevation (Fig. 3). Levelling data could be worked out from one of John Carter's sections, and the end-product was a three-dimensional computer model of the hall (Fig. 4).[18]

The hall as thus reconstructed was shown with a wooden floor structure based on that of the Painted Chamber. Clearly, such a floor was in existence by the time the access door to the chamber was created, and the documentary evidence suggests that after a major fire in 1298 a wooden floor required only to be replanked in the middle and strengthened by means of extra posts in the basement.[19] Whether, as we previously suggested, the hall was two-storeyed from the mid-12th century now seems less certain.[20] The floor may, for example, have been inserted after an earlier fire, of 1263, recorded in that year.

A little more consideration needs to be given to the date of the hall. The mid-12th-century style of the architectural features already mentioned (the chevron windows at the south end, and geminated windows and wall arcading of the internal east wall) is indisputable, and the upper parts of the medieval building may therefore probably be equated with the *noua aula* first mentioned in a pipe roll of 1166/7.[21] The earliest historians of the Palace claimed, however, to have observed evidence that the hall was of earlier date. William Capon's plan calls it 'The Ancient Hall of Edward the

FIG. 2. Engraving of the interior of the Lesser Hall after a sketch by Frederick Mackenzie
c. 1835
Rokewode, 'Painted Chamber' (as n. 17), pl. XXVI, detail 'G' (MPW 1106)

FIG. 3. Rectified version of Fig. 2

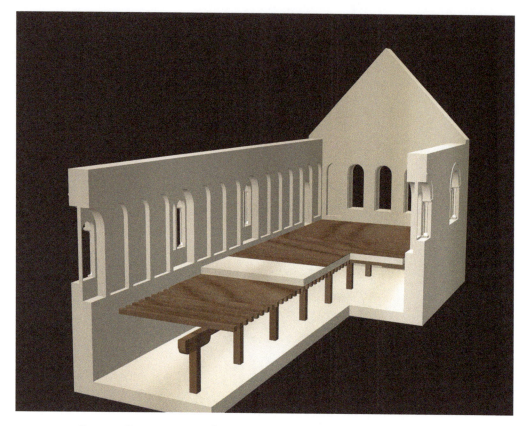

Fig. 4. Cut-away view of computer model of the medieval Lesser Hall

Confessor' and indicates that he believed it to have originally been a single-storey building. He was, however, wrong in his depiction of a cross-passage at the north end, as the extant plans of the works of 1722 show that before that date the two doorways in the side walls were not opposite each other; there is no reason to suppose that they were original features of the building. John Carter drew in 1800 and published in his *Ancient Architecture* an elevation, a section, and details of a 'Doorway in the basement story of the Court of Requests, Westminster' (Fig. 5).[22] With its steep chevron and cable mouldings, this could date from the late 11th century (see below). There must, however, be some doubt about whether Carter correctly gave its location, for an adjacent detail of the same plate depicts a 'View, looking east, into a place for occasional retirement [that is, a privy] at the north-east angle of the basement story of the Court of Requests'. This undoubtedly shows a garderobe in the Queen's Chamber,[23] as is clear from J. T. Smith's 'flat-pack' view of that building.[24] It is therefore possible that the door head was also in the basement of the Queen's Chamber, and that John Carter simply mislabelled the drawings, confused perhaps by the fact that the 'House of Lords' had moved from one building to another.

There are also problems of interpretation with an engraving from a drawing done by Frederick Mackenzie of another supposedly early feature in that cellarage, namely

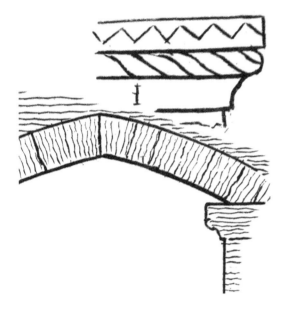

FIG. 5. Doorhead probably also in the basement of the Queen's Chamber, drawn by John Carter
Carter, The Ancient Architecture of England (as n. 22), detail of I, pl. XLIV (MPW 257)

a round-headed arch supported on detached jamb-shafts with Attic bases and foliate capitals, usually interpreted as a fireplace (Fig. 6). Another engraving of it was included by J. H. Parker when he republished Thomas Rickman's *Attempt to Discriminate the Styles of Architecture in England*,[25] differing somewhat in the detail of the foliate capital. It is regrettable that only engravings survive rather than the original drawings, which might have been a more objective record. Lethaby thought the arch might have dated from 'earlier than Henry II', and it is true that a date of around 1130 would be appropriate for the feature as depicted.[26] Where the early 19th-century observers could have seen it in the basement of the Lesser Hall is unclear, given that the brick vaulting inserted in the 1720s, replacing the medieval timber floor, would have masked much of the internal wall-face. The feature does not seem to be shown in the surviving plans of the basement, unless it be the rectangular feature at the south end visible in the Chawner and Rhodes survey. This would be below the three chevron windows at main level, which would require the fireplace to have been redundant by the time those windows were built. This dubious evidence apart, though, the whole building could well have been erected shortly after Henry II's accession in 1154.[27] Although the hall is recorded as having been severely damaged by the two 13th-century fires (1263 and 1298), after the second of which major repairs were made, the fact that 12th-century features survived at main level precludes these repairs' having involved a major reconstruction of the walls. The floor, on the other hand, which appears always to have been of timber until the 1720s, may have been built following the first fire, as suggested above; after the second fire it required only to be replanked in the middle and strengthened by means of extra posts in the basement.[28]

Even if the Lesser Hall was predominantly a mid-12th-century structure, it is likely to have replaced an earlier building on the same site. There was certainly a palace to the east of the Abbey in Edward the Confessor's day, and perhaps before that, and its buildings are unlikely have stood north or east of Rufus's hall, which would have been below high tide level. Indeed, it is surely more likely that the new Great Hall was constructed on a new, greenfield site, an area not hitherto used because it was so close to high-water level. The only available space for Edward's palace was to the south, the area that later developed as the Privy Palace.

THE PAINTED CHAMBER

PERPENDICULAR to the Lesser Hall, at its south end, was the Painted Chamber. The medieval origins of this building were more fully recognized in the early 19th century, and it was well recorded. In 1820, Edward Crocker produced a 'flat-pack' view of the main level, which, in conjunction with Chawner and Rhodes' survey and levelling data obtainable from our analysis of the Great and Lesser halls, would have the potential for computer modelling. Amongst other features, Crocker's drawings are of value in locating the precise positions of the Romanesque windows that preceded the well-known 13th-century remodelling discussed elsewhere in this volume. As noted above, the primary fabric of the chamber was even clearer after the fire, when the 12th-century origins of several of the windows, subsequently remodelled by Henry III, became apparent.

The basement was also recorded both by perspective drawings and watercolours and plans, some with measured dimensions inserted.[29] In this part of the building, too, there are indications of its Romanesque origins. Whereas the greater part of the building had a timber first floor, the eastern third of the undercroft was partitioned from the rest by a thick cross-wall, and at this end was a rectangular chamber oriented north–south with three bays of groin vaulting, suggestive of a date perhaps as early as the last years of the 11th century. It is likely that this was part of 'Marculf's Chamber', whose east wall appears to have formed part of the Thames waterfront in the early 14th century.[30]

THE QUEEN'S CHAMBER

A visitor exploring the medieval remains before 1823 could have left this undercroft via its external door and ascended the so-called 'Guy Fawkes' Stairs' at the south-east corner of the Painted Chamber block. This led to the lobby at the north end of the old House of Lords, located in the Queen's Chamber, with its chapel at the south end. As with the Lesser Hall, no medieval work was visible internally in the Queen's Chamber, though a watercolour of August 1823 shows 13th-century features being exposed by the removal of panelling,[31] and this was recorded by the office of Sir John Soane in the form of a 'flat-pack'.[32] The adjoining chapel, however, was still lit by its original lancets, with rere-arches of the typical Henry III form.

Various details visible in antiquarian drawings hint that this range, too, might have predated Henry III's obvious intervention. At the south-west corner of the Queen's Chamber was a two-storey lobby, and the doorway into the undercroft of the chapel has imposts that are clearly Romanesque, as shown in a watercolour drawing by Capon (Fig. 7). It is surely unlikely that Henry III's masons would have recycled a doorway in a completely new building, and the inference is that here, too, some elements of the Romanesque Privy Palace were reused as the foundations of the 13th-century work.

Views of the exterior of the Queen's Chamber and its chapel also show various redundant openings that seem to predate the 13th-century work, and there are

Topography of the Medieval Palace

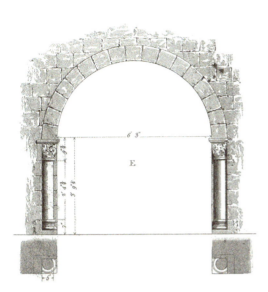 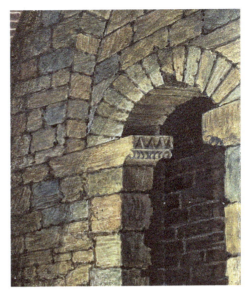

FIG. 6. Romanesque arch said to be in the basement of the Lesser Hall
Rokewode, 'Painted Chamber' (as n. 17), pl. XXVI, detail 'E' (MPW 281)

FIG. 7. Romanesque impost blocks in cellarage doorway, drawn by William Capon
Detail from WCA, box 57, no. 23 (MPW 597)

possibly some indications of Romanesque masonry, such as the round-headed doorway that peeks behind a half-demolished wall in J. T. Smith's 1807 engraving (Fig. 8).

To this evidence must be added the door head mentioned above, formerly attributed to the Lesser Hall. Its location is uncertain, and of course it is just possible that, despite the differences in the form of the arch and the lower moulding, Carter and Capon were depicting the same feature. The unusually steep, very simple chevron decoration, and the cable moulding, find a useful parallel in the nave and tower of St Andrew's Church, Great Dunham (Norfolk, Fig. 9), where other decorative features such as chip-carving suggest a late-11th-century date.[33]

After the Henry III reconstruction, the 'Queen's Hall' was another of the buildings damaged in the 1298 fire, and is therefore probably to be equated with the Queen's Chamber. Like the Lesser Hall, its floor was of timber, and, according to the *Memorandum* by the clerk of works for Westminster datable to 1284/5, 'The flooring of this hall, of which the greater portion had been burnt, and the remaining part was weak and decayed, was repaired and raised, and ceiled underneath'.[34]

EXTERIOR OF THE PAINTED CHAMBER, THE CHAPEL, AND THE RECEIPT

THE other buildings of the Privy Palace are analysed in this volume by Christopher Wilson, so our imaginary tour now returns northwards, up the east side of the Queen's Chamber and past the end of the Painted Chamber. At the time of the 1834 fire, this area was the Cotton Garden, named after Robert Cotton's house, but in the early

Fig. 8. Possible remains of a Romanesque arch at ground level on the east side of the Queen's Chamber, drawn by J. T. Smith, 10 October 1807
Sixty-two additional plates to Smith's Antiquities of Westminster (London 1807–09) (MPW 35)

Fig. 9. St Andrew's Church, Great Dunham (Norfolk): details of impost to blind arcading on north side of nave (left), and north-west tower pier (right)
John Crook

14th century the end of the building was in the Thames. In 1319, Peter de Skyrbeck received payment for building an arch buttress whose construction included 'long blocks of Aylesford stone', standing in the water at the end of Marculf's Chamber.[35] That the waterfront was on this alignment was confirmed in 1803, when a line of piles, interpreted by J. T. Smith as being 'to keep off the Craft', was discovered.[36]

By *c.* 1800, this corner was an architectural jumble, the main feature being a huge brick buttress that had been erected to compensate for the loss of abutment of a series of buildings, the last of which was the house, demolished in 1725, that Sir Robert Cotton had acquired in 1622. These buildings have left their mark in a number of features. In the 13th century, this was the site of Henry III's private chapel, with a squint in the communicating wall so he could see the altar from his bed.

FIG. 10. South-east corner of the Painted Chamber; detail of drawing by John Carter, c. 1809. To the right of the post-medieval brick buttress the remains of fan vaulting are visible, supported on heraldic corbels of the time of Richard II; below are the roundels that possibly held busts of the Caesars which gave their names to the bookshelves in the embrasures below.
WCA, box 57, no. 29C (MPW 589)

The remains of fan vaulting must be later still (Fig. 10). The surviving tas-de-charges are supported on heraldic bosses that include the arms of Bohemia impaling the Empire, suggesting that the vault dates from the time of Ann of Bohemia, queen consort of Richard II 1382–94. Below are oval-shaped recesses with ornate stone frames, evidently of later date. A plan from the office of Sir Christopher Wren indicates that Robert Cotton's famous library abutted this wall at first-floor level, and Tim Tatton-Brown has plausibly suggested that the bookshelves (whose position is indicated on Wren's plan) were located within the embrasures below the ovals, and that the portrait busts of the Caesars, after which the contents of each shelf were named, stood within the ovals.[37]

North of the Romanesque wing, which from the 13th century housed the Painted Chamber, was St Stephen's Chapel, corner to corner with the end of the Great Hall. The chapel in its final medieval form was erected in a series of interrupted phases by the first to the third Edward,[38] but there is documentary evidence for a Romanesque predecessor, probably on the same site. The design of the chapel as built is discussed by John Goodall elsewhere in this volume.[39] Linking the private chapel and St Stephen's Chapel in its final form was a timber-framed walkway or *alura*,[40] and it is therefore possible that the area enclosed by the three wings comprised a formal cloister. It seems likely that the 'Chapel of the Pew' was located over the east walk of this cloister, adjacent to and accessed from the east end of St Stephen's Chapel.

Running eastwards towards the river, from the north end of the Great Hall, was the 'Receipt of the Exchequer', which appears to have transferred here from elsewhere within the Palace in the later 13th century.[41] The Receipt was demolished in 1823, but its south-east corner was partially excavated in 1913. The position corresponded exactly with Capon's plan. The footings, with diagonally tooled blocks and a plain chamfer, were undoubtedly Romanesque,[42] and the thickness of the walls (shown on Richardson's plan) also hint at an early origin. The south side of the building was recorded by J. T. Smith,[43] and more analytically in an annotated sketch of *c.* 1810 by

John Carter.[44] Two round-headed window arches, which Carter noted were 'old', might be Romanesque.

THE COLLEGE

THE area between the chapel and the Receipt formed part of the site of the college of canons and vicars that Edward III founded in 1348. Accommodation had to be provided for a total of 38 people (a dean, 12 canons, 13 vicars, 4 clerks, 6 choristers, a virger, and the keeper of the Chapel of the Pew). By a charter dated 1 January 1354 the king granted them a long, approximately rectangular 'space' (*platea*) west of the Great Hall, between the chapel and the Receipt. This was intended for the cloister and 'houses' for the college. The canons may also have occupied this part of the Palace for a short time (though the dean initially occupied a house towards the northeast corner of New Palace Yard); as explained more fully below, by the end of the century they were accommodated on a plot of land further north, which the king had previously granted to the late earl of Kent together with another property formerly occupied by Roger of Heyton.[45] The situation was in effect a reversal of that of St George's College Windsor, another of Edward III's foundations and exactly contemporary with St Stephen's, where canons and vicars initially occupied the twenty-five 'chambers' of a purpose-built residential cloister, but where the vicars moved within a century into their own 'vicars' close', leaving the canons in sole occupation of Canons' Cloister.

The areas, both within and outside the Palace, described in Edward III's charter are confirmed by a *Composition* or agreement (*Compositio*) sealed in 1394 by the abbot and monks of Westminster Abbey and the dean and canons of St Stephen's College.[46] The *Composition* was intended to settle the question of whether the college should pay tithes and other dues to the Abbey's church of St Margaret, in whose parish the college theoretically lay. The *Composition* is more precise than the charter in that it gives the dimensions of each area, often to the nearest half-inch. Thus, the distance between the chapel and the Receipt, where the cloister and chapter-house were still to be built (*construenda*), measured 208 ft 10½ in. (63.67 m),[47] and the maximum distance from the wall-face of the Great Hall to the exterior east wall of the 'new houses of the vicars of the said college' was said to be 95 ft 8 in. (29.16 m), though there are difficulties with this dimension as explained below.[48]

The north–south dimension may be checked from Chawner and Rhodes's survey, which shows the outline of the Receipt, admittedly after the reconstruction of 1823 (Fig. 11). The distance from the chapel to the Receipt (excluding the chapel buttresses) may be scaled from this survey as 63.45 m, tolerably close to the 63.67 m specified in the *Composition*. The east–west dimension may also be checked, for, although the vicars' houses were demolished at the Reformation,[49] elements of the *lower* part of their west wall, facing what was then 'Speaker's Court',[50] appear to have survived until 1834. One of J. T. Smith's engravings clearly shows two 14th-century doors in the lower part of the wall (Fig. 12). The embrasures of those blocked doorways are shown on Chawner and Rhodes' ground-plan. There is, however, a problem. Scaling from Chawner and Rhodes' survey, the wall face between those features is 24.94 m from the east face of the Great Hall.[51] The *Composition* states that the width of 29.16 m (95 ft 8 in.) is the maximum (*nec ultra*) width of the site (which is indeed slightly wider at this end), and reiterates that this dimension included the width of the vicars' houses: 'infra quos octoginta quindecim pedes & dimidium & duas pollices

Topography of the Medieval Palace

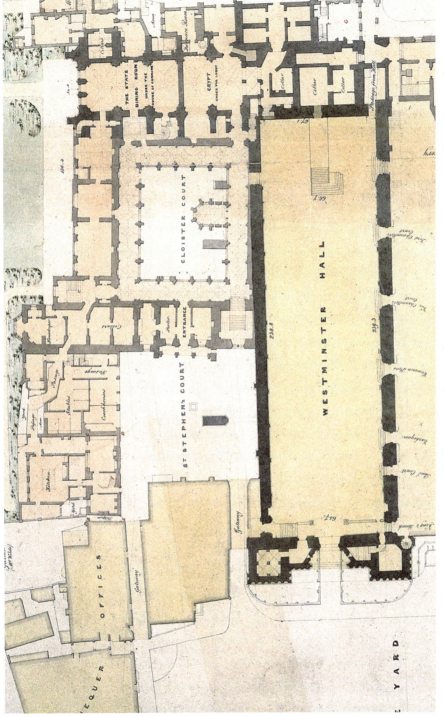

FIG. 11. Detail from T. Chawner and H. Rhodes's ground-plan of 1834 (east at top): 'No. 1. General Ground Plan of Westminster Hall, the Houses of Lords and Commons, and other public buildings situate between New Palace Yard ... and Parliament Place'
(*MPW 52*)

Fig. 12. View of the north-east corner of St Stephen's Court, showing two blocked 14th-century doorways surviving from the former vicars' houses
Smith, Antiquities *(as n. 24), facing 28 (MPW 826)*

etiam iam continetur latitudo dictarum domorum vicariorum'. Based on these measurements the houses would be only 4.22 m deep from east to west, including the thickness of their walls. It is surely more likely that the front to rear dimension of those houses is indicated by the thick interior wall that Chawner's survey (and Richardson's) show running parallel to the front wall-face of the buildings on the range on the east side of St Stephen's Court and New Palace Yard. Scaling from Chawner, this would give a more probable total depth (including the wall thicknesses) of 6.3 m. The discrepancy may perhaps be the result of scribal error in copying the extant manuscript of the *Composition*: the phrase 'octoginta quindecim pedes & dimidium & duas pollices', with its clumsy mixture of a half-foot and extra inches, looks suspect.

As already noted, the vicars' houses were already standing by 1394, but the cloister was still to be built. The south end of the range was, at the end of the 16th century, occupied by Mr Freke, the Auditor of the Exchequer.[52] His house was rebuilt as the east front of the Speaker's House by James Wyatt *c.* 1805–08,[53] and at the start of works in 1803, as noted above, a row of piles was discovered on the line of the east wall of that building, interpreted as being intended 'to keep off the Craft', and thus marking the old waterfront.[54] The outer face of that building, scaled from Chawner and Rhodes, was 31.29 m from the face of the south end of the Great Hall, so this suggests that there may have been a narrow strip of land between the back of the vicars' houses and the waterfront. The Thames is now about 65 m east of the rear of the vicars' houses.

Given the uncertainty over the width of the vicars' houses, it is difficult to take the analysis further and to suggest how far north the range might have extended. We know that there were thirteen vicars' houses on the east side of a plot that measured 63.67 m from north to south. Allowing 400 mm for the thickness of the walls between the houses, this would provide a house for each vicar of an internal width of around 4.5 m. Assuming that the depth of each house was around 6.3 m, as suggested above, the dimensions would be very similar to those of the canons' and vicars' houses at Windsor, which averaged 4.5 m wide by 6.2 m deep. There is no reason to assume that the range extended further north than the south wall of the Receipt.

Within the area later known as 'St Stephen's Court' a bell-tower was constructed in the 1350s. As mentioned, its upper storey (an addition of *c.* 1395) was removed in 1805 or just before,[55] and the lower storey was converted into a grand entrance staircase to the Speaker's House.[56]

North of the Receipt the building that later became known as the Star Chamber was rebuilt in the 1340s (Fig. 13).[57] Beneath it was a chamber that was also granted to the college, which Edward's charter of 1354 states was formerly occupied by the clerk of the royal kitchen.[58] In 1394, it was described in the *Composition* as a 'low room beneath the Star Chamber formerly called the chamber of the clerk to the royal kitchen'.[59] The Star Chamber was extended northwards as far as the Water Gate *c.* 1517, when a new house 'adjoining the Sterred Chamber, and leading to the gate of the bridge of the Palace of Westminster' was constructed.[60] Here an uncharacteristic error by the authors of the *History of the King's Works* must be corrected. They stated that the range was rebuilt again in 1599–1602, citing a clerk of works' account that refers to work on 'the framed tymber roofe of the longe raunge of the newe buildinges nexte the streete where the officers of the housholde do lye'.[61] The reference to a street (rather than New Palace Yard) should have aroused suspicion. In fact the document clearly locates these works at 'Whitehall alias ye newe Pallace of Westmynster wth other places adioyninge', not at the Old Palace, which presumably would not have been accommodating the 'officers of the household' at the end of Elizabeth's reign.

Equally uncertain is the authors' identification as the same building of a structure mentioned in the same set of accounts. It is there called an 'old timber range', surely distinct from the 'longe raunge of the newe buildings' previously mentioned. The range was being refurbished, a bricklayer being paid for 'digging of the foundacon bringinge upp with bricke the twoe sides of the olde tymber raunge being twoe stories and a halfe in heighte with xiij gable endes making with bricks and finishinge with mortar on both sides of the same buildinge'.[62] The context of the entry again suggests that this building, too, was at the 'new palace' of Whitehall rather than the Old Palace, and it is perhaps unlikely to be, as the authors of the *History of the King's Works* suggested, the row depicted in Wenceslaus Hollar's well-known view of the Palace from the north-east (and indeed other later drawings), showing a regular array of six gables running immediately south from the Water Gate.[63] The west side of the range was drawn by Carter,[64] and before it was truncated in 1808 had five gables, which makes a total of eleven gables on either side rather than the thirteen mentioned

Fig. 13. South-east corner of New Palace Yard, showing another 14th-century doorway, assumed by the caption writer to form part of the building known as the Star Chamber, rebuilt in the 1340s; unsigned early-19th-century vignette
WCA, box 56, no. 29D (MPW 1017)

in the account. True, both J. T. Smith and Brayley and Britton observed that a doorway near the passage to Speaker's Court bore the initials ER and the date 1602,[65] but that might be mere coincidence.

NEW PALACE YARD

Our imaginary tour of the medieval Palace continues with the outer court known since the early 16th century as 'New Palace Yard'. This area, north of the end of Westminster Hall and the Exchequer, was always an open space as it is today. This provided plenty of room for the temporary 'halls' that were erected for the coronation of Edward II — the accounts of that event suggest there was a long marquee along the north side with smaller ones running southwards towards the Great Hall.[66] New Palace Yard was illustrated countless times in the 17th century, though most engravings are dependent on Wenceslaus Hollar's 1647 view (Collins, Fig. 2, 208).

The main entrance to the Yard (as we shall call it for this period) was in the northwest corner, though a gate that was first built under Edward I in 1287–89, but was reconstructed in the late 1390s at the same time as the Great Hall was remodelled, and therefore probably also to a design by Henry Yevele.[67] John Stow almost certainly wrongly attributed the final remodelling of the gate to Richard III, and this dating was accepted by Brayley and Britton and other antiquaries.[68] It was mostly taken down in 1706. The lower part of the south side of the tower appears to have survived in a wall between two of the taverns in what was then Union Street, which were demolished in 1807. The wall fragment was subsequently recorded by William Capon, who indicated it by a black rectangle and the words 'Part of the South Wall of the Ancient Gateway built by K. RICH^d III. 1484 discovered 1807 in which Wall was found a very curiously sculptured Capital representing K. Rufus and G: Grispinus [*sic, recte* Gislebertus?] Sub Abbot of Westminster'. His drawings of the capital show a figure capital of late-11th-/early-12th-century date. It was sold to a collector, Sir Gregory Osborne Page Turner, 4th Baronet, in 1831 and its location is now unknown.[69] A second gate, in the south-west corner of the Yard, led into the area that later was called the 'Green Court', north of the Privy Palace. This gate was built by Henry III and was demolished only in 1731.[70]

The Yard was bounded on the east side by the water frontage of the Thames, with the Water Gate already mentioned, which by the early 16th century was abutted by the north end of the extended Star Chamber. Northwards again was the water frontage and then, from the mid-14th century, the 'Wool Bridge', the landing stage of the Wool Staple that had been founded by Edward III by 1354.[71] The mainly timber-framed buildings of the Wool Staple, including the Weigh House, were erected along the north side of the west end of the Yard, and a long east–west wall was built the following year. The *Composition* makes it clear that this was regarded as the north wall of the Palace.[72] At its east end it abutted a long wall 'over the Thames', which served as a reference point for the deanery and canons' houses, discussed below. A little to the north of the Palace wall was a roadway (which remained under the jurisdiction of the Abbey monks) running from the Wool Bridge to the gate of the Weigh House. The roadway, the clock tower, and indeed the site of the Wool Staple, seem to be indicated on Norden's survey of 1593, but it is dangerous to attempt to deduce too much from a tiny detail of a large bird's-eye view.

Within ten years the Palace wall was interrupted by the great storeyed clock tower (*orologium*), another of Henry Yevele's projects.[73] It housed three bells, the largest of which, 'Edward of Westminster', held the same place in people's hearts as Big Ben does today and was audible from the City. The clock tower served as a reference point in John Stow's description of the so-called 'Merciless Parliament' of 1397, which took place in a temporary building erected between the tower and the north end of Westminster Hall, then being remodelled.[74] The tower is a prominent feature of Hollar's view of New Palace Yard, which also includes the public fountain known as the Conduit; this is first mentioned in 1399, but by Hollar's day it had been rebuilt with an obviously Tudor ogee roof. Remains of the structure were discovered during the hasty excavation of the Houses of Parliament underground car park in 1973.[75] William Capon's plan was, of course, drawn up long after the demolition of the clock tower, so it is probably not safe to use it as an indication of the position of the north wall of the Yard. By Capon's day, the site of the tower was engulfed in rows of houses with a raised terrace in front of them overlooking New Palace Yard. He could well have taken the position of the tower from earlier plans, notably that of James II's coronation route published by Sandford in 1687.[76] The latter plan is of some interest in showing a street called 'The Woolstaple', but there is no particular reason to suppose that this was on the line of the roadway between the quay and the Weigh House. By 1761, as Fourdrinier's plan shows, all the ancient building, wall, and road lines had been obliterated.

THE COLLEGE DEANERY

AT the east end of the Palace wall, in the angle with the Thames Wall, a site was allocated by a grant of Edward III to William de Sleford, surveyor of the king's works at the Palace of Westminster and one of the first canons of St Stephen's, who was installed as dean of St Stephen's in May 1369.[77] Its location is precisely stated in a Patent Roll entry of 1438: it was

situated within and on the wall of the king's said palace, adjoining 'le Wolbrigge' of the king's staple there on the east, and the clock tower [*orologium*] of the palace on the west, and the palace wall on the south running along from the said clock tower to the Thames and bounded on the north by the way which runs between 'le Weyhouse' of the said staple, and the said 'Wolbrigge'.[78]

There was evidently a small strip of land between the wall and the roadway, but the site must have been restricted, and in 1438 Dean John Prentys petitioned to be allowed to pierce window openings through the Palace and Thames walls that formed the south and east sides of his house. Sleford occupied the house until his death in 1399, even though by 1394 (as explained in the *Composition* and discussed below) a new site for the deanery had been earmarked in the centre of Canons' Row. In 1438, Dean Prentys was adamant that the latter site was unsuitable for the deanery, describing it as 'a bare piece of ground which has never been built on and never can be for want of good foundations'.[79]

Despite Prentys's concerns about the suitability of the site for the deanery, the houses of the canons were certainly standing by 1394. The site was north of the Palace wall, and were therefore outside the precincts.[80] It comprised the greater part of a large 'close' (*clausura*) formerly occupied by the earl of Kent. According to the *Composition*, this area was bounded to the south by the Palace wall, and to the north by the far edge of a ditch formerly separating the earl of Kent's domain from a property belonging to the Abbey monks called 'Almayne'. The north–south dimension of the dean and canons' close measured 575 ft (175.3 m), including the width of the roadway along the southern limit.[81] The eastern boundary was a stone wall built above the Thames. The western limit was irregular, as explained in the *Composition*: 'non habet unam metam rectilinialem super quam abuttat sed diversas obliquas secundum quod partes magis vel minus versus occidentem extenduntur'. To illustrate this point, five typical east–west dimensions were then given. The maximum width of the close, on the north side of the roadway and measuring from the outer face of the Thames wall to the side of the Weigh House, was 346 ft, though the situation was made more complicated because the king was about to build six houses on the north side of the roadway, perhaps associated with the Wool Staple, though this is not stated in the *Composition*. The southernmost of the dean and canons' plots, assigned to Canon William Hanney, measured 209 ft from the outer face of the Thames wall to the outer face of a boundary wall at the west end (presumably the king's new houses were to the west of this). The house and garden plot assigned to Dean William Sleford (but never built on) was the seventh from the south, that is approximately in the middle of the row.[82] It was 175 ft long, and its western boundary wall faced the gateway into a plot that had been retained by the heirs of the earl of Kent. The tenth plot from the south, assigned to Canon William Winterton, was 206 ft long, and at the western end was the 'new great gate of the dean and canons'. Finally, the thirteenth and northernmost plot, assigned to William Beverley, was only 157 ft long, and bounded a property belonging to the Abbey monks, known as 'Les Gynes'.

Access to the thirteen tenements was from the west end, and the *Composition* mentions their 'gates' (plural), implying an access lane whose distant successor is modern Canon Row. Presumably the lane was entered from the west, through the close gate opposite the end of Canon Winterton's garden.

CONCLUSION

THIS paper has attempted to show the value — and the limitations — of using graphical evidence in conjunction with documentary records in the analysis of the lost Palace of Westminster. It is hoped that work will continue on the production of a digital base plan of the Palace, based on such sources, that will serve as a useful tool for future research into this significant group of buildings.

NOTES

1. See below, 3–4.
2. For the fire, see Caroline Shenton, *The Day Parliament Burned Down* (Oxford 2012).
3. Robert Billings, 'Parliamentary & other offices, courts, &c. Westminster', engraved 1 February 1835, published in E. W. Brayley and J. Britton, *The History of the Ancient Palace and Late Houses of Parliament at Westminster* (London 1836), pl. 2 (MPW 1107); C. J. Richardson, 'Plan of the parliamentary and other public buildings adjacent to Westminster Hall, from a survey made with the intention of supplying the necessary information for the proper consideration of the proposed new buildings', August 1835 (MPW 409).
4. The same convention had been adopted in Chawner and Rhodes' survey of 1834, which was the basis of Billings' and Richardson's plans.
5. *HKW* iv, 286–88.
6. See below, 17.
7. See Virginia Jansen's paper in this volume, 89–110.
8. See below, 15.
9. Victoria & Albert Museum, Print Room, acc. no. E.128-1924, pressmark PD 187BMPW 767. For its dating and artist, see Ann Saunders, 'Westminster Hall: a sixteenth-century drawing?', *The London Journal*, 12/1 (Summer 1986), 29–35.
10. Oxford, Ashmolean Museum (MPW 1086).
11. WCA, box 56, no. 11D (MPW 1042).
12. MPW 1475 (Morgan); MPW 607 (Francis Sandford, *The History of the Coronation of James II* (London 1687), pl. 1, 56).
13. Initially based at the University of Reading, the project received funding for its first stage from the Arts and Humanities Research Board (now the Arts and Humanities Research Council).
14. Now published as M. H. Port, *The Palace of Westminster Surveyed on the Eve of the Conflagration*, London Topographical Society (London 2011).
15. WCA, E.133 (107), formerly box 56, no. 9 (MPW 241).
16. See 22–71.
17. J. G. Rokewode, 'A Memoir on the Painted Chamber in the Palace at Westminster ... [Read 12th May 1842.]', SAL, *Vetusta Monumenta*, VI (London 1885), 1–37 and pls XXVI–XXXIX, pl. XXVI, detail 'G' (MPW 1106).
18. The process has been written up more fully in John Crook and Roland B. Harris, 'Reconstructing the Lesser Hall: an interim report from the Medieval Palace of Westminster Research Project', in *Housing Parliament: Dublin, Edinburgh and Westminster*, ed. Clyve Jones and Sean Kelsey (Edinburgh 2002), 22–61.
19. TNA, E 101/468/21 *passim*, cited in R. A. Brown, H. M. Colvin and A. J. Taylor, *The History of the King's Works: The Middle Ages*, 2 vols (London 1963), I, 506 and n. 1.

20. As stated in Crook and Harris, 'Reconstructing the Lesser Hall' (as n. 18), 40: 'The hall appears always to have been a two-storey building'.
21. *King's Works* (as n. 19), I, 492–93.
22. John Carter, *The Ancient Architecture of England*, I (1806 edn), pl. xliv and 37 (MPW 257).
23. Ibid., pl. xliii and 36 (MPW 256).
24. J. T. Smith, *Antiquities of Westminster* (London 1807), facing 39 (MPW 1009). The drawing adopts the useful convention of a plan surrounded by the four, folded-down, internal elevations, resembling a flat-pack construction kit.
25. J. H. Rickman, *An Attempt to Discriminate the Styles of Architecture in England* ... (Oxford 1862, 6th edn, ed. J. H. Parker), 123.
26. *pace* W. R. Lethaby, 'The Palace of Westminster in the Eleventh and 12th Centuries', *Archaeologia*, VI (1906), 131–48, at 142–46, for whom the undercroft was 'of Norman work earlier than Henry II'. He cited Rickman, for whom the features cited were of the time of William Rufus, and considered that 'It is probable [...] that this undercroft was the earlier Norman hall' that Henry II had remodelled, turning it into a two-storey structure. The features were also discussed by John Gage Rokewode in 'Painted Chamber' (as n. 17).
27. John McNeill has pointed out (personal communication) that much building work also took place at Westminster Abbey at the start of Henry II's reign, notably the infirmary hall and cloister. See Harrison and McNeill, this volume, Part I, 69–103.
28. TNA, E 101/468/21 *passim*, cited in *King's Works* (as n. 19), I, 506 and n. 1.
29. Best of these, despite some anomalies, is an annotated plan copied from a drawing in the Sir John Soane's Museum (MPW 551).
30. See below, 10.
31. Victoria & Albert Museum, Print Room, acc. no. 3304.2, pressmark 93.H.18 (MPW 1213).
32. WCA, box 56, no. 22, acc. no. 3319 (MPW 569).
33. I am grateful to Professor Sandy Heslop for this parallel.
34. TNA, E 101/468/21, cited in *King's Works* (as n. 19), I, 506. This paraphrase from Brayley and Britten, *History of the Ancient Palace and Late Houses of Parliament* (as n. 3), 113.
35. Ibid., 124. Aylesford stone is Kentish Ragstone.
36. See below, 11–12.
37. Tim Tatton-Brown, personal communication.
38. See 89–110. The development of St Stephen's Chapel is currently being investigated in a new AHRC-funded project, 'St Stephen's Chapel Westminster: Visual and Political Culture, 1292–1941', at York University.
39. *King's Works* (as n. 19), I, 493.
40. Brayley and Britton, *History of the Ancient Palace and Late Houses of Parliament* (as n. 3), 126–27.
41. *King's Works* (as n. 19), I, 541.
42. H. M. Colvin ed., 'Views of the Old Palace of Westminster', *Architectural History*, 9 (1966), 23–184, figs 26–28 (MPW 1091).
43. Smith, *Antiquities* (as n. 24), facing 28, reproduced in 'Views of the Old Palace' (as n. 42), fig. 23 (MPW 827).
44. WCA, box 58, no. 06C, reproduced in 'Views of the Old Palace' (as n. 42), fig. 24 (MPW 953).
45. See below, 18.
46. The *Composition* is in BL, MS Cotton Faustina A.III, fols 293r–314r.
47. *Composition* (as n. 46), fol. 294v: 'ducentos octo pedes & decem pollices & dimidiam in longitudine a predictam videlicet capella sancti Stephani versus dictam domum vocatam nunc le Resseyt borialiter'. Smith (*Antiquities* (as n. 24), 101) wrongly translates this dimension as 280 ft 10½ in., in which error he is followed by Brayley and Britton.
48. *Composition* (as n. 46), fol. 294v: 'nec ultra Octoginta quindecim pedes & dimidium & duas polices in latitudinem viz. a muro orientali magne aule Regie usque ad partem exteriorem muri orientali novarum domorum vicariorum dicti collegii versus Thamesiam orientaliter'.
49. As shown by the earliest views, such as that of Wyngaerde, showing the Palace from the river.
50. Chawner and Rhodes' survey still label it 'St Stephen's Court'. Smith (*Antiquities* (as n. 24), 29) says that the court was known as St Stephen's Court 'in the memory of persons now living'. It was also known as Star Chamber Court.
51. At the south end of the hall, the distance to the rear wall of the cloister may be scaled from Chawner as 23.25 m (the latter wall of course survives, and the distance as measured from the Plowman Craven survey is 23.31 m).

52. As shown in John Symands's plans (in the Hatfield House library) published in 'Views of the Old Palace' (as n. 42), figs 85–86.
53. J. Mordaunt Crook and M. H. Port ed., *The History of the King's Works*, VI: *1782–1851* (London 1973), 532–53. Illustrated in an engraving of 1810, WCA, E.133.6 (1) (MPW 831).
54. As shown in J. T. Smith's plan, *Antiquities* (as n. 24), facing 125 (MPW 31).
55. Smith, *Antiquities* (as n. 24), 91.
56. As shown in Brayley and Britton, *History of the Ancient Palace and Late Houses of Parliament* (as n. 3), pl. 334 (MPW 0277).
57. *King's Works* (as n. 19), I, 545, citing *CCR 1349–54*, 99. This is an account of a meeting of Council that took place in August 1349 'in the new chamber next the receipt of the exchequer'.
58. '[camera] quae quondam fuerat clerici coquinæ nostræ'.
59. *Composition* (as n. 46), fol. 299v: 'bassa camera subtus le sterrechambre situata vocata olim camera clerici coquine Regis'.
60. L&P, ii.(2), 3741 (on 1177) [document dated 17 October 1517 simply called 'R.O.', that is TNA] and 1476, discussed in A. F. Pollard, 'Council, Star Chamber, and Privy Council under the Tudors: 2. The Star Chamber', *English Historical Review*, XXXVII (1922), 516–39, here 517, and H. M. Colvin, D. R. Ransome and J. Summerson ed., *The History of the King's Works*, IV: *1485–1660 (part 2)* (London 1982), 288.
61. TNA, E 351/3236, fol. 4r.
62. TNA, E 351/3236, discussed in *King's Works* (as n. 60), 297.
63. MPW 261 and 1.
64. WCA, box 56, no. 38B (MPW 973).
65. Smith, *Antiquities* (as n. 24), 29; Brayley and Britton, *History of the Ancient Palace and Late Houses of Parliament* (as n. 3), 442–43.
66. Brayley and Britton, *History of the Ancient Palace and Late Houses of Parliament* (as n. 3), 117–18.
67. The development of the gate is well discussed in *King's Works* (as n. 19), I, 547–48. The authors doubt the assertion by John Stow (adopted by Brayley and Britton, *History of the Ancient Palace and Late Houses of Parliament* (as n. 3), 339) that it was rebuilt by Richard III.
68. Brayley and Britton, *History of the Ancient Palace and Late Houses of Parliament* (as n. 3), 444.
69. For a discussion of the capital, see Frank Barlow, *William Rufus* (Berkeley CA 1983), 114, n. 66, and by John McNeill, this volume, Part I, 88–90.
70. *King's Works* (as n. 19), I, 548, citing W. H. Maitland, *The History of London*, 2 vols (London 1756, 3rd end), II, 1341.
71. *King's Works* (as n. 19), I, 552, and references there cited.
72. The *Composition* (as n. 46), fol. 295r, refers to 'quodam longum murum lapideum dicti palacii Regii a Thamesia viz. usque ad quandam portam iuxta domum stapule nunc vocatam le Weyhous'.
73. The construction of the clock tower and its demise in 1698 is well described in *King's Works* (as n. 19), I, 509–10. Its position within the wall is accurately described in the *Composition* (as n. 46, fol. 295v) as 'longum murum supradictum cuius muro unus finis abuttat super Tamesiam versus orientem & medium transit campanile in quo pendet le clokke & alter finis abuttat super portam iuxta domum stapule nunc vocata le Weyhous versus occidentem'.
74. Quoted in Brayley and Britton, *History of the Ancient Palace and Late Houses of Parliament* (as n. 3), 283.
75. V. Horsman and B. Davison, 'The New Palace yard and its fountains: excavations in the Palace of Westminster, 1972–4', Antiquaries Journal, 69 (1989), 279–97.
76. See n. 12.
77. Smith, *Antiquities* (as n. 24), 179.
78. CPR *1436–41*, 192–93.
79. Ibid.
80. Because the dean and canons' houses were built at their own expense, they are not included in the *History of the King's Works*, as explained in *King's Works* (as n. 19), I, 525.
81. *Composition* (as n. 46), fol. 295v. 'Quingentos septuaginta quinque pedes legalis mensure Regie cum latitudine vie que ducit a dicta domo stapule nunc vocata le Weyhous usque ad pontem nunc vocatum le Wolbrigge'. See also G. Rosser, *Medieval Westminster, 1200–1540* (1989), 125.
82. It has been suggested that initially the dean had occupied a house in the north-east corner of the yard, between the clock tower and the Wool Bridge: *King's Works* (as n. 19), I, 525–26, citing CPR *1436–41*, 192.

Romanesque Westminster Hall and its Roof

ROLAND B. HARRIS and DANIEL MILES
with an appendix by THOMAS HILL

The Romanesque Great Hall at the Palace of Westminster survives today, but, bereft of its original roof and largely obscured by late-14th-century and more recent stonework, it has received scant attention in the last century. This article draws together the evidence for the form of the building as constructed in the 1090s, combining modern survey with antiquarian and archaeological records. It also considers the evidence for the form of the lost 11th-century roof, and, consistent with current understanding of contemporary roofs (mainly known from Continental examples), proposes a single-span, common tie-beam form.

PART 1: ROMANESQUE WESTMINSTER HALL (RBH)

INTRODUCTION

WILLIAM RUFUS'S Great Hall at Westminster retains a prominent position in state and public life, but its status amongst architectural historians and archaeologists is less assured (Fig. 1). This largely reflects the fact that, following the remodelling and reroofing of the 1390s, little of the Romanesque building is easily visible; an understanding of the original form of the hall requires a combination of archaeological, documentary and graphical evidence. Although much has been written on the subject of the works of the 1390s, the last significant analysis of the Romanesque hall is that by William Lethaby, published in 1906.[1] While much of his interpretation remains valid, the building merits reconsideration in this paper for three reasons. First, more evidence is available than Lethaby utilized: major works in 1914–23 revealed further details of the Romanesque masonry, modern archaeological survey allows better understanding of the visible fabric, and it has proved possible to assemble a more extensive corpus of antiquarian graphical evidence. Second, the lack of modern study has allowed myths and assumptions to propagate; these include the supposed boat-shape of the plan of the hall, and the fact that it must have had aisles. Third, the significance of the hall to the development of both secular and ecclesiastical architecture in the late 11th century has not been recognized widely; this is especially evident in the case of the sophisticated form of its combined fenestration and wall passage, which was at the forefront of clerestory design in England and Normandy.

DATE AND DOCUMENTARY SOURCES

THE documentary evidence for Westminster Hall prior to its remodelling in the 1390s is limited. Most usefully, it provides a date for completion of the building: the *Anglo-Saxon Chronicle* records that Westminster Hall was first used by William Rufus for a feast at Whitsun (29 May) 1099. Henry of Huntingdon, writing in the 1120s, is the

Fig. 1. Interior view, looking south
Roland B. Harris

earliest source for the well-known account that, on seeing the new hall, some of William Rufus's courtiers said 'that it was a good size, and others that it was too large. The king said that it was only half large enough'.[2] Adding to this story, the rather less reliable early-13th-century account in the *Histoire des Ducs de Normandie* also suggests that the hall may not have been quite ready in May 1099: perhaps rather implausibly, the king, realizing that the roof would not be covered in time for 'a' Whitsun (almost certainly that in 1099) scoured London for fine cloths (*escarlates*) as a temporary solution.[3] It is evident, nevertheless, that the masonry element of the hall would have been completed by the end of the 1098 building season, if not earlier. That building was under way in 1097, as would be expected, is clear from the *Anglo-Saxon Chronicle*'s entry that year for 'work on the king's hall, that was being built at Westminster'.[4] This reference has been taken as evidence for building work starting in 1097,[5] but a two-year construction period, while possible, is not implied; a longer duration is suggested by the scale of the building, and a start date of around 1095 is more likely. The architectural evidence (see below) does not support a long-drawn-out or interrupted building campaign (as found, for example, at the White Tower).[6] Thus, Goscelin of Canterbury's famous near-contemporary account of the wrecking of fourteen ships carrying cargoes of stone from Caen for building works at Westminster Palace (*regis palatium westmonasterii*), at some point between 1070–73 and 1087, evidently relates to works elsewhere at the palace.[7]

Later documentary references relate to repairs to the hall. These include accounts for shingles (*scindul*) on the roof, first appearing in the accounts of 1162–63.[8] That this was continued throughout the life of the roof is clear from references to the cutting of shingles and the purchase of 2,000 shingle nails for the hall in 1319, and for a further 8,500 shingle nails for the hall and the king's treasury in 1365.[9] As late as 1385, 10,250 shingles were placed on the roof.[10] The use of shingles for such a major roof is surprising and in sharp contrast to the lead roofs of Edward the Confessor's adjacent abbey;[11] it could suggest that a lighter roof covering was necessary. Other early unspecified works were undertaken in 1161–62,[12] and again in 1189–90.[13] There is also documentary evidence for repairs and modifications that were made shortly before the complete remodelling of 1394–1401. Statues were commissioned for the hall interior in 1385, and in 1385–87 at least one flying buttress was built to add support to the east wall of the hall;[14] the latter suggests that the roof and, thus, the wall head were spreading, and this is confirmed by the archaeological evidence (see below). As Howard Colvin noted, when John Godmaston was appointed clerk of works in January 1394, it was for the repair (*reparacio*) of the hall,[15] and it does indeed appear that the failing Romanesque roof instigated the transformation of the building under Hugh Herland and Henry Yevele.

GROUND PLAN

Dimensions and irregularities

THE north–south oriented hall has mean dimensions of 77.39 m × 25.01 m externally and 73.21 m × 20.79 m internally (Fig. 2). The use of averages reflects the irregularity in the ground plan: in reality the internal length of the east wall is, at 73.02 m, 380 mm shorter than the west wall, while the internal north wall, at 20.65 m, is 280 mm shorter than the south wall. More obviously and famously, the disposition of the bays of the east and west walls (as measured from the part-surviving clerestory windows and

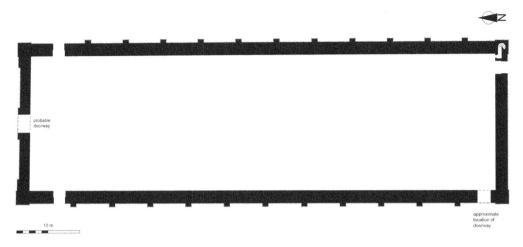

Fig. 2. Reconstructed ground plan
Roland B. Harris

pilaster buttresses) is irregular, so that those on the west side are positioned north of those on the east. Contrary to common assumption, however, this displacement is not consistent, but varies from 1.15 m at the southern end of the hall to 2.30 m at the north: the progressive increase in the displacement reflects the 6.04 m spacing of the west-wall bays compared with the 5.93 m-wide bays on the east. Colvin identified a second irregularity, in the form of the bowed plan of the side walls, and suggested that this derived from pre-Conquest halls.[16] The bowing, however, is only evident in the upper part of the walls, and modern tacheometric survey of the visible Romanesque fabric that forms most of the lower part of the west external elevation confirms that at ground level it is completely straight.[17] William Harvey's 1919 plan of the clerestory passage distinguishes between the deflection of the Romanesque wall passage and that of the 1919 wall face, making it clear that the internal refacing of the 1390s squared up the earlier bowed face.[18] Before 1394, the maximum deflection of the west wall head was 332 mm or more, and that of the east wall head was 405 mm or more. The bowing, which progressively increases towards the centre of the side walls, is evidently the result of the spread of the pre-1390s roof: significantly, the deflection is symptomatic of a single-span roof and is not at all consistent with the presence of aisles.

Foundations, ground level and the floor

THE late-11th-century external ground level of 1.60 m OD is evident from the intact Romanesque plinth along the exterior of the west side of the hall, and from an excavation directed by David Whipp against the northern end of this wall in 1975. The excavation exposed the construction trench and showed that the 1.2 m-deep foundations were laid on crushed chalk; the lower 800 mm comprised 'rubble bonded in place by mortar' (which sounds like banded foundations typical of the period), with the upper 400 mm having an 'even mortar face'.[19] While archaeological and engineering investigations within the hall in 1960 and 2005–06 recovered parts of the 13th-century king's high table,[20] the most significant evidence for the medieval hall floors comes from Sydney Smirke's record of the excavation of the floor in the 1830s (Fig. 3). As a requirement for the construction of the present floor, this involved digging out the entire floor to a depth of 4–5 ft (1.22–1.52 m). At a depth of 1 ft 4 in. (0.41 m), that is c. 3.26 m OD, he located an earlier Purbeck stone floor and, below that, successive strata of a compressed black soil (averaging 7–8 in. (0.18–0.20 m)); well-tempered pure clay (4–5 in. (0.10–0.13 m)); stone rubble, lime core, clay and sand make-up (3 ft (0.91 m)); artificially deposited clay (4–5 ft (1.22–1.52 m)); and natural (gravel and sand).[21] Smirke's identification of natural gravel and sand at c. 0.75 m OD corresponds with the level of the natural sand observed in the 1975 excavation. It is possible that his 'artificially deposited clay' equates to the thick blue-grey clay layer found lying above the natural sands in the 1975 excavation. The Purbeck marble floor may well be that laid for the coronation of Charles II in 1661, which followed levelling with 175 cartloads of earth and 78 loads of sand;[22] this quantity appears to account for the black soil layer below the Purbeck only. The date of the well-tempered clay and the deep rubble layer observed by Smirke is unknown, but it is unlikely that these are primary: the 11th-century doorway at the north end of the west wall, discovered in 1883, appears to have entered the hall around or just above the external ground level.[23] Perhaps most significantly, given his generally highly accurate observations and the depth of the excavations in the 1830s, Smirke was unable to find any trace of pier bases for what he strongly believed had been an aisled building *ab initio*. A ground-penetrating radar survey in 1999 also failed to locate any evidence for pier bases for any scheme of aisles (that is, two, three or five aisles).[24] In short, the below-ground archaeological evidence is consistent with that of the wall-head deflection, suggesting that the building was not aisled from the outset.

Doorways

MYTHS continue to be propagated about the primary doorway arrangements of Westminster Hall. Most disturbingly, in the recent paper on the king's table in Westminster Hall a supposed triple doorway arrangement at the north end and two doorways in the south wall were adduced as evidence for the width of assumed aisles,[25] although, in fact, only one of these doorways is known to have dated from the 11th century. For the north elevation, we are reliant on a sketch made by J. C. Buckler during restoration works in 1822 (Fig. 4).[26] This shows one unambiguously Romanesque blind arch, or recess, on the east with an apparently matching recess, but with a modified Gothic front arch, to the west, both filled with diaper work and flanking the late-14th-century cut through the wall for the great doorway. Significantly, the blind arches are too wide and closely spaced to relate to a three-aisled interior, although they do not preclude a central arcade: it is possible, perhaps even probable, however, that there was a smaller late-11th-century north doorway in this central position, as at the *Échiquier* at Caen. In the southern wall, Smirke identified a primary doorway near the south-east corner of the hall;[27] it is shown in section by Smirke,[28] and on the 1834 pre-fire plan by Chawner and Rhodes.[29] Similar evidence of 'square reveals and plain circular heads' led Smirke to identify three other primary doorways, one towards the south of the west wall, and opposing doorways in the side walls of the northern bay of the hall;[30] that on the east wall is shown in his longitudinal elevational section.[31] More evidence for the doorway at the northern end of the west wall was discovered when Sir John Soane's law courts, which had been built against the west side of Westminster Hall in the 1820s, were demolished in 1883. This revealed the lower parts of the plain Romanesque doorway, which were recorded by the

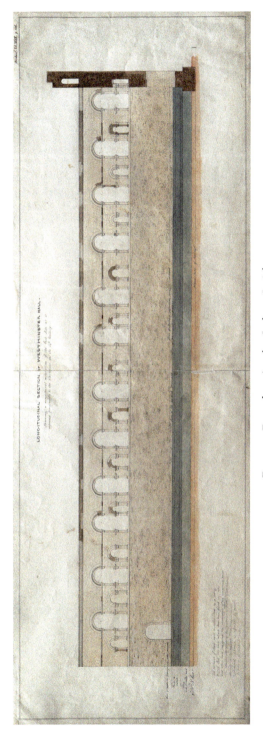

Fig. 3. East elevation by Sydney Smirke (*MPW* 439)

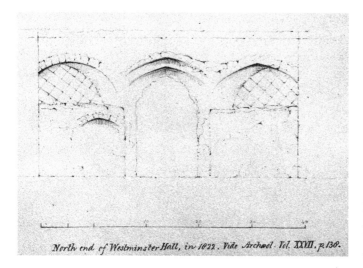

FIG. 4. Recesses in external face of north wall, recorded by J. C. Buckler in 1822 (MPW 434)

FIG. 5. Lower parts of Romanesque doorway at the north end of the west wall, revealed during demolition of Soane's Law Courts in 1883
(MPW 1446)
Photograph by Bedford Lemere

office of Joseph Loughborough Pearson[32] (probably by W. D. Caröe),[33] George Somers Clarke,[34] Edwin Freshfield[35] and, photographically, by Bedford Lemere (Fig. 5).[36] In addition to these doorways, we must assume that there was internal access to the clerestory wall passage (and the roof) via at least one spiral stair: Smirke observed a turret stair at the south-east corner.[37]

EXTERNAL ELEVATIONS

Side elevations

PEARSON'S 1886–88 replacement of Soane's law courts on the west side of Westminster Hall left the newly discovered Romanesque fabric largely exposed, and this remains the only visible part of the external face of the primary building (Figs 6 and 7). The lower part of nine and a half bays can be viewed, although the southernmost half-bay is within a boiler room, with the ashlar there obscured by white paint. The bays to the north are separated by pilaster buttresses, c. 500 mm deep and c. 850 mm wide. A plinth with a simple chamfer runs along all the exposed part of the elevation, except where cut by Pearson's doorways. Where the no-longer visible evidence of the doorway at the north end of the wall was exposed in 1883 (see above), the plinth was interrupted. Although preservation of the Norman wall was fought over in the 1880s, the primary fabric is less intact than Miele suggests:[38] in five of the bays there is convincing Romanesque ashlar (as determined by size, geological consistency with the stones below, and axe tooling) located where in 1883 there were doorways to Westminster Hall (created by Soane in the 1820s), and there were probably other areas of repair. The source of this *ex situ* Romanesque masonry is almost certainly the elevation above the blind arches of 1886–88: these arches and the projecting masonry above are very probably keyed into the external face of the hall, and, with Romanesque ashlar recorded above the level that is visible today, it must be assumed that this provided material for restoration of the lower part of the wall. The ashlar itself is of varied geological type, predominantly Caen stone, but with significant quantities of Reigate stone and Quarr stone. The different colours of the stones have been used for visual effect, with partial creation of a chequer or, rather, stepped pattern. This is most evident in the third and seventh bays from the south: the partial survival of this pattern arrangement in the lower courses above the plinth of other bays is, perhaps, another indication of the extent of later repairs, although it is by no means certain that the stonework pattern was rigorously and consistently applied in the 1090s.

The Romanesque fabric exposed in 1883 did not include any windows, which, as in the 1390s remodelling, were at the upper level, or clerestory, only. For understanding of the windows we are largely dependent on three antiquarian drawings. In 1823, John Soane recorded the upper half of a window at the north end of the west side of the hall (Fig. 8).[39] The top of the arch was hidden by the ceiling of the upper floor of the Exchequer building and the lower part of the window was lost by blocking masonry that Soane dated to the time of Henry III, but capitals and the full widths of the inner and outer orders of the window arch were preserved. The nook shafts were missing, but the measurement of the astragal is given as 9 in. (229 mm) on one of two details of the simple cushion capitals: this suggests shafts of a diameter of around 8 in. (203 mm). There is no evidence of the form of the archivolt, but it is depicted in detail by Frederick Mackenzie, in a drawing of 1842 (Fig. 9). This shows the southern part of the arch of the southernmost window of the east wall, and depicts a roll with two adjacent hollow rolls, or concave mouldings.[40] The third view is a small engraving by John Thomas Smith of a window exposed by the partial demolition of the belfry against the east side of the hall in *c*. 1805 (Fig. 10).[41] These sources combined give an external window opening 1.78 m wide and 4.15 m high. Windows of similar form and proportion are found in the external clerestory windows of relevant parallels, such as the clerestory at Winchester Cathedral. The combination of double concave mouldings and angle rolls on the archivolt adds to the corpus of similar mouldings dating to the 1090s, in the east arm of Chichester Cathedral, in Anselm's work at Canterbury Cathedral, and, most profusely, at Norwich Cathedral. Several unknowns remain for the windows; the principal of these is the form of the bases, which may well have varied from window to window (as they did on the interior arcade). Likewise the

Fig. 6. (*above*) West wall (fourth bay from north) during demolition of the Law Courts in 1883
(*MPW 1440*)
Photograph by Bedford Lemere

Fig. 7. The west wall today: third bay from south
Roland B. Harris

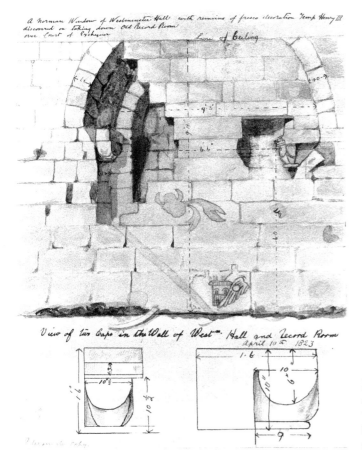

FIG. 8. Details of window at the north end of the west wall, recorded by John Soane in 1823 (MPW 940)

height of any sill is unknown, but the presence of a sill rising above the top of the string-course is likely, not least because the latter was only 395 mm above the floor of the mural passage: on the basis of parallels of windows of similar date, scale, form and function it is likely that the sill rose around another 300–350 mm above the external string-course. Finally, the evidence rules out sharply angled splays found, for example, in the rather smaller clerestory windows at Norwich Cathedral: the 1.78 m outer opening of the Westminster windows is only marginally narrower than the 2.17 m-wide concentric arch of the internal arcade, leaving little scope for any but the most negligible splay.

Mackenzie and Smith's 19th-century views also record other details of the upper parts of the elevation. Both show notched (sometimes called nutmeg) string-courses, in the former above the clerestory windows and in the latter immediately below. The lower string-course is further recorded on drawings by William Deeble (1809)[42] and R. W. Billings (1835),[43] which show the east side of the hall with the notched string-course continuing across the pilaster buttresses. Smirke also noted the lower external string-course, producing a measured elevation detail and section, making the parallel between it and that at Waltham Abbey (Fig. 11).[44] The extensive use of the same type

FIG. 9. Window, string-course, and corner buttress details, south end of the east wall, recorded by Frederick Mackenzie

Vetusta Monumenta, VI (1842, publ. 1885), pl. XXVI, detail 'A'

of moulded string-course on the exterior elevations of Norwich Cathedral is closer in date to Westminster Hall. The upper string-course matched the height of the top of the Romanesque wall head, above which Mackenzie's detail of the east elevation records a band of diaper work rising 850 mm, forming the wall of a parapet; Lethaby's 1906 reconstruction is confused in terms of levels, and he mistakenly added plain masonry above this diaper work to form the parapet wall.[45] On Mackenzie's detail the abrupt termination at an iron joist, which carries the later projecting ashlar above, suggests that the wall may have risen a little further, to some form of coping or weathering at least. On the wide south-east angle-buttress Mackenzie shows the diaper work rising higher, to c. 980 mm above the string-course; this is consistent with the fact that the angle-buttresses must have risen higher — as short turret stubs at least — to serve the primary wall passage in the southern gable wall at the level of the main wall head.[46] Comparable diaper work survives in the late-11th-century conventual buildings at Westminster Abbey, on the east face of the reredorter (at ground level) and near the wall head of the north-west corner of the refectory. In both these cases the chequer effect is created by the mix of limestones and glazed tile, although the external decoration of the hall may have used stone only. In addition to the use of different coloured stone types for effect on the west elevation of the hall (see above, and Fig. 12), Smirke noted a

FIG. 10. Window in east wall within belfry, recorded by J. T. Smith *c.* 1805
Smith, Antiquities *(as n. 41),* facing 45

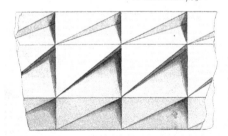

FIG. 11. String-course details, recorded by Sydney Smirke in 1835
(MWP 492)

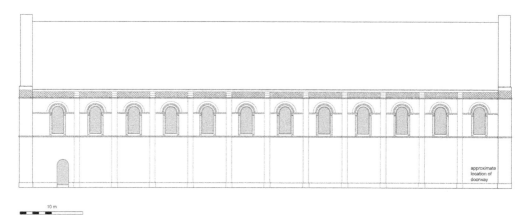

Fig. 12. Reconstructed west elevation
Roland B. Harris

diaper pattern of alternating Reigate stone and Caen stone 7 in. (178 mm) square high up on the southern gable.[47] The materials used in the diaper work of the north elevation recesses, exposed in 1822, are not recorded.[48]

End elevations

The north and south elevations of the hall appear to have followed the general form of the side elevations, albeit with the windows rather more widely spaced (see below), the large round-headed recesses of (at least) the north elevation, and the provision of gables. Although Smirke proposed three gables to each elevation (notwithstanding the implausibly long roof valleys implied, as well as aisles), it is difficult to reconcile this with his record of an upper wall passage in the south elevation, which had its floor at the level of the wall heads of the side elevations. Smirke's record of another detail of the south elevation 'considerably higher than the clerestory' is more ambiguous.[49] The diaper work here (see above) formed the wall face between two *in situ* shafts, c. 6 in. (150 mm) in diameter, complete with bases, which may have formed a continuous band of blind arcading, as reconstructed by Lethaby,[50] or smaller groups of blind arches. Smirke's observations provide strong evidence that the remodelling of the gables in the 1390s encased the Romanesque work, and that fabric from the 1090s probably survives; this is especially likely in the case of the north gable, where there has been less repair and where the interior face comprises intact Reigate stone from the 1390s.[51] In this context, a lower-pitched scar recorded in numerous antiquarian views of the northern gable may be significant:[52] this scarring may represent evidence of the Romanesque gable prior to the external refacing in the 1820s (Fig. 13).

INTERNAL ELEVATIONS

The high-level, or clerestory, Romanesque fenestration was rendered redundant by the works of the 1390s, since the reroofing at this date was accompanied by provision of new windows. It is remarkable, therefore, that repairs to the hall in 1834–37 and

Fig. 13. View of north elevation showing much-recorded crack possibly marking earlier gable, undated, late 18th century

(MPW 966)

1914–23 revealed sufficient evidence to allow a reconstruction of the 11th-century fenestration. That this was the case was the result of three factors. First, the eccentric disposition of the 14th-century roof trusses was in fact a modification of the still-greater earlier misalignment of the east and west walls, so that the new windows did not entirely correspond, and thus did not entirely obliterate, the earlier windows. Second, the 14th-century works, and, indeed, those of the 1830s, largely comprised cosmetic refacing of the walls and left much earlier fabric in place. Third, the Romanesque windows were part of a scheme that included a wall passage and intermediary arcading and, thus, much evidence of the overall scheme was unaffected by the renewal of windows in the 1390s.

Smirke combined the various fragments of evidence from the 1830s works for the east elevation to produce the first reconstruction of the Romanesque fenestration

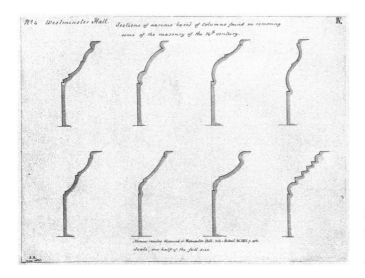

FIG. 14. Profiles of clerestory bases recorded by Sydney Smirke in 1835 (MPW 491)

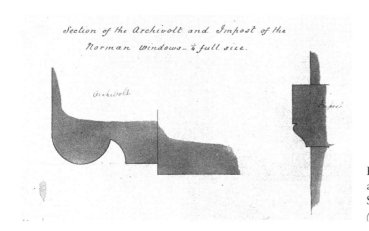

FIG. 15. Profile of window archivolt and impost by Sydney Smirke in 1835 (MPW 492)

scheme (Figs 14–16). His well-known drawing of the east elevation (Fig. 3) clearly distinguishes between the discoveries and his interpretation, and this was to prove crucial to Lethaby's reassessment of the evidence seventy years later: whereas Smirke had produced an extremely irregular arcade of alternating large and small arches, Lethaby was able to demonstrate that a more balanced and convincing scheme of pairs of arches between larger arches was possible. Lethaby's scheme published in 1906 suffered from some dimensional inaccuracies in Smirke's recording, but the subsequent 1914–23 repairs saw more accurate measurement of Romanesque details — both previously and newly discovered — by William Harvey (Fig. 17). The most important modification was in the east wall behind and adjacent to Truss 12[53] of the present roof, where Smirke incorrectly recorded the relationship between the upper nook shaft of a larger arch and the adjacent shafts and voussoirs of a smaller intermediary arch.

Romanesque Westminster Hall and its Roof

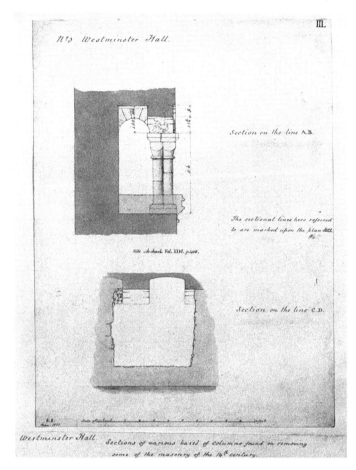

Fig. 16. Sections of the wall passage recorded by Sydney Smirke in 1835 (MPW 438)

This led Lethaby to conclude that the original scheme in which the clerestory was a continuous arcade of arches springing from clusters of four shafts had been less than perfectly achieved, and that occasionally narrow strips of ashlar separated these shafts into two pairs.[54] A more thorough examination behind Truss 12 by Harvey, however, revealed that the two arches were immediately adjacent and sprung from a cluster of four shafts without any separating band of ashlar. That Lethaby's scheme was indeed more rigorously applied than he had supposed was confirmed by further discoveries at this date of the same arrangement in the fabric behind Trusses 10 and 11, again in the east wall. During the works of 1914–23, several small areas of the clerestory were left accessible behind stone-faced cupboard doors.[55]

Harvey and Smirke's observations, together with the fabric visible today, reveal that the normal bay design for the clerestory arcade was of tripartite form, in which a large central opening matched the external window itself, the two being bisected by a continuous wall passage (Fig. 18). Each of the large openings was flanked by two smaller arches, the whole forming a symmetrical arrangement repeated in each bay of the side elevations, except the end bays, where the irregularity in the design of the hall either

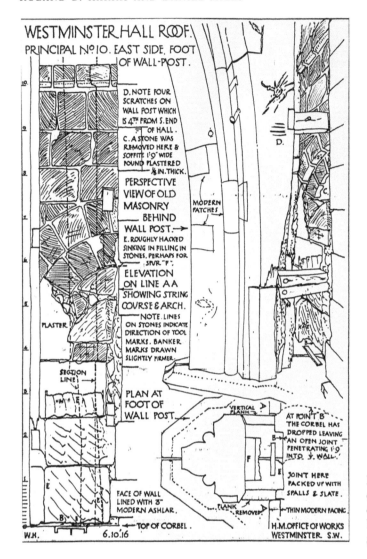

Fig. 17. Detail of Romanesque arcade found behind east side wall post recorded by William Harvey in 1916 (*MPW 1155*)

requires that one of the smaller arches is missing (east wall, south), an extra arch is required (west wall, north), or two extra arches are required (east wall, north) (Fig. 19).

The tripartite arcade of Westminster is notable for several features that had a varied influence on subsequent clerestory design. The most unusual feature of the arcade, given the comparisons with clerestories in great churches, is a result of the lack of articulation in the side walls of the hall: in the absence of an arcaded gallery or a main arcade below this 'clerestory' there are no shafts providing vertical accent and horizontal division into bays. Rather, the lower half of the internal walls was blank rubble, presumably plastered and very possibly painted. The only evidence for

Fig. 18. Wall passage today, west side
Roland B. Harris

shafts is the very slight, and questionable, trace of a corbelled-out pilaster above the clerestory, springing from the level of the window imposts, observed by William Harvey in December 1917.[56] The absence of the shafts usual in major church elevations means that the clerestory arcade at Westminster was continuous, the bays seamlessly running into each other without any need for solid ashlar between. A second distinctive feature of Westminster Hall is that the arcade springs from small (203 mm diameter) shafts grouped in fours: that is, two pairs front and back. The main arches of the tripartite arcade spring in different directions from the adjacent front capitals, while the rear shafts make separate provision for the springing of the vault over the wall passage. This latter is especially subtle, for not only do arches spring across the

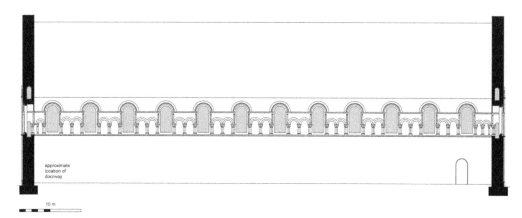

Fig. 19. Reconstructed west wall internal sectional elevation
Roland B. Harris

openings of the wall passage to the main window arch, but they also spring from the rear shafts of the intermediary pier of each bay between the smaller arches. The passage does not take the form of a simple barrel-vault cut periodically by the windows and the sub-arches, but consists of a series of transverse arches springing from the rear pairs of shafts of the arcade. Between these transverse arches there are segmental vaults oriented at right angles to the passage, thus creating distinct units in the wall passage behind each of the sub-arches of the arcade (Fig. 16). Other features in the Westminster Hall clerestory that are distinctive include the roughly 1:1 ratio of the lower and upper shafts, and, more significantly still, the presence of upper nook, or stilt, shafts to support the imposts of the main arches.

Following earlier development of clerestory passages in Normandy, as at Saint-Étienne, Caen (1060s) and Cerisy la Forêt (c. 1080, Fig. 20), the earliest known example of the tripartite clerestory is at Winchester Cathedral (begun 1079, Fig. 21). The closest parallel to that at Westminster Hall, however, is to be found at Norwich Cathedral (begun 1096, Fig. 22), which also has the stilted nook shafts. Eric Fernie recognizes the particular form with stilted nook shafts as being distinctively East Anglian,[57] while Stephen Heywood identifies the tripartite arrangement at Norwich as having 'its immediate source at Ely' (begun 1083);[58] inexplicably, Westminster Hall is missing from their discussions of Romanesque Norwich Cathedral. Evidently the cathedral clerestory is closely related to that at Westminster Hall and, given their chronologies, it must be concluded that Rufus's Great Hall was very probably the immediate source for the cathedral of his courtier, Bishop Herbert de Losinga. Indeed, Westminster Hall may have provided the source for other examples, such as Waltham Abbey (from c. 1125) and Romsey (c. 1140). Although just predating the clerestory at Norwich, that at Westminster Hall is every bit as sophisticated: the clustered shafts, and the complexity and subtlety of the passage vaulting, are two aspects that are not replicated at Norwich or in subsequent examples.[59]

The fenestration of the end walls of the hall is less easy to reconstruct, since both the 1834–37 and 1914–23 restorations involved little work in these areas. Barry's removal of the south window after the 1834 fire, however, did have a serious impact

Fig. 20. Cerisy la Forêt: nave north side
Roland B. Harris

on the south elevation. Fortunately, Smirke made one or two telling observations at that time: he reported evidence for the continuation of the clerestory wall passage across the south wall and was able to discern, through plaster, the outline of two openings corresponding to the main arcade arches of the side walls. The western of these openings is visible in an engraving in Brayley and Britton (Fig. 23),[60] and this shows the presence of a roll-moulded arch and the imposts, albeit in a sketchy form. That one of the niches of 1385 is set into the blocking of this arch supports Smirke's interpretation of these arches as an original continuation of the side wall clerestory arcade across the south wall. Smirke's observations and symmetry require us to place an identical main arch towards the south-east corner. The location of the western arch (and its implied eastern counterpart) preclude a central arcade dividing Westminster Hall into two aisles (the arches being wildly off-centre to the aisles in such a scheme), and, thus, it is quite logical to add a third central arch as Lethaby conjectured,[61] giving slightly wider spacing than for the main clerestory arches in the side walls. As for any sub-arches, it is tempting to flank the large arches with smaller arches in the manner of the side walls, but there is too little room on the outer side of the east and west windows in the south wall for such a scheme without seriously reducing their size. Moreover, since the northern interior elevation was 290 mm narrower, any use of similarly spaced arches here would have exacerbated the problem. It is most likely, therefore, that the large arches formed the outermost element of the end wall arcades. Between the large arches, however, there is scope for sub-arches in the manner of the

FIG. 21. Winchester Cathedral: south transept
Roland B. Harris

side walls. Significantly, the arrangement of the three main arches creates spaces sufficient for three subsidiary arches between each pair. That this should fit to within 6 mm is overstating the precision of the positioning of the results of geometrical rectification of the blocked arch shown in Brayley and Britton, but it does serve to demonstrate how neatly such a scheme would have worked and is, perhaps, sufficient to suggest that this scheme was applied to the south wall. Of course, it would be possible to place a respond or pilaster buttress in the position of the central or additional subsidiary arches, giving something of the effect of the end internal elevations of the Winchester Cathedral transepts, but this is improbable on two grounds. Firstly, there is otherwise a complete absence of vertical shafts or dosserets at Westminster Hall and, secondly, the exact correspondence with the width of a standard subsidiary arch would be unnecessary and improbable. The evidence, then, strongly suggests that the continuous wall passage arrangement of the side walls continued around the end walls, modified slightly to take account of the overall width of the hall and the wider window spacing (Fig. 24).

CONCLUSIONS

THE understanding and appreciation of Romanesque Westminster Hall has languished in the last century. Difficulties in accessing the visible remains of the 1090s fabric may be partly to blame: the ascent to the visible parts of the Romanesque clerestory requires

Fig. 22.   Norwich Cathedral: nave north side
Roland B. Harris

scaffolding or a hoist and is not for the faint-hearted, although creation of the Jubilee Café in 2002 opened up public access to the northern part of the exterior of the west wall. This reassessment of the evidence for William Rufus's Great Hall clarifies the form and significance of the clerestory — the hall's most sophisticated masonry component — as well as the form of much of the walls, from plinth to parapet. Along with a lack of interest in the 11th-century form of the hall has come a tendency to propagate myths and assumptions about it, typically in cursory summaries in discussions of later aspects of the hall, such as the existing roof structure or, most recently, the remains of the 13th-century king's high table. Such discussions have introduced bogus primary doorways and the fictitious bowed ground-level plan. Of most concern, however, has been the near-constant reassertion that the hall must have had two, three or more aisles, despite the negative findings of Smirke's excavation, the evidence for continuous clerestory wall passages and arcading in the end walls, the position and scale of the primary niches in the north elevation, the nature of the bowed wall heads (wholly inconsistent with the presence of aisles), and the implausible height of any aisle posts; the concern goes beyond roof forms, since the aisled interpretation has lead, most recently and bizarrely, to the closest parallels to Westminster Hall being identified in the naves of Westminster Abbey and Winchester Cathedral.[62] It is in this context that Christopher Wilson's comments on the 11th-century hall, in an article on Richard II's remodelling, stand out as the one recent reasoned assessment of the evidence: in addition to some of the structural

FIG. 23. South wall of Westminster Hall, showing a blocked Norman arch on the west side of the great south window
Detail from Brayley and Britton, History of the Ancient Palace and Late Houses of Parliament *(as n. 9), pl. 10*

evidence (he notes the Buckler drawing of the north elevation recesses and Smirke's excavation), Wilson also draws attention to the lack of documentary references to internal supports in the records of the law courts or in the accounts of the salvage of timber from the old roof in 1396–97; parallels (including the unaisled *Échiquier* at Caen, which appears to be closely related to Westminster Hall, and, more broadly, the invariably unaisled — and functionally related — monastic refectories);[63] and the absence of other examples in 11th- to 13th-century England of aisled halls with such high lateral walls as found at Westminster.[64] These broader considerations and, of course, the structural evidence reviewed in this article, provide a sufficient basis to consider the possible structural form — and context — of a clear-span roof, which is what Daniel Miles undertakes in the second part of this article.

PART 2: RECONSTRUCTING THE ROOF OF ROMANESQUE WESTMINSTER HALL (DM)

INTRODUCTION

IT has been postulated for many years that Westminster Hall as built by William Rufus in 1097 was an aisled hall, not unlike that of the bishop's palace at Hereford (Fig. 25). However, this dates from almost a century later, and there are technical problems with constructing such an aisled building on the scale of Westminster. The

Romanesque Westminster Hall and its Roof

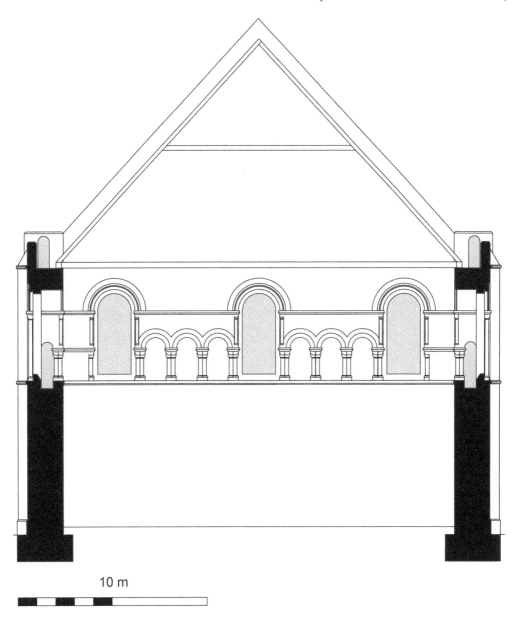

FIG. 24. Reconstructed north wall internal sectional elevation
Roland B. Harris

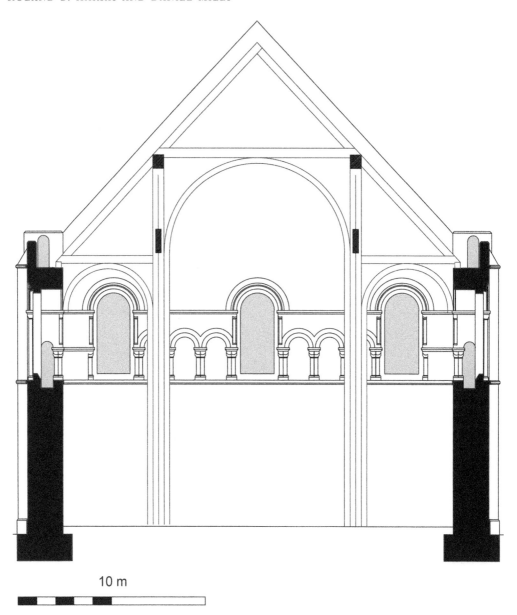

Fig. 25. Romanesque aisled-hall reconstruction of Westminster Hall as per Hereford
Daniel Miles

arcade posts for instance would need to be 59 ft (18 m) tall, with at least twenty-two of these. William Harvey's reconstructed aisled structure, which he drew up during his recording work in the early 20th century, is the best known,[65] but has no architectural precedent: the arcade posts interrupted by the aisle ties would be structurally unstable. In addition, given the extreme irregularity of the setting out of the windows between the east and west sides, the arcades would neither be aligning with the bays, nor equally spaced. If there was an arcade, then it would have more likely been of stone, like the Great Hall of Paris (early 14th century). This was about 90 ft (27.5 m) wide, divided by a central arcade of stone, giving two roofs of less than 45 ft (13.7 m) span.[66] However, Roland Harris has laid forth evidence strongly suggesting that there were no arcades in Westminster Hall originally, and the implication is that there was a single-span roof. This has usually been dismissed out of hand, but, given the weight of archaeological evidence, it is important to assess whether it was possible to construct a roof spanning 68 ft (20.79 m) without any intermediate support and, if so, what it might have looked like. To answer that, it is first necessary to review what wood-working technology was in use at the time, and what precedents there were for large-span roofs. Then consideration can be given to what types of roof may have been used and what sort of structural problems may have been encountered with these.

ENGLISH PARALLELS

SURVIVING early Norman roofs are rare and, in England, the only roof still standing is at Kempley (Gloucestershire). This dates from 1128–32, so is a generation later, but still before the end of the 12th century when carpentry techniques changed rapidly.[67] Kempley is unique in that it appears to have been an open roof, the earliest to be found in Britain.[68] But it does show the form of small scantling timbers used, with face-pegged lap joints and each truss a common rafter truss (Fig. 26). It was not double-framed. A second example from England was at Ely Cathedral, dating from about 1105–40 (Fig. 27). Although not standing, detective work by Gavin Simpson has allowed these reused timbers from the nave roof to be reconstructed on paper.[69] This roof was substantial, with a span of about 33 ft (10 m), and it had a 40-degree pitch. This was a common tie-beam roof, where every truss is composed of similar-sized scantling with a bottom cord or tie-beam on each truss, generally spaced 3 ft 3 in. (1 m) apart. The Ely roof was made up of a variety of smaller members and, again, it used lap joints. The tie-beams of a third roof, dating from 1056, survived at Odda's Chapel in Deerhurst (Gloucestershire) until receiving the unfortunate attention of the Ministry of Works in the 1960s, when it was replaced without recording. Although the roof above the tie-beams was replaced in the 17th century, Chris Currie was able to reconstruct its original form from the shadow of the truss on the gable end.[70] This had a similar span to Kempley, about 18 ft (5.5 m), with a 45-degree pitch, common tie-beams, and two angled struts (Fig. 28).

CONTINENTAL PARALLELS

MORE numerous contemporary examples can be found in northern Europe, despite the ravages of two world wars. Dating to about 1046, the choir roof of the Collégiale Sainte-Gertrude in Nivelles (Belgium) had a span of 33 ft (10 m), a 30-degree pitch,

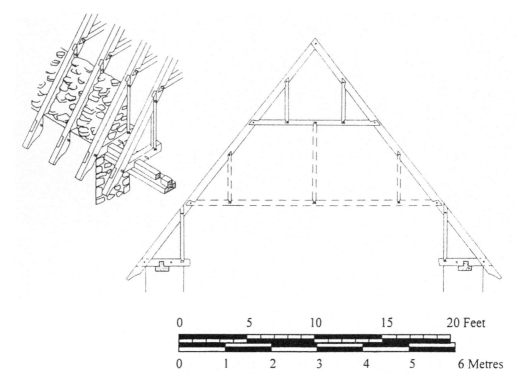

Fig. 26. Typical primary roof truss at Kempley Church
After Miles, Worthington and Groves, Church of St Mary, Kempley *(as n. 68)*

and two raking struts each side, identified from its masonry impression; the roof was replaced later in the medieval period.[71] It was most likely originally covered underneath with a ceiling of indeterminate form.

Another slightly earlier example is found in Paris, where reused timbers from the roof of the nave of Saint-Germain-des-Prés have been dendro-dated to 1018–38.[72] The roof had a series of radiating struts or hangers and a collar, again using lap joints and halvings (which suggests a collar). This also had a painted ceiling made up of boards 430 mm (17 in.) wide, nailed to the underside of the common tie-beams.[73] Somewhat later (1185–1200) than Westminster, but in our opinion typical of the second quarter of the 12th century, and similar to the lost roof of Jumièges, is the nave of the Collégiale Saint-Vincent Soignies in Hainaut (Belgium). This is a common tie-beam roof with a 30 ft (9.1 m) internal span and 43-degree pitch. It uses wall plates, and, again, there are lap joints and halvings on small scantling verticals and horizontal members.[74] The evidence for a ceiling in the nave is concealed, but the north transept, undated but possibly slightly earlier, is of the same main form and does have grooves cut in the sides of the tie-beams for boards, similar to the example at Boscherville in Normandy.[75] Lost roofs elsewhere also give us useful information, such as the *c.* 1067 roof at Jumièges. The form of this common tie-beam roof has been examined by Courtenay and Alcock.[76] A destroyed Carolingian example from Germany might also

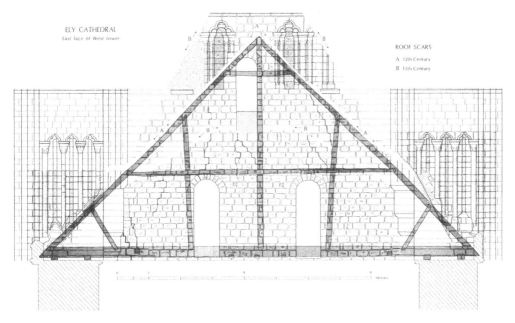

FIG. 27. Ely Cathedral: nave roof reconstruction
After Simpson and Litton, 'Dendrochronology in Cathedrals' (as n. 69)

be mentioned on account of its large span: Hersfeld Abbey, *c.* 1037, had a clear span of 43 ft (13 m).[77] Saint-Denis in Liège (1015–20), also has multiple common tie-beams and lap joints for hangers/struts.[78] This is a wide roof, about 33 ft (10 m) wide, with a 36-degree pitch.

RECONSTRUCTING THE FORM OF THE PRIMARY ROOF AT WESTMINSTER HALL

As we can see from this handful of 11th- and early-12th-century examples, and from other slightly later examples, none were double-framed roofs, with principal trusses and purlins. These did not really come in until the 13th century. A scissors-truss roof would have been equally anachronistic: this structural form was not developed for at least another century, and the jointing techniques to hold it together were not known to the Normans. So we can summarize that a roof, whatever the size, built at the time of Westminster Hall would not have been an open roof; would have had a common tie-beam arrangement; and would have consisted of a series of vertical or raking hangers and struts, with horizontal ties and collars. Spans were of course smaller, with few in England reaching much more than half the width of Westminster. It was not until almost a century later that the wide nave roof of York Minster was built, with a span of about 49 ft (15 m), but this was still only three-quarters the span of Westminster Hall.

In addition to being of a common tie-beam roof construction, the roof at Westminster most likely had a ceiling, as many of the comparable examples cited, which had primary or early ceilings. The stone arcading around all four sides of the roof strongly

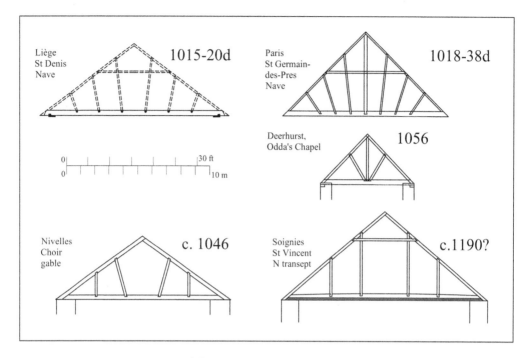

Fig. 28. Comparative roof drawings after Currie, 'A Romanesque roof' (as n. 70); Hoffsummer, *Les charpentes de toitures* (as n. 71); Hoffsummer, *Les charpentes du XIe au XIXe siècle* (as n. 72); Épaud, *De la charpente romane à la charpente gothique* (as n. 74)
Nat Alcock

suggests that it had a flat ceiling, possibly coffered, and spatially this produced a large room of pleasing proportions (Fig. 29). If there was no ceiling, the dark mass of structural timbers needed would have proved incongruous to the sophisticated stone arcading below. Of course this would have precluded an open hearth, so heating the hall would have been problematic.

The reconstruction in Figure 30 is one suggestion of what this roof might have looked like. It has a common tie-beam, outer rafters and three collars. Most importantly, we have hangers that keep the tie-beam from sagging and pulling the roof down with it. The dovetailed lap joint is employed at the ends of the horizontal and vertical members, which is quite efficient at withdrawal, and internally where they cross over they are halved, again a very simple and effective structural joint. By dividing the roof into a grid, no member is overstressed and triangulation is achieved by connecting the rafters to the ties by the collars and hangers.

One major consideration is obtaining sufficient number of timbers exceeding 68 ft (20.73 m) in a single length. Whilst it is still possible today to obtain timbers in excess of 70 ft (21.34 m) in length, the labour required to reduce this to a consistent section without the aid of sawing is not really an option for the 240 tie-beams and rafters needed. Figure 31 shows that a huge amount of waste would be needed to convert just one 70-ft-high tree to a single 1 ft (0.3 m) tie-beam.

Fig. 29. Conjectural interior view of Westminster Hall with some ceiling boarding
Thomas Hill, Helen Jones and Roland B. Harris

The problem of timber length is resolved by using simple splayed scarfs, a technique known in this period in ship building. The tie-beams would have been about 1 ft square; they do not want to be any larger as all they are doing is providing lateral restraint and would require support in the middle. This allows us to use trees of smaller size, no longer than 43 ft (13.11 m) for the tie-beams and rafters. The next longest timber is the king post, which at 37 ft (11.28 m) is also achievable. The illustration of a woodland (Fig. 32) — typical of woodlands in the late 11th century — at Mapledurham (South Oxfordshire) shows a large number of 40-ft-tall trees that would have been adequate to construct the roof at Westminster Hall.

Timber of the requisite length was therefore readily available during this period. The enormous extent of woodland at the time of the Domesday Book would have included mixed oak and beech woodlands, tall canopies, open glades, and trees of a variety of sizes.[79] The tall canopy has the effect of drawing up the small trees towards the light, making them very tall, straight, and with few branches until they reached the canopy. In short, ancient woodland was usually a far cry from the common modern perception of short, fat, stumpy veteran trees, which are not useful for structural building timbers. In medieval carpentry we normally find that a carpenter would select the smallest tree he could for each particular member, and this would be by simply squaring up the timber with the side axe, mainly chopping off the bark and sapwood. Timbers such as these were available throughout the medieval period and into the modern era.

A total of 1,760 trees would have had to be felled to construct the proposed 240-ft-long and 68-ft-wide roof. Half of these would have been immature trees big enough

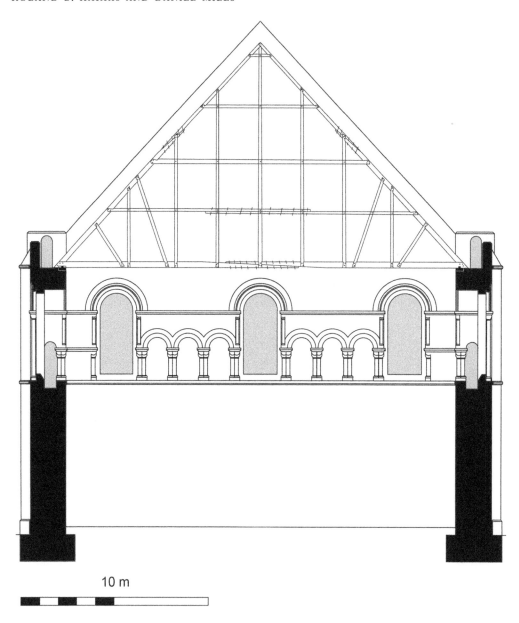

FIG. 30. Proposed reconstruction of single-span roof at Westminster Hall
Daniel Miles

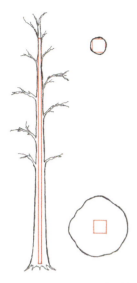 

FIG. 31. Section of tall tree illustrating the waste in chopping back to a single tie-beam or rafter (red)
Daniel Miles

FIG. 32. Typical naturally generating woodland at Mapledurham in south Oxfordshire
Daniel Miles

to convert into timbers 10–25 ft (3.04–7.62 m) in length. The remaining half would be larger trees, 25 ft (7.62 m) to more than 60 ft (18.29 m) tall, in order to obtain the 43 ft-long spliced tie-beams.

STRUCTURAL ANALYSIS OF THE RECONSTRUCTED ROOF

We have a proposed roof that uses the structural forms and the simple woodworking techniques of the time, and timbers that were readily attainable. But would such a roof actually stand up to the wind and snow loads? The proposed simple design was analysed by Thomas Hill of Mann Williams (Consulting Civil and Structural Engineers), who determined that it would stand up to the dead and live loads required of it. Further details of this analysis are found in the Appendix below. The design was based on 80 trusses spaced 3 ft (0.91 m) apart. Thomas Hill was able to reduce the tie-beams and rafters to 8-in.-square members, although they would probably have been at least 1 ft (0.3 m) square in reality. The internal members were all calculated at 4 in. square, although again they would more likely have been about 6 in. square or more. So massive timbers were not required structurally, and would only have the disadvantage of increasing the dead load of the roof. The connections between the members could be modelled as fully fixed, which transfers bending moment between members, or pinned, which has no moment transfer. As traditional timber connections are inherently somewhere in the middle, the model had some connections as

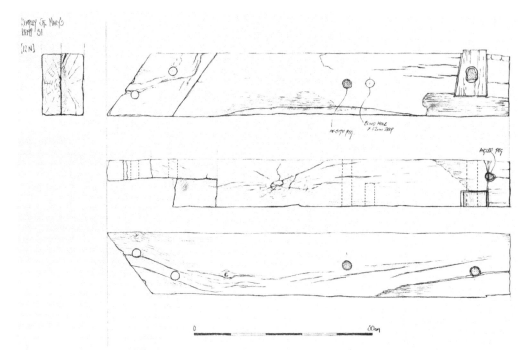

FIG. 33. Examples of Norman joints from Kempley Church
Rik Tyler

pinned and others as fixed, in order to replicate the actual effect of a timber frame. For instance, the internal members to the tie-beam and rafters have been taken as being pinned through the use of lap dovetail joints. However, where the internal members cross over each other, these were taken as fixed, given the fact that the timbers are halved over each other, which also interlocks them. The other structural connection is the splice or scarf to the tie-beams and the rafters. These are unsophisticated splayed joints with a series of skew pegs. The engineer calculated that about ten to twelve of these would have been required to provide the tensile strength needed, although the Normans might have used more (Fig. 33).

We know that the roof was repaired with shingles in the 1160s. This means it was almost certainly shingled before, which is interesting, because we know of no other large roof that was treated in this way. We would like to think that shingles were chosen because of their light dead load. In addition, the boarding required for the fixing of the shingles would have given a significant amount of additional strength by providing a stressed skin to the frames. This has not been taken into account in the engineer's calculations, so provides an inherent significant safety factor for the roof.

The total weight of the trusses would have been about 400 tonnes, although from an engineering perspective, the total could be reduced to 271 tonnes. The oak boarding and shingles would have weighed an additional 90 tonnes, and if the ceiling below was boarded, this would have weighed 31 tonnes. In comparison, the Richard II roof required about 600 tonnes of oak.

ERECTING THE ROOF

In order to construct this roof, the fact that the tie-beams and rafters are jointed makes it much easier to erect. Obviously there would have been a degree of scaffolding, but a full birdcage scaffold probably was not used. However, once both the sections of the tie-beam had been lifted up and pegged, with a temporary support, the two lower horizontal members and the lower section of the rafters could all have been fitted into place. Next, the shorter vertical members were put up and planks could have been placed on the horizontal members to get access to all levels. The upper stage of the roof truss could then have been fitted with a relative degree of safety. Indeed, the construction of this roof would have been considerably easier than the replacement roof of Richard II. Once a sufficient number of trusses was erected, the outer boarding could be fixed, and shingles applied, so several operations could be carried on concurrently. Ceiling boarding could also have been fixed at the same time, making use of the scaffolding needed to support the tie-beams.

FAILURE OF THE ROOF

Most Norman roofs had short life spans, and were being replaced a century or two later. Winchester, for instance, was pretty much complete by the 1090s, yet the roof of the nave was being replaced in 1250, and that of the south transept in 1320. The reason for these systematic failures was the extensive use of open lap joints. When first constructed, a roof composed of a number of members with such connections would have been exceptionally strong, but once the timbers had shrunk on seasoning, additional stress would have been placed on the pegs, and once one joint failed, adjacent joints would have been put under additional stress, resulting in progressive failure. These short-lived Norman roofs were replaced with more robust frames using the mortice and tenon joint, inherently stronger, and lasting 700 years or more. Yet Westminster appears to have survived for 300 years, despite being larger and longer: there is no documentary or, more significantly, structural evidence of a replacement roof before the 1390s. This is probably because of the multiple collars and hangers needed from the outset (because Westminster was so large), which gave the degree of structural redundancy required, as well as the stressed skin effect of the boarding.

However, the roof at Westminster did begin to fail, and progressively so during the 14th century, if not earlier. We have seen that by the 1390s the deflection at the top of the east wall was about 400 mm, and about 325 mm for the west wall. This shows that there was a certain amount of thrust being exerted on the walls by the roof, which would not have been the case if there were an arcade. The weakest part of this roof design is the joint between the rafter and the tie-beam; this would have most likely have been a halved joint, much like other contemporary examples. If this were to loosen, the rafters would push directly against the wall heads. This joint is also the one that is most susceptible to decay, being at the level of the parapet gutters, so some damage at this point would have been inevitable. Thomas Hill has modelled this situation as one possible mode of failure.

Generally in Romanesque roofs the rafters extended to or beyond the wall head, as seen at Kempley. However, the reconstruction offered here suggests that the rafters did not extend beyond the middle of the wall, since had they continued to the outer face of the walls in the same line scar as found on the internal gable ends, they would have clashed with the window heads. Also, as we have seen above, there is good evidence for a primary parapet, and the mass of the wall would have helped to retain the rafters and plate in position, not unlike the large contemporary 1090s roof of the White Tower at the Tower of London.[80]

No doubt some local failures of individual joints and members would have occurred owing to natural defects in the timber, as well as the loosening of the lap joints. Stress would have been placed on adjacent members and adjacent trusses, but eventually the whole would have come to a point of uneconomic repair. The roof almost certainly would have been strengthened from within, and repair accounts in the late 14th century bear this out. While we have no record of the roof actually collapsing, it is quite clear that it was deteriorating, if not in terminal decline, when Richard II decided to replace it with Hugh Herland's masterpiece in carpentry, which still stands today.

CONCLUSIONS

WE have demonstrated that it is possible to cover Westminster Hall with a single-span roof, if — as seems most likely — there were indeed no internal arcades. This roof would require a common tie-beam arrangement, the most structurally efficient method of achieving the span. Critical to this reconstruction is the use of two members with a long scarf to make up each tie-beam and rafter. Apart from one or two later examples,[81] no early buildings have been found with these composite tie-beams. However, no early buildings survive with such a wide roof. It is known that the keels of ships sometimes had long splayed scarfs,[82] and as the logic of such a joint is not out-of-this-world, it would have quickly been accepted that to construct such a large roof adequately, such a joint would need to be employed. As with other contemporary or earlier examples, the truss would be made up of one or more horizontal collars, and multiple canted or vertical struts or hangers would create a remarkably robust yet lightweight structure. The fact that it was shingled would have necessitated boarding, which would have given the roof additional strength, and if the ceiling below had also been boarded, then that too would have improved its capacity further still. Examples of Norman ceilings are more common than previously thought, and, in addition to that in Normandy at Saint-Georges (Boscherville), they are used further afield across the Continent, at Saint-Germain-des-Prés (Paris), Saint-Vincent in Soignies (Belgium), Maulbronn Abbey (Germany), and Sankt Martin in Zillis (Switzerland).[83] William Rufus's original roof appears to have lasted 300 years, which is more than can be said for any other large contemporary roof in England. Clearly the Norman builders of Westminster Hall got something right, and this reconstruction shows one way how that may have been achieved.

ACKNOWLEDGEMENTS

Daniel Miles is grateful to discussions with Damian Goodburn and Nat Alcock on points of Norman carpentry and structure, and Thomas Hill for kindly reviewing and analysing the structural design.

Romanesque Westminster Hall and its Roof

APPENDIX

Structural Analysis of the Roof

THOMAS HILL (Director, Mann Williams, Consulting Civil and Structural Engineers)

INTRODUCTION

WHILE the evidence both of the archaeology of Westminster Hall and of late-11th- and 12th-century parallels strongly suggests that the primary roof was of single span, it is important to assess the structural performance of such a roof. This appendix presents an independent structural analysis of the reconstructed roof form presented in the article above.

THE MODELLING

THE computational analysis of complex real-world structures is founded on a series of approximations and assumptions, reflecting the difference between an idealized computer model and the imperfect real world. Each assumption or approximation generates intrinsic inaccuracies, with varying implications on the true accuracy of results. Increasing detail and complexity of a computational model may reduce the magnitude and influence of assumptions and approximations, potentially generating greater accuracy of results. However, increased accuracy commonly offers a diminishing return, so engineering judgement is required to determine an appropriate complexity of structural modelling. The structural model for the proposed Norman Westminster Hall roof is comparatively crude, based on significant simplifications and assumptions of design parameters. The most significant assumptions and approximations made for the purpose of modelling the proposed roof are detailed below, with some explanatory commentary.

General form, dimensions and extent of the model

THE roof trusses span 21.6 m and are spaced at 900 mm centres. Ten trusses were modelled, although there would have been approximately 80–85 trusses in the roof structure based on this spacing. The structural performance of the entire roof was beyond the scope of this investigation.

Principal rafters and tie-beams were initially estimated as 200 mm × 200 mm, and all other internal sections as 100 mm × 100 mm.

The analysed arrangement and member sizes are indicated in Figure 34.

Precedent suggests a hardwood sarking (or boarding) layer to the roof and ceiling. The dead weight of the sarking has been incorporated into the analysis, although no associated beneficial diaphragm action or stiffness has been included. This is almost certainly conservative, as sarking would improve the structural performance of the roof generally if robustly connected to the supporting structure.

Materials

THE highest grade of oak available for structural design is grade THA, with a corresponding strength class D40 (therefore achieving a minimum ultimate bending stress of 40N/sqmm). THA grading is not strictly applicable to cross sections smaller than 100 mm × 200 mm, owing to the relevance of the scale and proportion of permissible defects compared with the dimensions of the member. However, it seems appropriate in this instance, given the prestigious nature of this structure and the likely availability and use of highest-quality oak, to assume a high structural grade.

Connections

CONNECTIONS between members are commonly modelled as either fully fixed, transferring bending moments between connected members, or pinned, with no bending moment transfer.

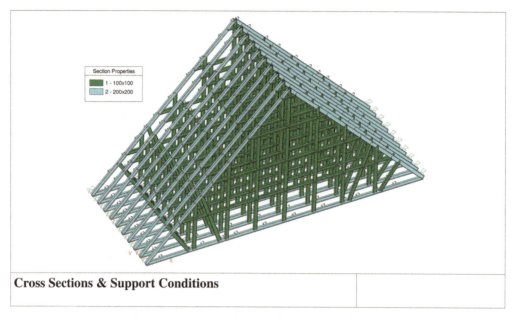

Fig. 34. Cross-sections and support conditions
Thomas Hill

This methodology is not particularly useful for traditional timber design, where connections are often inherently 'somewhere in the middle', neither fully fixed nor pinned.

Principal rafter and tie-beam splices are modelled as fully fixed, owing to the suggested length of the splices and the corresponding potential to transfer significant moments between the spliced members.

Connections between internal truss members and the principal rafter and tie-beam are modelled as pinned, as these connections are proposed to be a single- or double-pegged halved joint and there is no continuity of internal members.

Connections between internal truss members are modelled as continuous at their intersections, of a constant cross section and, therefore, fully fixed. In reality, where members are halved at connections the reduction in cross-section generates stress risers, which are discussed further in the results, and partial local 'hinges' in the members, the effects of which have not been considered in this model.

Defects

THERE is limited scope to allow for random, inherent or induced defects and irregularities in timber members, connections, workmanship, or the surrounding structure. The structural model of Westminster Hall roof is therefore effectively perfect. The real structure would certainly not be perfect, and imperfections and defects are obviously detrimental and often significant. However, the failure of the tie-beam to principal rafter connection at the supports has been simulated in the analysis.

Supports

THE boundary conditions or supports of a structural model have a fundamental influence on the behaviour and corresponding results generated by a computational model, the significance of which is easily underestimated. A selection of idealized support conditions is available to the designer, none of which readily represents typical support provided to components of building structures.

To generate the most significant forces in the tie-beam member one end of the truss was permitted to move laterally, by providing a 'roller' support. This replicates supporting masonry providing no resistance to lateral forces and corresponding horizontal displacements. It would be inaccurate to assume complete restraint from the supporting masonry, inferring an infinite stiffness, however, as per the connectivity between members, the reality is somewhere in the middle.

Sense check

THE computational modelling of even the most simple structures can be disproportionally sensitive to minor human mistakes inputting data. Therefore it is always critical to 'sense check' the results of computational modelling. Sense checking may involve simplified and approximate hand calculations to judge the expected magnitude and sense ('+' or '-') of forces. A simple and useful sense check is a comparison between graphical results and intuitive expectations, considering the nature of forces and deflected shapes.

RESULTS

SELECTED results for axial load, bending moments, the corresponding timber stresses and deflections are discussed for the loading combinations of (a) dead load only, and (b) dead + wind load (which is generally the most adverse and therefore governing combination).

Axial forces (kN)

A sense check inspection of the axial forces in the trusses indicates the largest axial forces for both load combinations are as expected, tension ('+') in the tie-beam, and compression ('-'), in the principal rafters (Fig. 35). The magnitude of these forces is large (25kN is a force approximately equivalent to a weight of 2.5T), although these are the members with the largest cross-sections. Axial forces within internal members are significantly lower in every load case, at <6kN.

Consideration of the nature of axial forces within internal members highlights the fundamental way in which these proposed trusses would function. Under gravitational loading the internal members are supporting only axial forces, with no bending moments (Fig. 36). The vertical internal members are working almost exclusively in tension, transferring the gravitational loading from the tie-beam to the principal rafters, which in turn transfer the loading to the supports in compression. The horizontal internal members are working in compression, therefore propping the principal rafters. Members working predominantly in tension and compression are efficient in trusses, and significant bending may necessitate considerably larger members.

Deflections (mm)

AN initial sense check of the deflected shape of the trusses for both dead load (Fig. 37) and dead + wind loading (Fig. 38) indicates that the deflected form of the trusses are intuitively correct.

The vertical deflections under dead loading only are small given the spans involved, 1–2 mm (shown with an exaggerated scale in Fig. 37). This is due to the efficient configuration of the truss, with members working principally in tension and compression rather than bending, but does not allow for any potential defects, either in members or connections, joint slip, etc.

Simulating a defect in the tie-beam indicates the trusses would be very sensitive to defects and failures in individual key members (Fig. 39). The vertical deflection under dead loading increases dramatically, from approximately 1 mm to nearly 90 mm. Such a failure also has significant, potentially catastrophic, consequences on the axial forces and bending moments in other truss members (Fig. 41).

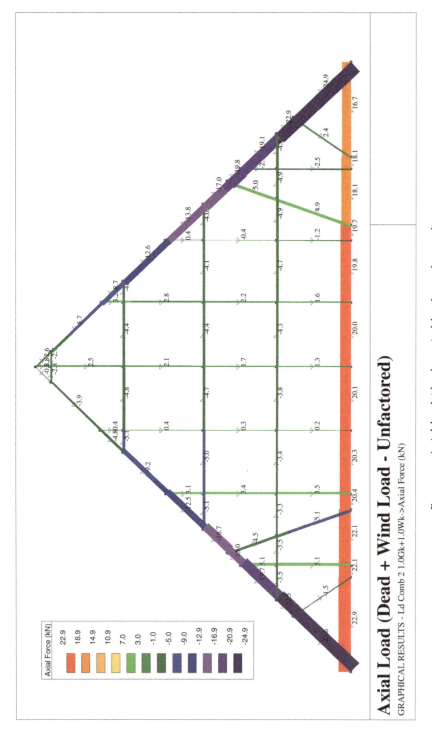

FIG. 35. Axial load (dead + wind load – unfactored)
Thomas Hill

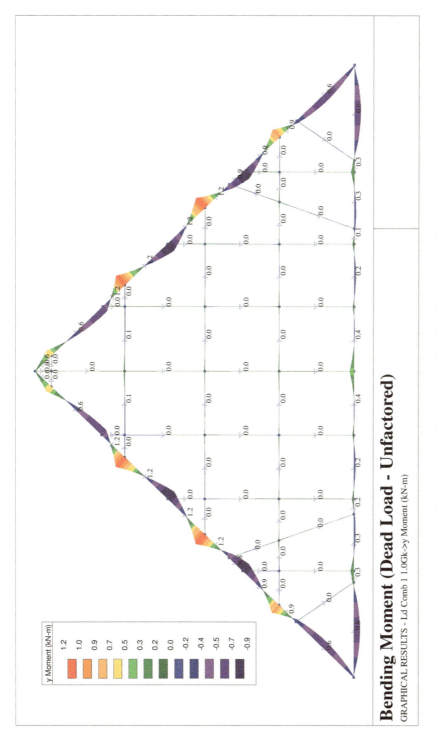

FIG. 36. Bending moment (dead load – unfactored)
Thomas Hill

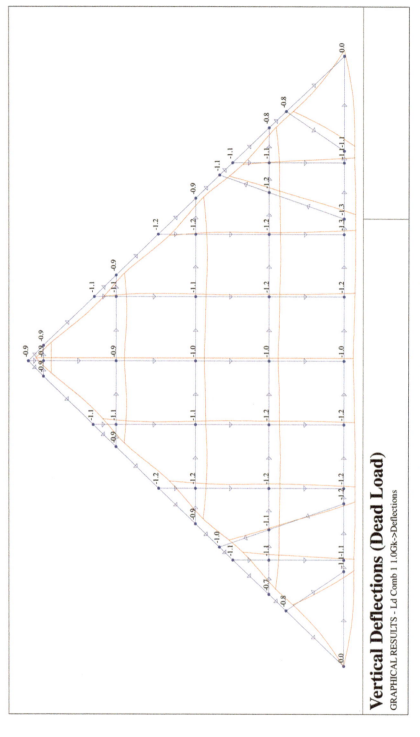

Fig. 37. Vertical deflections (dead load)
Thomas Hill

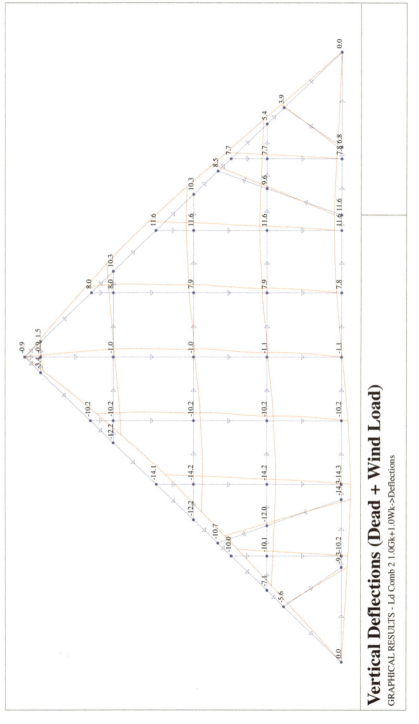

FIG. 38. Vertical deflections (dead + wind load)
Thomas Hill

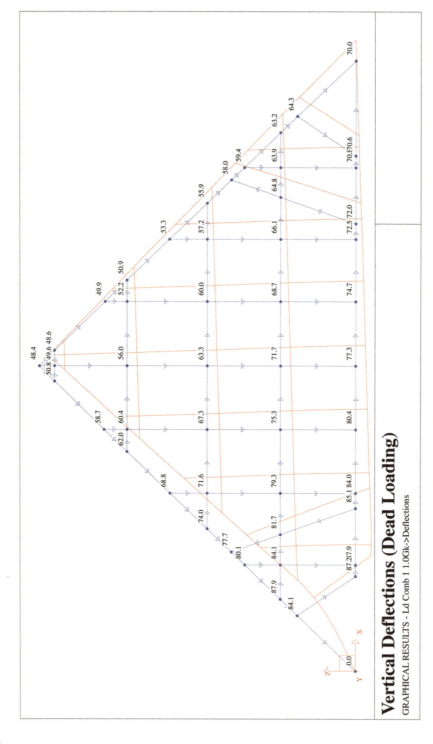

FIG. 39. Vertical deflections (dead loading)
Thomas Hill

Deflections under wind loading, for the complete and 'perfect' truss are significantly larger, at 14 mm+. While these deflections are reasonable and probably manageable (given the scale of the structure and potential consequences, lack of brittle finishes, etc.), the significant increase in deflections does indicate the relative inefficiency of the trusses and component members when working in bending, as induced by the twisting effect of the wind.

Bending moments (kNM)

UNDER dead loading the principal rafters and tie-beam are subjected to bending moments (Fig. 36), the pattern of which can be justified with a rudimentary sense check. The principal rafters are in positive (+ve), bending or 'hogging' at intersections with the horizontal internal members, which are in compression and therefore propping the principal rafters. Where vertical internal members, primarily working in tension, are supported from the principal rafters a 'sagging' bending moment is generated. Bending moments in the tie-beam are hogging at the points of effective support (vertical internal members), and sagging between supports.

Examination of the nature of forces within members under wind loading indicates that bending moments are generated within internal members due to the twisting effect of the wind (Fig. 40). These bending moments are small (<1kNM), although potentially significant when considering member stresses. The magnitude of bending moments in the principal rafter and tie-beam also increase, by a factor of three, and change in their distribution with more significant sagging moment in the windward principal rafter and hogging in the leeward.

The truss with a simulated tie-beam defect (Fig. 41) suggests the likely consequences of such a defect. Bending moments in the adjacent principal rafter under dead and wind loading increase significantly to more than 46kNM. Such an increased moment and corresponding stress could be potentially catastrophic, although the principal rafter cross-sections would be likely to be rectangular (say 250–300 mm deep × 150–200 mm wide) and the load-sharing effect generated by sarking would also help mitigate against such a failure.

Member stresses (N/sqmm)

TOTAL stresses in members are calculated by superimposing stresses generated by axial loading and bending moments, which are concurrent. D40 timber has a characteristic bending stress of 40N/sqmm, which is factored to generate a permissible stress depending on the nature and duration of loading, exposure conditions and other factors. The resulting permissible stress typically ranges between 10 and 22 N/sqmm.

Considering the members as modelled, with the full width section at connections, peak wind loading generates unfactored stresses not in excess of 6 N/sqmm. The maximum combined stress is generated at the intersections of internal members. In a half-width section stress would be doubled, so that the stress would reach 12 N/sqmm.

FURTHER ANALYSIS

VARIOUS aspects of the structural analysis would benefit from further investigation and refinement, potentially yielding interesting results and significant improvements in accuracy.

As discussed previously, boundary conditions within a structural model significantly affect results. The Norman roof trusses to Westminster hall were originally supported on masonry with an alternative configuration (Fig. 29). Substantial changes were made to the upper half of the walls during the 14th-century replacement of the roof; the original upper masonry was more voided and less structurally robust than the current configuration. Significant current horizontal deflections in the masonry are known to have existed before the reconstruction, presumably resulting from the thrust exerted by the original roof structure.

The horizontal deflection of the supporting masonry is an important consideration in the forensic analysis of any proposals for an original Norman roof and the circumstances leading to

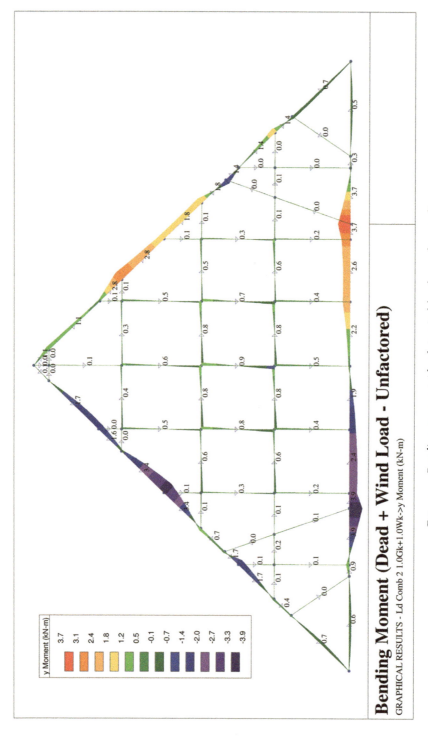

FIG. 40. Bending moment (dead + wind load – unfactored)
Thomas Hill

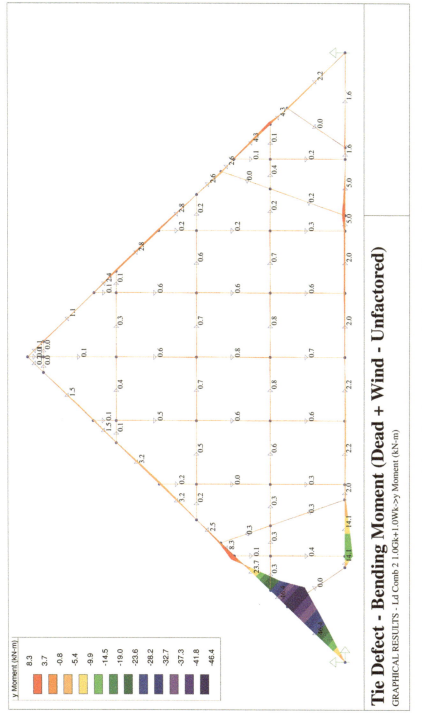

FIG. 41. Tie defect – bending moment (dead + wind load – unfactored)
Thomas Hill

its replacement. The structural performance of the original masonry can be simulated in a computational model utilizing finite element techniques; this would provide useful insight in the further evaluation of the original roof.

Ten independent two-dimensional trusses were included in the structural model, with no structural interaction between the trusses or load sharing. A three-dimensional analysis, considering the entire roof structure (including the beneficial structural characteristics of the sarking diaphragms and the accurate modelling of the supporting masonry) would inevitably generate more accurate and realistic results and conclusions.

CONCLUSIONS

THE structural analysis was two dimensional and relatively crude, with significant assumptions and approximations generating inherent inaccuracies. However, the fundamental parameters of greatest influence, support conditions, spans, loadings, truss geometry, configuration and member sections are representative of the suggested clear-span Norman roof. The analysis therefore provides relevant results for discussion, allowing the feasibility of the roof to be evaluated.

The structural performance of the proposed scheme, considering bending moments, axial forces and deflections for the different loading combinations, suggests that a clear-span roof, of typical Norman construction as proposed in the article above, is structurally feasible for Westminster Hall.

The simulation of a defect in the tie-beam member (Fig. 41) and the corresponding significant increases in deflections, bending moments, and timber stresses indicate that while the proposals represent a feasible scheme, individual trusses would be disproportionately sensitive to defects of workmanship, materials or maintenance.

The beneficial effects of the sarking boards may have helped mitigate such failures, distributing the additional loading between multiple trusses, although, given the probable 300-year life of the structure, it is conceivable that multiple trusses would experience such failures and, therefore, that the global performance of the roof structure would be severely impeded. This could potentially lead to significant thrusts imposed on the supporting masonry, ultimately necessitating complete replacement of the roof structure and the repairs to the supporting masonry.

NOTES

1. W. R. Lethaby, 'The Palace of Westminster in the Eleventh and Twelfth Centuries', *Archaeologia*, LX (1906), 131–48.
2. D. E. Greenway trans., *Henry of Huntingdon: The History of the English People, 1100–1154* (Oxford 2002), 48.
3. F. Michel, *Histoire des ducs de Normandie et des rois d'Angleterre* (Paris 1840), 65–66.
4. D. Whitelock, D. C. Douglas and S. I. Tucker ed., *The Anglo-Saxon Chronicle: A Revised Translation* (London1961), 175; J. Earle and C. Plummer, *Two of the Saxon Chronicles: Parallel, with Supplementary Extracts from the Others*, 2 vols (Oxford 1892, 2nd edn), I, 234.
5. See, for example, M. Collins, P. Emery, C. Phillpotts, M. Samuel and C. Thomas, 'The King's High Table at the Palace of Westminster', *The Antiquaries Journal*, 92 (2012), 197–243, at 203.
6. R. B. Harris, 'The Structural History of the White Tower, 1066-1200', in *The White Tower*, ed. E. Impey (New Haven CT/London 2008), 29–93.
7. R. Allen Brown, H. M. Colvin and A. J. Taylor, *The History of the King's Works: The Middle Ages*, 2 vols (London 1963), I, 491, n. 1; R. Gem, 'Canterbury and the Cushion Capital: a Commentary on the Passages from Goscelin's De Miraculis Sancti Augustini', in *Romanesque and Gothic: Essays for George Zarnecki*, ed. N. Stratford, 2 vols (Woodbridge 1987), I, 83–101, at 85.
8. Pipe Roll 8 Henry II, 69; Pipe Roll 9 Henry II, 72.
9. E. W. Brayley and J. Britton, *The History of the Ancient Palace and Late Houses of Parliament at Westminster* (London 1836), 121, 124, 191.
10. C. Wilson, 'Rulers, Artificers and Shoppers: Richard II's Remodelling of Westminster Hall, 1393-99', in *The Regal Image of Richard II and the Wilton Diptych*, ed. D. Gordon, L. Monnas and C. Elam (London 1997), 33–59 and 274–88, at 279, n. 40.

11. L. F. Salzman, *Building in England Down to 1540: A Documentary History* (Oxford 1952), 262.
12. Pipe Roll 8 Henry II, 43.
13. Pipe Roll 1 Richard I, 223.
14. *King's Works* (as n. 7), I, 528.
15. Ibid., 528–29.
16. Ibid., 47.
17. Metric survey undertaken by the author in 1999, under the auspices of the 'Medieval Palace of Westminster Research Project' funded by the Arts and Humanities Research Board.
18. House of Lords Record Office, Historical Collection, 3/6/2, dated January 1919.
19. D. Whipp and E. Platts, 'Westminster Hall Excavation', *London Archaeologist*, 2/14 (spring 1976), 351–55. The site archive has additional information, including a section drawing.
20. Collins et al., 'The King's High Table' (as n. 5).
21. S. Smirke, 'Second Letter from Sydney Smirke on the architectural History of Westminster Hall', *Archaeologia*, XXVI (1836), 415–21, at 415–16.
22. Collins et al., 'The King's High Table' (as n. 5), 231.
23. G. Somers Clarke, 'The west side of Westminster Hall', *Archaeologia*, L (1887), 9–16; SAL, BB 90/11868, B. Lemere, 5501 (MPW 1446).
24. Undertaken by the author in 1999, under the auspices of the 'Medieval Palace of Westminster Research Project' funded by the Arts and Humanities Research Board, using a Pulse EKKO 1000 GPR kindly provided by the NERC geophysical equipment pool.
25. Collins et al., 'The King's High Table' (as n. 5), 204–05.
26. SAL, Red Portfolio, Westminster, Houses of Parliament, 22 (MPW 434); S. Smirke, 'A further Account of the original Architecture of Westminster Hall', *Archaeologia*, XXVII (1838), 135–39. Brayley and Britton refer to a 'small tract' on Westminster Hall by J. Rickman, in which he interpreted the features discovered in 1822 as a 'triple doorway'; Brayley and Britton, *History of the Ancient Palace and Late Houses of Parliament* (as n. 9), 438.
27. S. Smirke, 'Remarks on the architectural History of Westminster Hall', *Archaeologia*, XXVI (1836), 406–14, at 410.
28. Smirke, 'A further Account of the original Architecture of Westminster Hall' (as n. 26), pl. 12.
29. TNA, WORK 29/21.
30. Smirke, 'Remarks on the architectural History of Westminster Hall' (as n. 27), 410.
31. Smirke, 'A further Account of the original Architecture of Westminster Hall' (as n. 26), pl. 12.
32. J. L. Pearson, *Report on Westminster Hall* (London 1884).
33. C. Miele, 'The Battle for Westminster Hall', *Architectural History*, 41 (1998), 220–44, at 228–29.
34. Somers Clarke, 'The west side of Westminster Hall' (as n. 23).
35. E. Freshfield, 'Masons' Marks at Westminster Hall', *Archaeologia*, L (1887), 1–4.
36. SAL, BB 90/11868, B. Lemere 5501 (MPW 1446).
37. Smirke, 'A further Account of the original Architecture of Westminster Hall' (as n. 26), 136.
38. Miele, 'The Battle for Westminster Hall' (as n. 33), 241.
39. MPW 940, published in J. Cherry and N. Stratford, *Westminster Kings and the medieval Palace of Westminster*, British Museum Occasional Paper 115 (London 1995), 55; and H. Colvin ed., 'Views of the Old Palace of Westminster', *Architectural History*, 9 (1966), 21–184, fig. 87.
40. MPW 1101: J. G. Rokewode, 'A Memoir on the Painted Chamber in the Palace at Westminster ... [Read 12th May 1842.]', SAL, *Vetusta Monumenta*, VI (London 1885), pl. XXVI, detail 'A'. This engraving is entirely convincing but for the fact the outermost order of the southern window arch of the east side is depicted as springing 5 ft 8 in. from the south-east clasping buttress; if this was really the case, then the southern window would be half a bay out of synchronization with the internal arcade (which is well recorded in this area) and would have coincided with the position of the southern buttress as predicted from the surviving buttresses on the east side, from the known disposition of the eastern clerestory arcade, and from the surviving buttresses on the west side and their relationship to the recorded western clerestory. Since 5 ft 8 in. approximates to the distance from the *centre* of the predicted position of the southern window to the south-east buttress, it may be that Mackenzie's error — for it is difficult to conceive of it as anything else — is the result of confusion when working up site sketches and notes of what was a very inaccessible detail.
41. MPW 1037: J. T. Smith, *Antiquities of Westminster* (London 1807, additional plates 1807–09), facing 45; 'Views of the Old Palace of Westminster' (as n. 39), 88B.
42. MPW 1167: J. Storer and J. Greig, *Antiquarian and Topographical Cabinet*, VI (London 1819), pl. 73c.
43. MPW 927: Brayley and Britton, *History of the Ancient Palace and Late Houses of Parliament* (as n. 9), pl. 9.

44. Smirke, 'Remarks on the architectural History of Westminster Hall' (as n. 27), 409.
45. Lethaby, 'Palace of Westminster' (as n. 1), 139–40.
46. Smirke, 'A further Account of the original Architecture of Westminster Hall' (as n. 26), 136 and pl. 12.
47. Ibid., 137–38.
48. Ibid., 138–39.
49. Ibid., 137.
50. Lethaby, 'The Palace of Westminster in the Eleventh and Twelfth Centuries' (as n. 1), 140.
51. Observed by the author in 2012, during conservation works to the north window and inner face of the north elevation.
52. MPW 852: Storer and Greig, *Antiquarian and Topographical Cabinet* (as n. 42), pl. 73a; MPW 880: J. Green del., Owen sculpt., *A view of north front of Westminster Hall* (1813), WCA, E.133.5 (34); MPW 942: Smith, *Antiquities of Westminster* (as n. 41), facing 30; MPW 950: R. B. Schnebberlie, del. *New Palace Yard, looking south-west*, WCA, box 58, no. 07A [formerly 7B]; MPW 966: 'Views of the Old Palace of Westminster' (as n. 39), fig. 30; MPW 1074: Green del., Owen sc. *Westminster Hall* (1805), WCA, box 59, no. 23B; MPW 1188: *S side of New Palace Yard, facing SW, showing N front of Westminster Hall, Exchequer buildings, etc.*, WCA, box 58, no. 20.
53. The trusses are numbered from the north in the manner of the Ministry of Works drawings.
54. Lethaby, 'The Palace of Westminster in the Eleventh and Twelfth Centuries' (as n. 1), 135, fig. 1.
55. These were investigated by the author in 1999, under the auspices of the 'Medieval Palace of Westminster Research Project' funded by the Arts and Humanities Research Board, and again, for this paper, in 2011. In 1999, David Park (Courtauld Institute of Art, London) examined the wall-paintings in the clerestory passage and concluded that they were of 13th-century date.
56. TNA, WORK 29/3414.
57. E. Fernie, *An Architectural History of Norwich Cathedral* (Oxford 1993), 152.
58. S. Heywood, 'The Romanesque Building', in *Norwich Cathedral: Church, City and Diocese, 1096–1996*, ed. I. Atherton, E. Fernie, C. Harper-Bill and H. Smith (London 1996), 73–115, at 111.
59. For discussion of the Romanesque clerestory at Norwich, see R. B. Harris, 'Reconstructing the cathedral-priory at Norwich: recent research on lost parts of the Romanesque church', *Norwich: Medieval and Early Modern Art, Architecture and Archaeology*, ed. Sandy Heslop and Helen Lunnon, BAA Trans., XXVIII (for 2012) (Leeds 2015), 57–74.
60. MPW 1147: Brayley and Britton, *History of the Ancient Palace and Late Houses of Parliament* (as n. 9), pl. 10.
61. Lethaby, 'The Palace of Westminster in the Eleventh and Twelfth Centuries' (as n. 1), 140.
62. Collins et al., 'The King's High Table' (as n. 5), 205.
63. For the *Échiquier* at Caen and parallels, see Edward Impey in this volume, 72–88.
64. Wilson, 'Rulers, Artificers and Shoppers' (as n. 10), 33, 43, and 280 n. 46.
65. TNA, WORK 29/3420.
66. H. Delhumeau, *Le Palais de la Cite: Du Palais des Rois de France au Palais de Justice* (Paris 2011).
67. D. Miles, 'Tree-ring dates', *Vernacular Architecture*, 39 (2008), 135–46, at 133.
68. B. M. Morley and D. W. H. Miles, 'Nave Roof, Chest, and Door of the Church of St Mary, Kempley, Gloucestershire: Dendrochronological Dating', *Antiq. J.*, 80 (2000), 294–96; D. W. H. Miles, M. J. Worthington and C. Groves, *Tree-ring Analysis of the Nave Roof, West Door, and Parish Chest from the Church of St Mary, Kempley, Gloucestershire*, English Heritage, Ancient Monuments Laboratory Report 36 (London 1999).
69. G. Simpson and C. Litton, 'Dendrochronology in Cathedrals', in *The Archaeology of Cathedrals*, ed. T. Tatton-Brown and J. Munby (Oxford 1996), 183–201.
70. C. R. J. Currie, 'A Romanesque roof at Odda's Chapel, Deerhurst, Gloucestershire', *Antiq. J.*, 63/1 (1983), 58–65.
71. P. Hoffsummer, *Les charpentes de toitures en Wallonie*, Ministère de la région Wallonne (Namur 1995), 78.
72. P. Hoffsummer ed., *Les charpentes du XIe au XIXe siècle: Typologie et évolution en France du Nord et en Belgique*, Monum. Éditions de Patrimoine 62 (Paris 2002), 100, 153, 168. English translation: *Roof frames from the 11th to the 19th century: Typology and development in Northern France and in Belgium* (Turnhout 2009).
73. *Les charpentes du XIe au XIXe siècle* (as n. 72), 153–54.
74. F. Épaud, *De la charpente romane à la charpente gothique en Normandie* (Caen 2007), 137.
75. L. T. Courtenay, L T, N. W. Alcock and E. A. Impey, 'An Early Common Tiebeam Roof: St Georges-de-Boscherville, Seine-Maritime, France', *Med. Archaeol.*, 42 (1998), 54–67.

76. L. T. Courtenay and N. W. Alcock, 'The Romanesque roof of Jumièges Abbey and its wider context in northern Europe', *Med. Archaeol.*, 59 (forthcoming).
77. K. J. Conant, *Carolingian and Romanesque Architecture 800–1200* (Harmondsworth 1973, 3rd edn), 73–74.
78. Épaud, *De la charpente romane à la charpente gothique en Normandie* (as n. 74), 138–39.
79. O. Rackham, *Ancient Woodland* (London 1980), 113.
80. Harris, 'The Structural History of the White Tower' (as n. 6), 75–85.
81. J.-P. Hunot in P. Hoffsummer ed., *Les charpentes du XIe au XIXe siècle: Grand-Ouest de la France* (Turnhout 2011), 48 and 279–94.
82. Damian Goodburn, personal communication.
83. Courtenay and Alcock, 'The Romanesque roof of Jumièges Abbey' (as n. 76), and Courtenay et al., 'An Early Common Tiebeam Roof' (as n. 75), 65.

The Great Hall at Caen and its Affinities with Westminster

EDWARD IMPEY

In the castle of Caen (Calvados), the second city of Normandy since the 1060s, stands a vast Romanesque hall, once part of the ducal palace, and known since the 19th century as the Échiquier. Long claimed to have had two storeys and to date from the reign of Henry I, it has now been shown on archaeological and structural grounds to have contained a single volume, and can be reattributed, for stylistic reasons, to the end of the 11th century. Given its similarities in form and date to Westminster Hall, and the circumstances surrounding Rufus's rule in Normandy, it is suggested that the Échiquier was built on his initiative and for a similar purpose. Furthermore, the recent archaeological discovery of a building near the Echiquier, perhaps of the same date and reminiscent of the Lesser Hall at Westminster, suggests that the two hall's affinity extended to possessing substantial camera-like structures close by.

THE ÉCHIQUIER: SITUATION AND DESCRIPTION

CAEN, unlike the ancient ducal capital at Rouen, is known only from the early 11th century, but was made the second city of Normandy by Duke William in the 1060s.[1] Here, on high ground to the north of the main settlement, he created a castle,[2] and within it a palace, at least parts of which were excavated by Professor Michel de Boüard in the 1960s.[3] Adjacent to these stands the best-preserved, the largest, and the earliest Romanesque hall to survive in Normandy, known since 1840 as 'The Hall of the Exchequer' or *l'Échiquier*[4] (Fig. 1).

The present form of the building dates from its restoration in the 1960s following partial destruction in July 1944.[5] In the 1960s, it was restored to what was, as then understood, its late medieval, single-volume form — owing, ironically, to the lack of detailed evidence for the form of its 'original' upper floor.[6] As a result, it was unwittingly returned to a close approximation of its primary form: a rectangle, orientated north-west by south-east, with the main entrance in the south-east façade, a window in the south-east gable, high windows in the side walls, and a single interior open from floor to rafters. Externally it measures (on average) 13.16 m (43 ft 2 in.) by 32.90 m (107 ft 11 in.), and internally 30.70 m (100 ft 9 in.) by 11.02 m (36 ft 2 in.), giving it a floor area of just over 338 m^2 (3,638 ft^2).[7] Inside, the walls are interrupted only by a string-course, chamfered at the lower edge, at the sill-level of the windows. Externally, except to the north, the elevations are articulated by pilaster buttresses, plinth, string-course, and (side walls) with a corbel-table (Figs 2–6).

Twentieth-century works apart, alterations to the primary building (period I) fall into three periods. In the later 12th century, a small structure was attached to the

Fig. 1. Aerial view of Caen Castle from the south-west. The *Échiquier* stands against the rampart to the north (left); immediately to the east of this stood the buildings of the 'palais de Guillaume'; the footings of the Henry I's *donjon*, surrounded by Philippe-Auguste's curtain wall, lie beyond

Reproduced by kind permission of the Musée de Normandie

south end of the north-east side, and in the first half of the 14th century the primary structure was reroofed, the ground floor flagged, a fireplace built into the west wall, a building attached to the east side (with a fireplace and chimney cut into its exterior wall),[8] and a vaulted storage room built against the north wall. The building then remained little changed until 1881, when a first floor was inserted in its southern half and new openings cut through the walls.[9]

THE ORIGINAL FORM OF THE *ÉCHIQUIER*

THE main question as to the *Échiquier*'s original form is whether it was, as de Boüard insisted, two-storeyed, an interpretation supported (with the occasional acknowledgement of debate), by all French authors[10] except Jean Mesqui (1993, 1997 and 2008):[11] the 'single-volume' interpretation, put forward by the author in the 1980s and in print in 1993, has found more favour (if indeed it was ever doubted), in England, and was assumed by Christopher Wilson in 1997.[12] This interpretation has since been confirmed in a recent article by the author and John McNeill, published in French,[13] and the arguments and counter-arguments need only be summarized here. De Boüard's

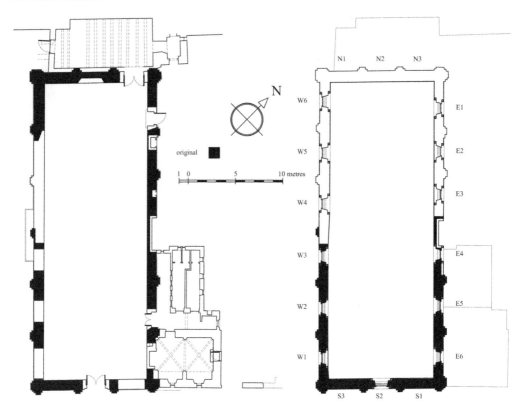

Fig. 2. Plans at entrance level and upper level (left, right)
Howard Jones

interpretation was based on four main points and observations. First, the absence of flagged paving and the presence of pits containing food remains implied to him a menial function, and thus, in a building of such obvious grandeur, the existence of an *étage noble* above.[14] Second, he believed that the existing windows, high up in the walls, would not have adequately lit a full-height interior.[15] Third, he saw their stepped sills as actual steps, and so necessarily close to a floor level.[16] He noted finally that as a storeyed building, it would have conformed to 'one of the best known types of domestic architecture of the 12th century'.[17] In fact, earth floors are known in comparable contexts elsewhere (including in Westminster Hall),[18] Romanesque interiors were routinely lit by high windows, and stepped sills are frequently found to windows far above floor level.[19] Finally, de Boüard's understanding of what was normal in the 12th century predated the identification of high-status ground-floor halls in France from before 1100,[20] and was coloured by an interpretation of Romanesque domestic buildings in England now known to be incorrect.[21] Moreover, it is worth noting that the *absence* of an upper floor obviates or answers de Boüard's own unanswered questions as to how smoke escaped from the ground floor,[22] how the ground floor was lit,[23] how the upper floor was supported,[24] why the rere-arch to

The Great Hall at Caen

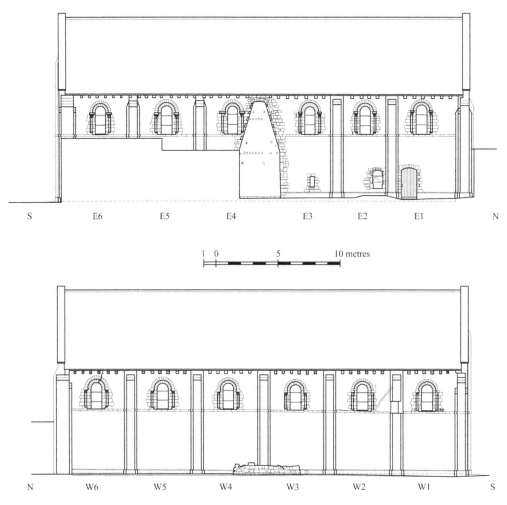

FIG. 3. East and west elevations (above, below)
Howard Jones

the south-east doorway rises above the postulated upper-floor level, and how to explain the absence of an original upper doorway.[25]

As an English readership will recognize, the single-volume, unaisled, high-windowed form of the *Échiquier* is common to numerous Romanesque halls in England, for example those at Westminster, Sherborne Castle (Dorset), and Old Sarum Castle.[26] Still more exact analogies can be found among monastic refectories, from which it has been suggested that the type derives,[27] including the late-11th-century refectory at Westminster Abbey,[28] the refectory or hall at Minster Court (Kent, *c*. 1120), or the refectory of Dover Priory (1130s).[29] The inescapable conclusion must be that the *Échiquier* was, as built, a single-storey structure (Fig. 7).

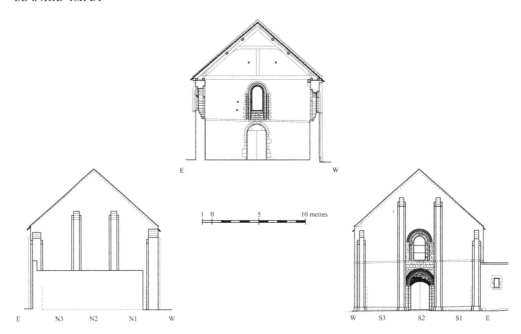

Fig. 4. Cross-section (facing south) and north and south elevations
Howard Jones

THE DATE OF THE *ÉCHIQUIER*

DE BOÜARD was cautious in dating the *Échiquier*. In 1962, he placed it simply in the '12th century', and only in 1965 and 1979 in the reign of Henry I.[30] In the two later publications he placed it on stylistic grounds only in 'in the first half of the 12th century';[31] his attribution to Henry I (that is, in Normandy, between 1106 and 1135) was based, his text implies, on the king's documented building of the *donjon* at Caen.[32] Lucien Musset,[33] Eric Carlson,[34] Jean Mesqui and other authors have agreed, some offering greater precision;[35] only Maylis Baylé demurred, placing the *Échiquier*, if without explanation, 'vers 1100'.[36] All this is understandable. On the face of it, Henry I is a good candidate: he was a frequent visitor to Normandy and did business in Caen in 1118, 1120, 1124, 1130–01, and twice between 1133 and 1135, although he went to Rouen at least forty-five times after 1105.[37] He was also a well-known architectural patron, and such a project could have been a fitting signal of his swift assertion of authority after Tinchebrai,[38] with Westminster serving as both model and incentive. Nevertheless, on the evidence presented to date, a firm attribution to either the 12th century or Henry, let alone 'the 1120s', could not be justified. In fact, at least two scraps of historical and archaeological evidence may specifically suggest otherwise, the first (*pace* de Boüard) being the *absence* of the *Échiquier* from de Torigni's detailed enumeration of Henry's works at Caen and elsewhere, which included a 'fittingly royal house' (*mansio*) at Rouen.[39] The second — the larger blocks and narrower joints

FIG. 5. The *Échiquier* from the east, overlooking the site of the 'palais de Guillaume'. All but the upper part of the three bays to the right is largely original, although there are traces of medieval alterations, notably the remains of a fireplace inserted to serve an attached building in the 14th century. The 1960s structure to the left conceals a vaulted room added in the 12th century

used in facing the *donjon* — implies that the *donjon* and the *Échiquier* were not built as part of the same campaign, nor, probably, by the same generation of masons.[40]

Positive evidence for the building's date, however, can be found in its design and decorative detailing. This is covered at length elsewhere, but in brief, there is nothing in the basic form of the building (rectangular, single-volume with high windows) that either indicates or precludes a date anywhere between the early 11th and the mid-12th centuries.[41] Nor can the elevational format be confined to a narrow chronological span: high windows resting on a string-course, pilaster buttresses and corbel-tables were a standard arrangement from the second half of the 11th century to the advent of Gothic, found locally, for example, at Saint-Nicholas in Caen (begun perhaps c. 1080x1082),[42] Lessay (eastern parts by 1098),[43] and the west front of Saint-Étienne in Caen (as completed by 1087). Examined at a more detailed level, however, there are indications of an early date. These include the articulation of the windows, with two unmoulded arches, a lower string-course, and coursed nook shafts inside and out supporting capitals and abaci, a variation on a repertoire well established by 1100; by the early 12th century, however, the angle shafts were more often monolithic colonnettes, and the outer arch usually moulded.

Fig. 6. The *Échiquier* from the south-west
Edward Impey

The most telling composition for dating purposes, however, is the south-east façade (Figs 4, 6 and 8). This is self-evidently the great decorative set-piece of the *Échiquier* and, as became commonplace in 12th-century Anglo-Norman architecture, the major decorative elements are geometric. From bottom to top these consist of diaper, chevron, a pattern based on intersecting circles (above the doorway), diaper again, mouldings (an angle roll and hollow) and multiple-billet (above the window). The façade has usually been dated by the presence of chevron, but this is one among several geometric forms, all of which properly require examination. From an Anglo-Norman perspective, the diaper, or *étoiles en creux et découpées en biseau*, is typologically the earliest form, appearing on the transept arches of La Trinité at Caen as early as *c*. 1059–66,[44] over the doorway to the Great Tower at Chepstow (Monmouth), and in the chapel at Durham Castle, the latter two examples having been built before *c*. 1090.[45] By the late 1080s and 1090s, *étoiles en creux* were beginning to be used more widely in Normandy, appearing in Caen at Sainte-Paix, in the south at Notre-Dame-sur-l'Eau near Domfront and Goult (Orne), and in the Seine valley at Graville-Sainte-Honorine (Seine-Maritime).[46] It is at its most prolific in the parish churches of the Bessin and the Orne valley, buildings that are notoriously difficult to date, but the distribution probably reflects an origin and early development in high-status buildings in Caen.[47] In the case of the *Échiquier*, the *étoiles en creux* of the tympanum and segmental arch are of the simplest and most common form: four-pointed stars, bevel-edged and inscribed within squares, arranged with only minor variations in scale,

The Great Hall at Caen

FIG. 7. Interior of the *Échiquier* looking south-east, engraved by James Basire from an 1836 sketch made by John Buckler, and printed as the frontispiece to vol. I of Thomas Stapleton's *Magni Rotuli Scaccarii Normanniae* of 1840. The roof was a 17th-century replacement and the door had been widened, but otherwise the interior remained much as built.
Thanks to the restoration of the 1960s it looks much the same today.
Reproduced by kind permission of the Society of Antiquaries of London

most noticeable on the radial voussoirs. If the intention was to create the illusion of a shimmering surface, the result must be counted a great success.

The tympanum in turn is framed by an arch made up of two rows of lateral centrifugal chevron with a cogwheel inner edge, a type among the most widely used and enduring in Anglo-Norman architecture.[48] The problem with dating chevron, however, is not its ubiquity or longevity, but that its origins have never been discussed in the detail necessary to form a view as to when it first entered the Anglo-Norman repertoire. There is not the space to do that here, but the essential point is that chevron is the result of combining a geometric pattern (a zig-zag) with a moulding profile, emerging from a series of experiments with radial-voussoir compositions initiated in western France during the third quarter of the 11th century.[49] By the late 1080s, instead of juxtaposing mouldings and geometric patterns, western French masons began to fracture the mouldings so they might themselves carry a geometric pattern. Two types of arch decoration — moulding and pattern — were effectively merged. The chevron used in the nave aisle portals at Le Mans Cathedral (Sarthe), datable to

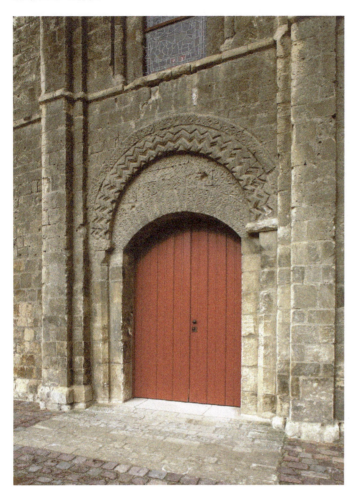

Fig. 8. *Échiquier*, south-east doorway. The main arch is carved with chevron ornament, while the hood-mould carries a design based on intersecting circles. Beneath this can be seen the segmental arch and tympanum embellished with *étoiles en creux*
Edward Impey

the early part of the episcopacy of Bishop Hoel (1085–96), is perhaps the earliest surviving example (Fig. 9).[50] Other likely late-11th-century instances of the use of chevron include the apse arch at Cerisy-la-Forêt (Manche) of perhaps *c.* 1090, the south aisle of Great Malvern Priory (*c.* 1085×1100?), and Anselm's choir at Canterbury as begun (*c.* 1096). The profile of the *Échiquier* arch is close to that of Le Mans, though Caen dropped the angled fillet between the two rolls and added a cogwheel edge. It is certainly much closer to Le Mans than to the apse arch at Cerisy, the only other 11th-century instance of chevron to survive in the duchy.

The hood-mould employs a pattern that was also derived from the same stable of designs that produced the chevron. The design itself is best described as a sequence of circles that contain a square with concave sides, a pattern that is based on intersecting circles.[51] It can be seen in the friezes of encircled concave-sided lozenges that were used on the west front of the new Cluniac priory of Saint-Jean-de-Montierneuf at Poitiers in 1086–96 (Fig. 10).[52] Thereafter the form is used on relief panels, string-courses and arches (particularly hood-moulds), becoming notably popular in England,

The Great Hall at Caen

FIG. 9. Le Mans Cathedral: south nave aisle portal. The type of chevron used on the outer arch at Le Mans is typologically close to that of the *Échiquier*. The lower stages of the west front at Le Mans date from the episcopacy of Bishop Hoel (1085–96)
Edward Impey

FIG. 10. Saint-Jean-de-Montierneuf, Poitiers: west front detail. The fragments of geometric ornament illustrated were reset in the present west front after its 11th-century predecessor was destroyed in the 17th century. The left-hand pattern is very similar to the design of the hood-mould above the south-east portal of the *Échiquier*. The original position of these fragments is uncertain, but it is likely that they were used as string-courses and date between *c.* 1087 and *c.* 1096
John McNeill

where its earliest dateable use is probably on the inner elevation of the crossing tower of Winchester Cathedral as rebuilt after the collapse of 1107.[53]

The portal is obviously the key to understanding and dating the ornamental repertoire of the *Échiquier*. Individual ornamental elements alone cannot date a building, but the prominence given to the juxtaposition of chevron and encircled concave-sided squares, both of which had been brought into use in the late 1080s or early 1090s, at Le Mans and Poitiers respectively, argue for a date in the 1090s for the *Échiquier*. They are the geometrically precocious elements within an otherwise well-established repertoire, alongside which the coursed angle-shafts, unmoulded arches, and shallowly carved plaits of the capitals look positively conservative. On balance, it is a repertoire far more likely to have come together just before 1100 rather than significantly later.

AFFINITIES WITH WESTMINSTER

WITH the original form of the *Échiquier* firmly established, its basic similarities to Westminster Hall are obvious: both house single-volume, ground-level, unaisled interiors, and share a simple rectangular plan. Similarities may extend also to access and circulation, if, as suggested in the case of Westminster, and is certain at Caen, both had their main doorways in a gable end. Finally, there are the basic similarities

81

in the external side elevations, both being articulated by pilaster buttresses and a mid-height string-course, framing a range of windows in the upper register. Differences in detail of course abound: the clerestory-like passage at Westminster, elaborate both in structure and effect, and the diaper-work to its parapet, contrast starkly with the austere simplicity of the *Échiquier*.[54] But the main difference is simply in size — Westminster Hall, with external measurements of 25.01 m (82ft 1 in.) by 77.39 m (253 ft 11 in.) and a footprint of 1,935 m² (20,828 ft²), is over four times larger than the *Échiquier*. If dating from the reign of Henry I, the patron and designers of the *Échiquier* could be assumed to have had a scaled-down version of the English building in mind. However, if the *Échiquier* was built or begun before c. 1100, its affinities with Westminster become more interesting, extending beyond similarities in form to those of authorship and purpose.

The creation of Westminster Hall by William Rufus is not in doubt, and is reaffirmed elsewhere in this volume.[55] In the case of Caen, if Henry I is excluded on grounds of date, the building must have been put up for either Robert Curthose or Rufus, in their capacities respectively as duke of Normandy and ruler during Robert's absence from 1096 to 1100. Of the two, Robert is by far the less promising candidate, partly as there were perhaps only two brief periods when he had both a reason and the resources to improve the palace at Caen. The first followed the 'inquest', jointly conducted by Robert and Rufus at Caen in July 1091, that produced the *Consuetudines et iusticie*:[56] affirming the importance of the *curia* would have underlined the need for a fitting venue at Caen, which the *Échiquier* could have provided, as indeed it later did. However, the rapid descent into chaos that followed suggests otherwise. The second occasion was in 1100, on Robert's return from Crusade, rich and promising peace, during which Caen was his first destination following a visit to Mont-Saint-Michel.[57] However, further chaos, his immediate relapse, as Orderic claimed, into 'sloth and idleness',[58] coupled with the absence of any single building project attributable to Robert (including the Orne canal that bears his name) all count against him.[59] Nor, while we must acknowledge Orderic's undoubted bias, are Robert's chronic insecurity, poverty, lamentable administration and inattention to formal process easy to reconcile with authorship of a major piece of governmental and ceremonial infrastructure. Rufus's candidacy is, by contrast, positively promising on several grounds. First, he was frequently resident, including for the Christmases of 1096, 1097 and 1098.[60] These may have been held at Rouen or elsewhere in Normandy, but his recognition at least of Caen's importance is underlined by its retention when ceding the county of Bayeux (in which it lies), and the cities of Bayeux and Coutances, to Henry in 1096.[61] Secondly, and perhaps most tellingly, Rufus famously had an interest in building and was rich enough to indulge it. Finally, there are reasons to suggest that Rufus had not only the means and opportunity to build the *Échiquier*, but also the motivation — at which point we move on to discuss the building's possible affinities of purpose.

Common ground between Westminster and Caen in this respect, beyond their obvious capacity as venues for assemblies and events, is suggested by Rufus's long-term intentions with regard to Normandy and his behaviour whilst in control. Rufus's position there from 1096 was as temporary ruler, to whom the duchy had been consigned or 'pledged', awaiting redemption by his brother on his return from the (First) Crusade.[62] However, Rufus was not only Robert's heir as duke, but must have doubted that Robert would return, and, it has been suggested, would have held it against him if he had — factors that would have encouraged him to take a long-term view.[63] This is not the place to elaborate on Rufus's (or his father's) interpretation and representation of royal status when in, and pertaining to, the French duchy of Normandy.[64] But whilst there is evidence that the Conqueror was wary of trading on his royal status in Normandy,[65] William of Poitiers asserts that in his master's youth Normandy was 'almost a kingdom', and certainly the Conqueror's grandiose gestures in founding two dynastic mausolea were on a more than kingly scale.[66] Rufus would therefore not have been short of precedent as to how regally the king of England might behave in the duchy. Moreover, as a king but not the duke — a title Robert seems to have maintained until his death — Rufus may have had both more reason and more leeway to emphasize his royal status, 'unencumbered with ambiguities that had surrounded the Conqueror's status in Normandy'.[67] In this context it is of interest that, between summer 1096 and January 1098, Rufus purchased from the monks of Saint-Étienne a set of royal regalia including 'the crown he [the Conqueror] wore on the festivals, his sceptre and rod'.[68] Why should he have done so? No reason is given in the relevant charter (surviving as a 15th-century *vidimus*), but it seems likely that he intended to use the regalia to replicate, in Normandy, the 'crown-wearing' ceremonies that he and his father held at the great festivals of the church in England;[69] the charter's reference to their use by William I 'on festivals', implicitly in the duchy, may indicate that he too had used it there to express his status as king *in* Normandy.[70] This would be consistent with Rufus's constitutional position, his robust interpretation of 'acting' authority (as shown for example by his attitude to Maine), and the sheer 'pleasure that he took in the royal title and dignity'.[71] However, occasions for such events required a fitting setting. Whilst provided for, perhaps, at Rouen, at Caen, if de Boüard is correct, Rufus had no such facility of his own — a problem to which the *Échiquier*, dwarfing the cramped buildings of his father, would have been a spectacular solution.[72]

Rufus, it can therefore be argued, built the *Échiquier* to help him assert his status, and particularly royal status, in the duchy, mirroring his political and propagandist motives in building Westminster Hall. If so, it would also help explain the building's design, an issue that arises because its free-standing and architecturally dominant form was, it seems, quite alien to ducal and palatial architecture in Normandy before c. 1100:[73] in keeping with his motives, he chose, it could be argued, a form associated with kings, not merely dukes. This apparent use of an 'English' form at Caen also suggests — as might be assumed but remains unprovable — that Westminster was the first of the two buildings to be designed.

Finally, thanks to recent archaeological work in Caen, there are hints that the affinity between the two buildings extended to the complexes of which they were part. By the 1160s, as has long been known, the hall at Westminster was accompanied by the Lesser Hall: a two-storey building, 14.96 m (49 ft 1 in.) by 40.92 m (134 ft 3 in.), standing to the south of the hall on the same axis, and which substantially survived until the fire of 1834.[74] This, it is assumed, served as a residential rather than exclusively ceremonial space, complementing the hall as a *camera* or chamber-block might do, albeit on a gigantic scale, for less exalted houses. At Caen, Benedicte Guillot has uncovered the lower parts of a building measuring 13.65 m (44 ft 9 in.) by 24.65 m (80 ft 10½ in.), ashlar-faced inside and out, part basemented, and possibly with an upper floor, 45 m (147 ft 8 in.) to the south-west of the *Échiquier* (Fig. 11).[75] The excavator dates the building on stratigraphic grounds to about 1200, but the masonry (upright blockwork and wide joints) suggests a building roughly contemporary with the *Échiquier*. Its form and location, meanwhile, although not axial to the hall, as

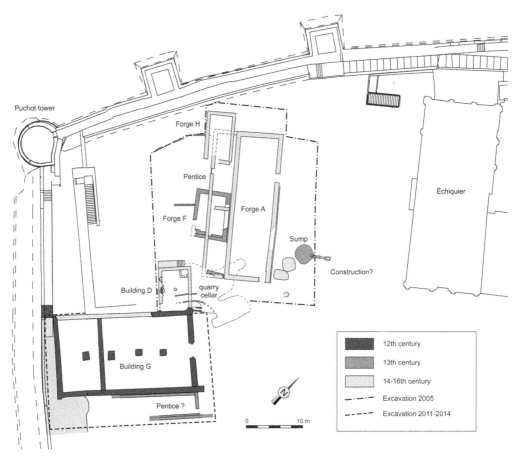

FIG. 11. Plan showing the position of the *Échiquier* (top right) in relation to the second Romanesque building ('Building G'), discovered in 2011. It is suggested here that the two buildings are roughly contemporary and that the respective purposes of the *Échiquier* and Building G were equivalent to those of Westminster Hall and the Lesser Hall, or (depending on its actual date), the latter's precursor

Reproduced by kind permission of Bénédicte Guillot

was the case at Westminster, hint at a function akin to the Lesser Hall's in the 12th century. If so, it would in turn strengthen the case that a precursor to the Lesser Hall existed at Westminster in the time of Rufus.

ACKNOWLEDGEMENTS

I am grateful to many people and organizations for help with the preparation of this article, in particular Howard Jones, for his survey of the building; Jean-Marie Levesque and Pascal Leroux, for repeated access to the *Échiquier*, its annexes and de Boüard's archive; and to John McNeill for contributing a section on the geometric sculpture of the *Échiquier*.

NOTES

1. L. Jean-Marie, *Caen aux XIe et XIIe siècles: Espace urbain, pouvoirs et société* (Condé-sur-Noireau 2001), 31; M. de Boüard, *Le Château de Caen* (Caen 1979), 9–10. For the charters, see M. Fauroux, *Recueil des actes des ducs de Normandie (911–1066)*, Mémoires de la Société des Antiquaires de Normandie XXXVI (Caen 1961), nos. 34 and 58; D. Bates, *Normandy Before 1066* (London 1981), 13, 152, 178–79.

2. E. Chatel ed., *Quartum Chronicorum Librum ... qui vulgo Anonymus Cadomensis nuncupatur*, Mémoires de la Société des Antiquaires de Normandie XXXIII (Caen 1892), 138; G. Burgess and A. Holden, *The Roman de Rou* (St Helier 2002), 22, lines 5170–71; L. Musset, *Les actes de Guillaume le Conquérant et de la reine Mathilde pour les abbayes caennaises*, Mémoires de la Société des Antiquaires de Normandie XXXVII (Caen 1967), 69, no. 6, by which in 1080–82 the Conqueror granted to La Trinité a house '[...] in castello Cadomi'; and ibid., 85, no. 8, also of 1082, which mentions the 'ecclesia Sancti Georgii de Castro Cadomi'.

3. De Boüard, *Le Château* (as n. 1), 9. De Boüard considered the mention of 'Le Palais' at the beginning of the 15th century to be a reference to this complex; ibid., 21 and n. 35.

4. The name was first applied by Thomas Stapleton in *Magni Rotuli Scaccarii Normanniae* (2 vols (London 1840, 1844), I, xxix), based on his partly correct assumption that it was used by the Norman Exchequer; ibid., I, xxvii and xxxi; de Boüard, *Le Château* (as n. 1), 67. The name was popularized by Eugène de Beaurepaire in *Caen Illustré: son histoire, ses monuments* (Caen 1896), 47, and endorsed by the architect Lucien Sallez in 1904 (Archives des Monuments Historiques 12852), and again in 1908 (Congrès Archéologique de France, 75/1, plan facing 110).

5. The main damage, including the crater mentioned by de Boüard (*Le Château* (as n. 1), 71) was probably done on the 16 July, although more may have followed before the last bombardment on the 15 August; J. Poirier, *La Bataille de Caen* (Caen 1944), 30, 68.

6. '[...] faute de témoins suffisants d'un état plus ancien'; de Boüard, *Le Château* (as n. 1), 70.

7. Internally at ground level the long sides each measure 30.86 m (101 ft 3 in.), but while the south-east entrance gable wall is 11.18 m (36 ft 8 in.) wide, the north-west end gable is 130 mm (5 in.) narrower.

8. On the 14th-century work (including the removal of the allegedly original upper floor) and its dating, see de Boüard, *Le Château* (as n. 1), 77–79.

9. The date of 1881 is given in the legend of a plan of the castle of 1882 (Archives Départementales de Calvados, CPL 660): 'étage construit en 1881. Salle de harnachement'. A drawing showing this as proposed or after completion, undated, but bearing the legend 'PROJET D'ETABLISSEMENT D'UNE SALLE D'ARMES DANS LE BATIMENT', is published by de Boüard (*Le Château* (as n. 1), 89, fig. 31). The original cannot now be located. See also a number of post-war photographs. The new masonry in the positions of the 19th-century openings in the eastern three bays shows clearly in Merlet's photograph of 25 February 1963.

10. J.-M. Laurence, *Caen* (Condé-sur-Noireau 2001), 79; A. Renoux, *Fécamp: Du Palais ducal au Palais de Dieu* (Paris 1991), 32 (although recognizing that this is a matter of debate); J. Decaëns, 'Le premier Château, de Guillaume le Conquérant à Richard Cœur de Lion (XIe–XIIe siècles)', in *Mémoires du Château de Caen*, ed. J.-M. Levesque and J.-Y. Marin (Caen 2000), 15–22, at 20; P. Leroux, 'Un chantier archéologique pionnier (1956–66)', ibid., 83–87, at 86; J. Decaëns and A. Dubois, *Le château de Caen: Mille ans d'une forteresse dans la ville* (Caen 2009), 42–45 (although acknowledging uncertainty, at 42).

11. J. Mesqui, *Châteaux et enceintes de la France médiévale: De la défense à la résidence*, 2 vols (Paris 1991–93), II, 81–82; idem, *Châteaux forts et fortifications en France* (Paris 1997), 86; *Le château de Lillebonne des ducs de Normandie aux ducs d'Harcourt*, Mémoire de la Société des Antiquaires de Normandie XLII, 90.

12. E. Impey, 'Seigneurial Domestic Architecture in Normandy, 1050–1350', in *Manorial Domestic Buildings in England and Northern France*, ed. G. Meirion-Jones and M. Jones (London 1993), Society of Antiquaries Occasional Paper no. 15, 82–120, at 84–85; C. Wilson, 'Rulers, Artificers and Shoppers: Richard II's Remodelling of Westminster Hall, 1393-99', in *The Regal Image of Richard II and the Wilton Diptych*, ed. D. Gordon, L. Monnas and C. Elam (London 1997), 33–59 and 274–88, nn. 5 and 46.

13. E. Impey and J. McNeill, 'La grande salle des ducs de Normandie à Caen', in *La demeure seigneuriale dans l'espace Plantagenêt*, ed. G. Meirion-Jones (Rennes 2013), 95–131; for a version in English, see E. Impey and J. McNeill, 'The Great Hall in the Castle at Caen', in *Castles and the Anglo-Norman World: Proceedings of the Conference held at Norwich Castle Museum in 2012*, ed. J. Davies, A. Riley, J.-M. Levesque and C. Lapiche (Oxford forthcoming).

14. De Boüard, *Le Château* (as n. 1), 70, 71.

15. Ibid., 70.

16. Ibid., 70: 'que les appuis des fenêtres furent primitivement en gradins'; 74.

17. M. de Boüard, 'Le Château de Caen', *Le Mois à Caen*, 9 (November 1962), 17–18; idem, *Le Château* (as n. 1), 70, para 2: 'notre bâtiment se rattache à l'un des types les mieux connus de l'architecture civile du XIIe siècle'.

18. For Westminster, see S. Smirke, 'Remarks on the architectural history of Westminster Hall', *Archaeologia*, XXVI (1836), 406–14; Roland B. Harris and Daniel Miles in this volume, 22–71. See examples given by M. E. Wood in *The English Medieval House* (London 1964), 389–93, and L. F. Salzmann in *Building in England Down to 1540: A Documentary History* (Oxford 1952), 147.

19. Locally, for example, in the church of Saint-Nicolas-des-Champs.

20. J. Mesqui, *Le Château d'Angers* (Paris 2001), 36–37; J. Brodeur, P. Chevet and J. Mastrolenzo, 'Construction sur le site du château d'Angers d'après les fouilles récentes', in *La Construction en Anjou au Moyen Age: Actes de la Table ronde d'Angers des 29 et 30 mars 1996*, ed. D. Prigent and N.-Y. Tonnerre (Angers 1998), 101–12, at 107, fig. 4.

21. P. Faulkner, 'Domestic planning from the twelfth to the fourteenth centuries', *Archaeol. J.*, 105, 150–83, at 151 and 163–64; Wood, *English Medieval House* (as n. 18), 14–34; J. Blair, 'Hall and Chamber: English Domestic Planning 1000–1250', in *Manorial Domestic Buildings* (as n. 12), 1–21.

22. De Boüard, *Le Château* (as n. 1), 72–73.

23. Ibid., 72.

24. Ibid., 71.

25. Ibid., 79.

26. On Roger of Caen (Sarum), see E. Kealey, *Roger of Salisbury, Viceroy of England* (Berkeley/Los Angeles/London 1972); for Sherborne Castle, see RCHME, *An Inventory of Historical Monuments in the County of Dorset*, I: *West* (London 1952), 64–66. For the courtyard house at Old Sarum and its relationship with Roger's work at Sherborne, see J. Ashbee, 'Cloisters in English Palaces in the Twelfth and Thirteenth Centuries', *JBAA*, 159 (2006), 71–90, here 73–77, and for a general assessment of Roger's patronage, see R. Stalley, 'A Twelfth-Century Patron of Architecture: A Study of the Buildings Erected by Roger, Bishop of Salisbury 1102–1139', *JBAA*, 3rd ser., XXXIV (1971), 62–83.

27. Blair, 'Hall and Chamber' (as n. 21), 13.

28. Tim Tatton-Brown, personal communication.

29. P. K. Kipps, 'Minster Court, Thanet', *Archaeol. J.*, 86 (1929), 213–23; E. Impey, 'The Origins and Development of Non-conventual Monastic Dependencies in England and Normandy, 1050–1350', 3 vols (unpublished doctoral thesis, Oxford, 1991), III, 177–203; T. Hudson Turner, *Some Account of Domestic Architecture in England from the Conquest to the end of the Thirteenth Century* (Oxford 1851), 43–45 and intervening views and plan. The hall or refectory at Minster measured (internally) c. 8 m (26 ft 3 in.) × 19 m (62 ft 4 in.), the Dover refectory 8.22m (26 ft 11 ½ in.) × 30.48 m (100 ft).

30. In 1965 (in 'La Salle dite l'Echiquier, au Château de Caen', *Med. Archaeol.*, 9 (1965), 64–81, 67), and in 1979 to Henry I (*Le Château* (as n. 1), 12, 69).

31. De Boüard, 'La Salle' (as n. 30), 67; idem, *Le Château* (as n. 1), 69.

32. De Boüard, *Le Château* (as n. 1), 12, citing Robert de Torigni; see the *Chronica Roberti de Torigneio*, in R. Howlett ed., *Chronicles of the Reigns of Stephen, Henry II., and Richard I*, 4 vols (London 1884–89), IV, 106. Caen was captured in 1105.

33. L. Musset, *Normandie Romane*, I (La Pierre qui Vire 1987, 3rd edn), 50: 'sa façade austère presente le même décor purement géometrique que les églises du temps'.

34. E. G. Carlson, 'The Abbey Church of St Etienne at Caen in the 11th and early 12th centuries' (unpublished Ph.D. thesis, Yale University, 1968), 88.

35. F. Neveux, *La Normandie des ducs aux rois, Xe–XIIe siècle* (Rennes 1998), 399; J. Decaëns, 'Le premier château' (as n. 10),19; Decaëns and Dubois, *Le château de Caen* (as n. 10), 40; J. Mesqui, *Le château de Lillebonne* (as n. 11), 90.

36. M. Baylé, *Les Origines et les Premiers Développements de la Sculpture Romane en Normandie*, Art de Basse Normandie, no. 100 bis (Caen 1992), 29, 104. Lord Methuen, although he would not have regarded his own opinion as expert, placed it in the 'late 11th century'; idem, *Normandy Diary: being a record of survivals and losses of historical monuments in north-western France, together with those in the island of Walcheren, and in that part of Belgium traversed by 21st Army Group in 1944–45* (London 1952), 201.

37. C. H. Haskins, *Norman Institutions* (Harvard 1918), Appendix G, 309–20.

38. W. M. Aird, *Robert Curthose, Duke of Normandy (c.1050–1134)* (Woodbridge 2008), 245.

39. 'Turrem nihilominus excelsam fecit in castello Cadomensi, et murum ipsius castelli, quem pater suus fecerat, in altum crevit'; *Chronicles* (as n. 32), IV, 106. 'et aedificia ad mansionem regiam congrua infra eundem murum parat'; ibid., 106.

40. The original facing of the *donjon* survives on the west side, where it includes an original buttress; de Boüard, *Le Château* (as n. 1), 103 and 127, fig. 45.

41. For a fuller account, see Impey and McNeill, 'La grande salle' (as n. 13), 112–23.

42. M. Baylé ed., *L'architecture normande au Moyen Age*, 2 vols (Caen 2001, 2nd rev. edn), I, 62.
43. Musset, *Normandie Romane*, I (as n. 33, 3rd edn), 171. The founder's son was buried in the middle of the choir in February 1098.
44. M. Baylé, *La Trinité de Caen: sa place dans l'histoire de l'Architecture et du Décor Romane* (Geneva 1979), 57, and eadem, *Sculpture Romane en Normandie* (as n. 36), 102.
45. R. Turner, *Chepstow Castle* (Cardiff 2002), 5–8, 27–30, and J. Goodall, *The English Castle* (New Haven CT/London 2011), 86–87.
46. Musset, *Normandie Romane*, I (as n. 33, 3rd edn), 295–96 and pl. 117.
47. Whether it was used in Odo's 11th-century cathedral in Bayeux is unknown. Of the parish churches, Secqueville-en-Bessin (Calvados) is likely to be among the earliest, and stylistically fits most comfortably in the 1090s. For a broader discussion of the *étoile en creux* in the development of sculpturally enriched Anglo-Norman architecture *c.* 1100, see Baylé, *Sculpture Romane en Normandie* (as n. 36), 102–05.
48. The descriptive vocabulary used here is taken from R. Moss, *Romanesque Chevron Ornament: The language of British, Norman and Irish sculpture in the twelfth century*, BAR International Series 1908 (Oxford 2009), particularly 3–4, but see also the admirable 'Chevron Guide' of the Corpus of Romanesque Sculpture in Britain and Ireland; http://www.crsbi.ac.uk/the-chevron-guide/ (accessed 21 January 2015).
49. The best discussion of this is A. Tcherikover, 'Romanesque sculpted archivolts in western France. Forms and techniques', *Arte Médiévale*, 2nd series, 3 (1989), 49–75.
50. The dating has been much discussed. See A. Mussat, *La Cathédrale du Mans* (Paris 1981), 31–32, and F. Salet, *La Cathédrale du Mans*, Congrès Archéologique de France 119 (Paris 1961), 34. The attribution of the west front to Hoel, who could only have had the means and opportunity to build it between 1085 and 1090, derives from the 12th-century *Gesta Domni Hoelli Episcopi*, which says that he 'exteriores etiam parietes, quos alas vocant, per circuitum consummavit'; G. Busson and A. Ledru ed., *Actus Pontificum in Urbe Degentium*, Archives historiques du Maine 2 (Le Mans 1901), chapter xxxiv, 382–97, at 383.
51. Reticulated designs based on intersecting circles were a commonplace of Roman and late Antique pavements, and survive in significant numbers, particularly at ecclesiastical sites in 4th–7th-century Italy. As early as the 2nd century, Roman designers had started to isolate and reconfigure the individual motifs created by intersecting circles, as can be seen on a funerary stele in the Museé Archéologique at Saintes, for example. Although the individual elements were widely used in the Roman and late Antique periods, they do not seem to have been among the early wave of geometric motifs revived and used in decorative masonry patterns in the Poitou and Loire valley in the course of the 11th century. Rather, their adoption seems to date from the last quarter of the 11th century.
52. The nave and west front of Saint-Jean-de-Montierneuf (Vienne) were rebuilt in 1643–44 following the partial collapse of the crossing. A number of carved stones from the earlier west front were then reused in this reconstruction, consisting for the most pat of shallowly carved geometric designs on voussoirs or ashlar blocks that were probably originally arranged as string-courses and spandrel decoration. The variety of geometric forms in use at Montierneuf was clearly considerable, and their position, on the west front of the most important building to be created in the last quarter of the 11th century in Poitiers, lends them a peculiar significance. The west front campaign can be closely dated, and will have been undertaken between the reburial of Duke Guy-Geoffroi-Guillaume immediately in front of the altar of the Holy Cross in 1087, and the consecration of one of the two altars in the choir by Pope Urban II on 22 January 1096. The nave and the west front are likely to have been finished some time before the papal consecration. See R. Favreau, *Poitiers: Saint-Jean-de-Montierneuf* (Poitiers 1996), 18–23 and 26–29, and M.-T. Camus, *Sculpture Romane de Poitou: Les grands chantiers du XIe siècle* (Paris 1992), 191–94.
53. If the restoration of the tympanum at Beaumais (Orne) was accurate, it may be that there was a direct connection between Saint-Jean-de-Montierrneuf at Poitiers and buildings in and around Caen. Beaumais shares a significant number of relatively unusual geometric motifs with Saint-Jean-de-Montierneuf. See Baylé, *Sculpture Romane en Normandie* (as n. 36), fig. 339.
54. See Roland B. Harris and Daniel Miles in this volume, 22–71.
55. Ibid., 22–24.
56. Haskins, *Norman Institutions* (as n. 37), 277–84; F. Barlow (*William Rufus* (London 1983), 283) and Aird (*Robert Curthose* (as n. 38), 146) are of the view that the 1091 date is not proven, and that these events could perhaps have taken place in 1096.
57. For the visit to Mont-Saint-Michel, M. Chibnall ed. and trans., *The Ecclesiastical History of Orderic Vitalis*, 6 vols (Oxford 1969–80), V (1975), 300; for the visit to Caen, hinted at by Wace, see G. S. Burgess and A. J. Holden ed., *The Roman de Rou* (St Helier 2002), lines 9691–98, 304;C. W. David, *Robert Curthose, Duke of Normandy* (Cambridge MA 1920), 124; Aird, *Robert Curthose* (as n. 38), 199, 201.
58. Aird, *Robert Curthose* (as n. 38), 246; *Orderic Vitalis* (as n. 57), VI (1978), 96: 'Nam ex quo dux de Ierusalem rediit, et ducatum Normanniae recepit, torpori et ignaviae nimis subiacuit', and V (1975), 86.
59. Jean-Marie, *Caen* (as n. 1), 9–101.

60. D. Whitelock ed., *The Anglo-Saxon Chronicle* (London 1961), 174–75.
61. Barlow, *William Rufus* (as n. 56), 364; J. Green, *Henry I* (Cambridge 2009), 36; *Chronica Roberti de Torigneio* (as n. 32), 54.
62. David, *Robert Curthose* (as n. 57), 91; Barlow, *William Rufus* (as n. 56), 369; Green, *Henry I* (as n. 51), 36; Aird, *Robert Curthose* (as n. 38), 162. The sources include Hugh of Flavigny (*Chronicon*, ed. J.-P. Migne, *Patrologia Latina*, CLIV, cols 21–404, at col. 354) and Eadmer (*Historia Novorum in Anglia*, ed. M. Rule (Rolls Series, LXXXI, London 1884), 74), both of whom used the word *tradere*. Orderic simply says that Rufus 'received' (*recepit*) Normandy; *Orderic Vitalis* (as n. 57), V (1975), 26. Robert de Torigni (interpolation, *The Gesta Normannorum Ducum of William of Jumièges, Orderic Vitalis and Robert of Torigni*, ed. E. M. C. van Houts, 2 vols (Oxford 1992–95), II, 204); *Regesta Regum Anglo-Normannorum, 1066–1154*, ed. C. Johnson and H. A. Cronne, 3 vols (Oxford 1956), II, 377 *concordia*; and *Roman de Rou* (as n. 57), line 9671) '*gage*'.
63. C. Warren Hollister, 'Normandy, France and the Anglo-Norman *Regnum*', *Speculum*, 51/2 (1976), 202–42, at 213. See Barlow, *William Rufus* (as n. 56), 365: 'No official record of the treaty of 1096 between Robert and William has survived'.
64. B. English, 'William the Conqueror and the Anglo-Norman succession', *Bulletin of the Institute of Historical Research*, 64/155 (1991), 221–36, at 234. J. Le Patourel (*The Norman Empire* (Oxford 1976), 238) asserts that 'there is a good deal of evidence to confirm the idea contained in the phrase used by the author of the *Gesta Stephani*, that the Norman kings were kings "in" Normandy as well as in England'. The words of the *Gesta* (ed. K. R. Potter, *Gesta Stephani* (Oxford 1976), 8) are as follows: '[...] regem eum in Angliam et Normanniam [...] sacravit et iniunxit'. On the Conqueror's adoption and use of the royal title in preference to that of *dux*, see Hollister, 'Normandy' (as n. 63), 206.
65. L. Nelson, 'The Rites of the Conqueror', in *Anglo-Norman Studies IV: Proceedings of the Battle Conference 1981*, ed. R. Allen Brown (Woodbridge 1982), 117–32, at 131; Hollister, 'Normandy' (as n. 63), 207–08.
66. R. H. C. Davis and M. Chibnall ed., *Gesta Guillelmi* (Oxford 1998), 44, 45; Hollister, 'Normandy' (as n. 63), 208; D. Douglas, *William the Conqueror* (London 1964), 263–64; Nelson, 'The Rites' (as n. 65), 131.
67. Hollister, 'Normandy' (as n. 63), 213.
68. Barlow, *William Rufus* (as n. 56), 368. Seeing death approaching, William gave to Saint-Étienne 'coronam, qua in celebrioribus festivitatibus inter sacra missarum sollemnia, coronabatur, cum sceptro, & virga; & prætiosi lapidis calice, aureisque candelabris, & cæteris ad coronam pertinentibus, Regalium insignium'; A. du Monstier, *Neustria Pia, seu de omnibus et singulis abbatiis et prioratibus totius Normaniæ* (Rouen 1663), 638. See also L. Musset, *Les Actes de Guillaume le Conquérant et de la Reine Mathilde pour les Abbayes Caennaises*, Mémoires de la Société des antiquaires de Normandie XXXVII (Caen 1967), no. 24, *vidimus* of 1424, 132–34, the Latin quotation at 133.
69. Barlow, *William Rufus* (as n. 56), 368; M. Biddle, 'Seasonal Festivals and Residence: Winchester, Westminster and Gloucester in the Tenth to Twelfth Centuries', *Anglo-Norman Studies VIII: Proceedings of the Battle Conference 1985*, ed. R. Allen Brown (Woodbridge 1986), 51–72; Nelson, 'The Rites' (as n. 65), 130–21 and n. 143.
70. William could perhaps have worn it at Caen, where he may have spent the Christmases of 1079 and perhaps 1068; D. Bates ed., *Regesta Regum Anglo-Normannorum, The Acta of William I (1066–1087)* (Oxford 1998), 84.
71. Barlow, *William Rufus* (as n. 56), 99–100; *Oxford Dictionary of National Biography*, 60 vols (2004), LIX, 'William Rufus', 63–73, at 70.
72. It is possible however that William had another residence within the precincts of Saint-Étienne. A tradition to this effect is recorded by P. D. Huet (*Les Origines de la Ville de Caen et des Lieux Circumvoisins* (Rouen 1706), 180), and buildings which could have served such a function for later dukes or royalty stood there until the mid-19th century.
73. Impey and McNeill, 'La grande salle' (as n. 13), 118–20.
74. J. Crook and R. Harris, 'Reconstructing the Lesser Hall: An Interim Report from the Medieval Palace of Westminster Research Project', *Parliamentary History*, 21/1 (2002), 22–61.
75. B. Guillot, *Calvados, Caen, Le Château, Un Edifice de la fin du XIIe siècle. Campagne 2012–13 rapport intermédiare 2012*, Institut National de recherches archéologiques préventives (Caen 2012), 22, fig. 2; idem, 'Recent Excavations at Caen Castle (2005 to 2014): Medieval Forges and Renaissance Stable', in *Castles and the Anglo-Norman World* (as n. 13).

Henry III's Palace at Westminster

VIRGINIA JANSEN

In memory of Richard K. Morris

Under Henry III (1216–72), Westminster became a key royal residence, referred to as a palace rather than a house. This study discusses what we know of Henry III's palace before the 1263 fire, focusing on the King's Great Chamber of c. 1232–36, the Queen's Chamber and Queen's Chapel of 1237–38, and the new Exchequer, built in c. 1240. It considers what these structures looked like on the basis of abundant royal records and antiquarian illustrations; to which buildings they may be compared, such as Winchester Castle Hall, Salisbury Cathedral, the choir of the Temple Church, London, and Windsor Castle; and how they may have been furnished and used for alms-giving, great assemblies, and quotidian functions.

INTRODUCTION

WESTMINSTER was one of Henry III's best-loved houses, and 'the largest and most impressive group of domestic buildings in the kingdom'.[1] Indeed, contemporaneous sources referred to Westminster as a palace unlike any other of the king's houses.[2] Its importance was closely linked to Westminster Abbey, which by the 13th century was the recognized site for coronations. The adjacent Palace was not only significant for ceremonial events, but had also become, or was becoming, the financial, administrative, and judicial centre of the realm, adjoining its most wealthy and populous city. From the earliest years of his reign, Henry's itinerary shows that he was spending considerable time there. Allied with the Abbey for centuries, the Palace became particularly significant for Henry, whose devotion to St Edward the Confessor, enshrined at the Abbey, developed into religious fervour by the 1230s.[3] Not only did Henry sponsor the rebuilding of Westminster Abbey, beginning in 1245, but earlier he had contributed to the construction of the Lady Chapel of the Abbey. In addition, he had both the administrative and the residential areas of the Palace reworked, beginning with his Great Chamber,[4] rendering the entire complex an immense royal building site at the heart of his monarchy.

This paper discusses what we know of Henry III's Palace before the fire in 1263 damaged many of the residential buildings and their interior decoration (Fig. 1). Although the Palace is now gone, much survived until the fire of 1834 and its aftermath, recorded in abundant drawn and written sources. As a result, this paper is able to summarize what these structures looked like, to which buildings they may be compared, and how they were used, in addition to giving an idea of the richness of the written and visual resources.[5] An important caveat, however: working with antiquarian images rather than the actual fabric means that the documentation may be neither consistent nor accurate, even in the most exacting architectural drawings, so that conclusions should be considered somewhat more tentative than usual.

VIRGINIA JANSEN

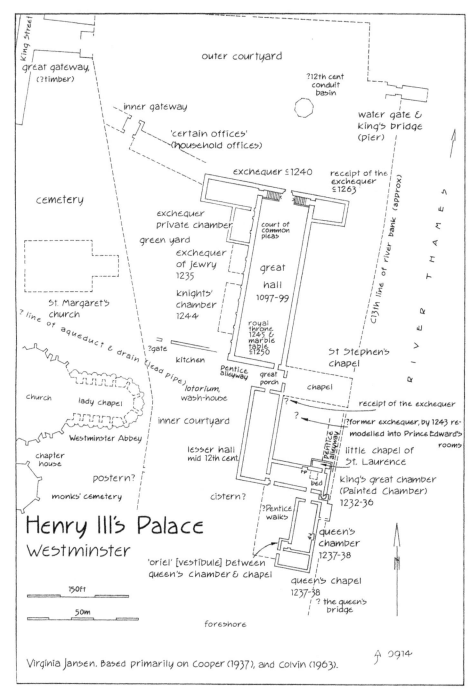

FIG. 1. Plan of Westminster Palace during the reign of Henry III
Drawing by Jill Atherton after V. Jansen

EARLY WORK

WHEN Henry III ascended the throne in 1216 at the age of nine, England was in the middle of a civil war with rebellious barons in league with the French, who had invaded the country — an inauspicious time for any domestic construction. At Westminster, there existed already a substantial palace, mainly erected by Henry's grandfather Henry II, although much was in poor condition.[6] During the minority, the regents focused on defence and practical needs, as the writs show: repairs to buildings, quays, precinct walls, and gates occurred here as elsewhere.[7] By 1227, £800 had been expended.[8] The walls and gates may have been rebuilt in stone during this period, certainly by 1235.[9] The considerable majority of references, however, cite payments for activity on houses.

In 1227, although the king had acquired regal powers, he was still subject to supervisory control and yet to affect major cultural production. Royal orders were directed mainly toward producing small-scale objects and wainscoting for the chapels, especially for St Stephen's, and refurbishing buildings then in heavy use, such as the Exchequer. This chamber was at this time located east of the Great Hall, but moved subsequently to the north-west end by 1243.[10] In the 1230s, new construction occurred, including a timber almonry using recycled 'old wood', and a two-storey Exchequer of the justices of the Jewry, presumed to be situated on the west side of the hall in 1235.[11] An early personal order directed the upgrading in 1234 of the waterworks, on which Henry expended funds throughout his reign. Henry ordered a specialist conduit-maker hired, a Master William from Reading;[12] even for plumbing Henry sought the best. Furthermore, in 1244 he ordered a *lotorium*, a round structure for washing, to be located between the kitchen and the entrance to the Lesser Hall.[13] Later, a conduit for water was made to feed the royal baths, which included a bath tub, and water was collected in a cistern ornamented with a tinned statue between the king's and queen's chambers, where there was a garden.[14]

ROYAL APARTMENTS

BEFORE these last works, however, the king started to renovate his Great Chamber in March 1232, when he ordered his master carpenter to select quality timber, presumably for the roof.[15] Even though considerable funds had been spent recently on repairs to the houses and the king was complaining about his lack of money, upgrading the locus of rule may have been an astute response to the political tumult occurring at this moment. Hubert de Burgh, the justiciar, was trying to maintain his hold on power, as Hubert's enemy, the bishop of Winchester, Peter des Roches, who had been the king's former guardian and tutor, had again become Henry's closest advisor, and as previously in the 1220s, there ensued contention over rule and the king's favour.[16] These factors, as well as the several functions of government now located at Westminster, together transformed the Old Palace of Henry II. Henry's ideas about aristocratic luxury and display were undoubtedly shaped by both Hubert and Peter, both of whom were exceedingly rich, and the flamboyant bishop of Winchester especially must have encouraged Henry to build fit for a ruler.[17] In any case, Henry now began to effect changes in the Old Palace buildings and to order those updated amenities, for which he is famous, that advanced his sense of modernity and visual display.[18]

Remodelling the Great Chamber was not, of course, simply an exercise in fashion. The space served as the king's reception and audience hall. Called the Painted Chamber by 1307, it was the third largest building in the Palace (about 24.19 m (80½ ft) long, 7.93 m (26 ft) wide, and 9.68 m (31¾ ft) high), after the Great and Lesser halls.[19] It, too, had been part of Henry II's Palace, and its thick walls provided a solid scaffolding for Henry III's modernizing and elaborate improvements, as occurred also at Windsor.[20] Even such a rich patron as the king did not waste money on needless demolition. Instead, resources could be applied to magnificent enrichment: elaborate doorways and mouldings, traceried windows, and paintings with expensive colours. In the next decade, a fortune was expended: almost £2,000 was dispersed on the royal apartments; after the approximately £15,000 paid out at Windsor during the reign, the expenditures on the Palace of Westminster and the castles of Winchester and the Tower of London followed at nearly £10,000 each, trailed by £3,600 at Clarendon and £3,300 at Woodstock.[21] Yet the outlay at Westminster is even more impressive, since little was expended on the great defences that surrounded Windsor, Winchester and the Tower.

Although many images survive of the architecture of the 1230s and 1240s, the main period of Henry III's building at the Palace, the interiors were burned in the fire of 1263. Thus, textual evidence provides the only information for the roof, floors and decorative work, whereas antiquarian illustrations show rebuilt elements of the king's room, including windows and doors. The structure was presumably complete by 27 February 1236, when it was called 'the new chamber of the king', and finished with murals ordered between May 1236 and August 1237.[22] Adjoining the north-east wall was a 'little chapel in the corner of the king's chamber', probably the one dedicated to St Laurence.[23] Also connected with the chamber, perhaps near the stairs, was a small wardrobe in addition to the large one that was probably located underneath the room.[24] Like most chambers in medieval palaces (as opposed to ground-level halls), including most of the major buildings at Westminster, this structure consisted of two storeys, the main floor above a ground-level undercroft.

Illustrations of the interior show twin two-light windows in plate tracery at the east end, the lancets surmounted by a lozenge (Fig. 2). Drawings that depict an oculus rather than a lozenge reflect a refurbishing after 1818 for new governmental functions.[25] The former pattern, however, was used in the lateral walls; the south wall had two such windows and the north wall three. Since one entered the chamber facing east, the richer treatment is appropriate. The lateral walls also reveal traces of round-headed windows from the 12th-century predecessor of the chamber.[26]

Plate tracery showing a geometric figure atop two lights is typical of the second quarter of the 13th century, before the advent of the Decorated style, and can be found throughout England, including in the archbishop's palace at Canterbury of c. 1220, but the lozenge pattern is rare. It exists as an updated motif on the exterior of the chapter-house at Lincoln, probably of c. 1215–30.[27]

More specific to the architecture of the reign of Henry III — a motif that has become one of its hallmarks — is the doorway with a segmental arch on short vertical springers that replaced one of the 12th-century windows in the south-western corner of the room (compare Figs 6a, 6c, 9a).[28] Such doorways exist throughout England, for example, at St Albans, Lincoln and Fountains, as well as in northern France, at the Sainte-Chapelle, Paris. Within the greater Henry III context, the device is found not only at Westminster Palace and Westminster Abbey, but also at Beaulieu, Netley and Romsey abbeys (all in Hampshire); Winchester Castle Hall; Lambeth

FIG. 2. Westminster Palace: King's Great Chamber (Painted Chamber), looking east, 1799; watercolour by William Capon
Society of Antiquaries of London

Palace Chapel in London; Wells, Salisbury and Rochester cathedrals, and so on. As an expedient way of creating a wider opening without increasing height, it is favoured for internal openings, but seldom used externally.

So far I have not located any drawn mouldings of the south-western doorway. The simple mouldings of the windows and their capitals bear resemblance to mouldings in Winchester Castle Hall, Jocelyn's palace at Wells, the Temple Church, London, and the north cloister walk and doorway to the refectory at Canterbury of 1226–36; all use a series of plain rolls and hollows with an occasional filleted roll marking a major element (Figs 3 and 4). Nearly the same capital profile can also be found in Winchester Castle Hall and the triforium of the eastern transept of Salisbury Cathedral.

More details survive from the queen's apartments built south of the King's Chamber. In January 1236, the king married Eleanor of Provence. His marriage produced a spate of building, as the queen and her household naturally needed updated accommodation in major royal houses. At Westminster in 1237–38, on an earlier undercroft recorded in an antiquarian illustration, a chamber was constructed, and adjacent to the south a large two-storey chapel (later referred to as the 'Prince's Chamber') was built under the supervision of Brother John of Waverley, a mason; painting was undertaken during 1238–39.[29] The Queen's Chamber ran north–south, with the chapel oriented. Whether there were connecting pentices at this time, or even additional buildings that formed a cloister — such as existed in Henry III's Palace in both the Upper and Lower Wards at Windsor in the late 1230s and 1240 respectively — is unknown, but it has been reasonably proposed.[30] Since the 19th-century plans show walls thinner than those of the Queen's Chamber and Queen's Chapel, these representations might indicate later construction instead.[31] Although a cloister would have facilitated movement, access to the queen's apartments would have been restricted without one, a consideration to be borne in mind after the 1238 assassination attempt. For now, the question of a cloister in this location remains open.

Both the chamber and the chapel (internally respectively 21.34 × 8.23 m (70 × 27 ft) and 13.11 × 6.44 m (43 × 21 ft 1½ in.)), connected via an *oriolum*, an 'oriel' or vestibule, are spacious rooms, indicating that the queen's entourage was large.[32] Indeed, it was the capacious chamber that became the location for the House of Lords until 1800. Illustrations show the two-storey palace construction in the process of demolition in 1823 (Fig. 5). The Queen's Chamber was an elegant room with a splendid fireplace, such as Henry had in his chamber and in several other spaces.[33] Similarly, two-light windows in plate tracery surmounted by a simple oculus occurred here, as well as a doorway with a segmental arch on vertical springers opening to the vestibule (Fig. 6a). In the chapel, however, the windows were simple pointed lancets, three on the east side, and five on the long south side, rather than traceried windows. These lancets widened considerably into the interior, their rere-arches sitting on short vertical springers (Fig. 6c). The north wall, up against the chamber, had blank walls; the fenestration of the west wall is unknown.

A few deteriorated arches remain from the queen's residence in the Sir John Soane's Museum, London (Figs 6a and 6c), but details are clearer in Soane's drawings, especially for the two fine doorways of the 'oriel', and a chapel window.[34] These arch mouldings now have regular unfilleted rolls and hollows; some rolls were probably beaked, that is, with a sharp edge marking the point of the reversal of the curve (Figs 3 and 4). Comparisons found are limited to individual elements rather than to

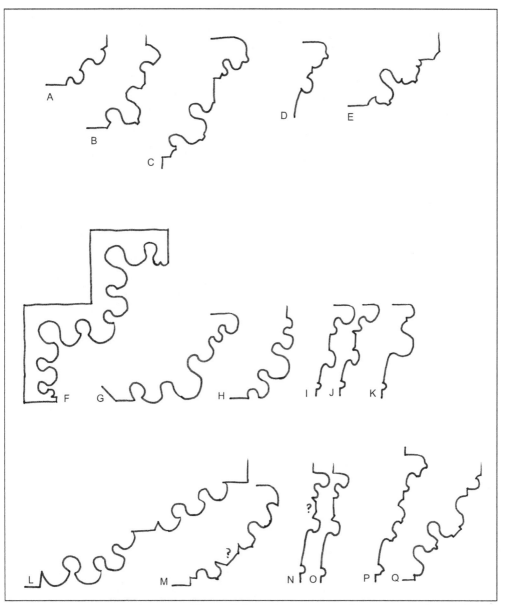

FIG. 3. Westminster Palace: mouldings of the 13th-century royal apartments, derived from various sources, including the author's personal observations (not to scale).
A–E King's Chamber: A cornice; B–D east window, exterior arch, interior arch, capital to centre shaft; E quatrefoil opening
F–K Queen's Chamber: F–G doorway arches, vestibule to chamber, chamber to vestibule; H lateral window, arch; I–J capitals; K doorway arch from vestibule to chamber, jamb capital
L–Q Queen's Chapel: L doorway arch from vestibule to chapel; M–O lateral window, arch, capitals; P–Q east window, capital and arch

V. Jansen

VIRGINIA JANSEN

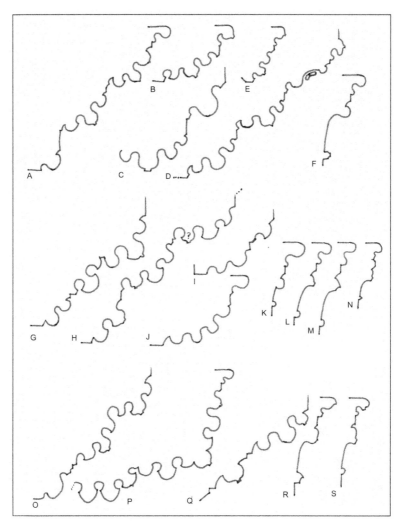

FIG. 4. Westminster Palace: selected comparisons for mouldings of the 13th-century royal apartments (not to scale).
A Winchester Castle Hall, doorway, arch; B Wells, Jocelyn's palace, doorway, arch; C Temple Church, London, arcade, arch; D Canterbury, refectory doorway, arch; E Woodchurch (Kent), piscina, arch; F Canterbury, Prior's Chapel, doorway jamb, capital
G Salisbury Cathedral, east transept triforium, arch; H Beaulieu (Hampshire), monks' doorway to church, arch; I Winchester Cathedral, retrochoir, south-east chapel, upper arch; J Temple Church, London, lancet, rere-arch; K Examples include Winchester Castle Hall (arcade), Salisbury (east transept triforium), Titchfield (Hampshire, chapter-house), Woodchurch (Kent, sedilia), capitals; L Wells, Jocelyn's palace, capital; M Temple Church, London, arcade, capital; N Examples include Winchester Cathedral (retrochoir dado), Beaulieu (refectory), Chichester Cathedral (St Richard's porch), East Meon (Hampshire, chancel arcade), capitals
O Beaulieu, refectory doorway, arch; P Salisbury, presbytery arcade, arch; Q Westminster Abbey, east cloister walk, wall arcade, arch; R Westminster Abbey, St Faith's Chapel, capital; S Westminster Abbey, chapter-house vestibule, capital

V. Jansen

Henry III's Palace at Westminster

FIG. 5. Westminster Palace, views of the Queen's Chapel (exterior, interior) and Queen's Chamber (interior) in process of demolition, 1823
Gentleman's Magazine, 93/2 (December 1823), pl. I, facing 489

VIRGINIA JANSEN

FIG. 6. Westminster Palace, extant arches in the Monk's Yard, Sir John Soane's Museum: a. Queen's Chamber, doorway to vestibule (MY 13); b. Exchequer, doorway from 'Queen Elizabeth's Chamber' or Court of Equity into the Court of Exchequer (MY 27); c. Queen's Chapel, window arch (MY 15)
Stephen Astley © Sir John Soane's Museum

entire mouldings, such as examples found at Salisbury Cathedral, Beaulieu Abbey (to which Henry contributed), Winchester, Jocelyn's palace at Wells, the Temple Church choir, and others in the south and south-east, where the capital type, with small variations, was also common; this form was used not only throughout the Palace, but also continued in the Abbey. The comparisons range in date mainly from the 1220s and the 1230s, thus appropriate to the 1237–38 date documented for the queen's apartments.[35]

Something of the sculpture of the chapel also survives in William Capon's brilliantly painted watercolours of headstops depicting a king and queen flanking the central east window (Fig. 7). Orders for paint appear frequently in Henry's writs, and Capon has noted on his drawing that the queen's head was painted 'in oil colors [sic] & gilt', and that the mouldings are 'blue / red / dark / gold hollow / greenish / fillet gilt / red / gilt hollow / green / hollow dark red / gold / blue / moulding gilt'.[36] It may seem foolhardy to attempt comparisons from such sketches, but one might note heads in the Temple Church (Fig. 8, late 1230s), on the pulpitum screen at Salisbury (c. 1236) and at Windsor, such as a painted head in the cloister of the Lower Ward (c. 1240), as well as some heads in the early parts of the Abbey (for example, the north arm of the transept, St Faith's Chapel, and the eastern triforium).[37] The adjacent capitals and arch mouldings, however, show profiles like the slightly later ones of the Exchequer and the east walk of the Abbey cloister (Figs 3, 4 and 10). Might these reflect remodelling after the fire of 1263?

BUREAUCRATIC PRECINCT ('GREAT PALACE')

WHILE the residences were being upgraded, building was proceeding in the bureaucratic area of the Palace (later called the 'Great Palace') to keep pace with its increasing importance. Whether because of Henry's fastidious sense of propriety, undoubtedly increased after his marriage, or because of additional space required Thames-side for his expanding family (or both), a distinction between the administrative precinct of officials and the more restricted areas of residences was emerging. Governmental buildings were moved north-west of the Great Hall. Earlier, however, repairs were needed after the enormous flood in 1236, when the best means for transversing the hall was by boat; in 1242 it was by horse.[38] In 1240, the wall of the inner ward from

FIG. 7. Westminster Palace, head-stop with a queen's head; watercolour by W. Capon, 1823

City of Westminster Archives Centre, Gardner Collection, box 57, no. 54c

FIG. 8. Temple Church, London, head corbel from northern arch between choir and nave
V. Jansen

the almonry to the gateway was ordered crenellated, surely for display rather than defence; if so, it may be the earliest known instance in England of using the motif to signify status.[39] Its timber gate was rebuilt in stone in 1244–45. Sometime between 1235 and the spring of 1243 (when the chamber of the old Exchequer east of the Great Hall was being fitted up for Prince Edward), probably in the late 1230s, the Exchequer must have been relocated to adjoin the hall at the north-west corner, where stairs still lead up through a 13th-century doorway (Fig. 9).[40] New rooms were constructed, again large and spacious, including the Exchequer, which measured 23.16 m (76 ft) in length (almost as long as the King's Great Chamber), and a building for knights, built in 1244, south of the Exchequer, along the west wall of the hall.[41] Although we have no visual evidence for the knights' chamber, the writs describe it as 'a long and ample chamber', to be built like the Exchequer with two storeys; its upper chamber should contain two fireplaces, and the chamber below, one; and the 'timber roof should not block the windows of the great hall'.[42]

Although textual documentation on the Exchequer, which was pulled down in 1822–23, is sparse, more visual evidence survives. Typical of the period of Henry III there is a plate-tracery window with two lights under a quatrefoil crowned by a segmental rere-arch on vertical springers in the west wall; such an arch can be seen in other doorways and arches of the Exchequer (Fig. 9a). A precedent for the window form occurred in the archbishop's palace at Canterbury of c. 1218–20; later examples with trefoil-headed lancets can be found in Winchester Castle Hall, begun in 1222 and finished in the early 1230s; the hall in the great tower of Chepstow Castle, of the later 1230s; Elias of Dereham's house Leadenhall in the close of Salisbury and the

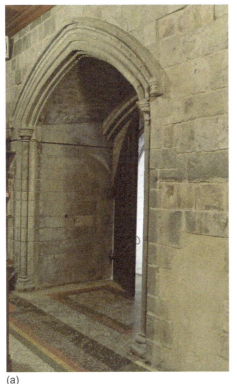 

(a)   (b)

Fig. 9. Westminster Palace, former Exchequer–Westminster Hall doorways: a. from former Exchequer to hall; b. from hall to former Exchequer

a: V. Jansen; b: Roland B. Harris

heavily restored Bishop's Jocelyn's palace at Wells (both of the same period as Winchester); and the piscina of the Temple Church choir (1230s).[43] As Henry III was born in Winchester and spent several Christmases there, there is no doubt that the king and his men regarded the great aisled hall of Winchester Castle as a significant model.

The moulding profiles of the Exchequer are well represented among the 19th-century antiquarian drawings. Additionally, one of the arches in the Sir John Soane's Museum has been identified as deriving from this building (Figs 6b and 10).[44] These mouldings are full of hollows and bowtells (rolls), some filleted as in the doorway to the Great Hall, whereas those in the chambers have beads astride the rolls; a few scroll mouldings appear, typical of Westminster Abbey profiles. The profiles of the hall doorway are earlier in appearance, most similar to those of the hall at Winchester as well as of St Faith's Chapel in the Abbey. The nailhead capitals on the north jamb share the same profile with those in the chapel of Clifford's Tower, York (1245), a royal work with which the Windsor and Westminster master, Henry de Reyns, was involved.[45] The more up-to-date profiles of the chamber arches, however, resemble those in the south cloister of the Lower Ward at Windsor Castle (1240), profiles that

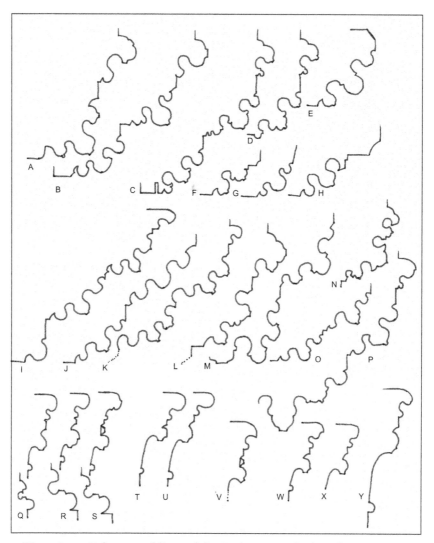

FIG. 10. Westminster Palace, mouldings of the Exchequer and selected comparative examples (not to scale).
A–H Exchequer: A doorway arch to Westminster Hall; B doorway arch from Westminster Hall; C–F west window, exterior arch, interior arch, interior arch (architrave), quatrefoil; G doorway, arch to inner chamber; H doorway, arch from inner chamber
I Winchester Castle Hall, south doorway, exterior arch; J Westminster Abbey, St Faith's Chapel, doorway, arch; K Netley Abbey (Hampshire), east window, arch; L Winchester Cathedral, cloister doorway to dormitory, arch; M Temple Church, London, north arch between choir and nave; N St Albans, west wall niche, arch; O Windsor Castle, chapel doorway to Galilee, arch; P Westminster Abbey, presbytery, arcade, arch
Q Exchequer to Westminster Hall, doorway, capital and base; R–S Westminster Hall to Exchequer, doorway, capitals and bases (south jamb, north jamb); T Corfe (Dorset), St Edward's, chancel, capital; U Temple Church, London, window arch, capital; V York, Clifford's Tower, chapel, corbel; W Westminster Abbey, St Faith's Chapel and cloister east walk, capital; X Salisbury Cathedral, nave triforium, second eastern bay, capital; Y Netley Abbey, choir arcade, capital

V. Jansen

are continued in the Abbey, especially in St Faith's Chapel and the eastern cloister. They thus demonstrate the probable use of the same workers at Windsor and Westminster; so too might the crocket capitals of the central window shafts in the west wall, as drawn by Buckler, that appear similar to capitals of the 1240s work at Windsor Castle and Westminster Abbey.[46] Similar profiles occur in related buildings, such as Netley Abbey, founded by Peter des Roches. All these connections underscore the royal axis of Winchester–Windsor–Westminster.

Whereas the window tracery of the Exchequer followed older precedents, the mouldings show its architecture as current. It is unsurprising that the forms of large, visible features such as window tracery might be considered up to date longer than elements that only designers and historians might notice.

INTERIORS AND USES

So far, discussion has focused on examining the Palace buildings. The records also allow a glimpse of the life that these walls witnessed. Henry ordered murals frequently to add meaning to the rooms. Since the 1263 fire destroyed most of the paintings, evidence is textual. Only brief mention of these can be made here, omitting writs for the several chapels. Much of the painting had an ornamental nature, such as painted green curtains forming a dado. Dating most likely to the 1230s, similar painted curtains remain in the chamber block of the Lower Ward at Windsor.[47] Green was a favourite colour of the king, and it may have carried Solomonic connotations.[48] There were figures of birds, lions, and other beasts, as well as a *magna historia*, a great narrative; although the text does not cite the subject, it proves that history painting existed before the 1263 fire.[49] In addition, angels, lions for the gable wall, a *mappa mundi* and Evangelists were ordered for the King's Chamber, as well as Evangelists for the queen's and Prince Edward's rooms.[50] In the lavatory ('in garderoba'), 'where the king washed his head', Henry must have taken solace after 1256 from a daily viewing of the story of the king of the Garamantes, saved from rebellious subjects by his dogs, painted at a time when he was having political trouble.[51] In 1240, in the Queen's Chamber, a fire's welcome was enhanced by a figure painted on the chimney, whose 'sad look and miserable appearance may properly be likened to winter'.[52] In 1259, when the king's fireplace was remade, the mantel was painted with a Tree of Jesse, emphasizing the king as sanctioned ruler and God's appointed vicar, based on the generations of the gospel of Matthew.[53] Allegorical figures also graced the large surfaces of the thick 12th-century window embrasures.[54] The location of two rooms are not precisely known: a painted Antioch Chamber, such as also was fashioned at Clarendon and Winchester and ordered here in 1251 for the king's garden as a low, one-storey structure with a fireplace; and a chamber with the buttress standing in the Thames and the Marculf story portrayed in the gable window.[55] Since the depiction was located in the gable, I disagree with Colvin's placing the Marculf structure beneath the King's Chamber. As another low edifice, perhaps it too was a garden building.

The Great Chamber held at least one magnificent piece of furniture: the royal bed. Monumental and expensive, these beds of estate represented their owners' wealth, status and hence authority; they were meant to be viewed.[56] Henry III's is the first such bed for which there is evidence, and its location at the east end of the room indicates its pre-eminent focus. The canopy bed and bedding were thoroughly sumptuous. Its posts were painted green and covered with gold stars and silver decoration. Its tester was hung with green linen, ordered in December (1243) to provide enclosure against the cold — and others' vision. Green cloth covered the bedding.[57] The bed stood against the north wall, adjacent to a small chapel that projected beyond, so that whenever Henry woke up, he could see the altar from his bed through a 'squint' framed by a roundel, or quatrefoil, window that was glazed in 1236.[58]

Since the King's Great Chamber was used as a royal audience room, it is fitting that it should display magnificence to show paramount royal authority. Furthermore, the Great Chamber served additional uses: as a room for enacting daily orders and consulting both magnates and staff, such as the exemplary royal administrator, Edward of Westminster. It was a multi-purpose space, where the various administrative aspects of rule and living were personally and intimately linked. The chamber must thus have been fitted out with many handsome pieces of furniture. Accounts document tables made for the royal chambers in 1253.[59] Judging from references to other aristocratic rooms, since no such documentation survives for Westminster, there were also probably buffets for the display of and service from plate, chests, chairs, rugs and even stalls along sections of the walls, situated to convey status.[60] Equally, there would have been at least tables and chairs of fine quality in the Queen's Chamber, such as the 'fair table' that the queen had at Woodstock.[61]

Royal magnanimity was especially noticeable during the great alms-giving occasions.[62] Of all of the residences, Westminster Palace was used most for Henry III's massive outlays in an age when generous charity was expected. Thousands were fed throughout the year, accommodated usually in the Great Hall and sometimes in the Lesser Hall. Henry was thus not only displaying kingship emphatically, but what is more important, seeking salvation.[63] When in 1236 he ordered a motto to be painted on the west gable of his chamber beneath a representation of the parable of Dives and Lazarus, he underscored his duty of alms-giving and hope for salvation.[64] These paintings faced the east end, speaking to the king's view, but were also visible to those present when they left. When numbers were especially large, all the great rooms were used, such as in 1243 when at least 6,000 were fed; the 'old and feeble [ate] in the Great and Lesser Halls, the less feeble and middle-aged in the king's chamber, and the children in the queen's chamber'.[65] Since Queen Eleanor also gave substantial alms, her chamber served on other occasions as well.[66]

Yet grander occasions included the great councils, which, because of the turmoil of the previous reign, Henry's long minority, and several Continental wars, became frequent during his reign. During the years 1235–57, of the fifty-four meetings, Maddicott calculates that thirty-nine occurred at Westminster or London, taking place in the Abbey as well as the Palace.[67] Although information seldom relays the exact location, they may have occurred often in the King's Great Chamber, then newly remodelled, a space that signified the union of monarch and council. From the shifting nature of these great assemblies parliament developed; the first use of the word *parliamentum* is documented in 1236.[68] At least by 1259, parliamentary meetings were opened in this chamber, which served as the assembly room for parliament into the modern era.[69]

For the most significant ceremonial occasions the Great Hall was used.[70] During Henry's reign, additions here concentrated on furnishings. Henry embellished the hall with a large Purbeck marble table and a superlative throne. The high table, remains of which have been recently excavated and dated to *c.* 1250, was situated at the south dais end.[71] The throne, dating to 1245 and rendered in the brilliant metals beloved during the Middle Ages, imitated the throne of Solomon, but it exists only textually:

The king to Edward of Westminster, greeting. Since we recall that you told us that it would be rather more splendid to make the two leopards which are to be on either side of our throne at Westminster of [gilded] bronze instead of cutting them out of marble, we command you to have them made of metal as you said.[72]

This quotation confirms that the trusted Edward and King Henry worked in tandem to create the sumptuous and brilliant works that have determined the artistic legacy of Henry III.

The accounts give further insight into the personality of the king. Work was to be done 'decently and well': sculpture should be 'beautiful and well-painted', painting ought to use the 'best colours' possible; even lavatory freestone was to be 'polished'.[73] Location was considered: an image of the Virgin should be painted in St Stephen's Chapel so that it could be seen 'as one enters the chapel coming down from the hall'.[74] Since ceremonial movement was intrinsic to the royal person, Henry ordered a porch 'in keeping with so great a palace' so that he could dismount from his palfrey 'with befitting dignity'.[75] Some writs testify to his sense of refinement: in 1259 Henry paid for making a conduit so that 'the filth of the king's kitchens at Westminster [would be directed] to flow into the Thames, which the king ordered to be made because of the stench of the dirty water which was carried away through his halls, which used to infect persons spending their time there'.[76] Finally, his orders must always be accomplished quickly: 'get it done for the king's arrival'.[77] The knights' chamber was to be completed in six weeks 'even if a thousand workmen are required every day'![78]

CONCLUSION

DETAILS indicate that the architecture of Henry III's Palace employed the typical forms of the 1220s and 1230s associated with his reign, rather than initiating innovative work, such as that which appeared in the 1240s at Windsor Castle and Westminster Abbey. Informative models appear to have been Salisbury Cathedral, Winchester Castle Hall and the Temple Church — unsurprising, since Henry was born in Winchester and declared his wish to be buried at the Temple in both 1231 and 1235.[79] What is significant at the Palace instead are the added features, elaboration and expanded spaces, underlying the importance of Westminster during the reign. Here, as elsewhere, Henry III worked with existing structure, but he dressed it up by adding modern conveniences and superlative material qualities associated with his ideas of kingship. He was constantly ordering improvements, such as wardrobes and lavatories or wash-houses, oriels, porches, covered walkways (pentices), conduits, traceried and glazed windows, elaborately moulded doorways, fireplaces, wainscoted walls for decoration and warmth, and paintings, both ornamental and figurative, applied with expensive, beautiful colours. In fact, Henry III might be called the 'king of amenities'. These elements went a long way towards creating the atmosphere of 'accustomed delights and rest' that Henry had uttered about his Palace, according to Matthew Paris.[80] But without the survival of copious, detailed royal records, most of this work would not be known, nor without the abundant 19th-century illustrations would almost anything be visualized; they supply a picture of what was destroyed in 1834 and its aftermath.

VIRGINIA JANSEN

ACKNOWLEDGEMENTS

Appreciative thanks go to the Arts Research Institute and the Academic Senate Committee on Research of the University of California, Santa Cruz, for contributing to research expenses for this study and for travel to the conference; to Nicola Coldstream for, as ever, fruitful discussions; to Richard Morris for providing me with mouldings related to my Henry III project; to the editors and the reader for their comments; and to the institutions and photographers who granted me permission to publish their images.

NOTES

1. R. A. Brown, H. M. Colvin and A. J. Taylor, *The History of the King's Works: The Middle Ages*, 2 vols (London 1963), I, 86.
2. Ibid., I, 120, n. 4.
3. D. A. Carpenter, 'King Henry III and Saint Edward the Confessor: The Origins of the Cult', *English Historical Review*, CXXII (2007), 865–91, here especially 869–72, for the beginning of the cult in *c.* 1233.
4. T. Craib, 'Itinerary of Henry III', unpublished typescript held at TNA (1923); revised version by S. Brindle and S. Priestley, unpublished, English Heritage (2000), copies deposited in London at the BL, SAL, and the Institute of Historical Research.
5. Excellent discussions figure in *King's Works* (as n. 1), I and II, and P. Binski, *The Painted Chamber at Westminster*, Society of Antiquaries of London, Occasional Papers, n.s., 9 (London 1986), but references in this paper generally cite the original sources. Most illustrations pertaining to the Palace can be found in H. M. Colvin ed., 'Views of the Old Palace of Westminster', *Architectural History*, 9 (1966), 21–184. Many of these, especially those by William Capon, John Carter, and the Soane office, are in WCA, Gardner Collection (no longer in the Westminster City Library, as cited in Colvin, 'Views'); the Buckler drawings are in the BL; and Soane's drawings and measured plans are in the library of the Sir John Soane's Museum. Antiquarian authors include J. Carter, *Ancient Architecture of England* (London 1887, new edn); J. G. Rokewode, 'A Memoir on the Painted Chamber in the Palace at Westminster ... [Read 12th May 1842.]', SAL, *Vetusta Monumenta*, VI (London 1885), 1–37 and pls XXVI–XXXIX; J. T. Smith, *Antiquities of Westminster* (London 1807), and the *Sixty-two additional plates to Smith's Antiquities of Westminster* (London 1807–09). To avoid excessive citation of the illustrations, I usually restrict references to the figures in Colvin, 'Views'. See also Mark Collins' paper in this volume, 206–56.
6. See John Crook in this volume, 1–21; J. Crook and R. B. Harris, 'Reconstructing the Lesser Hall: An Interim Report from the Medieval Palace of Westminster Research Project', in *Housing Parliament: Dublin, Edinburgh and Westminster*, ed. C. Jones and S. Kelsey (Edinburgh 2002), 22–61, at 28, n. 20.
7. T. D. Hardy ed., *Rotuli Litterarum Clausarum in Turri londinensi asservati*, 2 vols (London 1833, 1844), and *CLR 1226–40*; the relevant entries are given in *King's Works* (as n. 1), I, 494, n. 3; however, the reference to *Rotuli Litterarum Clausarum*, II, column 18, should be corrected to 18b.
8. *King's Works* (as n. 1), I, 494, n. 4.
9. C. Thomas, R. Cowie and J. Sidell, *The royal palace, abbey and town of Westminster on Thorney Island: Archaeological excavations (1991–8) for the London Underground Limited Jubilee Line Extension Project*, MoLAS Monograph 22 (London 2006), 94. An entry in *Rotuli Litterarum Clausarum* (as n. 7), I, 586, directed a sizeable outlay for stone toward the work of the walls in 1224.
10. For the chapels: *CLR 1226–40*, 10, 38; *CR 1231–34*, 9, 10, 207, 378; *CR 1234–37*, 239. Carpenter, ('Saint Edward the Confessor' (as n. 3), 872), cites the writ at *CR 1231–34*, 10 as the first one known showing Henry's interest in religious art. For the Exchequer: *CLR 1226–40*, 103; perhaps located above the Receipt of the Exchequer: *King's Works* (as n. 1), I, 538–40.
11. For the almonry wood, perhaps from the Great Chamber: *CR 1231–34*, 114; for the Exchequer of the Jewry: *CR 1234–37*, 100; I. M. Cooper, 'Westminster Hall', *JBAA*, 3rd series, 1 (1937), 168–228, here especially plan I between 170 and 171.
12. *CR 1231–34*, 530–31; the 1244 new conduit: *CLR 1240–45*, 239, 248; 1259 repairs in H. M. Colvin ed., *Building Accounts of King Henry III* (Oxford 1971), 342–45, 384–85.
13. *CR 1242–47*, 272.
14. In 1259: *CR 1256–59*, 380; *CLR 1251–60*, 507; the existence of a bathtub inferred from *King's Works* (as n. 1), I, 550; for the cistern, *Building Accounts* (as n. 12), 422–23, 426–27, 352–53.
15. *CR 1231–34*, 41, 56 (May), for the directive of timber, which was ordered in March at the same time that the barons refused a military aid. See also *CR 1231–34*, 56 (May). A few months later, the king

is recorded acknowledging his lack of money; D. A. Carpenter, 'The Fall of Hubert de Burgh', in D. A. Carpenter, *The Reign of Henry III* (London/Rio Grande 1996), 45–60, at 50, citing Matthew Paris, *Chronica Majora*, ed. H. R. Luard (Rolls Series, LVII, 7 vols, London 1872–83, repr. 1964), III (1876), 211–12, 219; *PR 1225–32*, 466; and *CR 1231–34*, 140.

16. Carpenter, 'The Fall of Hubert de Burgh' (as n. 15), 45–60; N. Vincent, *Peter des Roches: An alien in English politics, 1205–1238*, Cambridge Studies in Medieval Life and Thought, 4th series, 31 (Cambridge 1996), especially 357–62 for the fall of Hubert de Burgh; C. Ellis, *Hubert de Burgh: A Study in Constancy* (London 1952), 126–43; F. A. Cazel, 'Hubert de Burgh' (unpublished Ph.D. dissertation, Johns Hopkins University, 1948), 315–49. Thanks to the reader for suggesting a consideration of Hubert's fall on the king's reworking of his Great Chamber.

17. On Hubert de Burgh's wealth, see Cazel, 'Hubert de Burgh' (as n. 16), 246–47; Ellis, *Hubert de Burgh* (as n. 16), 172–73, 203–28; *PR 1232–47*, 5 (reprinted in Ellis, 206–07). Henry had spent Christmas 1231 in Winchester with Bishop Peter; Craib, 'The Itinerary' (as n. 4). Carpenter ('Saint Edward the Confessor' (as n. 3), at 868–70 argues that Henry III's particular interest in St Edward begins only after 1232.

18. Also at Windsor, for example, the 1227 temporary kitchen was rebuilt during 1233–34: *CR 1227–31*, 12; *CLR 1226–40*, 215; V. Jansen, 'Henry III's Windsor: Castle-building and Residences', in *Windsor: Medieval Archaeology, Art and Architecture of the Thames Valley*, ed. L. Keen and E. Scarff, BAA Trans., XXV (Leeds 2002), 95–109, at 98.

19. *King's Works* (as n. 1), I, 495 (dimensions), 496, fig. 47 (plan and elevations).

20. Jansen, 'Henry III's Windsor' (as n. 18), 95–109.

21. T. B. James, *The Palaces of Medieval England c. 1050–1550* (London 1990), 78, and *King's Works* (as n. 1), I, 113, 120, and II, 859 (where the castle-building sums of £9,683 for the Tower of London, £9,655 for Winchester and £7,500 for Dover are cited).

22. *CR 1234–37*, 245; ibid., 271; *CLR 1226–40*, 283; *CR 1234–37*, 484.

23. *CR 1237–42*, 26; *King's Works* (as n. 1), I, 498. This secluded space served for the secret marriage of Eleanor, Henry's sister, to Simon de Montfort; M. Howell, *Eleanor of Provence: Queenship in Thirteenth-Century England* (Oxford 1998, paperback edn 2001), 26.

24. *CR 1234–37*, 271, *King's Works* (as n. 1), I, 502; the small one may have been where the king washed his head: *CR 1254–56*, 326. It was perhaps located near the stairs between the king's and queen's chambers, since in 1252 (*CR 1251–53*, 57) a reference to the 'small garderobe of the queen and king' ('parvam garderobam regine regis (*sic*)') in the singular suggests a shared space; possibly only one was needed, since Henry may have often slept in the queen's room rather than in his Great Chamber. We know this detail, since he escaped assassination at Woodstock in 1238 because the king was 'quiescens cum regina'; Matthew Paris, *Chronica Majora* (as n. 15), III (1876), 497. As the queen's wardrobe was beneath her chamber (*CR 1237–42*, 26), the king's large one might have been similarly located. Ground level would also have been convenient for the delivery of shoes and tunics to the wardrobe in waiting for alms-giving: *CLR 1240–45*, 306; also S. Dixon-Smith, 'The Image and Reality of Alms-Giving in the Great Halls of Henry III', *JBAA*, CLII (1999), 79–96, at 88–89. Furthermore, at Winchester there was an 'upper' wardrobe (or lavatory) (*CLR 1251–60*, 96); also P. Eames, 'Furniture in England, France and the Netherlands from the Twelfth to the Fifteenth Century', *Furniture History*, XIII (1977), vii–xxiv, 1–303, pls 1–72, at 6.

25. 'Notes and Remarks, by the late Mr. William Capon, to accompany his Plan of the ancient Palace of Westminster [Read 23d December, 1824.]', SAL, *Vetusta Monumenta*, V (London 1835), 1–7, pl. XLVII, at 4–5. The west wall was redone in the later Middle Ages, probably during the reign of Edward IV: *King's Works* (as n. 1), I, 537.

26. Rokewode, 'Painted Chamber' (as n. 5), 1–2, 7, and pl. XXXIX; Binski, *Painted Chamber* (as n. 5), 3–4, 10–11, and pl. XXVb. See also John Crook in this volume, 1–21.

27. Thanks to Jennifer Alexander for discussing the chapter-house with me. Although the lowest levels were laid out by *c.* 1200, the vault may be as late as *c.* 1230: J. S. Alexander, 'Lincoln Cathedral Cloister', *The Medieval Cloister in England and Wales*, ed. M. Henig and J. McNeill, *JBAA*, 159 (2006), 222–48, at 241, 244–45. R. R. Laxton, C. D. Litton and R. E. Howard (*Timber: Dendrochronology of Roof Timbers at Lincoln Cathedral*, EH Research Transactions, Research and Case Studies in Architectural Conservation, 7 (London 2001), 49) suggest a date just before the *c.* 1216–20 timbers of the vestibule.

28. V. Jansen, 'Dying Mouldings, Unarticulated Springer Blocks, and Hollow Chamfers in Thirteenth-Century Architecture', *JBAA*, 135 (1982), 35–54, at 36. A good example of a doorway with vertical springers on the inside but regular springers on the outer face can still be seen in the north-west corner of Westminster Hall (Fig. 9).

29. Chamber and chapel are illustrated in Colvin, 'Views' (as n. 5), figs 122–42; figs 134–35. WCA, Gardner Collection, box 57, no. 3, probably depicts the undercroft of the Queen's Chamber documented in the reign of Henry II; compare John Crook in this volume, 1–21, and *King's Works* (as n. 1), I, 492, n. 3.

For Henry III's work: *CR 1237–42*, 26; *CR 1234–37*, 425, 500; *CR 1237–42*, 12–13; *CLR 1226–40*, 258, 276, 298, 301, 389, 393, 399 and 404.

30. Thomas, Cowie and Sidell (*The royal palace* (as n. 9), 161) suggest a cloister in the period of *c.* 1230–*c.*1350; the reign of Henry III is suggested in M. Collins, P. Emery, C. Phillpotts, M. Samuel and C. Thomas, 'The King's High Table at the Palace of Westminster', *Antiq. J.*, 92 (2012), 197–243, at 202. Thanks also to Chris Thomas for his communication on the issue. See further my remarks on courtyards and medieval planning in 'Henry III's Windsor' (as n. 18), 101, as well as J. Ashbee, 'Cloisters in English Palaces in the Twelfth and Thirteenth Centuries', in *The Medieval Cloister* (as n. 27), 71–90, at 85–87, including association of some cloisters with queens.

31. Capon, 'Notes and Remarks' (as n. 25), pl. XLVII; Smith, *Antiquities* (as n. 5), pl. facing 125, with excavated foundations; Sir John Soane's Museum Library, drawings 37/1/16–17 and 3/1/20, which show wall thicknesses clearly; Colvin, 'Views' (as n. 5), figs 1 and 103; Thomas, Cowie and Sidell, *The royal palace* (as n. 9), fig. 45.

32. Howell (*Eleanor of Provence* (as n. 23), 267) estimates it at roughly one hundred various staff; thanks to Steven Brindle for pointing out this reference. The dimensions are taken from an 1823 plan by Soane in WCA, Gardner Collection, box 56, no. 22. See *King's Works* (as n. 1), I, 121–22 for varying definitions of *oriolum*. Another oriel ordered in 1236 mediated between the King's Chamber and the Receipt of the Exchequer; ibid., 539; *CR 1234–37*, 245.

33. *CR 1234–37*, 100.

34. As this part of the Sir John Soane's Museum is under conservation I have been unable to examine the arches in person, but Curator Stephen Astley, to whom I owe an enormous debt of gratitude, generously took detailed photographs before the scaffolding went up, as well as helping me in the library. The arches are identified in catalogue box 54 and described in P. M. Rogers, 'Medieval Fragments from the Old Palace of Westminster in the Sir John Soane Museum', in H. S. Cobb ed., *Parliamentary History, Libraries and Records: Essays presented to Maurice Bond* (London 1981), 1–8. For the drawings, see Colvin, 'Views' (as n. 5), figs 123–24, 127–30.

35. For fuller information contact the author. V. Jansen, 'Architectural Remains of King John's Abbey, Beaulieu (Hampshire)', in M. P. Lillich ed., *Studies in Cistercian Art and Architecture*, 2, Cistercian Studies Series, 69 (Kalamazoo 1984), 76–114, figs 1–39, here figs 11–15, and 96–97 for beaked rolls. R. Morris, 'An English glossary of medieval mouldings: with an introduction to mouldings c. 1040–1240', *Architectural History*, 35 (1992), 2–17.

36. WCA, Gardner Collection, box 57, no. 54C; Colvin, 'Views' (as n. 5), fig. 139.

37. V. Jansen, 'Light and Pure: the Templars' New Choir', in *The Temple Church in London: History, Architecture, Art*, ed. R. Griffith-Jones and D. Park (Woodbridge 2010), 45–66, pls 36–43 and pl. III, at 52; L. E. Tanner, *Unknown Westminster Abbey* (Harmondsworth 1948), pls 16, 20, 21, 33.

38. Paris, *Chronica Majora* (as n. 15), III (1876), 339 and IV (1877), 230; *CR 1234–37*, 245. Thomas, Cowie and Sidell, *The royal palace* (as n. 9), 49.

39. *CR 1237–42*, 178. Colvin (*King's Works* (as n. 1), I, 124) cites Woodstock (1249) and Havering (1251) as 'perhaps the earliest recorded instances' of 'ornamental' usage.

40. For the gate: *CLR 1240–45*, 267, 325; *CR 1242–47*, 344; *CLR 1245–51*, 10, 16, 89. For the Exchequer: *CR 1234–37*, 100, and *CR 1242–47*, 160; Buckler's plan with the extant doorway in Colvin, 'Views' (as n. 5), fig. 57. I am especially grateful both to Roland Harris for alerting me to this doorway and for sending me photographs, and to David Harrison for arranging for me to view it in 2013 and 2014.

41. *King's Works* (as n. 1), I, 504, 540–41; chamber illustrated in a Buckler drawing, ibid., pl. 30A, and Colvin, 'Views' (as n. 5), fig. 67.

42. *CR 1242–47*, 160 ('fieri faciant unam cameram longam et amplam ad estagium apud Westmonasterium in longum magne aule versus occidentem ad opus militum, sicut aliquando inter ipsos et regem fuit provisum, ita quod visus fenestrarum ejusdem aule non impediatur'), 167; *CLR 1240–45*, 239.

43. Elias of Dereham was supervising the work at Winchester Hall in 1233; *King's Works* (as n. 1), II, 859. The dado of the cathedral 'retrochoir' also shows the pattern of a quatrefoil between two trefoil arches. For Chepstow, see N. Coldstream and R. K. Morris, 'The Architecture and Decoration of the Marshals' Great Tower', in *Chepstow Castle, Its History & Buildings*, ed. R. Turner and A. Johnson (Almesley 2006), 101–12.

44. The arch in the so-called Monk's Yard, numbered MY 27, is described in the catalogue as deriving from the 'Old House of Lords' ('the queen's chamber'), but Rogers ('Medieval Fragments' (as n. 34), 2), noticed that the moulding is the same that Buckler drew (Colvin, 'Views' (as n. 5), fig. 62), showing a doorway into the main Exchequer Chamber from the inner room, later called either the Court of Equity or 'Queen Elizabeth's Chamber' (the confusion perhaps deriving from Buckler's title on the drawing, 'the queen's chamber'). The Exchequer is well represented in ibid., figs 55–82. The Sir John Soane's Museum and the WCA hold many Soane drawings, but the sketch-like quality of the mouldings are less precise than Buckler's antiquarian attention.

45. *King's Works* (as n. 1), I, 104–05; II, 889–91; CR 1242–47, 293. Nailhead capitals occur contemporaneously in the nave of Christchurch, Dublin, in c. 1234–40; see R. Stalley, 'The construction of the medieval cathedral, c. 1030-1250', in *Christ Church Cathedral, Dublin: A History*, ed. K. Milne (Dublin 2000), 53–74, at 70 (dating) and pls 16a and 16c. Another Dublin relationship existed in the hall of Dublin Castle, which had windows based on Canterbury analogous to those in the Exchequer at Westminster; see CR 1242–47, 23.

46. Illustrated in Colvin, 'Views' (as n. 5), fig. 70. Henry III's itinerary shows much travel between Windsor and Westminster, with stays often on the same or adjacent days. Many of the Windsor stays are followed by a longer period at Westminster; Craib, 'The Itinerary', as n. 4.

47. D. Park and R. Pender, 'Henry III's Wall Paintings of the Zodiac in the Lower Ward of Windsor Castle', in *Windsor* (as n. 18), 125–31, at 126–27.

48. Binski, *Painted Chamber* (as n. 5), 40. Eames ('Furniture' (as n. 24)) cites many examples of green cloth, however, which do not bear such a meaning, for example at 76, 81–85, 88.

49. Rather than repeating all the entries in the Rolls here, see *King's Works* (as n. 1), I, 129, 497–501, 540; also *Building Accounts* (as n. 12), 326–27, 426–27, passim, as well as Binski, *Painted Chamber* (as n. 5), especially 16–17, 22, 35.

50. CR 1234–37, 271; *King's Works* (as n. 1), I, 497; CR 1243–47, 45.

51. D. J. A. Ross, 'A Lost Painting in Henry III's Palace at Westminster', *Journal of the Warburg and Courtauld Institutes*, XVI (1953), 160 and pl. 22. CR 1254–56, 326.

52. CLR 1226–40, 444.

53. Thanks to the reader for clarifying the significance.

54. Rokewode, 'Painted Chamber' (as n. 5), pl. XXXIX; WCA, Gardner Collection, box 57, nos. 52–53; *King's Works* (as n. 1), I, frontispiece, and Colvin, 'Views' (as n. 5), 132–33.

55. CR 1247–51, 283, 464; *King's Works* (as n. 1), I, 129 (for the Antioch Chamber), 502 (for the Marculf painting), and CR 1251–53, 290.

56. Eames, 'Furniture' (as n. 24), 77, 85–86, 228, and eadem, 'Documentary Evidence Concerning the Character and Use of Domestic Furnishings in England in the Fourteenth and Fifteenth Centuries', *Furniture History*, VII (1971), 41–60, at 47–48.

57. CLR 1240–45, 205; CR 1242–47, 169; CLR 1226–40, 376.

58. *Building Accounts* (as n. 12), 426–27; Binski, *Painted Chamber* (as n. 5), 13–14, figs 2, 3; Colvin, 'Views' (as n. 5), figs 101–03, 108, 114. CR 1234–37, 270, where the window is called a 'rotunda', but Buckler's drawing shows a quatrefoil (BL, Add. MS 36370, fol. 207v; in Colvin, 'Views' (as n. 5), fig. 119). To the medieval scribe the term may have meant the same, or, more likely, the elaborate quatrefoil surmounted by a gable could have been remodelled after the fire.

59. *Building Accounts* (as n. 12), 248–49; *King's Works* (as n. 1), I, 224.

60. Eames ('Furniture' (as n. 24), 203) cites references; see also ibid., 198–99, for various types of furniture. She emphasizes that the Lords' Chamber had nearly the same needs as the hall; ibid., 217. See also Binski, *Painted Chamber* (as n. 5), 35.

61. CLR 1251–60, 67.

62. Dixon-Smith, 'Alms-Giving' (as n. 24). Throughout she analyses the workings and goals of charity, according to the entries in the Liberate Rolls. The feedings recorded took place particularly during the 1240s according to research undertaken by both her and Johnstone: H. Johnstone, 'Poor-Relief in the Royal Households of Thirteenth-Century England', *Speculum*, 4 (1929), 149–67.

63. Dixon-Smith, 'Alms-Giving' (as n. 24), 87, 90.

64. Eames, 'Documentary Evidence' (as n. 56), 21; eadem, 'Furniture' (as n. 24), 181–82, 201–02; CR 1234–37, 271, and Binski, *Painted Chamber* (as n. 5), 13: 'Ke ne dune ke ne tine ne prent ke desire' ('Whoever does not give up what he possesses shall not receive what he desires').

65. CR 1242–47, 150 ('Pascantur autem omnes debiles et senes in magna aula et minori, minus debiles et mediocres in camera regis, et pueri in camera regine'), 199; Johnstone, 'Poor-Relief' (as n. 62), 150, 154–56, 164, n. 1. Calculations of the food costs corroborate the high numbers fed; see Dixon-Smith, 'Alms-Giving' (as n. 24), 87, and eadem, 'The Image and Reality of Almsgiving in the Halls of Henry III: The Pursuit of Salvation and the Presentation of Kingship' (unpublished M.A. dissertation, University of London, 1997, 6), where she argues that the number was 10,000. Appreciative thanks to Sally Dixon-Smith for sending me a copy of her dissertation with its very useful appendices.

66. Johnstone, 'Poor-Relief' (as n. 62), 157.

67. J. R. Maddicott, *The Origins of the English Parliament, 924–1327* (Oxford 2010), 163–64. See also David Harrison in this volume, 133–51.

68. Maddicott, *English Parliament* (as n. 67), 157, citing the Curia Regis Rolls, XV (1233–37), no. 2047.
69. I. M. Cooper, 'The Meeting-places of Parliament in the Ancient Palace of Westminster', *JBAA*, 3rd series, III (1938), 97–138, at 112.
70. See Nicola Coldstream, this volume, Part I, 301–11.
71. M. Collins et al., 'The King's High Table' (as n. 30), 210.
72. CR 1242–47, 293: 'Rex Edwardo de Westm', salutem. Quia reducimus ad memoriam quod nobis dixistis quod parum plus erit sumptuosum facere duos leopardos eneos qui erunt ex utraque parte sedis nostre de Westm' quam eos facere ex marmore insciso vel sculpto, vobis mandamus quod eos fieri faciatis ex metallo sicut dixistis ...'; translation in *King's Works* (as n. 1), I, 102; Eames, 'Furniture' (as n. 24), 181.
73. CR 1242–47, 45; CR 1231–34, 207; CR 1253–54, 165; *Building Accounts* (as n. 12), 296–97, 348–49; *King's Works* (as n. 1), I, 94–95, passim.
74. CR 1242–47, 287; also Binski, *Painted Chamber* (as n. 5), 15, 35–44 on the placement of wall-paintings.
75. CR 1242–47, 273.
76. CR 1256–59, 377–78; CLR 1251–60, 507.
77. CR 1234–37, 271.
78. CR 1242–47, 160.
79. Jansen, 'Templars' New Choir' (as n. 37), 48, 64–65.
80. Paris, *Chronica Majora* (as n. 38), IV, 385, 'ad solitas delicias et requiem Westmonasterialem'.

St Stephen's Chapel, Westminster

JOHN GOODALL

This short essay considers the history of St Stephen's Chapel at Westminster prior to the fire of 1834. It sets the chapel in the context of the medieval Palace and explains the ways in which its design was to influence the future of English medieval architecture and British political life.

AFTER the great fire of 1834 swept through the Palace of Westminster, one building more than any other amidst the ruins attracted the attention of artists and visitors. This was the vast shell of the Chapel of St Stephen. It had two claims on popular attention. The upper floor of this building had served since 1548 as the debating chamber of the House of Commons, and its ravaged remains testified, therefore, to the defining importance of the fire in the life and history of the Palace. But the ruin itself was also manifestly fascinating. Revealed by the fire were the bones of a great medieval chapel that had itself long attracted antiquarian interest and attention. Hitherto it had been necessary to probe into the recesses of a working building — presided over by sometimes awkward officials — to glimpse the remains of this structure. Now these were laid bare for all to see in the charred remains.

In the ensuing reconstruction of the Palace of Westminster, St Stephen's was completely reconfigured. Its lower vaulted chapel was preserved and extravagantly redecorated by Crace. This splendid interior, exceeded in grandeur only by the new interior of the House of Lords, remains in use today as the Chapel of St Mary Undercroft. Meanwhile, the upper chapel was rebuilt as St Stephen's Hall, a stately corridor that connects Westminster Hall with Central Lobby. The observant visitor passing through this busy thoroughfare can find a series of brass markers and inscriptions that identify the former position of the original lobby of the House of Commons, the Speaker's chair, and the clerks' table. From these they can also get an impression of the scale of the medieval building as well as the intimacy of the former chamber of the House of Commons. This latter space, it should be said, was consistently inadequate for the number of MPs returned to Parliament.

The medieval history and documentation relating to this cannibalized chapel have been very well studied and have generated a literature commensurate with its great importance.[1] Today — in 2015 — all this material is under review in a major three-year government-funded research project overseen by the University of York. Given that this research project is due to report so soon, this will be short article, the aims of which is to set out the importance of the chapel and to explain in detail the thinking behind a reconstruction drawing produced by Stephen Conlin for a short article in *Country Life* (1 April 2015). For part of the interest of St Stephen's is that it is a touchstone for a debate about the character of medieval architecture; the disagreements between scholars over the history of its construction say as much about the limitations of the evidence as their contrasting conceptions of the process of its creation.

In broad outline, the history of St Stephen's well known.[2] A chapel of this dedication is first documented in 1184, though nothing is securely known about the form or location of this building in the Palace. In 1292, however, Edward I began a completely new chapel of this name on a monumental scale. Why he chose to do so is not entirely clear, but historians have long suggested that he wanted to create a building that rivalled the royal chapel of the French kings on the Isle de la Cité in Paris, the Sainte-Chapelle. This French building, created in 1240–48 by Louis XI at stupendous cost as a life-sized reliquary for the Crown of Thorns worn by the crucified Christ, clearly astonished contemporaries and was imitated across Europe.

Voluminous surviving building accounts identify the mason initially in charge as Michael of Canterbury. To him can certainly be attributed the essential form of the building, on a rectangular plan with an upper and lower chapel. The foundations for the new building were laid in the gap that existed between the two largest and most important buildings in the Palace, the vast Westminster Hall — where the royal courts sat — and, aligned with it, the Lesser or White Hall. The chapel stood at right angles to these halls to form with them a group of buildings on a T-shaped plan. But the three buildings were not fully integrated; instead, they sat corner to corner with a courtyard at their intersection.

In 1297, the financial difficulties of the Crown brought work to a close, and the operation was mothballed, with materials laid in store. Then, in 1320 work resumed for another five years. It was probably at this moment that the only substantial change to the design of the chapel was made: a clerestory and vault were planned for the building. Timber was cut for the latter structure, but the vault was not constructed. During this period, Thomas of Canterbury succeeded Michael in his direction of the project. But again, the disastrous culmination of Edward II's reign brought work to a close. The project resumed briefly in 1331–34, this time under Thomas's sole direction. Finally, in 1340–48 the building was brought to architectural completion by William Ramsey, who had succeeded to the role as the king's master mason.

As completed, St Stephen's comprised a lower and upper chapel. The former was one storey in height and vaulted in stone, while the latter was lofty and richly ornamented. Immediate inspiration for this design probably did come from the Sainte-Chapelle, which is conceived in the same form. Notwithstanding this connection, it is worth observing that double chapels of this kind have a long history in relation to royal palaces across Continental Europe. Romanesque examples of the form in England would include the forebuilding chapels in the great tower at Dover Castle, built in the 1180s by Henry II.

In conjunction with this point it is worth observing that modern authorities assume that the upper and lower chapel served essentially the same function for discrete audiences, respectively the king and the household. Yet in the case of both St Stephen's and the Sainte-Chapelle, this analysis is entirely without documentary basis (though in the former case it must be admitted that the prolonged construction of the chapel does complicate any interpretation of the available evidence).[3] As an alternative parallel it is worth pointing to the great two-storey basilica of San Francesco at Assisi, effectively a convent church attached to a papal palace. In this case the upper and lower churches were used for distinct elements of the liturgy.[4]

The upper chapel of St Stephen's was a lofty interior five bays in length with an elevation of three registers. At floor level there was a continuous stone bench divided into seats by ornamental canopies. Above this dado rose tall windows set beneath a deep horizontal cornice, which could plausibly be read as an intended termination to the elevation. Nevertheless, the upper chapel was completed with a clerestory and a timber vault. The choice of lightweight timber rather than stone for the vault may itself be further evidence that the vault was added as an afterthought to a building that was originally designed without one. Unfortunately, however, the physical evidence that would allow for certainty on this point has vanished: the clerestory and vault were removed during repairs in 1692 before any detailed record of them was made.[5] All attempts to reconstruct them are necessarily dependent, therefore, on inference from building accounts and early topographical views of the Palace. It is from these that much of the external outline of the chapel as depicted in Fig. 1 derives.

To my reading, the clerestory wall appears to have sat on the inside face of the structure below. This is a very unusual detail in an English building, where the depth of the wall was commonly used to create an additional layer of internal ornament. In this case the arrangement created an external wall passage that was spanned by flying buttresses. Rising behind these on the buttresses themselves were pinnacles of stone that rose roughly to the height of the apex of the roof. There also existed much bigger pinnacles at the corners of the building. These gave the building a very distinctive outline not unlike that of Battersea Power Station in the modern cityscape of London. Something of its prominence, indeed, is suggested by its inclusion as a background detail in Van Dyck's *The Great Piece* portrait of Charles I with Henrietta Maria and his children (1632). Presumably these massive angle turrets were designed like the Eleanor Crosses and incorporated multiple pinnacles. Many later chapel buildings, such as King's College, Cambridge, pick up on this distinctive treatment of the angle turrets.

It should be observed that most of the early drawings — particularly those by Hollar — suggest that the clerestory windows must have been about the same size as the lower windows of the upper chapel. This must be mistaken, because the one certain detail known about the height of the building is from *The King's Avyse*, compiled by Henry VI for Eton College early in 1449. This states that Eton College chapel was to have walls 80 ft high and taller than those of St Stephen's.[6] The reference indicates the degree to which the chapel remained in the 15th century a benchmark of architectural grandeur. It also suggests that the clerestory could only have been about a quarter of the height of the entire chapel elevation. This proportion is also suggested by the detailed anonymous 16th-century view held at the Victoria & Albert Museum.

This and other drawings show that the eastern gable was very elaborately decorated, as befitted its position overlooking the thoroughfare of the Thames. One problematic detail is the decoration of the uppermost level of the gable with a band of arches. The evidence is equivocal, but I would interpret this feature, which was destroyed in 1692, as an external band of blind arcading. Part of the reason for concluding this is bound up with the reconstruction of the vault and roof, which in itself is a very thorny issue.

Though many of the drawings show slightly different treatments of the roof of the chapel, nearly all make it clear that the outline of the building was curved and that the roof rose to the line of the gable. In addition, the Victoria & Albert Museum view suggests that the gable was defined by a deep cornice and punctuated by projecting ornaments, perhaps crockets of stone. There are 14th-century English parallels for both curved and polygonal gables that closely match the line of the roofs they bookend. The most obvious are the hall of Berkley Castle, the chapter-house of Canterbury

Cathedral, and the south gable of Gloucester Abbey (now the cathedral). On this basis it seems reasonable to reconstruct the lost roof accordingly. There comes a problem, however, when you try to postulate the relationship of this structure with the internal vault.

All the drawings show a clerestory with the apex of the arches rising to the parapets of the wall head. The vault, therefore, must internally have risen to at least this level, but this would leave very little space between the leads and the upper surface of the vault. This is precisely the treatment of the chapter-house at Canterbury, but with the important difference that the latter possesses a ceiling that can follow the line of the roof. Assuming that St Stephen's had a vault, however, and that this sprang from above the level of the internal cornice (as it must have done), this creates an odd disposition of elements. Either the vault was very strangely distorted as a penetrated barrel vault, or there existed large spaces of walling between the clerestory windows on the interior. It is to step beyond the evidence, but in Figure 1 I suggest the latter arrangement with decorative panels between the windows.

Of the form of the chapel windows, only those of the lower chapel can be reliably reconstructed from the evidence available. These were of four lights and possessed ogees with tightly formed points termed 'Kentish tips'. The principal lateral windows were also of four lights, though no detailed evidence remains for their form. Here, the drawing copies the perfectly plausible designs proposed by Mackenzie; presumably they followed in the same tradition of Decorated tracery as those in the chapel below. Other parallels that could be invoked include the Lady Chapel at St Albans. Finally, the form of the clerestory windows is unknown. Any reconstruction of its putative tracery depends on the supposed date of the clerestory, and opinion differs as to whether it was an afterthought; it probably was. Nevertheless, they are shown here with reticulated tracery, a form that might have been created at any date between 1292 and 1348.

The east end of the building terminated in a large window, which is known from numerous 17th-century illustrations to have comprised six lights. The window was cited in an early-14th-century contract as the model for the surviving window of St Anselm's Chapel, Canterbury,[7] a five-light window that clearly matches the known style of the other tracery in the building. What it lacks are the trefoil cusps, ornamented with blind tracery, that survived in the head of the Westminster window even after the fire. Cusping of this kind is unusual on a large scale, but there are 13th-century parallels for it, such as the terminating screen of the south aisle of Gloucester Abbey.

At the very moment that St Stephen's was completed architecturally, Edward III changed its constitution. On 6 August 1348 he founded two colleges of priests at the nerve centres of his realm: one attached to St Stephen's at Westminster, the other to St George's Chapel Windsor. The structure of both colleges was modelled on that of the Sainte-Chapelle in Paris.[8] Although Windsor additionally incorporated the members of the Order of the Garter, the constitution of the colleges is clear evidence that they were conceived in rivalry to their French royal counterpart.

The college's domestic buildings — including a cloister, clock tower, and a series of timber-frame houses that gave the street Canon's Row its name — were erected in the area of land between Westminster Hall and the Thames. Meanwhile, to accommodate this body of clergy a choir was created for them within the upper chapel. This was done in a conventional way, by dividing the interior in two with a screen or pulpitum. Choir stalls were then erected along the sidewalls and across the back of

St Stephen's Chapel, Westminster

Fig. 1. A reconstruction drawing of St Stephen's Chapel in *c.* 1530 by Stephen Conlin commissioned by *Country Life*, showing the building viewed from the north-west, with the corner of Westminster Hall outlined in the foreground and the gable of the White Hall beyond. A corner of the college cloister, built *c.* 1526, is visible to the left

the screen. This arrangement must have compromised the architectural clarity of the original design. Nothing is securely known about the pulpitum, though it is again referred to as a model in another document relating to the design of Eton College, the king's will of 1448, according to which it was 12 ft deep.[9] In the reconstruction drawing, the form of the pulpitum has been copied from the eastern wall of Bristol Cathedral, a building otherwise closely linked to St Stephen's.[10]

No evidence survives either for the form of the stalls.[11] These must have been relatively low built. Those depicted here are shown with canopies modelled on those erected in the choir at Gloucester. It is possible that some elements of the stalls survived the conversion of the chapel into the debating chamber of the House of Commons. Certainly, the bench ends shown in several early images are very angular. The closest comparable designs of which I am aware are depicted by Hollar in the Royal Chapel in the Upper Ward at Windsor.[12] Whether the Windsor stalls were also 14th-century or Tudor creations is not clear.

In tandem with this important change in the status of St Stephen's, a massive programme of painting and decoration was initiated. From the fragments of this that survive in the British Museum or are recorded in numerous drawings, prints and engravings, this was evidently of the very highest quality. The royal colours of England — red and blue — featured prominently in the detailing of the architecture, and the whole was picked out with copious quantities of gold. Narrative cycles were painted in the infilled lower register of the windows and the windows filled with stained glass.[13] As completed in the 1360s this spectacular creation would easily have rivalled the interior of its Parisian rival.

As far as it is possible to tell from drawings of the chapel in its damaged state, there is no evidence that there ever existed steps for a high-altar podium at the east end of the building. This could simply reflect the fact that the damage done to the fabric obscured all evidence for this detail. Alternatively, perhaps the altar steps were demarcated in the Purbeck marble floor. Nor is it clear whether there were any squints that permitted views of the high altar from the royal closet in the Chapel of Our Lady of the Pew at the south-east end of the chapel.

The main entrance to the upper chapel was integrated within a raised western vestibule decorated inside and out with panelling. This structure may have been the inspiration for the later 14th-century broad porches to Westminster Hall and the north transept Galilee of the Abbey. Its detailing, however, particularly the treatment of niches, bears comparison to that found on cosmopolitan mid-14th-century furnishings. The closest overall parallel is the pulpitum of Old St Paul's, which shares many details with it. Surviving furnishings that reflect its direct influence include the throne of Bishop Hatfield at Durham (built 1362–71) and the canopy over the tomb of Edward II. The latter's bulbous cusped lights on a large and small scale seem to relate straight back to this exquisite Westminster design.

The sumptuous doorways of the vestibule are particularly interesting. That opening into the west end of the chapel possessed a central trumeau, a relatively unusual feature in English buildings (though examples do exist in contemporary French-inspired work such as the chapter-house door at York Minster). Two doors in a similar idiom are to be found at Westminster Abbey — one to the infirmary and the other to the refectory — but there are more exact parallels too. That separating off the internal porch has internal cusping and a frame of quatrefoils that suggest a direct connection to the surviving entrance to the Aerary Porch at Windsor, completed in the 1350s.[14]

As late as the 15th century, doorways echoing the vestibule design continue to appear, as for example the doors flanking the altar in the Beauchamp Chapel at Warwick. All these connections serve as a further reminder that St Stephen's remained admired into the late Middle Ages.

As well as giving access to the upper chapel, the vestibule also formed a connection between the two adjacent buildings: the Great Hall and the White Hall, which were respectively set at ground and first floor level. By the end of the 14th century, the canons approached the chapel from a lobby in the south-west corner of the cloister. This gave direct access both to the west end of the lower chapel as well as to an internal porch within the vestibule. Presumably there was another stair — or possibly even two — that connected to either end of the upper vestibule.

Such vestibule arrangements are know in other important chapel buildings, as for example the Lady Chapel at Westminster and the original chapel of St George at Windsor. One parallel that has previously escaped notice, however, is the chapel of Beaumaris Castle on Anglesey, built by Edward I. In this case, the chapel vestibule runs through the depth of the wall. To judge from the squints cut through from it to the body of the chapel, this also served as a space for the household to attend divine service and witness the elevation. At Beaumaris there are also small, raised closets — presumably for the king and queen — that open off the vestibule.

In architectural terms the new building articulated several technical ideas that were to transform 14th-century English architecture. The seats and their canopies in the lowest register of the upper chapel, for example, imitated the treatment of the principal windows and their surrounds. This consonance of miniature and full-scale elements was borrowed from the example of French architecture.[15] From it grew a highly inventive late medieval English tradition of exchanging ideas between full-scale and miniature design.

No less important was the treatment of the exterior, which incorporated distinct registers of ornament and moulding at each level. From this idea there developed an architectural language — unparalleled in Continental Europe — in which moulding and decoration were used to underline function. Structural or defensive elements, for example, were boldly detailed in a way that suggested strength: the scissor arches supporting the crossing at Wells, for example, are detailed with three wave mouldings that convey an idea of muscular strength. Sometimes overlaying this idea was the application of different registers of ornament to different layers of a building. One of the clearest expressions of these related ideas is the gatehouse of St Augustine's Abbey, Canterbury, completed by 1308, which preserves visual coherence despite rising from an austere entrance level to richly ornamented corner turrets.

At the same time the chapel's side elevations were visually integrated by an overlaid grid of masonry shafts. Directly from the example of St Stephen's there developed the idea of turning the walls and vaults of buildings into lattices of stone, a fundamental aesthetic principle of the so-called Perpendicular style that would remain in currency through the late Middle Ages and beyond. Finally, assuming the design dates to the 1290s, the vault of the lower chapel incorporates one of the first known examples of a lierne, a decorative rib that does not rise from the spring from the wall or connect to the central boss (slightly earlier liernes once existed in the choir vault of St Albans Abbey). Liernes made possible the creation of complex star-shaped and net vault patterns that would henceforth be the meat and drink of great church architecture.

The most important late medieval alteration to the college fabric was the reconstruction of the cloister, probably around 1528. This dating derives from the appointment in that year of Henry Redman to the post of master mason of the college. There are very close parallels between the vault forms in the cloister and those found in St George's Chapel Windsor and the chapel Redman designed for Abbot Islip at Westminster Abbey.[16] Whatever the case, the cloister must have been begun before Henry VIII's divorce from Katherine of Aragon in 1533, because her emblems of the castle and pomegranates appear within the vault. The most obvious source for this remarkable structure, with a two-storey polygonal projection on its western side (presumably a chapel with the collegiate chapter-house above), is the cloister and chapter-house of Old St Paul's. Later damaged by fire and bombing, the two-storey cloister of St Stephen's is nevertheless one of the finest structures of its kind to survive in Britain. It remains almost totally unknown to the public.

A snapshot of the college and its buildings in the 1540s is provided by the documentation associated with its suppression at the Reformation. An inventory describes the rich contents of its sacristy and a valuation of its estates shows it was wealthier than many of England's greatest monasteries, with an annual income of over £1,000.[17] The House of Commons sat in its new chamber following major works to the interior in 1547–48. It is not quite clear from the documentation how the interior was adapted at this time. It was probably floored over and also ceiled in for warmth. Certainly, Wren describes an existing ceiling of plaster when he came to propose his alterations of 1692.[18] Partly for the same reason, tapestries were hung on the walls during sessions of Parliament into the 17th century. These are shown on the view of the chamber that appears on the Great Seal of the Commonwealth. The defunct chapel fittings, meanwhile, seem to have influenced — or been incorporated into — the new furnishings.[19]

The screen that formerly divided the choir from the so-called antechapel was apparently preserved and the two spaces to either side of it reconstituted. The choir became the new debating chamber, while the antechapel became the lobby of the Commons. It must be admitted that there is no explicit evidence for this transmutation of space, but it does seem reasonable to infer it from the circumstance of the change. Even more significantly, the seats for MPs were arranged in exactly the manner of choir stalls. That is to say, they were ranged along the side walls and then returned at right angles against the internal screen that divided the chapel from the antechapel. It is this confrontational arrangement of seats that has done so much to shape the style of debate at Westminster. The Speaker's chair, meanwhile, was placed in front of the former high altar. This position was the natural focus of the interior, but it may possibly have been informed by the former position of the gospel lectern. Certainly, lecterns in chapter-houses were the places from which the community was addressed.

The seating of the old house was of course imitated in the new chamber and then — at Churchill's insistence — recreated again following war damage. It is fascinating to speculate on how different our parliamentary system might have been — indeed, our history — if in the 1540s the Commons had been given another of its former chambers for regular use. Might the octagonal chapter-house at Westminster Abbey, the first meeting place of Parliament in 1265 and the documented chamber of the Commons for a period from 1352, have encouraged consensual British politics?

NOTES

1. See in particular J. Topham, *Some Account of the Collegiate Chapel of St Stephen, Westminster* (London 1795); J. T. Smith, *Antiquities of Westminster* (London 1807), and *Sixty-two additional plates to Smith's Antiquities of Westminster* (London 1807–09); E. W. Brayley and J. Britton, *The History of the Ancient Palace and Late Houses of Parliament at Westminster* (London 1836), and F. Mackenzie, *The Architectural Antiquities of the Collegiate Chapel of St Stephen* (London 1844); *The Gentleman's Magazine Library: Architectural Antiquities*, part I (London 1890), 65–94; J. M. Hastings, *St Stephen's Chapel* (Cambridge 1955); R. A. Brown, H. M. Colvin and A. J. Taylor, *The History of the King's Works: The Middle Ages*, 2 vols (London 1963), I, 510–27; H. M. Colvin ed., *The History of the King's Works*, IV: *1485–1660 (Part II)* (London 1982), 291–92 and 296, 525–32; and C. Wilson, 'The Origins of the Perpendicular Style and its Development to c.1360' (unpublished Ph.D. thesis, University of London, 1980), 34–80.
2. For an outline of the building chronology as it is currently understood, see *King's Works* (as n. 1), I, 510–27.
3. That the low chapel was used by the royal family is demonstrated by the queen's documented presence in 'The low chapel of the Lord King [*capella bassa predicti Domini Regis*]' at Westminster in 1315; I. S. Leadham and J. F. Baldwin ed., *Select Cases before King's Council 1243–1482* (Cambridge MA 1918), 27–28.
4. D. Cooper and J. Robson, *The Making of Assisi* (New Haven CT/London 2013), 3–4.
5. *Wren Society*, 11 (1934), 46–48.
6. R. Willis and J. W. Clark, *The Architectural History of the University of Cambridge*, 4 vols (Cambridge 1886), I, 367.
7. C. Wilson, *The Gothic Cathedral* (London 1992), 194.
8. R. Bowers, 'Music and the Musical Establishment of St George's Chapel in the Fifteenth Century', in *St George's Chapel Windsor in the Late Middle Ages*, ed. C. Richmond and E. Scarff (Windsor 2001), 174–75.
9. Willis and Clark, *Architectural History of the University of Cambridge* (as n. 6), I, 354.
10. C. Wilson, 'Gothic metamorphosed: The Choir of St Augustine's Abbey in Bristol and the Renewal of European Architecture around 1300', in *The Medieval Art, Architecture and History of Bristol Cathedral*, ed. J. Cannon and B. Williamson (Woodbridge 2011), 69–147.
11. C. Tracey, *English Gothic Choir Stalls 1200–1400* (Woodbridge 1987), 49–55.
12. As reproduced in W. H. St John Hope, *Windsor Castle: An Architectural History*, 3 vols (London 1913), I, pl. XXVII (facing 284).
13. The SAL has extensive watercolour records and drawings of this painting, including images by John Carter.
14. J. Goodall, 'The Aerary Porch and its Influence on Late Medieval English Vaulting', in *St George's Chapel Windsor in the Fourteenth Century*, ed. N. Saul (Woodbridge 2005), 165–202.
15. For Michael of Canterbury's career, see J. Harvey, *English Mediaeval Architects: A Biographical Dictionary down to 1550* (Gloucester 1984), 45–46, and Wilson, 'Origins of the Perpendicular Style' (as n. 1), 27–111.
16. J. Goodall, 'The Jesus Chapel or Islip's Chantry at Westminster Abbey', *JBAA*, 164 (2011), 260–76, here 271–72.
17. J. R. D. Tyssen and M. E. C. Walcott, 'Inventory of St Stephen's Chapel', *TLMAS*, 4 (1873), 366–75.
18. *Wren Society*, 11 (1934), 46.
19. See also Harrison's paper in this volume, 147 and Fig. 8.

The Late-14th-Century Reconstruction of Westminster Hall

JULIAN MUNBY

The rebuilding of Westminster Hall by Richard II in the last years of his reign is the supreme expression of his kingship and resulted in one of the most spectacular creations of the medieval office of works — to be seen alongside the Wilton Diptych as a measure of the artistic refinement of the age. As the king's great hall in the Palace of Westminster, it performed major functions in every sphere of national life and was the backdrop for key events and for long the home of the central courts of justice.[1]

RICHARD II

THE international links of a monarch whose queens were from Bohemia and France respectively is reflected in the curious discovery in 1896 of three brass pots in the palace of King Prempeh of the Ashanti in Kumasi (Ghana).[2] One of them was made in London and bears the arms of Richard II, and raises the question of how they got there — one thinks inevitably of English trade and links to Portugal, and of the abbey at Batalha with its very English architecture, begun in 1380s.

Richard 'of Bordeaux' was crowned at the age of ten in 1377, and famously showed great personal bravery during the Great Revolt of 1381, but his early years under the care of the Council ended in disaster in 1388, when his household was dismembered at the 'Merciless Parliament' in Westminster Hall. He had married Anne of Bohemia (the daughter of the Emperor Charles IV) in 1382, but had no children by her; when she died in 1394 at Sheen he had the palace destroyed in his grief. Her crown is an example of the finery and delicacy of Richard's court — which is also shown by his use of handkerchiefs and baths in the Privy Palace.[3] While his patronage of the arts is remarkable, it was a remarkable age, with the growth of English as a literary language, the development of manuscript illumination, and the Perpendicular style in architecture.[4]

In 1389, Richard II declared himself of age and inaugurated his personal rule, which began well enough, with a truce with France, which cemented with his second marriage; he then turned his attention to pacifying Ireland, where he famously taught English table manners to Irish kings. He began to reassert his authority by a building programme at Westminster (where the rebuilding of the Abbey nave had already begun), and two works of art, the Westminster Abbey portrait and the Wilton Diptych, were to be part of the process.[5] Where the portrait displays the public face of kingship, the diptych reflects the private side: Richard in the presence of King Edmund (whose slippers he wore at his coronation); Edward the Confessor (whose coat and crown he wore, and arms he took); and St John the Baptist (whose tooth was in his possession) — all of them associated with kingship and Westminster.[6] Richard's personal rebus of the white hart and the Plantagenet broompod (*planta genista*) are also present, and the angels wear the broompods, as if his retainers, while Richard (it has been suggested) offers England to the Virgin.[7]

WESTMINSTER HALL

WHEN Richard came to the throne he inherited the results of several centuries of royal building activity, and not least his grandfather's great rebuilding of Windsor Castle that had recently approached completion. While serious royal castles were somewhat reduced in number; there was no lack of building activity on castles and town walls, especially on the south-east coast in response to French attacks and fear of invasion. The building of a small set of palace apartments within Portchester Castle in the 1390s was perhaps a one-off royal building enterprise against the expected arrival of the French consort Isabella of Valois in 1396, while the king's own houses were much fewer in number in the vicinity of London.[8] Richard's decision in 1393 to reconstruct the principal locus of the king's authority in Westminster may have been influenced by striking Continental examples, which would have been more or less known by experience or repute: the Grand-Salle of the Palais de la Cité, Paris, built for Philippe IV le Bel in *c.* 1300,[9] or the mid-14th-century Salón del Tinell in the royal palace of the kings of Aragon in Barcelona, and the audience and banqueting halls of the papal palace at Avignon, built by Benedict XII and Clement VI between 1334 and 1352.[10]

Richard's reworking of Westminster Hall was the principal survivor of the great royal Palace largely destroyed in 1834 by fire (caused, it must not be forgotten, by the over-enthusiastic destruction of medieval financial records).[11] Partly, but not only because of this destructive episode, the Palace of Westminster, and especially the great hall has been a *locus classicus* for the archaeology of medieval buildings. Setting aside the Guy Fawkes lantern (one of Oxford's oldest museum objects, acquired in 1641),[12] the buildings of the Palace of Westminster attracted architectural antiquaries from long before 1834; for example, William Capon (1757–1827) had planned the extent of the ancient Palace, and made observations on the masonry when a door was made in the west wall in 1793.[13] The reconstruction of the north end of the hall by Soane in 1818–20 had been preceded by recording episodes by several individuals. In *c.* 1780, John Carter had made observations in the reopened porter's lodge at the north end of the hall, and was to note 'innovations' made in refacing the north plinth of the hall,[14] while Capon, Soane and John Buckler drew the north elevation prior to its major restoration.[15] Plans and illustrations of the buildings featured in the increasing number of works devoted to Gothic architecture, such as the publications by J. T. Smith, John Britton and A. C. Pugin.[16] In 1821, Pugin noted the rebuilding of the north end of the hall, and made a drawn record of the south window that was later removed for the entrance to the Houses of Parliament, while his thoughtful description of the roof was illustrated by a section, elevation and details of angel and hammer post.[17]

The investigation and recording of the superb medieval murals in the Painted Chamber is a well-known episode, and it must be remembered that the records exist partly because of rival claims and competitive recording of the newly discovered paintings by Stoddart and Capon.[18] On a lesser scale, the uncovering of the Norman arcade by Sydney Smirke (the architect's brother) in 1823 resulted in a neat drawing of the remains and the permanent display of the unblocked window reveals, and it was at this time that the absence of obvious remains of footings for aisle posts was noted.[19]

Gothic masonry was always more likely to attract attention than carpentry, and J. C. Buckler's record of the dismantled louvre in 1821 displayed an unusual interest in this material; see further below.[20] The destruction of so much of the Palace in the fire of 1834 brought artists flocking to the smoking ruins, and a series of detailed record drawings came about, though not so many of the undamaged hall.[21] The interest aroused in the Palace by its destruction led to the publication of Brayley and Britton's account in 1836.[22] In a signal episode from later in the century, Pearson's contribution to 1880s debate concerning the building of a 'cloister' on the west side of the hall[23] involved expert witness evidence on the date and character of the masonry and buttresses on the west side; the resulting drawings (reproduced in the 1885 report of the parliamentary committee) included an elevation showing stones coloured for the different phases,[24] in an 'early' (post-Willis) example of building archaeology, just predating William St John Hope's coloured phase plan of Lewes Priory published in 1886.[25]

The carpentry of the roof attracted attention nationally and internationally. In the third volume of the *Dictionnaire* of Viollet le Duc (1858) it merited three illustrations in the entry for *charpente*,[26] and of course it appeared in Friedrich Ostendorf's magisterial study of European carpentry published in 1908, though perhaps not based on his own observation, since it seems he did not visit England.[27]

The 20th century saw a number of archaeological episodes in and around the hall in response to intrusive works of building and repair,[28] of which the most significant for present purposes was the Museum of London's uncovering of further remains of the marble table legs from the 'king's bench' at the high end of the hall, and part of a programme of consolidation for the floor support.[29]

RICHARD II AND THE REBUILDING OF WESTMINSTER HALL

The works on Westminster Hall began in 1384 with the commissioning from the Corfe marbler Thomas Canon of thirteen statues of kings of England (presumed to be from Edward the Confessor to Richard II), flanking the high table (in three niches on either side of the king's throne) and on the rebuilt north wall. Those remaining outside have been much restored, and the remaining kings were taken inside and carefully conserved in the 1986–94.[30] The idea of a new roof and the preparation of the masonry shell began within ten years of the start of work on the hall.[31] In January 1394, John Godmeston was appointed clerk of works for the 'repair' of the hall, with Hugh Herland as the Comptroller, and was granted with powers to take men and materials and sell the old timber.[32] Hugh Herland, also the master carpenter for the works, was 'disposer of the king's works of carpentry' after the death of William Herland in 1375, and since 1366 had a little house in the Palace of Westminster 'for keeping his tools [*instrumenta*] and for making his patterns [*formis*] and moulds [*moldis*]'.[33]

The reconfiguration of the hall commenced with the refacing and heightening of the side walls, with a contract issued to two Gloucestershire masons, Richard Washbourne and John Swallow, for moulded cornice according to 'a pattern and mould made by the advice of Master Yevele' and delivered by his warden Watkin Walton; it was to be of Reigate stone, and was to contain twenty-six corbels of Marre stone (hard Magnesian limestone from just west of Doncaster).[34] Henry Yevele, now of advanced years, was the still the king's chief mason and may also have been involved in rebuilding the north end of the hall.

One surviving roll of 'particulars of account' for 1395–96 survives to document the earlier stages of work in gathering and transporting materials.[35] A large quantity of oak timber was purchased to make scaffolding, and boards were obtained for making masons' moulds. Timber had previously been obtained from the Hampshire royal forests of Odiham and Alice Holt (respectively 8 miles north-west, and 3½ miles south-west of Farnham), and was worked in Farnham in Surrey at a place called 'the Frame', possibly in the vicinity of the bishop of Winchester's castle, where William of Wykeham, now back in favour with Richard II, was still lord of the manor. While timber has to be sawn and converted, a large flat area would have been necessary for the prefabrication of the roof trusses, before they were disassembled and transported by road to the Thames near Chertsey (some 23 miles) and thence by water to Westminster. In June 1395, thirty waggons were ordered to cart timber five times (450 loads in all) from 'the Frame' to 'the Hamme', a name now represented by the moated Ham Farm south-east of Chertsey Mead, near the confluence of the River Wey and the Thames.[36] Other timber, from the abbot of St Albans' Barvin Park (Hertfordshire)[37] and William Croyser's park in Stoke d'Abernon (Surrey), would have been taken directly to Westminster.[38]

Carved elements in the decoration of the roof carpentry included the series of greater than life-size angels holding shields on the ends of the hammer-beams. Whether, as has been suggested at St Mary's, Bury St Edmunds, they were classed as Cherubim, Seraphim, Powers etc., we may not know, but they were certainly ranked in value, at 26s. 8d., 20s. and 15s. apiece, even if the distinction is not very apparent today.[39] Lead for the roof was purchased in 1395–96, and the glazing of the louvres in 1397–98 must imply that the whole roof was in place.[40] The hall was associated with the coronation of Queen Isabella in 1397, when the roof was partly covered with a coarse woollen cloth called 'wadmole', though perhaps not used for the actual feast. For the opening of parliament later in the year a special 'hale' or temporary hall (perhaps more like a tent) was constructed in the Palace yard as the theatrical backdrop for Richard's public act of revenge on his former enemies, the Lords Apellant.[41]

Following the commissioning and construction of the roof, the north end of the hall was rebuilt from 1398, with a central porch and lodges flanked by two towers containing vaulted upper rooms.[42] These may have been intended to provide the final security for the much rebuilt and extended side walls, with the roof now in place; they did of course provide a cathedral-like approach to the hall on the north side, similar indeed to Westminster Abbey. The works were still incomplete at the downfall of Richard II in September 1399, though the hall was used for the accession of his successor Henry IV.

THE ORIGINS OF THE ROOF CARPENTRY

It has been remarked that discussion of the roof of Westminster Hall has rather overshadowed consideration of the masonry, and while undoubtedly true, this is about the only building in England for which this is so, such is the usual balance of Gothic scholarship. Much of the discussion has actually been about the structure of the roof and how its load is delivered unto the walls (on which see more below); the aesthetic impact of the roof has perhaps been rather less discussed. The double motif of arch and hammer-beam created an interior that must have been as astounding when it was first seen as it remains today. There was not, as now, an entrance from the south end, no steps, and a lower floor, so when entered from the north end the view was directly towards the king's throne on a dais beneath the south window, framed by the profile of the roof carpentry. The succession of massive moulded trusses effectively forms a vault or great receding canopy leading the eye towards the most honorific seat in the room.

Although there are precedents of sorts in England, one has to go elsewhere for parallels: for massiveness (and a 81 × 27 m span without arcades) there is the Palazzo della Ragione in Padua, or the Grand-Salle of the Palais de la Cité in Paris, built by Philippe IV le Bel in *c.* 1300 (with twin roofs and a central arcade over a 27-m span).[43] For design, the most remarkable roof is the 13th-century Gothic arch of trefoil form, repeated in each rafter truss, over the infirmary hall of the Ghent Bijloke Hospital.[44] For a closer parallel as a public hall there is the Ridderzaal in the Binnenhof in The Hague, the manorial hall of Floris V, count of Holland, with its huge roof of base-cruck form, built in the 13th century and later used as a meeting place for the States General of the Netherlands.[45] English antecedents must naturally include the roof of St George's Hall in the upper ward of Windsor Castle (1360s), whose depiction by Hollar raises many questions, not wholly explained by post-fire discoveries in the hall masory.[46] Here the Gothic form appears to be arch braces rising from a cornice (below the wall head) to the collar beam and providing a canopy of receding arches, above which are open traceried panels filling the spandrels between the braces, collars and principal rafters. The rafters, whose curve is necessarily eccentric to the curve of the braces, are shown with an ogival terminus at the apex, though on this point Hollar's accuracy may perhaps be questioned. The late-14th-century Guard Room at Lambeth Palace also has a prominent arch-braced roof with spandrels decorated with quatrefoils and mouchettes;[47] this is really of base-cruck form in the tradition of Stokesay Castle (1280s), with its great Gothic arch over the hall, in the manner of the late-13th-century stone arches seen at Conway Castle and Mayfield Palace (Sussex, another house of the archbishop of Canterbury).[48] Direct parallels with the Windsor roof are hard to find, except in the curious case of the hall of Exeter College, Oxford, dating from 1618, which has similar open panelling between arch brace and rafters that could have been copied from Windsor.[49]

As for large 'engineered' roofs, the history of the hammer-beam is clear in outline if not particular: appearing in the 1290s or later in Chichester and Winchester, both in a mature form. The use of the cantilever principal to reach out across large spans was employed at York in the Chapter House roof in the 1280s, where the large brackets rise from the walls in the vault pockets to support the great square base that supports the roof, thus reducing the (octagon) span of *c.* 18 m to a (square) span of *c.* 14 m.[50] By the time the Ely Octagon was designed in the 1320s the same principal reduced the octagonal masonry span from *c.* 21 m at the base corbels to *c.* 16 m at the octagonal timber base that mounts the lantern.[51] In Chichester, the pyramidal roof of the large square Bishop's Kitchen was formed by mounting a four-square frame on the ends of paired hammer-beams springing from the four corners of the masonry walls, reducing a span of 10.5 m to 5.6 m. The curves of the lower braces continue into the supporting braces in the upper stage, creating a series of intersecting trefoils arches that introduce Gothic form to a humble building, wreathed with smoke and steam.[52] The same may have been true at the Winchester 'Pilgrim's Hall', which may also have had a mundane use, despite being a showcase of carpentry and roofing techniques of *c.* 1300: the building displays successively a hammer-beam hall, a base-cruck and an aisled frame (all beneath a crown-post roof).[53] The Winchester hammer-beams (which share characteristics with Chichester while displaying several features found in high-status carpentry of the early to mid-14th century) span a hall of 9.3 m and, as often commented, obviate the need for aisle posts. So by the time a hammer-beam is used in the hall at Tiptofts, Wimbish (Essex) in *c*. 1330 in a more modest manorial setting, its appearance is unsurprising.[54]

If the hammer-beam and the transverse arch were familiar elements by the mid-14th century, when the Black Death brought something of a caesura to half a century or more of great creativity in English carpentry,[55] their reappearance together in Westminster will certainly have been novel. The roof carpentry still awaits a full re-examination at close quarters, but it was subject to a very detailed study a century ago under the Office of Works architect Sir Frank Baines (1877–1933), a somewhat mysterious figure who was highly influential in establishing principles of monument conservation.[56] Baines' illustrated report was published as a Blue Paper in 1916, and the remarkable original drawings are preserved in the Parliamentary Archives.[57] The detailed drawings of construction and jointing show the unusual degree to which the roof was a complex puzzle piece locked together with tenons, trenching, and moulded elements. Some key elements may now be described (Fig. 1).

A In the base triangle, the huge (6.09 m high, 0.6 × 0.5 m) wall post has staggered offsets for the springing of the two braces to the centre and front of the hammer-beam. As can be seen from the partial example preserved in the Museum of London (Fig. 2),[58] these have a moulded base as far as the springing point, and tenons to hold the ends of the braces; above the junction the post reverts to a plain T-profile in plan. As Pacey has observed, the offsets were of variable height, and were cut as required to meet the lower ends of the two braces.[59] Courtenay has remarked that the evidence of the Baines survey drawings shows that the posts were not placed flush with the masonry wall sockets, but stood forward, and were partly held in place by an additional spur-piece tenoned into their backs at the lower end.[60] Clearly, the relationship with the Marre-stone corbel was deemed more important than contact with the wall above that point. The brace nearest the wall is the lower portion of the great arch, which here as above is formed of a central brace flanked by a pair of outer mouldings, and another purely decorative pair of mouldings on their outsides. Both of the lower spandrels are filled with tracery panels.

B The hammer-beam has three supports, from the wall post, the central member of the great arch, and the inner brace rising to the swirl of fabric at the angels' feet; it mounts the next sector of the great-arch central member (with double tenons), and the hammer post (with double tenons) that rises above the angels' shoulders. Both sides of the hammer-beam are trenched to take the larger outer moulding of the great arch, which introduces a degree of locking together the principal members at this stage. At the back of the hammer-beam it receives the wallplates at the base of the roof, though this arrangement has been disturbed by later alterations and is not entirely clear.

C The hammer post receives the two inner parts of the great arch (the brace up from the wall post and the one down from the collar), mortised to its front and back faces. Again, these are flanked by the outer mouldings of the arch, trenched through the sides of the hammer post. The Baines survey seems to show that the main outer mouldings are in two sections, with the break between upper and lower lengths occurring in the spandrel behind the hammer post, but the break is covered by the outermost moulding that continues over the break. Again, the spandrels are filled with

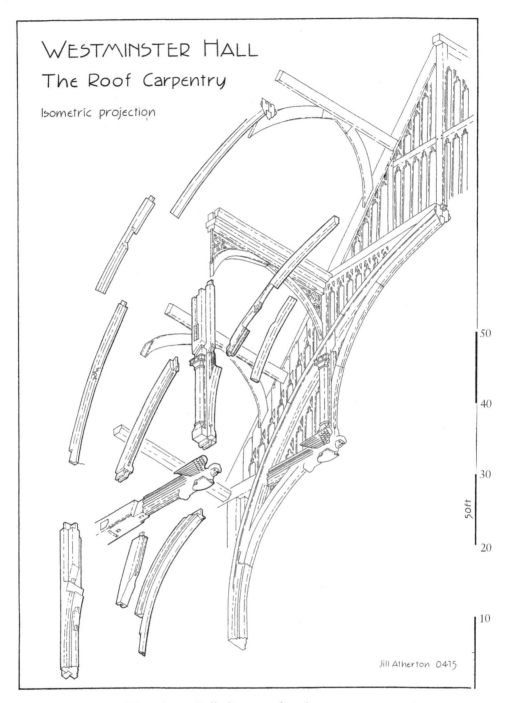

FIG. 1. Westminster Hall: diagram of roof carpentry construction
Jill Atherton

FIG. 2. Westminster Hall: part of a hammer post in the Museum of London (overall length 1.57 m)
Reproduced courtesy of Mark Collins

traceried panels, held in place by slots in the adjacent members. The upper section of the hammer post carries the braces for the longitudinal arcades with their traceried panels, and the group of upper wallplates: the head timber of the arcade, a more substantial wallplate that passes over the top of the hammer post, and the moulded upper plate that mounts the ashlar posts of the upper 'base triangle', which is itself tenoned into the collar beam.

D The upper section of the great arch, rising from hammer post and dying into the centre of the collar beam, is once more a complex structure. The inner arch of trefoil profile springs from offsets on the hammer post and dies midway into the outer arch. The outer arch has a substantial brace from the hammer post to the soffit of the collar, and is double tenoned to the downstanding part of the pair of beams forming the collar; meanwhile the outer mouldings intercept the collar, and the outermost mouldings ride over the collar to complete the illusion of a single arch to which the collar is wholly subservient.

E In the upper roof its 'tie-beam' is the double collar, and the rafters are double tenoned to the king-post at the apex (and to the collars at their feet), while the upper purlins have double tenons to the rafters. The upper collar, which exists to articulate the panels of tracery, does not span between the rafters, but runs between the king-post and queen-posts, and it is the latter that are tenoned vertically into the rafters.

One remaining part of the roof was happily subject to an archaeological episode of importance, when one of the louvres was carefully recorded by J. C. Buckler (1793–1894) on its removal in 1821. Buckler had an unusual regard for medieval timber

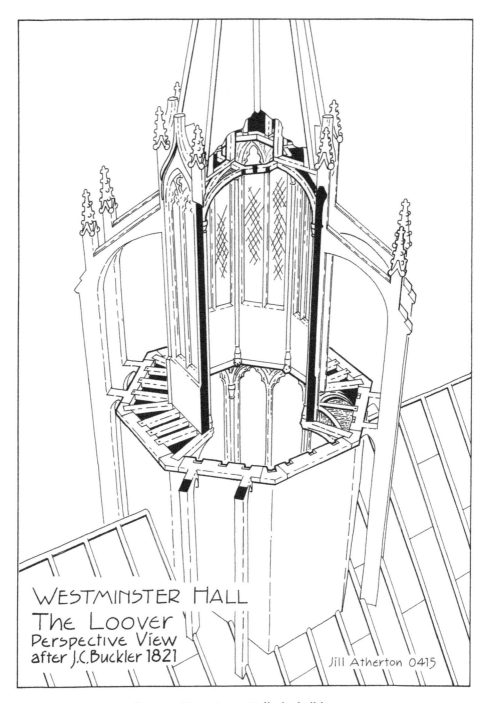

Fig. 3. Westminster Hall: the hall louvre
Jill Atherton, after J. C. Buckler, 1821

construction, and his series of drawings form a valuable record of a splendid timber lantern, being drawn 'immediately after its removal from the roof, April 10, 1821'.[61] Its replacement, having survived the great fire of 1834, was later destroyed, and the current one no longer has the elegant profile of the original. The form of Herland's louvre is not without interest (Fig. 3): there is a broader octagonal base with blank two-light traceried windows, supporting a narrower lantern stage with eight tall traceried openings. The transition between the two stages is formed by small hammer-beams (0.76 m long) held on curved braces that support the octagonal base plate of the lantern.

There is continuing speculation and debate about the mechanical function of the roof. The topic received considerable attention, first in the 1920s,[62] then in the 1960s,[63] and again in the 1980s–90s, with approaches ranging from high science with computerized and physical modelling[64] to geometric reasoning.[65] The contention has been between seeing the arch as the principal agent in delivering the load to a lower point in the wall, and the hammer-beam as the key factor in placing the load on top of the wall. Baines considered that his steel repairs allowed the timber elements to work 'according to the constructive principal of the roof', while leaving its precise nature somewhat opaque.[66] One imagines that both possibilities were in the mind of the designer, but the question remains, as does the fascination in this hugely impressive remnant of the medieval Palace that has continued to function for over 600 years as the iconic ceremonial location that it was intended to be from the start.

ACKNOWLEDGEMENTS

The two drawings, which were made especially for this article by Jill Atherton, were most generously sponsored by Mr Frederick Uhde. I am grateful to Nigel Saul for his comments on the first draft of this paper.

NOTES

1. Dorian Gerhold, *Westminster Hall: Nine Hundred Years of History* (London 1999). For an interesting if little-known piece, see F. W. Maitland, 'From the Old Law Courts to the New', *Cambridge Law Journal*, 8 (1942), 2–14.

2. John Cherry and Neil Stratford, *Westminster Kings and the Palace of Westminster*, British Museum Occasional Paper 115 (London 1995), 98–100.

3. On royal magnificence, see Jenny Stratford, *Richard II and the English Royal Treasure* (Martlesham/ Rochester NY 2013).

4. Gervase Mathew, *The Court of Richard II* (London 1968); Jeremy Catto, 'Written English: the Making of the Language 1370–1400', *Past and Present*, 179/1 (October 2003), 25–59; J. H. Harvey, *The Perpendicular Style 1330–1485* (London 1978). And Jane Spooner, this volume, Part I, 262–90.

5. For the role of art and architecture in Richard's policies in the 1390s, see N. Saul, *Richard II* (New Haven CT/ London 1997), chapter 11.

6. For Richard and the saints, see Saul, *Richard II* (as n. 5), 303–19.

7. Dillian Gordon, *Making and Meaning: The Wilton Diptych* (London 1993), 58; D. Gordon, L. Monnas and C. Elam ed., *The Regal Image of Richard II and the Wilton Diptych* (London 1997).

8. R. A. Brown, H. M. Colvin and A. J. Taylor, *The History of the King's Works: The Middle Ages*, 2 vols (London 1963), I, 237, 343–45; Barry Cunliffe and Julian Munby, *Excavations at Portchester Castle*, IV: *Medieval: The Inner Bailey*, Society of Antiquaries Research Report 43 (London 1985).

9. Herveline Delhumeau, *Le Palais de la Cité: du Palais des rois de France au Palais de Justice* (Arles 2011).

10. See Christopher Wilson's essential study, 'Rulers, Artificers and Shoppers: Richard II's Remodelling of Westminster Hall, 1393–99', in *The Regal Image of Richard II and the Wilton Diptych*, ed. D. Gordon, L. Monnas and C. Elam (London 1997), 33–59 and 274–88.
11. Caroline Shenton, *The Day Parliament Burnt Down* (Oxford 2012).
12. http://britisharchaeology.ashmus.ox.ac.uk/highlights/guy-fawkes-lantern.html (accessed 15 March 2015).
13. See William Capon's *Plan of the Ancient Palace of Westminster, by the late Mr William Capon measured and drawn between 1793 and 1823* (SAL, *Vetusta Monumenta*, V (London 1828), pl. XLVII), together with the 'Notes and Remarks, by the late Mr. William Capon, to accompany his Plan of the ancient Palace of Westminster [Read 23d December, 1824.]' (ibid., 1–7). See also H. M. Colvin ed., 'Views of the Old Palace of Westminster', *Architectural History*, 9 (1966), 21–184; figs 1–2 there reproduce part of his plan in the Society of Antiquaries of London. See also Mark Collins paper in this volume, 206–56.
14. *The Gentleman's Magazine*, LXXVIII/2 (November 1808), 977, pl. II.
15. 'Views' (as n. 13), figs 31–41.
16. J. T. Smith, *Antiquities of Westminster* (London 1807); J. Britton and A. C. Pugin, *Illustrations of the Public Buildings of London with Historical and Descriptive Accounts of Each Edifice*, 2 vols (London 1825, 1828). In general, see J. M. Crook, 'John Britton and the Genesis of the Gothic Revival', in *Concerning Architecture*, ed. John Summerson (London 1968), 98–119; and N. Pevsner, *Some Architectural Writers of the Nineteenth Century* (Oxford 1972), chapters 3 and 4.
17. A. C. Pugin, *Specimens of Gothic Architecture Selected from Various Ancient Edifices in England*, 2 vols (London 1821, 1823; 2nd edn 1823), pls XXXII–XXXV.
18. Paul Binski, *The Painted Chamber at Westminster*, Society of Antiquaries of London, Occasional Papers, n.s., 9 (London 1986). See also Christopher Wilson in this volume, 152–86.
19. Sydney Smirke, 'Remarks on the Architectural history of Westminster Hall', *Archaeologia*, XXVI (1836), 406–14, and XXVII (1837), 415–21. For his 1835 drawings in the Society of Antiquaries of London, see Cherry and Stratford, *Westminster Kings* (as n. 2), 51–53.
20. 'Views' (as n. 13), figs 46–48.
21. R. J. B. Walker, 'The Palace of Westminster after the fire of October 1834', *Walpole Society*, 43 (1972–74). Many are reproduced in 'Views' (as n. 13), and also in Cherry and Stratford, *Westminster Kings* (as n. 2).
22. E. W. Brayley and J. Britton, *The History of the Ancient Palace and Late Houses of Parliament at Westminster* (London 1836).
23. See Chris Miele, 'The Battle for Westminster Hall', *Architectural History*, 41 (1998), 220–44.
24. *Report of the Select Committee on Westminster Hall Restoration*, House of Commons Sessional Papers 1884–85, XIII (166), App. No. 1 'Copy of a Report on Westminster Hall by Mr. J.L. Pearson' and plates.
25. W. St J. Hope, 'The Archaeological History of the Cluniac Priory of St Pancras at Lewes', *Sussex Archaeological Collections*, 34 (1886), 71–106.
26. E.-E. Viollet le Duc, *Dictionnaire raisonné de l'architecture française du XIe au XVIe siècle*, III (Paris 1858), 42–45, figs 32–34.
27. F. Ostendorf, *Die Geschichte des Dachwerks* (Leipzig 1908), 108–09, fig. 184a. For Friedrich Ostendorf (1871–1915), who fell at Arras, see the proceedings of 2009 colloquium in Karlsruhe: J. Kleinmanns ed., *Friedrich Ostendorf Bauten und Schriften*, Schriften des Südwestdeutsches Archiv für Architektur und Ingenieurbau (SAAI) 1 (Salzburg 2010). There is no evidence from his drawing archive in Karlsruhe that he visited England (Dr Ulrich Schumann, personal communication, 6 June 2012), though this is curious, given the number of English examples that he illustrated, and deserves further investigation.
28. D. Whipp and E. Platts, 'Westminster Hall Excavation', *London Archaeologist*, 2/14 (1976), 351–54; David Sturdy, 'Mid Pleasures and Palaces: Archaeological Work at the Royal sites of London', *London Archaeologist*, 2/16 (1976), 417–22; V. Horsman and B. Davison, 'The New Palace Yard and its Fountains: Excavations in the Palace of Westminster, 1972–4', *Antiq. J.*, 69 (1989) 279–97.
29. M. Collins, P. Emery, C. Phillpots, M. Samuel and C. Thomas, 'The King's High Table at the Palace of Westminster', *Antiq. J.*, 92 (2012), 197–243; and see George Nash, 'Stopping the rot: subsidence and structural damage at Westminster Hall', *London Archaeologist*, 11/11 (2007), 290–97.
30. The statues are not of Purbeck, but of Reigate and Totternhoe stone; Malcolm Hay, *Westminster Hall and the Medieval Kings* (London 1995), 12. See also Cherry and Stratford, *Westminster Kings* (as n. 2); and P. Lindley, 'Absolutism and Regal Image in Ricardian Sculpture', in *The Regal Image of Richard II* (as n. 7), 60–83 and 288–96.
31. A fully documented account of 'the rebuilding of the great hall 1394–1401' appears in *King's Works* (as n. 8), I, 527–33.
32. *CPR 1391–96*, 348–49.

33. John H. Harvey, 'The King's Chief Carpenters', *JBAA*, 3rd ser., 11 (1948), 13–34; John Harvey, *English Mediaeval Architects: A Biographical Dictionary down to 1550* (Gloucester 1984, rev. edn), 137–41; *CPR 1391–96*, 707 (28 April 1396), 725 (20 June 1396).

34. L. F. Salzman, *Building in England down to 1540: A Documentary History* (Oxford 1952; 2nd edn 1967), 472 (45); E. A. Gee, 'Stone from the Medieval Limestone Quarries of South Yorkshire', in *Collectanea Historica: Essays in Memory of Stuart Rigold*, ed. A. Detsicas (Maidstone 1981), 247–55.

35. Account of Master Hugh Herland of the payments made by John Godmaston, clerk of the works, for the repair of Westminster Palace, etc., from Easter 1395 to Easter 1396 (that is, 18–19 Ric. II); BL, Add. Ch. 27018. John Godmeston's particulars of the account for 21–22 Richard II are in TNA, E 101/473/12; see also E 101/470/17 and E 101/683/82. For 22 Richard II to 1 Henry IV, see TNA, E 101/473/11. The enrolled accounts for this period occur on the Foreign Account Rolls of Richard II, TNA, E 364/30 (19 Richard II) to E 364/34 (23 Richard II to 1 Henry IV).

36. *CCR 1392–96*, 352; H. E. Malden ed., *A History of the County of Surrey*, III (London 1911): 'Parishes: Chertsey', 403–13; http://www.british-history.ac.uk/vch/surrey/vol3/pp403-413 (accessed 21 March 2015).

37. In Northaw parish, about three miles east of Potters Bar; see William Page ed., *A History of the County of Hertford*, II (London 1908), 'Parishes: Northaw', 357–60; http://www.british-history.ac.uk/vch/herts/vol2/pp357-360 (accessed 21 March 2015).

38. On timber sources, see *King's Works* (as n. 8), I, 529. Croyser was the tenant of the earl of Gloucester's manor; 'Parishes: Stoke d'Abernon', in *History of the County of Surrey* (as n. 36), 457–62; http://www.british-history.ac.uk/vch/surrey/vol3/pp457-462 (accessed 21 March 2015).

39. *King's Works* (as n. 8), I, 529–30; these costs are £1.33, £1 and 75p in decimal.

40. *CPR 1391–96*, 352, 372 (and expenditure of £604 on Godmeston's roll of 1395–96) for lead. For the louvres, see TNA, E 101/473/12 and E 101/470/17.

41. *King's Works* (as n. 8), I, 530–32.

42. Compare the entrance with the 'welcoming' porch to that in Westminster Abbey (built in the 1340s) and the late-14th-century north porch (now removed); see Tim Tatton-Brown, 'Westminster Abbey: Archaeological Recording at the West End of the Church', *Antiq. J.*, 75 (1995), 171–88, and in Part I of this volume, 312–24.

43. Delhumeau, *Le Palais de la Cité* (as n. 9).

44. L. van Puyvelde, *Un Hôpital du Moyen Âge et une abbaye y annexée: La Biloke de Gand, étude archéologique* (Ghent 1925); the Bijloke hospital is now a concert hall, adjacent to the STAM Museum of Ghent in the Cistercian abbey.

45. Ostendorf, *Geschichte des Dachwerks* (as n. 27), 159, fig. 247. The Ridderzaal was rebuilt in replica c. 1900 after a careless demolition, and is the equivalent of Westminster Hall in the Dutch Parliament.

46. Steven Brindle and Brian Kerr, *Windsor Revealed: New Light on the History of the Castle* (London 1997).

47. T. Tatton-Brown, *Lambeth Palace: A History of the Archbishops of Canterbury and their Houses* (London 2000), 41, 45.

48. Anthony Emery, *Greater Medieval Houses of England and Wales, 1300–1500*, III: *Southern England* (Cambridge 2006), 373–76 (Mayfield). For English antecedents, see also Lynn T. Courtenay, 'The Westminster Hall Roof and its 14th-Century Sources', *Journal of the Society of Architectural Historians*, 43/4 (December 1984), 295–309.

49. H. E. Salter and Mary D. Lobel ed., *The Victoria History of the County of Oxford*, III (Oxford 1954), 116–18. The roof became more Gothic and less Jacobean after a 19th-century reworking; unpublished Oxford Archaeology client report for Exeter College.

50. J. Q. Hughes, 'The Timber Roofs of York Minster', *Yorkshire Archaeological Journal*, XXXVIII (1955), 474-95; C. A. Hewett, *English Cathedral Carpentry* (London 1974), 74–77; idem, *English Cathedral and Monastic Carpentry* (Chichester 1985), 107–10. The dendro date supplied for the RCHM was announced at the 34th International Medieval Congress, Kalamazoo, in May 1999 in an unpublished paper: J. Munby, 'The Chapter House Roof, York Minster'. It is reported in full in Sarah Brown, *York Minster: An Architectural History c 1220–1500* (Swindon 2003), Appendix 4, 294–97; chapter 2 discusses every aspect of the chapter-house with only a brief note on the roof, at 69.

51. Hewett, *English Cathedral Carpentry* (as n. 50), 82-89; idem, *English Cathedral and Monastic Carpentry* (as n. 50), 114-22.

52. J. Munby, 'Medieval Carpentry in Chichester: 13th-century Roofs of the Cathedral and Bishop's Palace', in *Chichester Excavations 5*, ed. A. Down (Chichester 1981), 229–53; see also idem, 'Thirteenth-century Carpentry in Chichester' and 'The Bishop's Palace', *Archaeol. J.*, 142 (1985), 13–17 and 32 respectively. The kitchen is illustrated in Walter Horn and Ernest Born, *The Plan of St. Gall: A Study of the Architecture and Economy of, and Life in a Paradigmatic Carolingian Monastery*, 3 vols (Berkeley Los

Angeles 1979), I, 276; see further J. Munby, 'Cathedral Carpentry', in *The Archaeology of Cathedrals*, ed. T. Tatton-Brown and J. Munby, OUCA Monograph 42 (Oxford 1996), 177.

53. J. Munby with John Fletcher, 'Roof Carpentry in the Cathedral and Close at Winchester', in *Medieval Art and Architecture at Winchester Cathedral*, ed. T. A. Heslop and V. Sekules, BAA Trans., VI (Leeds 1983), 100–11; John Crook, 'The Pilgrim's Hall, Winchester. Hammerbeams, Base Crucks and Aisle-Derivative Roof Structures', *Archaeologia*, CIX (1991), 129–59.

54. 'Wimbish', in RCHM, *An Inventory of the Historical Monuments in Essex*, I: *North West* (London 1916), 349–57 (no. 14).

55. See the unpublished paper by C. R. J. Currie, 'The Age Of Carpentry: The New Art And Society In Plantagenet England' (1989, 1991), available at http://history.eserver.org/medieval-carpentry.txt (accessed 23 March 2015).

56. In the life of his son (Brian Mooney, *Frank Baines: A Life Beyond the Sea* (London 2011)), something is revealed of Baines' private life and career, but not all. See now also the new life by C. C. Pond, 'Baines, Sir Frank (1877–1933)', *Oxford Dictionary of National Biography*, October 2014; online edn January 2015 at http://www.oxforddnb.com/view/article/60657 (accessed 17 March 2015). For the context, see Simon Thurley, *Men from the Ministry: How Britain Saved Its Heritage* (New Haven CT 2013).

57. Frank Baines, *Westminster Hall: Report to the First Commissioner of H.M. Works &c. on the Condition of the Roof Timbers of Westminster Hall, with Suggestions for Maintaining the Stability of the Roof* [Cd. 7436] (London 1914); L. T. Courtenay, 'The Westminster Hall roof: a new archaeological source', *JBAA*, 143 (1990), 95–111; Parliamentary Archives HC/LB/1/114/42, volume of 38 drawings.

58. Acc. no. 27.32/12 (no longer displayed and now in store).

59. Arnold Pacey, *Medieval Architectural Drawing: English craftsmen's methods and their later persistence, c.1200–1700* (Stroud 2008), 114–15, illustrated at fig. 4.17.

60. Courtenay, 'Westminster Hall roof' (as n. 57).

61. Buckler's drawings of the louvre, in BL, Add. MS 36436, fols 430–35, are all reproduced in 'Views' (as n. 13), figs 46–48.

62. William Harvey, 'Westminster Hall Roof and the Woodman', 'Westminster Hall Roofs, Old and New', 'Westminster Hall Roof and Mechanical Science', *The Builder*, 121 (1921), 220–21, 374–75 and 440–41 respectively; 'Westminster Hall Roof', *RIBA Journal*, 3rd ser., 30 (1923), 8–14; 'Westminster Hall Roof. An instructional model', *RIBA Journal*, 3rd ser., 31 (1924), 579–81; Herbert Cescinsky and Ernest R. Gribble, 'Westminster Hall and its Roof', *The Burlington Magazine*, 40 (1922), 76–84.

63. Jacques Heyman, 'Westminster Hall Roof', *Proceedings of the Institute of Civil Engineers*, 37 (1967), 137–62; discussion by R. J. Mainstone and others in *Proceedings of the Institute of Civil Engineers*, 38 (1967), 785–96.

64. Lynn T. Courtenay and R. Mark, 'The Westminster Hall Roof: A Historiographic and Structural Study', *Journal of the Society of Architectural Historians*, 46/4 (December 1987), 374–93; Yun Sheng Huang, Robert Mark and Avery M. Wellman, 'Westminster Hall's Hammer-Beam Roof: A Technological Reconstruction', *Association for Preservation Technology Bulletin*, 20/1 (1988), 8–16.

65. Gene Waddell, 'The Design of the Westminster Hall Roof', *Architectural History*, 42 (1999), 47–67.

66. Frank Baines, 'Repair of Westminster Hall Roof', *RIBA Journal*, 3rd ser., 30 (1923), 14–15.

Parliaments, MPs and the Buildings of Westminster in the Middle Ages

DAVID HARRISON

This paper examines how parliamentarians, and MPs in particular, used the buildings at Westminster, including the major spaces associated with formal proceedings in Parliament: the Painted Chamber, where Parliament was usually opened in the Middle Ages; the White Chamber, where the peers regularly sat until 1801; and the various places where the Commons met before settling in St Stephen's Chapel, namely the Painted Chamber itself, the Lesser Hall, Westminster Abbey chapter-house, and the refectory. How MPs debated in these meeting places and how they and others regarded their work is also considered, as is the role of Westminster Hall in parliamentary or quasi-parliamentary proceedings. But MPs did not spend all their time in formal session during a parliament. They required accommodation and places to eat and be entertained. As the paper discusses, Westminster was amply provided with inns and other buildings to provide for these needs.

AT the heart of medieval Westminster were the two great complexes of the Abbey and the Palace. Around them the topography was very different from that seen today: there was no Parliament Street or Whitehall, no Parliament Square or Bridge Street, and no Margaret Street funnelling traffic between the Abbey and the Palace. There were two major long streets bounded by densely packed buildings: Tothill Street, which led west from the west gate of Westminster Abbey, and the now-lost King Street which ran from north to south towards the Abbey's north porch, parallel to, and to the west of, the modern Parliament Street and through what is now Parliament Square (Fig. 1). Linking King Street and Tothill Street, and bordering the Sanctuary of the Abbey, was Thieving Lane (later Bow Street). The main public entrance to New Palace Yard, which was larger than today, was from the west through King Street (see prelim Plan B, p. x). The whole site had a steepish slope down to the river, as one can still tell by comparing the original floor levels of the Abbey and Westminster Hall.

The buildings of Westminster and how parliamentarians and MPs in particular used them are the subject of this essay, which considers both the architectural gems where MPs met to conduct their official duties, and the vernacular buildings, including lodgings, taverns and inns, that were also essential to the functioning of Parliament. Some of the buildings survive, particularly those associated with the Abbey, but others have disappeared, including both the vernacular buildings in the streets and many of the buildings in the Palace, which were lost in the 19th century. The footings of two of these buildings, the Lesser Hall and the Painted Chamber, probably survive under today's Old Palace Yard. The other major building to be destroyed was the Parliament Chamber, where the House of Lords sat until 1801; any remains would lie under the Victorian palace, behind the west front.

FIG. 1. View south from the roof of the Banqueting Hall, 1807, showing King Street, right, with the new mid-18th-century Parliament Street parallel to it on the left
Palace of Westminster Collection, WOA 324

The medieval English Parliament has been studied intensively for centuries by a long list of historians, including bishops, knights and MPs,[1] the period from 1386 has been thoroughly examined by the History of Parliament Trust. Although constitutional developments have been the main concern of many scholars and MPs' biographies have all been the focus of the Trust, there is a considerable literature on most aspects of the institution. Rosser has published a fascinating survey of medieval Westminster, making full use of the extensive records of Westminster Abbey, which owned many properties in the vicinity.[2]

ORIGINS OF PARLIAMENT

PROTO-PARLIAMENTARY meetings were held at Westminster long before the first reference to a parliament. The early history of the institution has recently been rewritten by Maddicott.[3] He finds that, from King Æthelstan's time, kings were able regularly to summon lay and ecclesiastical magnates, as well as lesser landholders, from all over England to assemblies where the king took counsel on gifts, appointments, legislation, justice and war — what William Malmesbury called the 'vital business affecting the realm' — and sought to forge political consensus. Business was supplemented by feasting as well as by demonstrations of royal charisma, such as crown-wearings. From Cnut's reign, assemblies increasingly met in London or Westminster.[4] In 1065, Edward the Confessor summonsed a great concourse 'from the whole of Britain' to Westminster to celebrate Christmas and witness the consecration of the rebuilt Abbey.[5]

After the Norman Conquest, councils and crown-wearings continued. According to the *Anglo-Saxon Chronicle*, William I 'wore his royal crown three times each year, as often as he was in England [...] at Easter he wore it in Winchester, at Pentecost in Westminster, at midwinter in Gloucester; and there were often with him all the powerful men over all England', including thegns and knights.[6] The tradition was continued by his successors, and during this period the buildings where the crown-wearings took place can be identified. At Pentecost 1099, William II 'held his court for the first time in his new building [the great hall] at Westminster' when King Edgar of Scotland carried the Sword of State before his overlord.[7]

According to Maddicott, the post-Conquest kings governed through a smaller, permanent inner council, but occasionally called a great council of additional nobles and senior churchmen to gain their approval for decisions. The great council's meetings sometimes took place at Westminster: in 1163 Henry II considered the liberties of St Albans amidst a large assembly of ecclesiastical and lay magnates in St Catherine's Chapel, Westminster, the ruins of which remain off Little Cloister (Fig. 2).[8] A key role of these assemblies was to consent to heavy taxes and hopefully make them more palatable to the country. Magna Carta enshrined the requirement of consent to taxation, and the minority of Henry III continued the practice of conducting political business in such assemblies.

Henry III spent far longer at Westminster than his predecessors and held many assemblies there. In the period 1235–57, there is evidence for fifty-four parliamentary type assemblies; about forty of them met at Westminster. Sometimes these meetings are called parliaments, and the first official use of the term dates to 1236.[9] Occasionally, the locations of meetings were recorded; among them, all in the Abbey, were St Catherine's Chapel, in 1237, when the king swore to observe the Magna Carta; the Abbey refectory, in 1244 and 1252 (Fig. 3); and the chapter-house, which is discussed in more detail below.[10]

In the 1260s, civil war broke out. After victory over Henry at Lewes in 1264, Simon de Montfort called his own parliament to Westminster in January 1265; this has been seen as the forerunner of the modern institution because it included not only the men of the great council, but also representatives from each county and from cities and towns. Simon was killed later in 1265, but Henry III's successor, Edward, continued to call parliaments and increasingly summonsed knights and burgesses, especially as wartime demands for money became more pressing. Between 1294 and 1307, the Commons were summoned to eleven out of twenty parliaments. In Edward II's reign the Commons were in some form represented in twenty-one out of twenty-seven parliaments. A convention was being established that the Commons had to assent to taxation and to have a role in legislation, petitions and the provision of advice.[11] From Edward III's reign, Parliament included the Commons, and met frequently, usually at Westminster. Between 1340 and 1440, there were about 100 parliaments, of which only a dozen did not meet at Westminster. The Commons deliberated separately from the king and his nobles, and from this period there are more detailed accounts of what happened during parliaments and more references to where it met.[12]

Fig. 2. Westminster Abbey, St Catherine's Chapel: internal view looking west
© *Dean and Chapter of Westminster*

FROM SUMMONS TO ARRIVAL IN WESTMINSTER

The summonsing of Parliament followed a standard routine. In 1295, a writ to the sheriffs of each county informed them that that the king, wishing to consult '[...] the earls, barons and other great men [...] concerning the measures to be taken against the perils threatening [the] kingdom [...]' had summonsed these magnates to Westminster on 'the Sunday next after the Feast of St Martin'. The sheriffs were then ordered '[...] to choose without delay from your county two knights, and from each city two citizens, and from each borough two burgesses, [...] [all] men of discretion and able to perform their duty'. Usually the suitors of the county court met to elect the MPs in the 13th and 14th centuries. Although elections were often uncontested and knights of the shire were, with exceptions, usually selected by the mutual agreement of a small number of the constituency's elite, a statute of 1429, finding that elections had recently been crowded by people of 'small means or no worth', decreed that only freemen who owned freehold land worth 40s. had the vote. This remained the county franchise until the Great Reform Act of 1832.[13]

The 14th-century treatise *Modus Tenendi Parliamentum* states that forty days' notice should be given before Parliament met, and such notice was normally provided from the 14th century, though MPs often arrived after the appointed day.[14] The main reason for the lengthy notice period was the organization of the elections rather than the time taken to get to Westminster. Travelling from many parts of England was speedy on a road system that had been improved by the construction of impressive

FIG. 3. Westminster Abbey, refectory: the ruined north wall, seen from the south-west in c. 1864, with the unrestored chapter-house above it, on the right
© Dean and Chapter of Westminster

stone bridges.[15] One day's expenses was allowed for MPs travelling from Cambridge to Westminster, a journey of about 50 miles. Representatives of Cornwall and Cumberland were allowed eight days' expenses for their journey.[16]

Once the MPs arrived at Westminster they had to find accommodation, usually for a short period. In the century after 1340, half of the ninety or so parliaments lasted fewer than six weeks.[17] Great magnates had their own great houses, many on the banks of the Thames, but most MPs did not. Fortunately, the streets of Westminster were lined with inns, as Rosser records. The Abbey records provide a detailed account of improvements made to its properties: in 1396–97, £41 was spent on a new stable block for the Boar's Head on King Street, roofed with 18,000 tiles; in 1401, £30 was spent on another four stables with accommodation above; in 1417–20, the main block of the inn was rebuilt at a cost of £160. An inventory of 1479 lists sixteen bedchambers in the inn containing twenty-seven beds with a number of larger rooms, including St Mary's and St John's, and the Falcon Chamber. The Saracen's Head by the Palace gate, together with neighbouring houses at the southern end of King Street, was rebuilt in 1486–87 at a cost of £230. The high costs were reflected in complaints about the exorbitant price of wine at such establishments.[18] In addition, lodgings could be rented in private houses; we know that John de Whalley, a Cistercian monk, found accommodation in a house at Westminster, because he was found naked in bed with the owner, Alice, by her husband.[19] MPs rented lodgings too, as they did in later centuries; in 1403–04, the Abbey had to make repairs to houses broken during the parliament.[20] Not all parliamentarians stayed in the immediate vicinity of Westminster: John Paston I, who was MP for Norfolk, lodged in the Inner Temple. Some, such as John Tiptoft, earl of Worcester, whose house was in Thames Street near the river, lived or stayed in the city. In May 1468, Henry Stafford and Margaret Beaufort stayed at the Mitre Inn in Cheapside at the time of an important meeting of Parliament, where the king announced his intention to invade France.[21]

The initial stages of parliaments were set in the Palace. The main public entrance was from the east side of King Street, through the great gateway and into New Palace Yard; on the opposite side of the yard was the Water Gate, which was approached from a jetty, known as the King's Bridge (Fig. 4). At the south end of New Palace Yard was Westminster Hall. This was always a vast space of a single span.[22] It was the location of the major law courts and was accessible to the public; Pollard described it as crowded with people on legal business.[23]

Archbishop Stratford's attempts to attend Parliament in 1341 provide interesting insights into access to the Palace, in particular that the public entered by the north

FIG. 4.   King's Bridge
Palace of Westminster Collection, WOA 2981

door, and that it was possible to pass through the complex to the Lesser Hall, where serjeants-at-arms guarded access to the Painted Chamber. When the archbishop arrived on 23 April with 'a great multitude of clerks and esquires', his way was barred there by the steward of the king's household; on the next day, royal officials waited for him at the same door, clearly knowing he would have to pass that way. The archbishop was told he must go to hear charges against him at the Exchequer, which was entered from the hall up steps on the west side; the door to the Exchequer built in Henry III's reign survives. After appearing in the Exchequer, the archbishop was able to proceed freely through the hall, up the steps in the south-east corner, along the landing past the entrance to the upper chapel and into the Lesser Hall (Crook, Fig. 1, 2). At the far end of this room however, outside the Painted Chamber, he was halted by serjeants-at-arms. There followed adjournments to await the arrival of more parliamentarians until Thursday 26 April, when in the king's presence Parliament finally proceeded to business in the Painted Chamber. During the sitting there was a scene outside: it was the archbishop with his entourage, who had once again being forced to wait in the Lesser Hall while his message was taken to the king. He was finally admitted and subsequently returned to the king's favour.[24]

Neither the Commons nor Lords normally sat in the Great Hall, although there were exceptions when it did, as in 1265.[25] The hall was used for big public occasions. Announcements were made here so that they might reach a large audience: at the conclusion of the 1259 parliament, the Provisions of Westminster were read aloud before magnates and 'innumerable people'. In 1285, the Statute of Westminster II was 'read aloud in the hall in the presence of the whole people'. During the parliament of 1395, Lollard tracts were affixed to the doors of the hall.[26] A few major parliamentary events took place in the hall. At a crowded meeting in the hall in 1327, which included lords, commons, and Londoners, Roger Mortimer announced the decision to depose Edward II; sermons by bishops followed, as did a reading of the 'articles of accusation', which were acclaimed by the assembled people.[27] When Richard II was deposed, the duke of Lancaster (soon to become Henry IV) heard mass in the Abbey and then returned to the newly remodelled hall 'with Sir Thomas Erpingham going ahead of him carrying his [...] bejewelled sword, at which time the crowd of people there was so great that it filled not only the hall itself but also the adjacent courtyard outside'.[28]

OPENING OF PARLIAMENT

BEFORE a parliament assembled, an invitation was issued in Westminster Hall to the public to submit petitions.[29] The hall was also the place where the Commons were usually mustered at the state opening.[30] In the best medieval eyewitness account of the event, the Colchester MPs note that the Commons assembled at 9 a.m. on 7 November 1485 in the Great Hall, where the Lord Steward held a roll call of MPs, checking their names against the sheriffs' election returns.[31] The Colchester diaries also observe that the king and Lords had assembled in the Painted Chamber (Wilson, Fig. 1, 153) and went from there to the Abbey for a mass of the Holy Ghost while the Commons roll call was held.[32] A more detailed account of the state opening in 1510 records that the young Henry VIII and the Lords were met outside the Abbey by the abbot and chapter; the king sat in a pew at the south end of the high altar and, after mass, went to the Painted Chamber. An image survives of the young king, preceded by the Sword of State and Cap of Maintenance, in procession from the Abbey on 4 February 1512.

First came mitred abbots, followed by bishops; next Henry carrying a sceptre, under a canopy held by monks; then the secular peers in robes. This practice of visiting the Abbey continued until 1679, when it was cancelled for security reasons; it was abandoned thereafter. Following Henry's acquisition of Whitehall Palace in 1529, there was a procession from there to parliament, establishing a tradition of royal processions to parliament that still continues.[33]

After the mass, the king and peers returned to the Palace. The peers were robed and sat in the Painted Chamber, a spacious room 24.5 m × 7.9 m and 9.7 m high, which had been rebuilt in the 13th century as a state bedroom. The wall-paintings from which it took its name included the coronation of Edward the Confessor, personifications of Virtues and a cycle derived from the Book of Maccabees; these were destroyed in the early 19th century, but copies had been made, and 20th-century copies of these adorn the area off the Lower Waiting Hall of the present Palace.[34]

The Commons were summoned to the Painted Chamber to join the peers. A speech was given, usually by the Lord Chancellor, explaining why Parliament had been summoned. In the parliament of 1380, the Chancellor declared that 'a very large sum' was needed and must be raised quickly to provide for the immediate needs of defence and of the war.[35] The clerk of the parliaments read out names of receivers and triers of petitions. The Commons were then ordered to elect a Speaker, and the Lords and Commons separated. In 1411, after the opening speech by the bishop of Winchester, the Commons were told to meet at the typically early time of 7 a.m. the next morning to elect their Speaker and to present him to the king an hour later; in fact, he was not put forward until some days later. On other occasions, the election period was more realistic: in 1485 the Commons were told to return in two days to present the Speaker.[36] Two representatives for Colchester described how the House of Commons chose Thomas Lovell as Speaker on 8 November that year and the next day went to the 'Parliament Chamber' (NB not the Painted Chamber) to present him:

[On 8 November], be ix of the clokke, so for to procede un to a (leccion for) [...] a Speker. So the lection gave his voyse unto Thomas Lovel, a (gen tilman) [...] Lyncolnes Inne. That doon, it pleased the Knyghts there there [*sic*] present (for to rise from) their sets and to for to goo to that plase where as the Speker stode and [...] set hym in his sete [...] [On 9 November], at x of the cloke, sembled Maister Speker and all the Knyghts, sitteners and burgeyses in the parlament house [that is, the Commons' Chamber], and so departed in to the parliament chambir [that is, the Lords' Chamber] (be fore) the Kyngis grace and all his lords spirituall and temporall and all his Jugs (and so) presented our Speker [...][37]

The Wriothesley Garter Book, produced by Sir Thomas Wriothesley, Garter King of Arms from 1505 to 1534, contains the famous and first contemporary picture of a meeting of parliament (Fig. 5). Several commentators, including the Parliament website, have described this image as the opening of Parliament in 1523, but the image does not show this, since the Speaker of the Commons is present. It seems to show the presentation of the Speaker to the king, or perhaps the closing of the session, but may also be meant to represent all three occasions rather than anything too specific.[38] The image shows Wriothesley himself in a prominent position to the right of the monarch, as well as an earl holding the Cap of Maintenance, and two earls to the left, one with the Sword of State. The Lords Spiritual sit on benches to the right of the king, and the Lords Temporal to the left. The judges and serjeants-at-law occupy four woolsacks in the centre, and the clerks kneel behind, writing the record. The Commons stand at the bar.[39]

Parliaments, MPs and the Buildings of Westminster

FIG. 5.   Image said to be the *State Opening of Parliament*, Henry VIII, 1523
Royal Collection Trust/© Her Majesty Queen Elizabeth II 2015

DAVID HARRISON

MEETING PLACES

The Lords

As the Colchester diaries indicate, the Lords normally deliberated in a building known as the Queen's or White Chamber, and in the later Middle Ages as the Parliament Chamber (Fig. 6). It had been built by Henry III for his wife, Eleanor, and was in the upper storey of a building running north–south at the south-eastern end of the Painted Chamber. With occasional exceptions — such as at the time of the rebuilding of Westminster Hall during the 1397 parliament, which prevented access to both the Painted and Parliament chambers — the Lords met in the same location until 1801, when they moved to the Lesser Hall.

The Commons

WHILE the Lords normally sat in the same room, the Commons used a number of locations.[40] Before finally settling permanently on St Stephen's Chapel, they met in at least four places in Westminster: the Painted Chamber, the Abbey chapter-house, the Lesser Chamber and the Abbey refectory; there was possibly a fifth location in 1545 and 1547. The evidence does not permit us to say where the Commons met in every parliament, but there is information for a number of parliaments, particularly from the Parliament rolls. The first parliament where the meeting place of the Lower House is recorded, met in 1343: on 28 April that year Edward III opened Parliament in the Painted Chamber, then he and the magnates withdrew into the nearby White Chamber, leaving the Commons in occupation of the Painted Chamber, where presumably they transacted their business over the next three weeks. The Parliament rolls also mention the Commons using 'la Chambre de Peinte' in 1365, 1366 and 1373 (see the table below).

WESTMINSTER BUILDINGS WHERE THE HOUSE OF COMMONS MET BEFORE THE 16TH CENTURY

Name of building	Location and possible remains	Main parliamentary function	Known dates at which the Commons met in the building
Painted Chamber (also known as the King's Chamber)	East of statue of Richard the Lionheart; remains of the west end may survive under Old Palace Yard.	Opening of Parliament	1343, 1352 (the first day), 1365, 1366, 1373[41]
Lesser Hall (also known as the White Hall)	North of statue of Richard; remains may survive under Old Palace Yard.	Court of requests from the 15th century; Lords 1801–34	1368,[42] 1834–50
Abbey chapter-house			1352, 1376, 1377 (twice),[43] 1384,[44] 1395 (met here or refectory)
Abbey refectory	The north and east walls survive, south of cloisters.		1395?, 1397, 1404, 1414, 1416 (twice);[45] probably the venue for every 15th-century parliament

142

Parliaments, MPs and the Buildings of Westminster

FIG. 6. *A View of the House of Peers*, Cole, 1755 , in the Parliament chamber
(earlier the 13th-century Queen's chamber)
Palace of Westminster Collection, WOA 885

On 17 January 1352, at the opening of Parliament, Chief Justice Shareshill expounded the reasons for summonsing the parliament and ended his exposition with instructions to the Commons to reassemble in the Painted Chamber to consider what he had said the following morning. He also told them that, before completing their work, they were to choose twenty-four or thirty from among themselves, who were to confer with a number of Lords sent to meet them in the Painted Chamber. When the delegation from the Upper House arrived, those MPs not involved in the conference were to leave, and go to the chapter-house in Westminster Abbey, where they were to continue with their business.[46] Once the conference was over, the representatives from the Commons rejoined their colleagues in the chapter-house, where they reported on the outcome, and the matter was further discussed. Access to the chapter-house was presumably via the Postern Gate in Old Palace Yard, leading to a lane, which still exists, running between the chapter-house and the Lady Chapel. At the end is a fine 13th-century door into the south transept.

The chapter-house would in some respects have seemed the perfect meeting place (Fig. 7). As Carpenter has stressed, Henry III saw the building as a place for his business, and there are indications that the building was designed as a place where Henry would on great occasions take the President's seat: the sculptured Annunciation faced the President's seat, and tiles run in bands from east to west, framing the seat, with the grandest depicting the king's coats of arms. State business was indeed discussed in the chapter-house, but not always as Henry III would have wished. The building was in use by 1257, when in Henry's absence the archbishop of Messina sought support for the Sicilian adventure before a multitude, but with a singular lack of success. It was here, on Valentine's Day during the parliament of 1265, that Henry III, who had been captured the year before, confirmed Magna Carta and the Montfortian constitution, and promised not to revenge himself on the opposition.[47]

Traditionally, the chapter-house was seen as the main meeting place of the Commons in the 14th century, because the Parliament rolls of 1376 state that at the close of the opening ceremony, Chancellor Knyvet told the Commons to withdraw to 'lour auncienne place' in the chapter-house, and nine months later, in January 1377, the new chancellor (Houghton) repeated this instruction. Here 'auncienne' denotes former: the Commons had used the chapter-house in 1352.[48] In fact, the Commons are recorded as meeting in the chapter-house on just five occasions between 1352 and 1384; a sixth meeting may have taken place in 1395. In the late 14th century, John of Northampton began his series of wall-paintings in the chapter-house, which may have been related to the Commons' ceasing to meet there.[49]

The parliament of 1376, known as the Good Parliament, is one of the best recorded of the Middle Ages, no doubt because of interest in what occurred. By the closing years of Edward III's reign, there was much opposition in the country to the corrupt influence of his son, John of Gaunt. After the opening, the two Houses separated. The *Anonimalle Chronicle* describes what happened, including the process of debate. 'Chiualers et communes' assembled, entered the chapter-house and seated themselves throughout, one next to the other. (Remember that this was an octagonal building, unlike any of the other buildings used by the Commons.) As there were about 250 MPs, they could not all have had seats by the walls, and some must have sat in the central part of the building. The MPs started to debate and spoke from the lectern, presumably the one near the central column,[50] where a knight argued that the people were too poor, and straitened by recent circumstances, to be able to contribute to yet another tax; other knights went to the lectern to voice their objections.[51] It has been

Parliaments, MPs and the Buildings of Westminster

FIG. 7. Westminster Abbey, chapter-house: restored interior, looking east
Malcolm Crowthers

argued that this description suggests that the knights who spoke sat sufficiently close to the lectern to reach it without undue inconvenience before they started to address the assembly.[52]

After the other knights had spoken, Sir Peter de la Mare, one of the knights for Herefordshire, and the steward of the earl of March, a leading opposition magnate, recapitulated what had been said so far.[53] De la Mare was chosen to speak on behalf of the Commons throughout the parliament and has been seen as the first Speaker. He laid before the duke of Lancaster and the rest of the council a demand for an examination of the public accounts and criticized the shameful financial transactions of courtiers. Two of the chief offenders were impeached, in what is the earliest example of impeachment where the Commons brought charges before the Lords.[54]

In addition to the Painted Chamber and the chapter-house, the Commons also met during the second half of the 14th century in 'la petite salle' (probably the Lesser Hall). In 1368, after the opening in the Painted Chamber, the Commons moved to this room. From the 15th century, this room was used as the Court of Requests. It became the House of Lords in 1801, and after the fire of 1834 was the chamber of the Commons again while the Palace was rebuilt.[55]

At the opening of the parliament of 1395, members were told to meet 'en la maison de Chapitre ou le Refectaire' ('the chapter-house or refectory') of the Abbey, and in January 1397 the Commons sat in the refectory. In 1404, the refectory was described as the 'maison d'hemble' ('house of assembly') for the Commons, as it was again for the parliaments of 1414, 1415 and 1416. Many references in the 15th century simply refer to the Commons meeting in their accustomed place, which clearly meant the refectory.[56] The refectory was a big room measuring 130 ft long by 37 ft wide, and its north and east walls survive as part of Westminster School. Some of the lower walls and arcading date from the 11th century, the blocked windows from the 14th. Presumably the Commons used the monks' furniture. As Hawkyard has noted, the alignment of the dining furniture is likely to have determined and established what has become the preferred layout of the Commons, with the Speaker's chair placed on the dais in front of the President's table at the east end, opposite the entrance in the west; the clerk's table was presumably in front of the Speaker's chair, with the rows of benches either side of a central gangway. At the west end, opposite the Speaker's chair, was a screens passage with a gallery above, where in February 1533 the papal nuncio and the two French ambassadors presumably listened to the debate.[57] It is possible that the screen was used for divisions, just as the former pulpitum in St Stephen's Chapel was later. Just before and after the Dissolution of the Abbey on 16 January 1540, the refectory continued to be used by the Commons, in 1539 and 1540, and for all three sessions of the parliament of 1542, but seven months later, on 5 November, the new Dean and Chapter decided to demolish the building, which they no longer needed, and the Abbey was at last able to rid itself of Parliament.[58]

It is not known where the Commons met in 1545 or 1547. Hawkyard has suggested either St Catherine's Chapel, which, as we have seen, was used for assemblies in earlier centuries, or the monastic dormitory, which was redundant; part of it is now the main hall of Westminster School, although it was badly bombed during the Second World War.[59]

In 1547, the act to dissolve colleges was passed and Edward VI subsequently handed St Stephen's Chapel to the Commons. Large sums were spent on its secularization, including £15 in 1547–48 and £344 in 1549–50.[60] The classic depictions post-date Wren's classical alterations, but there are earlier images (Fig. 8). In the 14th century,

Fig. 8. *La maniere et ordre de la Sceance de la maison basse ou de communes*, the House of Commons in session between 1630 and 1640, sitting in the former St Stephen's Chapel
Palace of Westminster Collection, WOA 351

a pulpitum had been erected between the second and third bays, dividing the building into an outer and inner chapel. The pulpitum screen was used for divisions, and the gallery above may have been a viewing area for distinguished visitors to view the debate. Internally the chapel measured 90 ft in length and 26 ft in width, but the inner chapel was 54 ft long by 26 ft wide. The arrangements were probably similar to those used in the refectory, though the space available was considerably less. Four rows of seating provided for members in the late 1540s occupied the space previously used by the stalls. At the raised east end of St Stephen's Chapel, in front of where the high altar had stood, was the Speaker's seat.[61]

The outer chapel provided a space where visitors could wait until individual members could speak to them; this led to the outer chapel's acquiring its new name, the lobby. It also provided space for the clerks to work: there was a room off the south-west corner of the chapel, possibly between the buttresses, which for a short period served as the clerk's office.[62] A lobby and office space for the clerks must have been available in earlier meeting places. The screens passage in the refectory is likely to have been used for these purposes, as may the two-storeyed structure, described as a *cawagium*, at the west of the building. The vestibule in the chapter-house probably served the same functions.[63]

THE LIFE OF THE MPS AT WESTMINSTER

IN the Middle Ages as now, MPs were much criticized. They were seen as useless and impotent. The late medieval poem, Mum and Sothsegger, provides a savage caricature of a parliament *c*. 1400:

Some members sat there like a nought in arithmetic, that marks a place but has no value in itself [...] Some members slumbered and slept and said very little. Some mumbled and stammered and did not know what they meant to say [...] Some were so pompous and dull-witted that they got hopelessly muddled before they got to the end of their speeches. No one whether he sat on the bench or whether he was a burgess, could have made out what they were driving at, their meaning was so stupid and bald and thin.[64]

MPs were also accused of vandalism. Mats in the chapter-house, presumably to protect the tiles, were destroyed by MPs in 1377–78 and 1379–80; a table in the refectory was damaged in 1383–84, the cloisters in 1448–49.[65] MPs were also accused of advancing their own interests. Lawyers were the subject of particular criticism: they were accused of abusing the petitioning process to aid their private clients, and in 1372 the Commons sought to ban their election as knights of the shire.[66]

The medieval MP's life had its disadvantages. The chamber must at times have been extraordinarily boring. The Colchester MPs record that on 14 November 'there were arguments for such to non conclusion'.[67] Bills were read from start to finish; no wonder the MPs fell asleep. Moreover, high politics was dangerous: Peter de la Mare, the hero of 1376, was imprisoned when John of Gaunt regained control.[68] Casual violence was always a concern, and weapons were forbidden to discourage this; in 1332 'hacquetons, breastplates, swords, long knives, or any other dangerous weapon, either in [...] London, or in any place between the city and the Palace of Westminster, or within the palace itself' were banned.[69]

There were nevertheless advantages in being an MP. Most liked the position enough to carry on doing it. Under Edward III, 124 knights served in three consecutive parliaments, forty-two in four, nineteen in five, and one in eight.[70] There was the status and pleasure of being an insider and getting insights into key events, which would have been an important factor in an era of limited and slow communications. For some, there was the opportunity to act in what they saw as the nation's interest, to attack the policies of incompetent or corrupt regimes, as the members of the Good Parliament sought to do. The expenses were a major bonus, and were significantly more generous than any subsequent system, especially for the knights of the shire. At a time when the daily wage of an artisan was about 2d. or 3d., expenses in 1327 were set at 4s. day for knights (twice the rate for military service) and 2s. for burgesses.[71]

Finally, there was the social life with its feasting and festivities. At the opening of the 1260 parliament, Henry III spent £229 on a great feast and listened to water music played on the Thames.[72] At the time of the Whitsun parliament of 1306, to which the Commons were summonsed, Edward I knighted his son Edward and over 250 other young men in the Abbey, including Piers Gaveston and Roger Mortimer. This was followed by the 'feast of the swans' when 'a magnificent device, featuring two gilded swans was brought in by a host of minstrels'.[73] A great dinner was often held at the dissolution. On 21 May 1368, the last day of the parliament, all the Lords and several of the Commons dined with the king. Before the dissolution of the parliament in 1402, on 25 November all Lords spiritual and temporal and all the Commons were invited to dinner with the king the next day.[74] Less salubrious activities included visits to the large number of brothels. Trade in the stews (licensed brothels) at Southwark was prohibited when Parliament was sitting, but there were many other opportunities. Jane Apryce ran a brothel within the precinct of the Palace in Henry VIII's reign.[75]

London also offered other entertainments, including tournaments. To celebrate the betrothal of Charles, Comte de Charolais and Philip the Good's heir, to Margaret, Edward IV's sister, Antoine, the Bastard of Burgundy, and Anthony Woodville, Lord Scales, met in the lists at Smithfield on 11–12 June 1467, a few days after the parliament was dissolved. Crowds of thousands turned out to watch.[76] While a tournament would lure some to stay on in London, without such an attraction most wanted to get home. According to Guy, in March 1532 — just when, according to Elton, the House of Commons was reaching the apogee of political importance over the Supplication against the Ordinaries — the fact remained that all MPs wanted to do was to persuade Henry VIII to end the session as quickly as possible.[77]

The return to the constituency produced a variety of reactions. It could bring problems, such as explaining the heavy taxes that had been agreed. Sometimes the decisions Parliament made were disastrous: the Peasants' Revolt of 1381 was a direct consequence of the poll tax levied at 1s. per head, to which MPs had consented in the parliament of November 1380. But the home-coming could be more agreeable: payments are recorded in 1332 and 1351–52 for wine provided for the MPs for Leicester on their return from Parliament while they regaled the assembled company with their news.[78]

NOTES

1. See, for example, W. Stubbs, *The Constitutional History of England in Its Origin and Development*, 3 vols (Oxford 1874–78); Sir Goronwy Edwards, *The Second Century of the English Parliament* (Oxford 1979); J. E. Powell and K. Wallace, *The House of Lords in the Middle Ages* (London 1968).
2. G. Rosser, *Medieval Westminster 1200–1540* (Oxford 1989).
3. J. R. Maddicott, *The Origins of the English Parliament, 924–1327* (Oxford 2010).
4. Maddicott, *Origins* (as n. 3), 47.
5. F. Barlow, *Edward the Confessor* (London 1997), 244–45.
6. M. Swanton trans. and ed., *The Anglo-Saxon Chronicle* (New York 1996), 219–20, 234.
7. *The Anglo-Saxon Chronicle* (as n. 6), 234; F. Barlow, *The Feudal Kingdom of England 1042–1216* (Harlow 1999, 5th edn), 135.
8. N. Vincent, 'The Court of Henry II', in *Henry II: New Interpretations*, ed. C. Harper-Bill and N. Vincent (Woodbridge 2007), 313.
9. Maddicott, *Origins* (as n. 3), 157–58.
10. Maddicott, *Origins* (as n. 3), 164, 457; D. Carpenter, 'King Henry III and the chapter house of Westminster Abbey', in *Westminster Abbey Chapter House: the history, art and architecture of 'a chapter house beyond compare'*, ed. R. Mortimer and W. Rodwell (London 2010), 32–39.
11. Maddicott, *Origins* (as n. 3), 335.
12. Edwards, *Second Century* (as n. 1), 1–3. The key source is the Parliament rolls, the official parliamentary record, compiled by royal clerks. Some rolls survive from the 13th century, but from early in Edward III's reign there is a virtually unbroken series for each parliament: *Rotuli Parliamentorum; ut et petitiones et placita in Parliamento tempore Edwardi R. I [- Henrici R. VII, 1278-1503]*, ed. J. Strachey et al., 6 vols (London 1767–77).

13. J. R. Maddicott, 'Parliament and the Constituencies, 1272–1377', in *The English Parliament in the Middle Ages*, ed. R. G. Davies and J. H. Denton (Manchester 1981), 61–87, at 72–73; *English Historical Documents*, IV: *1327–1485*, ed. A. R. Myers (London 1969), 465.
14. N. Pronay and J. Taylor text and trans., *Modus Tenendi Parliamentum*, Parliamentary Texts of the Later Middle Ages (Oxford 1980), 213–15.
15. D. F. Harrison, *The Bridges of Medieval England* (Oxford 2004).
16. H. W. Cam, *Liberties and Communities in Medieval England* (New York 1944), 237–38.
17. Edwards, *Second Century* (as n. 1), 1.
18. Rosser, *Medieval Westminster* (as n. 2), 79, 123, 130, 420.
19. J F Merritt, *The Social World of early modern Westminster* (2005), 146–54; Rosser, *Medieval Westminster* (as n. 2), 132.
20. Rosser, *Medieval Westminster* (as n. 2), 39.
21. H. Castor, *Blood and Roses* (London 2004), 152; W. Thornbury, *Old and New London* (London 1878), 17–28; M. K. Jones and M. G. Underwood, *The King's Mother: Lady Margaret Beaufort, Countess of Richmond and Derby* (Cambridge 1992), 47.
22. C. Wilson, 'Rulers, Artificers and Shoppers: Richard II's Remodelling of Westminster Hall, 1393–99', in *The Regal Image of Richard II and the Wilton Diptych*, ed. D. Gordon, L. Monnas and C. Elam (London 1997), 33–59 and 274–88. See also Roland B. Harris and Daniel Miles in this volume, 22–71.
23. A. F. Pollard, *The Evolution of Parliament* (New York 1964, 2nd edn), 52.
24. Powell and Wallace, *House of Lords* (as n. 1), 336–38.
25. Maddicott, *Origins* (as n. 3), 204, 234.
26. J. M. Bowers, *The Politics of Pearl: Court Poetry in the Age of Richard II* (Cambridge 2001), 26.
27. Maddicott, *Origins* (as n. 3), 284, 361, 449.
28. C. Given-Wilson ed., *Chronicles of the Revolution 1397–1400* (Manchester 1993), 164–65.
29. Pollard, *Evolution of Parliament* (as n. 23), 37.
30. A. L. Brown, 'Parliament, c.1377–1422', in *English Parliament in the Middle Ages* (as n. 13), 109–40, here 121.
31. *Modus Tenendi Parliamentum* (as n. 14), 185.
32. Ibid., 185.
33. Trinity, College, Cambridge, MS 0.3.59; H. S. Cobb, 'The Staging of Ceremonies of State in the House of Lords', in *The Houses of Parliament: History, Art, Architecture*, ed. C. and J. Riding (London 2000), 32–38.
34. P. Binski, *The Painted Chamber at Westminster*, Society of Antiquaries of London, Occasional Papers, n.s., 9 (London 1986), 9, 38–42, 82–86. See also Christopher Wilson's paper in this volume, 152–86 and Mark Collins's paper, 206–56.
35. Edwards, *Second Century* (as n. 1), 34.
36. *Modus Tenendi Parliamentum* (as n. 14), 185.
37. Ibid., 185.
38. I am grateful to Dr Paul Seaward for this suggestion.
39. The description is taken from Cobb, 'Ceremonies of State' (as n. 33).
40. For the meeting places of the House of Commons, see I. M. Cooper, 'The Meeting-Places of Parliament in the Ancient Palace of Westminster', *JBAA*, 3rd series, 3 (1938), 97–138; Edwards, *Second Century* (as n. 1); A. Hawkyard, 'From Painted Chamber to St Stephen's Chapel: The Meeting Places of the House of Commons at Westminster until 1603', *Parliamentary History*, 21/1 (2002), 62–84.
41. *Rotuli Parliamentorum* (as n. 12), II, 136, 237, 283, 289, 316.
42. Ibid., II, 294.
43. Parliaments in January and October 1377.
44. *Rotuli Parliamentorum* (as n. 12), II, 237, 322, 363; III, 5, 185, 329.
45. Ibid., III, 329, 338, 523; IV, 34, 70, 94.
46. Edwards, *Second Century* (as n. 1), 8–9.
47. D. Carpenter, *Chapter house*, 32–39.
48. Edwards, *Second Century* (as n. 1), 5.
49. P. Binski and H. Howard, 'Wall paintings in the chapter house', in *Westminster Abbey Chapter House* (as n. 10), 184–208, here 195.
50. '[...] une chiualer del south pais leva suse et ala a la lectrone en my lieu le chapiter qe toutz purrount oier, et enpellaunt sur le dit lectrone comenca a dire'; Carpenter, 'King Henry III and the chapter house of Westminster Abbey' (as n. 10), 36.
51. V. H. Galbraith ed., *Anonimalle Chronicle* (Manchester 1927), 80–83.
52. Hawkyard, 'Meeting Places of the House of Commons' (as n. 40), 68.
53. *Anonimalle Chronicle* (as n. 51), 80–83.

54. *Rotuli Parliamentorum* (as n. 12), II, 321.
55. J. Crook and R. B. Harris, 'Reconstructing the Lesser Hall: an interim report from the Medieval Palace of Westminster Research Project', in *Housing Parliament: Dublin, Edinburgh and Westminster*, ed. C. Jones and S. Kelsey (Edinburgh 2002), 22–61. See also Mark Collins's paper in this volume, 206–56.
56. Cooper, 'Meeting-Places of Parliament' (as n. 40), 119.
57. Hawkyard, 'Meeting Places of the House of Commons' (as n. 40), 77.
58. Ibid., 73–77.
59. Ibid., 77. See also Eddie Smith, this volume, Part I, 372–415.
60. H. M. Colvin ed., *The History of the King's Works*, IV: *1485–1660 (Part II)* (London 1982), 291–92.
61. Hawkyard, 'Meeting Places of the House of Commons' (as n. 40), 77–79.
62. W. R. Lethaby, 'Early Plans of Part of the Palace of Westminster, 1593', *The Home Counties Magazine*, V (1903), 1–4 with plates, here 3.
63. Hawkyard, 'Meeting Places of the House of Commons' (as n. 40), 74, 68.
64. *English Historical Documents* (as n. 13), IV, 453–54.
65. Rosser, *Medieval Westminster* (as n. 2), 39.
66. Edwards, *Second Century* (as n. 1), 51.
67. *Modus Tenendi Parliamentum* (as n. 14), 186.
68. M. H. Keen, *England in the Later Middle Ages* (London 1973), 265.
69. E. W. Brayley and J. Britton, *The History of the Ancient Palace and Late Houses of Parliament at Westminster* (London 1836), 203.
70. Maddicott, 'Parliament and the Constituencies', 75.
71. Ibid., 78.
72. Carpenter, 'King Henry III and the chapter house of Westminster Abbey' (as n. 10), 36.
73. Maddicott, *Origins* (as n. 3), 280; M. Prestwich, *Edward I* (London 1988), 121.
74. Powell and Wallace, House of *Lords* (as n. 1), 291, 367.
75. Rosser, *Medieval Westminster* (as n. 2), 143–44.
76. S. Anglo, 'Anglo-Burgundian Feats of Arms at Smithfield, June 1467', *Guildhall Miscellany*, II/vii (1965).
77. J. Guy, *Tudor England* (Oxford 1990).
78. M. Bateson ed., *Records of the Borough of Leicester*, 3 vols (Leicester 1899–1901), III, 11, 75.

A Monument to St Edward the Confessor: Henry III's Great Chamber at Westminster and its Paintings

CHRISTOPHER WILSON

This paper considers four aspects of the 13th-century king's great chamber in Westminster Palace that have been neglected or inadequately treated in earlier studies of the topic: the unique form of the chamber's structure as remodelled in the early 1230s; the nature and scope of the work on the wall-paintings carried out under Henry III and his two successors; the significance of the chamber's bedroom function in relation to the cult of St Edward the Confessor; and the underlying iconographic unity of the paintings.

IN April 1323, when they will still have been pristine, the wall-paintings in the king's great chamber in Westminster Palace provoked a highly enthusiastic response from Symon Semeonis, an Irish Franciscan who was passing through England en route for the Holy Land:

Almost immediately adjacent to the said monastery [of Westminster] is the very famous palace of the kings of England, in which is that well-known chamber on whose walls are all the warlike stories of the entire Bible, painted in a manner beyond praise and all described very fully and perfectly in French, to the great admiration of beholders and with the greatest royal magnificence.[1]

Had this description been our sole source of information about the appearance of these paintings, it might have been reasonable to assume that the imagery of the chamber was in the nature of a celebration of the martial exploits of Old Testament heroes. However, in 1819 substantial fragments of the paintings were briefly uncovered and recorded prior to their destruction, and it immediately became apparent that the predominant theme, far from being glorificatory, was the downfall of tyrannical rulers. There have been several attempts to reveal the thinking behind this uniquely extended narration of stories illustrative of bad governance and of resistance to it,[2] but it will be argued here that the key to understanding why these scenes were included has so far been missed and that it was located in the very paintings that Symon Semeonis failed to mention, those that celebrated England's foremost royal saint, Edward the Confessor. Offering an account of the intended import of the paintings will entail reaching a view as to their dating within the long period during which work on the chamber's decoration is known to have been in progress, namely 1236–1308. Before turning to that evidence, some consideration must be given to the functions and the singular architectural form of the chamber itself.

A Monument to St Edward the Confessor

THE ARCHITECTURAL FORM OF THE CHAMBER AND ITS FUNCTIONS

THE king's chamber at any major English royal residence was in essence a combined bedsitter and office, 'the inner, private sanctum of the [king where he] slept, and often dined or worked away from the hubbub of the household, closeted in privacy with a small circle of friends and counsellors'.[3] At Westminster Palace, as at any substantial seigneurial residence, the chamber, together with the hall and the chapel, formed a core of three rooms frequented by the lord and his household. In the king's other main metropolitan residence, the Tower of London, the hall, chapel and chamber took up the whole of the main floor of the principal building, the late-11th-century White Tower.[4] Westminster's household hall, chamber and chapel were each contained in discrete structures, but their arrangement attained a high degree of formality in that they were set around three sides of a rectangle, with the hall forming a west range and the chapel and chamber forming north and south ranges respectively (Fig. 1). The hall and chapel were joined at only one of their corners, leaving their entrance fronts free, but the chamber abutted the south end of the east wall of the hall, an

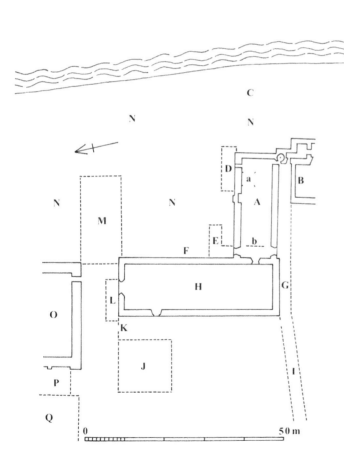

FIG. 1. Westminster Palace, plan of the king's lodging after 1263. In the interests of clarity some documented features have been omitted from the space to the west of St Stephen's Chapel.
A. king's great chamber; B. queen's chamber, north end; C. Marculf and Antioch chambers, approximate site; D. king's oratory of St Laurence; E. covered stair and lobby; F. Receipt of the Exchequer, approximate site until 1263; G. stair and upper-level passage flanking the king's chamber; H. small hall (household hall); I. pentice linked to south transept of Westminster Abbey; J. kitchen serving small hall; K. entrance to king's houses (Privy Palace); L. covered stair and lobby; M. St Stephen's Chapel; N. king's garden; O. Great Hall (Westminster Hall), south end; P. household knights' chamber; Q. kitchen serving Great Hall; a. king's bed; b. spere
Graphic by C. Wilson

arrangement implying a greater measure of interdependence. There must be a very good chance that this layout went back to Edward the Confessor's foundation of Westminster Palace in the middle years of the 11th century. Of course, this is only a hypothesis, but the general practice of piecemeal rebuildings of major residential complexes, a practice followed here, tended to favour continuity in layouts over radical replanning.[5] Another pointer towards a mid-11th-century date is the placing of the hall, chapel and chamber due east of, and almost on the same axis as, the great church that the Confessor built at Westminster Abbey.[6]

The date of the king's Chapel of St Stephen that was in existence during most of the 13th century is not known, but it was certainly not a new building and it was single-storeyed, unlike the celebrated structure that succeeded it on the same site from 1292.[7] The hall, on the evidence of antiquarian drawings made before its final demolition in the mid-19th century, was an early-12th-century building. It, too, was single-storeyed originally, but after a major fire in February 1263 it was subdivided by the introduction of a timber floor. This change would have provided the opportunity to insert a door in the north wall leading directly into the king's chamber, which will always have been at first-floor level.[8] The chamber that survived down to the 19th century was a little later, to judge from its recorded details, and in all probability it belonged to the work done on 'the king's houses of Westminster' for which £190 was paid in 1165–66.[9] The dimensions of the main chamber at first-floor level were generous by any standards — 24.19 m (80½ ft) long, 7.93 m (26 ft) wide, and 9.68 m (31¾ ft) high — although there is no sign that its architecture was particularly elaborate (Figs 2 and 3). Most of the 12th-century masonry seems to have been retained when Henry III remodelled the chamber c. 1232–36. Early-19th-century drawings of the exterior face of the east wall suggest that the main arches of the two large windows were still essentially 12th-century, and no doubt that was also true of the four openings with semicircular internal heads near the west ends of the lateral walls. Those in the north wall were retained as windows by Henry III, whereas those in the south wall were blocked.[10] One of the south windows was unblocked in the early 19th century and found to retain non-figural painted decoration that was almost certainly original work of the later 12th century.[11] The imposts from which the internal window heads sprang were strikingly simple.[12] The west window in the north wall was placed at a greater distance from the west wall than its southern counterpart, an asymmetry indicating that Henry II's chamber was entered from a door at the west end of the north wall (Fig. 4). There is good evidence that the same point of access was retained by Henry III.[13] The central and eastern parts of the north wall of the 12th-century chamber probably incorporated a sequence of features similar to that recorded in late-18th- and early-19th-century antiquarian drawings: a large fireplace, solid walling forming a backing to the king's bed, and a door leading to the oratory of St Laurence set against the outer face of the north wall (Figs 1D and 3). The nearest thing to a pre-13th-century reference to the oratory is to be found in Geoffrey Gaimar's poem *L'Estoire des Engleis*, which has William II hearing mass in the upper storey of his chamber (*en sun estage*) during the celebrations marking the inauguration in 1099 of Westminster Hall (Fig. 1, O). Geoffrey wrote his poem in 1136–37, but his modern editor is inclined to think that his account of the 1099 festivities was based on an eyewitness account.[14] The dedication of the oratory to St Laurence will have been chosen by someone who understood that it made a pair with the dedication to St Stephen borne by the king's main chapel, and that the crown of victory alluded to

A Monument to St Edward the Confessor

Fig. 2. Westminster Palace, king's great chamber, interior views and details. Part of engraving by Frederick Mackenzie, 1842, after *Vetusta Monumenta*, VI (1885), pl. XXVII
C. Wilson

in both names made them very suitable for places of worship created for the use of kings.[15]

In practically every year of his long reign, Henry III spent more time at Westminster than at any other of his residences, and it is therefore not surprising that his very earliest recorded act of art patronage was his commissioning in 1231 of embellishments to the two main chapels of Westminster Palace, painted frontals and retables

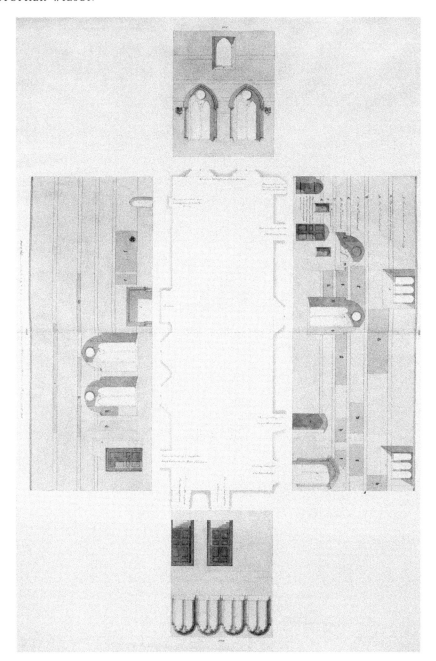

FIG. 3. Westminster Palace, king's great chamber, plan and interior elevations. Watercolour by Edward Crocker, *c.* 1820. The areas of wall surface shown in the darker tone indicate the parts of the 13th-century paintings uncovered in 1819. The shallowest horizontal bands bore the series of inscriptions that identified each of the narrative scenes

Ashmolean Museum, Oxford

Fig. 4. Westminster Palace, king's great chamber, reconstruction of north interior elevation and king's bed canopy as in mid-1260s
Graphic by C. Wilson

for their altars.[16] The remodelling of the king's chamber at Westminster could well have been begun around the same time, as the earliest mention, in 1232, concerns the selection of timber for the roof.[17] References to the paintings in 1236 indicate that the structure had been completed by then. What is a little unexpected, given the high ambition of most of the buildings commissioned by Henry III, is that the architecture produced by the remodelling was fairly modest. The semicircular internal heads of the retained 12th-century windows in the north wall coexisted with new windows of similar format but with pointed-arched heads, and all openings were given simply treated plate tracery. Somewhat more ambitious were the modifications made to the windows in the east wall: the insertion of plate tracery incorporating two lights and unusual diamond-shaped openings, and the addition of the sort of moulded rear arches and marble-shafted jambs that one might have expected to find in all the windows. Moulded rear arches borne on marble shafts were also included in the new door inserted at the west end of the south wall.[18] Like the entrances to the king's chambers in other of Henry III's residences, it will have been reached by an external covered stair with a lobby or *oriolum* at the top. The most likely site for such a stair was against the southern end wall of the household hall, where it could have connected directly with the pentice that enabled Henry III to walk dry-shod all the way from his chamber to his private door into the south transept of Westminster Abbey (Fig. 1G, I).[19] Most of the rather scanty documentary evidence for the structural repairs to the rooms gutted by the 1263 fire concerns roof timbers, but the purchase of boards is also mentioned, and there can be little doubt that those were mostly destined for the boarded ceiling of the chamber that remained in place until 1819 (Fig. 2).[20] The lack of any references to masonry in the documents relating to the repairs of the mid-1260s could simply be due to loss of records, but on balance it seems likely that the pre-existing stonework was retained with little modification.

The single most remarkable feature of the remodelling of the chamber in the 1230s is one that has been completely ignored in the literature: the zone of solid walling that rose above the lateral windows and occupied around 40 per cent of the elevations

(Figs 2–4). This windowless upper zone was at variance with contemporary northern European usage in two important respects. Firstly, it represented a rejection of the standard and wholly rational practice of making windows rise almost to the wall head, a practice exemplified at the Palace by the queen's chamber built to the south of the king's chamber in 1237 (Figs 1B, 5) and by the Exchequer chamber erected in the outer court of the Palace in the late 1230s or early 1240s.[21] Both of those rooms were covered by open timber roofs of steep pitch such as one would expect to find over practically any unvaulted structure of 13th-century date, whereas the covering installed over the king's great chamber in the 1230s (and recreated after the chamber was burned out in 1263) took the highly unusual form of a flat ceiling, a choice indicating that those responsible had recognized that a steeply pitched covering would have combined with the windowless upper walls to produce an unacceptably ill-lit interior. The second abnormal attribute of the chamber's masonry was the fact that the inclusion of the windowless upper zone made the walls rise some 3.35 m (11 ft) higher than those of the household hall, the traditionally pre-eminent component in any seigneurial residence. That pre-eminence, which had been expressed clearly at Westminster by the considerably greater area of the hall vis-à-vis the chamber, was partly practical, in that the hall was a dining room intended to accommodate all or most of the household, and partly an expression of the fundamental importance of the bond between a lord and his men, which eating together regularly was a way of fostering. The overtopping of the walls of the hall by the chamber is very apparent in the earliest visual record of the exterior of the chamber, that included in an anonymous mid-16th-century drawing of the Palace viewed from Lambeth (Fig. 6).[22]

What was the aim in making the upper walls of Henry III's chamber windowless? The explanation would seem to be that it was a way of providing unbroken wall surfaces capable of accommodating an unusually extensive scheme of painting. All that can be said of that scheme is that it was probably a single narrative, for a royal writ of August 1237, reinforcing an earlier one of May 1236, ordered that partly executed paintings simulating flat textile hangings (*panelli*) decorated with lions, birds and other beasts, which were on the walls below the chamber's 'great story' (*magna historia*), be abandoned in favour of painting in the manner of a green curtain, the explicitly stated aim being to avoid impairing the effect of the 'great story'.[23] Putting together the visual evidence for the building and the documentary evidence for its paintings, the decoration of the chamber can be reconstructed as two horizontal zones, the lower given over to painted simulations of green hangings, the upper consisting of a narrative cycle occupying all the solid walling added above window level (Fig. 4). No doubt the fictive hangings resembled the real green curtains with which the king's bed is known to have been hung.[24] Although the first sign of the name most frequently applied to the chamber in the later Middle Ages, the Painted Chamber, occurs only in 1290[25] (Fig. 7), this would have been a perfectly valid appellation at any time from the mid-1230s onwards.

In what was technically the kingdom's only royal palace and by far the most frequented of the king's residences, it might be expected that the king's great chamber would have been a bedroom in name only, a grand antechamber to the real bedroom beyond. This kind of arrangement seems to have existed at some other royal houses and it certainly existed at Westminster from the next reign onwards, but in Henry III's time there is no evidence at all of a second chamber functioning regularly as a bedchamber.[26] Unequivocal evidence that Henry III slept in the bed in his great

A Monument to St Edward the Confessor

FIG. 5. Westminster Palace, queen's chamber, exterior of west wall, during demolition in 1823. Graphic based on part of watercolour by Edward Blore (BL, Add. MS 42022, fol. 21r)
Graphic by C. Wilson

FIG. 6. Westminster Palace, king's great chamber and household hall from the east. Graphic based on part of an anonymous mid-16th-century drawing (London, Victoria & Albert Museum, E.128-1924) KEY A. roof of small hall (household hall); B. roof of the queen's chamber; C. top of stair turret at south-east corner of the king's great chamber; D. wall-walk linking C and E; E. 'Outlook tower' over north-east corner of the king's great chamber; F. king's oratory of St Laurence
Graphic by C. Wilson

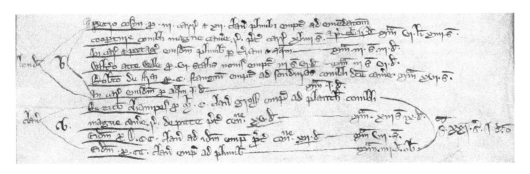

FIG. 7. Detail of particulars of account of clerk of the king's works at Westminster for 22 February 1290–Easter 1291, showing purchases of lead and nails made in connection with repairing the roof of the king's great chamber in 1290 (TNA, E 101/468/2, roll 9, mem. 15). The entry recording the purchase of 1100 large nails 'for the boarding of the roof of the king's great painted chamber' (*ad plancham combli magne camere regis depicte*) appears in the seventh and eighth lines shown. Compare the reference to the king's great chamber *tout court* in the second line shown
C. Wilson

159

chamber is the statement made in a writ of 1244 that the curtains around the bed were to safeguard the king's privacy.[27] Moreover, the order of 1236 that a round window beside the king's bed be glazed has very reasonably been interpreted as the draught-proofing for the king's benefit of the quatrefoil-shaped opening just east of the bed that gave a view into the oratory (Figs 4 and 8).[28] The thinking that might have lain behind the decision not to add a second more private chamber will be considered in the third section of this paper. Of course one should not visualize Henry III spending his entire time at Westminster in his great chamber, for he had a considerable number of other rooms that he could have used for sleep, leisure and relaxation, and presumably also for business if the need arose. These included at least one chamber underneath his great chamber (Fig. 2, lower right) and also the Antioch and Marculf chambers, both of which were single-storey structures. Significantly, all of these ground-floor rooms adjoined the king's garden, which occupied much of the space between the great chamber and St Stephen's Chapel as well as the ground between those buildings and the river (Fig. 1C, N).[29] Henry also had the option of sleeping with his queen in her chamber, as we happen to know he was doing on a night in early September 1238, when an intending assassin succeeded in breaking into his chamber at Woodstock Manor.[30] Other rooms at his disposal at Westminster included a 'privy chamber' for the king's ablutions, which was somewhere conveniently close to the Thames, a wardrobe, which will probably have been on the ground floor below the great chamber,[31] and the small room at second-floor level in the turret, which rose from the north-east corner of the chamber (Fig. 6E). This turret, which could have been either a 12th-century survival or a new structure, had comparatively large windows overlooking the king's garden and commanding spectacular views towards the city of London, and is therefore interesting as a possible ancestor of the outlook towers that began to proliferate in the late Middle Ages and Renaissance.[32] Henry III had its interior painted in 1251.[33]

Apart from the bed, the only permanent fitting of the king's great chamber will have been the 'spere', the timber barrier forming a lobby at the entrance end of the room (Fig. 1b). No examples are known to survive of what was probably once a ubiquitous component of medieval chambers, but in form speres were no doubt closely akin to the screens that are still to be found at the low ends of a good number of medieval and Renaissance halls in England.[34] The spere to the great chamber could well have been among the unspecified number of speres that were being installed in the king's chambers in 1288–89 and if so it will have been the successor to an earlier screen of the same kind.[35] Edward I's reign saw the provision of much movable furniture for the king's and queen's chambers at Westminster, mostly tables of different sizes and various kinds of seating. There can be little doubt that most of the pieces were being used in connection with the taking of meals.[36] By the early 13th century, to the dismay of some, the elites of England were ceasing to bond with their households in the proper traditional way by dining and supping with them in hall on a regular basis, and there is no reason to suppose that Henry III was conservative in this respect.[37] The fact that the east wall of the great chamber had two large windows rather than the more usual uneven number suggests that the central pier was intended to function as the backing for the king's seat and its cloth of honour.[38] During meals the king's table, the high table, will have been set north–south. The bed projecting from the north wall (Figs 1a and 4) would have tended to create two separate zones, reinforcing the hierarchical distinction between the high table and the tables set lengthwise that would have occupied the western two-thirds of the chamber. The meals served

A Monument to St Edward the Confessor

in the king's great chamber in the 13th century will have ranged from daily dinners and suppers, when the king probably ate in the company of senior household officers and a few guests, to the banquets on 13 October, the principal feast of St Edward, and the periodic feedings of large numbers of the poor as part of the king's almsgiving.[39]

On 7 April 1259, Henry III ordered his treasurer to have the defective chimney of the chamber pulled down and rebuilt immediately after the ending of the king's parliament then in session.[40] While this reference does not conclusively prove that parliament was occupying the king's chamber, it is hard to imagine what else might have been thought to warrant delaying a repair that seems to have been urgently needed. The chamber is known to have been used for the opening session of each parliament held at Westminster from 1339 onwards,[41] and there must be a fair chance that it had been fulfilling the same function since Henry III's reign. How early this usage occurred cannot be known, but it is very suggestive that the holding of the earliest assembly 'officially' referred to as a parliament, in January 1237, should have coincided with the completion of Henry III's remodelling of the chamber.[42] Henry's readiness to allow parliament to meet in his chamber will have cost him some inconvenience, for he will have had to find other places to eat and sleep for the duration, but no doubt it will have seemed to him an apt usage, given that taking counsel was one of the traditional functions of a chamber. The relative accessibility of what was primarily the king's main living space is perhaps the most striking thing to emerge from this sketch of the functions of the king's great chamber at Westminster in Henry III's reign.[43]

THE DATING OF THE PAINTINGS

THE documentary evidence for the paintings in the king's great chamber at Westminster has been reviewed in detail on a number of occasions, and for that reason the following discussion will focus only on the salient elements. The decorating of the remodelled 12th-century chamber was probably imminent by May 1236, when the king issued instructions that the walls be painted in the manner of a green curtain and that a specified aphoristic text be painted on the end wall next to the entrance (see below, 170). Fifteen months later came the already-mentioned reinforcing writ, which reveals that the main decoration of the room above the simulated green hangings was an unidentified 'great history'. In April 1243, pictures of two facing lions were ordered to be added to the end wall near the text, followed in October by figures of the Evangelists, one on each wall. Presumably all of these additions covered or displaced parts of the painted hangings.[44] The rebuilding of the chimney in 1259 was completed with the painting of a Tree of Jesse on the chimney breast. All of this work will have been to a greater or lesser degree wrecked by the fire of 7 February 1263, which burned out not only the chamber but the oratory of St Laurence and the household hall as well as other lesser rooms. An authorization to issue money for paintings in the chamber dated 6 November ordered that the work be completed by Christmas of the same year. A further writ dated 17 September 1264 describes the chamber as 'now painted' but lacking gilding. In fact writs relating to the chamber's paintings continued to be issued almost to the very end of Henry III's reign, but none of them reveals to us the state of the work at any given moment.

The most important specifics provided by the documentation from the last years of Henry III's reign are the following: the name of the painter in charge of the post-1263 work, Master Walter of Durham; a statement of the cost of materials used between Christmas 1266 and Michaelmas 1267 ('And for gold leaf, and other things necessary for the paintings around the king's bed in the king's chamber there, £53 5s. 2½d.'); and a payment of 20s. made on 13 January 1268 for gold needed for the 'perfection' of the chamber.[45] The payment of 1266–67 has been interpreted by Paul Binski as the cost of making the large picture of the coronation of St Edward, which occupied the wall at the head of the bed (Fig. 8), the images of St Edward and St John the Evangelist in the guise of a pilgrim in the embrasures of the window opposite, and the images of the triumphant Virtues in the other window embrasures.[46] However, the payment seems to be for materials rather than workmanship and for that reason it should probably be seen as connected with the gilding noted as lacking in September 1264. The high cost of the materials and the reference to the king's bed could be explained by the fact that the large painting of the Confessor's coronation was framed by particularly elaborate fictive metalwork, but it is perhaps more likely that what was being referred to was the gilding applied to all of the paintings at the bed end of the chamber. A longitudinally phased execution of the gilding would have enabled part of the chamber to remain in use at any one time, and a possible indication that this approach had been adopted in the earliest work of painting carried out after the 1263 fire is the observation made in the early 19th century that only half of the ceiling had been painted with a short-lived scheme of saints' heads.[47]

During the first two decades of Edward I's reign, the accounts of the clerk of works for Westminster Palace contain a sprinkling of references to painting in the chambers of the king and queen. Some of this work was done by the painter William of Nottingham, who, to judge from other commissions entrusted to him, was an esteemed

FIG. 8. Westminster Palace, king's great chamber, north wall, painting of the Coronation of St Edward; watercolour by Charles Stothard, c. 1820
Society of Antiquaries of London

A Monument to St Edward the Confessor

artist,[48] but the only mention of painting in the king's great chamber, the purchase in 1289 of colours and other materials used for repairs (*emendaciones*), is accompanied by an entry for Master Walter's wages, a clear indication that he was once more in charge there. In the following year, Walter was working on a painting of Christ in Majesty and the Evangelists in the king's new stone-built chamber known as the Green Chamber on account of the predominant colour of its walls.[49] Work in the great chamber would have been impossible in that year, because the fabric of the room was undergoing extensive repairs, which included mending the chimney and roof timbers and strengthening the foundations.[50] It seems likely that these structural works were intended to be preparatory to the extended programme of repair (*emendacio*) to the chamber's paintings that was inaugurated on 28 April 1292 along with Edward I's most important venture in the field of ecclesiastical architecture, the rebuilding of St Stephen's Chapel. The simultaneous start of work on these two projects, which made it necessary for the king to decamp to the nearby residence of the archbishop of York, is a clear indication that Edward had embarked on a concerted campaign of improvement to his principal residence. The painting of the chamber, like the building of the chapel, seems to have moved ahead quickly, but in 1297 both projects were halted by the financial crisis brought about by the king's determination to wage war on three fronts simultaneously.

Work on the paintings resumed only at the start of Edward II's reign, in September 1307, when Walter's son Master Thomas of Westminster was summoned from Peterborough 'for the ordaining, repairing and mending [*ad ordinandum reparandum et emendandum*] of certain defects existing in divers stories [*historiis*] in the Painted Chamber and [. . .] the mending of divers paintings and designs [*depicturas et protracturas*] in divers chapels, chambers and rooms in the palace'. The defects that Thomas was to remedy will have been largely or entirely the result of Edward I's total neglect of the Palace following a disastrous fire, which left large parts of it gutted in March 1298. Thomas's work on the chamber was most intensive towards the end of 1307, when twelve painters were assisting him, and it can be assumed that they succeeded in refreshing the paintings in time for the coronation of Edward II on 18 February 1308, as little more was done after that. An interesting detail contained in the accounts for this phase of work is the payment in October 1307 of 6d. to Thomas for the carriage of all his 'stories [*istoribus*] and colours' from London to Westminster Palace.[51] The 'stories' that needed to be fetched from Thomas's base in the city of London were evidently too large or too bulky to be carried by Thomas in person, and it is hard to see what they could have been other than drawings comparable to those made in 1352 in connection with the still partly extant paintings in St Stephen's Chapel. The latter were on sheets of 'royal' paper,[52] but Thomas's were presumably on parchment. The fact that Thomas needed to have access to those drawings while working on the paintings in the chamber is in itself a strong indication that his work was in the nature of a restoration of what already existed. After 1308, there appear to be no further references to painters' work in the chamber.

How should the four major phases of activity between the early 1230s and the first decade of the 14th century be related to the visual records made during the brief exposure of the surviving paintings in 1819–20? The artist responsible for making one of the two extant sets of copies of the murals, Charles Stothard, reportedly observed the presence of multiple layers indicative of several periods of work, and noted that one of the triumphant Virtues in the window splays had been repainted twice. None of the early-19th-century observers indicates whether any formal or iconographic differences between the layers could be detected.[53] There can be no question of dating the topmost layer, the one recorded, to the first campaign of the 1230s. The facial types, the elongated proportioning of bodies, and the 'broad-fold' draperies are unmistakably based on mid-13th-century northern French art, an influence which began to make itself felt in England in the 1250s and which will have become more powerful with the creation of the Westminster Retable in the late 1250s or early 1260s, to all appearances by top-flight Parisian artists.[54] It is therefore not surprising that there has been unanimity that the paintings recorded in 1819 postdated the fire of February 1263. By Michaelmas 1267, when the large payment mentioned above was made for the paintings around the king's bed, it is likely that what had been achieved was not only those paintings but the repainting of the entire chamber along the pre-1263 lines, with a new version of the 'great history' above simulated green hangings. The last five years of Henry's reign could have seen the partial replacement of the fictive hangings by the four lower bands of narrative scenes whose remains on the south wall were recorded in 1819. It is certain that painted green hangings were present in the post-1263 chamber, because some portions remaining on the lower part of the west wall were observed by one of the most assiduous antiquarian recorders of the medieval Palace during the disastrously destructive years around 1800.[55]

Until fairly recently, there was general agreement that all the paintings in the chamber belonged to the post-1263 phase, albeit overpainted to a now-indefinable extent in 1292–97 and 1307–08. That consensus was broken in 1986 by Paul Binski, who proposed that the work of the 1260s was confined to the painting of the coronation of St Edward the Confessor behind the king's bed, the images of St Edward and St John the Evangelist on the embrasures of the window opposite the bed, and the triumphant Virtues painted on the other window embrasures. According to Binski, the Old Testament narrative scenes forming the great majority of the paintings were created under Edward I from 1292. It is clear from his 1986 monograph that this dating has to do with his view of the scenes 'as responding to and commenting on prevailing concerns of the Edwardian court of the 1290s', but it is also clear that he is unable to decide which of those concerns, if any, can be thought to explain the existence of the Old Testament scenes. Though noting 'that these scenes probably had some moralizing importance which went beyond the celebration of knightly heroism in Judas Maccabeus', and suggesting, somewhat as an afterthought, the possibility that in the paintings begun two years after Edward I's general expulsion of the Jews from England in 1290 the king 'can be seen openly to celebrate [his] wanton cruelty [...], recounting and mocking Jewish history with a blunt self-confidence', Binski admits that 'the significance of these narratives will remain a matter of informed conjecture'.[56]

In his 1986 monograph, and also in the long article on the Old Testament scenes that he published in 2011,[57] Binski shows no sign of being aware that a stumbling block to his late dating is the fact that every time the nature of Edward I's work on the paintings is spelled out in the accounts the word used is *emendacio*. In medieval Latin *emendacio* means more or less exactly what emendation means in modern English: mending, amending, repair, reworking, revision, improvement. Together with the verb *emendare*, *emendacio* occurs countless times in the 13th- and 14th-century records generated by the king's works organization, and whenever evidence is available for the nature of the work in hand, the term is found to refer to the modification of something already in existence rather than the creation of something

A Monument to St Edward the Confessor

new. In the documents relating to the painting of the chamber it occurs at least three times between 1255 and 1289, and the references in question are all accepted by Binski as indicating repair work.[58] The present writer finds it impossible to imagine how Binski could have become persuaded that the great majority of the paintings in the chamber resulted from the process of *emendacio*. In the 1307 'brief' to Master Thomas, cited earlier, the first of the three gerunds employed to characterize the nature of his work on the paintings, *ordinandum*, denotes organizing or arranging, one of the key functions of a master craftsman in charge of a team, and the other two gerunds, *reparandum* and *emendandum*, are a binomial frequently used to signify 'mending' or 'repairing' in royal building accounts of the 13th and 14th centuries. In legal language the use of binomials was a device for overcoming ambiguity, although it is evident that in non-legal contexts it often amounted to little more than a stylistic trait. The verb *reparare* along with its derivatives was thoroughly ambiguous, for it could relate either to repair or to totally new work, and it is only by considering the context that one can see which meaning was intended; but no-one could have been in any doubt about the meaning of the binomial *reparandum et emendandum*.[59]

Which features shown in the early-19th-century copies of the Old Testament narrative scenes are indicative of date? There is probably nothing about the records of the figure style, drawing or composition that can be viewed as clearly diagnostic of a date in the 1260s or one in the 1290s. That is not altogether surprising, for English painting underwent comparatively little stylistic change in the three decades following the advent of intense French influences around 1260. Nevertheless, if these scenes really were new designs of the 1290s, as Binski insists, one might expect to see some sign that the angularity characteristic of mid-century broad-fold drapery had been toned down and made a little more fluid, in accordance with the general trend evident in late-13th-century French and English art. There are one or two details of dress that look more at home in the 1260s than the 1290s. For instance, the hat of the woman who drops a millstone on to King Abimelech (Judges 9, 53) incorporates a flaring crown-like element of a kind that was completely out of fashion by the 1290s, when much more compact headdresses were favoured. Moreover, the late 13th-century version of this headgear would probably have included a hanging kerchief concealing the hair, whereas here the netted hair is very visible.[60] Outdated costume details were certainly sometimes included in 13th-century art-works in order to imply cultural distance from the Old Testament, and an example here is the early 12th-century style of episcopal mitre worn by the priests of the Jerusalem Temple who are laying a curse on Nicanor, one of the foes of Judas Maccabeus,[61] yet there is no obvious reason why King Abimelech's assailant should have been made to sport an archaizing hat.

The detailing of the architectural settings of the Bible scenes is a rather different case, for English architectural style was starting to undergo radical and rapid change during the years around 1290. As far as southern England was concerned, the main catalysts to this process were the two most ambitious royal building projects of the early 1290s, the Eleanor Crosses and the new St Stephen's Chapel in Westminster Palace, where micro-architecture, a previously almost unknown aspect of the French Rayonnant style, was being used to generate designs of unprecedented originality.[62] If, as seems clear, the work done on the paintings of the king's great chamber in the 1290s and the first decade of the 14th century had as its main objective a thoroughgoing repair of any areas that had become damaged since the end of Henry III's reign or more recently, it would have been natural to give rein to the normal human urge to be fashionable by modernizing whatever seemed particularly out of date, in this case the very prominent architectural component to the paintings. As Jean Bony noted in 1979, the hollow cornices topped by miniature parapets formed of continuous rows of openwork quatrefoils under miniature crenellations have close analogues in St Stephen's Chapel and other works of the 1290s and early 1300s by the same architect, Michael of Canterbury.[63] The character of the architectural settings that the paintings are likely to have possessed in their original 1260s incarnation can probably be gauged from two of the four structures found in the group of scenes devoted to the miracles of Elisha. In the structure at the far right the surface of the flanking pinnacles is punctuated by small black lancets and foiled shapes and the terminations to the pinnacles are of a strikingly schematic triangular shape with a surface decoration of continuous zigzags (Fig. 9). Both features would look completely at home in the Douce Apocalypse, a royal manuscript contemporary with, and stylistically extremely close to, the post-1263 phase of work on the king's great chamber (Fig. 10).[64] There could hardly be a more marked contrast than that between these pinnacles and the up-to-date Rayonnant type flanking the adjacent structure, and the most obvious explanation for the contrast would be that the pinnacles of the rightmost structure are survivals from the post-1263 phase of work. It could be that the work of modernization in the 1290s and 1300s had missed out these pinnacles, or that the repainting fell off at some later date. There are further indications that substantial parts of the architectural settings had survived from the mid-1260s. One is that the pinnacles on the second structure from the left are akin to those on the Westminster Retable, another major art-work of around 1260, whose figure painting and decoration are very closely related to the post-1263 work in the king's great chamber. Another is the foliate cornices on the lower storeys of this and the rightmost structure. These are of mid-13th-century types that were seemingly never used in England and were out of

Fig. 9. Westminster Palace, king's great chamber, south wall, painting of episodes from IV Kings 4, 38 – 5, 27; watercolour by Charles Stothard, *c.* 1820
Society of Antiquaries of London

FIG. 10. Douce Apocalypse (Oxford, Bodleian Library, MS Douce 180, p. 6). Detail after M. R. James, *The Apocalypse in Latin and French (Bodleian MS Douce 180)*, facsimile edn, Roxburgh Club ([Oxford] 1922)
C. Wilson

FIG. 11. Paris, Sainte-Chapelle, canopy over reliquary of the Crown of Thorns. Detail of late-17th-century drawing made for François-Roger de Gaignières (Paris, Bibliothèque nationale de France, Estampes Va 9, fol. 54 bis), after Branner, 'The Grande-Châsse' (as n. 102), fig. 1
C. Wilson

date in France well before the end of the 13th century. Yet another is the marked resemblance of the pendant pointed and trefoiled arches framing many of the Old Testament scenes to the cusping in the arches surmounting the scene of Edward the Confessor's coronation, the latter attributed to the 1260s by all students of the chamber's paintings. As with the headgear of the woman dropping the millstone on to King Abimelech, there is no iconographic reason why any of these details should have been made archaic in order to convey cultural distance.[65]

Attributing the Old Testament paintings to Henry III rather than to Edward I makes good sense when they are viewed within the context of the two kings' art patronage. Henry installed two further Old Testament cycles in his Westminster apartments: the story of Joseph painted on the wall above and behind his seat in the oratory of St Laurence in 1238, and the story of Nebuchadnezzar painted in St Stephen's Chapel in 1258. Another Joseph cycle was painted in the new chapel of Winchester Castle in 1250. Of course, these commissions represent only a small part of the many dozens of wall-painting schemes known to have been ordered in the course of his reign, but the prominence accorded to Old Testament subject matter at Westminster is still remarkable.[66] Edward I by contrast, is known to have commissioned only two new wall-paintings with figural components: the already-mentioned images of Christ in Majesty and the Evangelists painted in 1289 by Master Walter of Durham in the Green Chamber only a few metres away from the great chamber at Westminster, and a scheme consisting of fifty-four heraldic shields and four knights 'seeking a tournament' painted in the hall at King's Langley Manor in 1292.[67] On the available evidence, which there is no reason to think misleading, Edward I emerges as someone reluctant to commission any form of wall-painting other than the repetitive patterns routinely applied to 13th-century interiors, and one can only wonder whether that attitude was a reaction against his father's tastes or the consequence of witnessing the progressive decay of the schemes that his father had commissioned.

Since Edward I differed from his father in not being a prolific patron of figural wall-painting, one has to ask why he caused so much effort to be lavished on the repair of those in the great chamber at Westminster. The most important consideration will have been simply the need to maintain an ensemble likely to have been perceived as the principal glory of the main English royal residence. A ruler who asserted his kingly authority as much as Edward I did could hardly have failed to appreciate the chamber's value as a backdrop for such important events at court as the homage of Alexander III of Scotland in October 1278.[68] Moreover, Edward's sense of filial piety was strong,[69] and for that reason alone removal or concealment of his father's work would probably have been unthinkable. Another factor that must have favoured retention was the very slow rate of change in dress in the 13th and early 14th centuries, which will have ensured that the paintings continued to look fairly modern. As to the causes of their evidently rather rapid deterioration, one can only speculate. It is possible that their technique was inherently fragile, but the close proximity of the river will have created damp conditions inimical to any wall-paintings and especially to those whose medium was oil.[70] Late-18th- and early-19th-century views of the exterior of the chamber indicate that its walls were largely rubble-built,[71] and if the render covering the rubble were not constantly maintained that too could have caused damage. The fabric of the chamber, particularly its unusually low-pitched roof, will almost inevitably have suffered some deterioration during the nine years following the fire of 1298 when Edward I no longer lived in the Palace and undertook no repairs.[72] The paintings will have looked old-fashioned for the first time in the 1340s, when the dress of both sexes changed dramatically.[73] At some point in the late Middle Ages they will have become vulnerable to decay and to the ascendancy of tapestry as the preferred form of wall decoration in elite residences. Large parts of the 13th-century paintings were destroyed by the series of undocumented late medieval modernizations that appear in late-18th-century and early-19th-century views: the replacement of the upper part of the west wall by a continuous band of two-light windows, the rebuilding of the fireplace and chimney breast flush with the surrounding wall surface, and the insertion of two rectangular three-light windows into the top of the south wall (Figs 2–4).[74]

THE KING'S BED AND ITS ASSOCIATED PAINTINGS

IT is a curious fact that none of the art-historical accounts of the great chamber mentions that during the Middle Ages this will have been thought of by many as the chamber in which Edward the Confessor had lived and died.[75] The names most commonly used in the 13th century, the king's chamber or great chamber, reflected the reality that the room functioned as the principal chamber of the ruling king, but it is not impossible that it was sometimes referred to as St Edward's Chamber, a name which was said to be in common use in 1477.[76] In Henry III's reign there might or might not have been a general awareness that the existing structure was essentially the work of Henry II, but we can be sure that even those conscious of the chamber's architectural history would have considered the association of the site with St Edward immeasurably more significant than the date of the structure currently occupying the site. That Henry III's remodelling of the chamber was conceived as an act of devotion to the Confessor is very strongly suggested by the fact that the date of the work, c. 1232–36, coincides almost exactly with David Carpenter's dating of 1233–38 for Henry's adoption of St Edward as his special patron and exemplar and his elevation of the saint's cult to a new level of importance.[77] Much later in his reign, Henry would describe himself in an inscription on the base of St Edward's shrine as the friend of the saint,[78] and it will surely have been a quest for spiritual closeness to the Confessor that lay behind his decision in the early 1230s to continue sleeping in the saint's chamber rather than turning it into the anteroom to a new and more private bedchamber. It is telling that Henry would choose as his place of eternal rest the grave that had been the Confessor's.[79]

The focal point of the site of memory that his great chamber will have represented for Henry III was inevitably the bed. As befitted the object that enabled the room's most basic function to be fulfilled, this was the largest piece of furniture and almost certainly the only one continuously in place. But as well as being a very prominent feature of the actual chamber of Henry III's day, the king's bed was the setting for an extraordinarily large number of the episodes that form the version of the Life of St Edward commissioned by Henry III for presentation to his queen around the end of the 1230s, *La Estoire de Seint Aedward le Rei*. In the only surviving copy of this text, which dates from the later 1250s, no fewer than thirty of the illustrations show the Confessor either reclining or sitting and only eight show him standing,[80] and there can be no doubt that this presentation of the saint as a kind of benign *roi fainéant* was intended to underscore the point made right at the start of the text, that St Edward was one of those sainted kings of England who were not 'mighty and very bold' but 'wiser and more peaceable and even-tempered'.[81] In the eyes of Henry III, who aspired to be a king of the second kind, it will have seemed entirely apt that the Confessor be commemorated in the great chamber in a way that evoked his characteristic recumbent and sitting postures, that is, by a large and splendid representation of his coronation painted on to the wall at the head of the bed (Fig. 8).[82] Whether there was an image of this kind in the chamber before the 1263 fire is unknown, but if there was it would help to explain the existence of a fine rendering of the same scene in a manuscript of Matthew Paris's *Flores Historiarum* that is known to have been illuminated at Westminster around 1250.[83]

A documented feature of the pre-1263 chamber that can reasonably be viewed as referring to St Edward's distinctive style of kingship is the aphoristic text ordered to be painted by the entrance in May 1236: '*Ke ne dune ke ne tine ne prent ke desire*' ('Whoever does not give what he has shall not have what he desires').[84] Like the earlier Life by Ailred of Rievaulx on which it draws, *La Estoire de Seint Aedward le Rei* includes a story illustrating the Confessor's unworldly attitude to wealth whose setting is the king's chamber at Westminster. The king, having been briefly left alone, is resting on his bed when he sees a serving boy enter and take gold from the chest where the royal treasure is kept. Edward makes no attempt to intervene, and when his chamberlain returns and realizes that the treasure has been depleted the king tells him to calm himself as plenty of gold remains.[85] It may well be that Henry III had a particular interest in the Westminster setting of this instance of the Confessor's extreme generosity to the poor because the manifestation of that trait which gave rise to the standard iconography of St Edward, the giving of the ring to St John the Evangelist in the guise of a pilgrim, took place not at Westminster but at Clavering in Essex.[86] There is also the possibility that in ordering the text to be painted at the entrance to his chamber Henry was alluding to the room's function as the setting of one of his own regularly performed acts of charity, the feeding of large numbers of paupers on the two feasts of St Edward.[87]

Flanking the painting of St Edward's coronation, but outside the area of the bed canopy, were paintings of single armed guards, a reference to the sixty guardians of Solomon's bed described in the Song of Songs. The co-opting of the guardians as protectors of Henry III's sleeping place will have been understood by contemporaries familiar with the Lives of St Edward, in which the saint attracts comparisons with Solomon on account of his wise and pacific nature and his wealth.[88] The use of the same iconography in 1250 for a painted panel next to the king's bed in Winchester Castle, a residence founded after the Confessor's time, suggests that Henry considered the Solomonic reference to be applicable to himself without the saint's mediation.[89] Another possibility is that the Winchester guardians echoed imagery associated with the pre-1263 bed at Westminster. Paul Binski has suggested that the bed's green hangings mentioned in the 1240s alluded to the *lectulus noster floridus* of the Song of Songs, and it could be that the gold-patterned columns carrying the bed's canopy (for which see the next paragraph) were intended to evoke the silver-sheathed columns of Solomon's litter (*ferculum*), which some influential commentators, including Bede, conflated with the *lectulus*.[90]

There are several documentary references to the bed that stood in Henry III's great chamber before the 1263 fire, enough to indicate that it was a splendid affair. In December 1243, forty-eight ells of green linen were supplied for it, and in the following year it was ordered that the columns around it be repainted green and patterned with small gold motifs.[91] The curtains mentioned in 1244 will have defined a kind of chamber within a chamber, a private space considerably larger than the bed within it. Unfortunately, there is no documentary evidence for what the columns carried at this stage, but Paul Binski has assumed that the canopy over and around the bed was essentially a curtained box, a version of the four-posters familiar from late medieval representations of bedrooms, with the difference that at Westminster the bed did not occupy the whole of the area under the canopy. He has compared the effect of the canopy when its curtains were drawn back to the cloths of honour carried over kings in processions.[92] The green accoutrements of the bed were very much in line with

A Monument to St Edward the Confessor

other orders for interior decoration by Henry III,[93] but here the colour will have been exceptionally prominent because the drapes were matched by the painting of most of the walls of the chamber as a simulation of green curtains. It is possible that the canopy was replaced in the 1250s by something more elaborate than a cloth of honour carried on columns, for in or around 1258 20 marks for painting it were paid to Brother William,[94] the Westminster monk who was Henry's most favoured painter before that role was taken over in the mid-1260s by Master Walter. The word used in the payment, *tabernaculum*, could sometimes denote a cloth of honour, but starting in the second half of the 13th century it was regularly being applied to architectural canopies incorporating arches or vaulting.[95] One of William's most important earlier works was his painting in 1248 of the timber-vaulted Chapel of St Edward in the lower ward of Windsor Castle,[96] and it is not impossible that on the strength of that commission he was thought to be a specialist in painting timber vaults. If there was a coronation painting over the bed before the 1263 fire the canopy, whatever its form, would have had to be set quite high up in order not to cast heavy shadows over such a significant image.[97]

Documentary references to the bed installed after the 1263 fire indicate that its canopy was at least as elaborate as its predecessor.[98] In 1284, gold and colours costing slightly over £3 were used on its decoration;[99] between Michaelmas 1288 and Michaelmas 1289 a wooden buttress was supplied, presumably as a replacement for one which had become damaged;[100] and in November 1289 a master glazier called John was paid 1 mark for repairing a boss.[101] The only 13th-century object existing today that can be described as a wooden canopy incorporating a boss, buttressing, polychromy, gilding and glass adjuncts is the vaulted canopy surmounting the platform that supported the reliquary of the Crown of Thorns in the Sainte-Chapelle in Paris (Fig. 11). This wonderfully elegant piece of applied architecture was apparently installed during the 1250s and if it was not yet in place when Henry III first visited the chapel in 1254 it would almost certainly have been visible during his second visit in 1259.[102] Confirmation that the canopy in the Sainte-Chapelle was a major influence on the design of the post-1263 bed ensemble is provided by the form of the arches that surmounted the scene of St Edward's coronation at the head of the bed, for their segmental profile, an extreme rarity in the Gothic period, and their formation as alternating strips of imitation enamels and goldsmith's work is a combination that recurs nowhere else than on the east face of the reliquary (Figs 8, 12).[103] The basic meaning of an arched or vaulted canopy is very similar to that of a cloth of honour, for both function as indicators of high status by being evocations of heaven. Yet the architectural type is more visually impressive and also symbolically richer by virtue of the capacity of its arched forms to recall the eternal connotations of circles and spheres.[104] The idea of modelling the immediate surroundings of his bed on features of Louis IX's chapel that honoured relics of Christ presumably seemed to Henry III no more than the appropriate expression of what was due to his special patron and to the sacral nature of English kingship in general.

THE IMPORT OF THE OLD TESTAMENT PAINTINGS

IN his 2011 article on the Old Testament paintings Paul Binski proposed that the 'in some ways abstruse' scenes that account for most of the imagery in the king's chamber 'belonged to a substantial tradition of political reflection on monarchy' and that they

FIG. 12. Paris, Sainte-Chapelle, detail of the east face of the reliquary of the Crown of Thorns. Detail of S.-J. Morand, *Histoire de la Sainte-Chapelle royale du Palais* (Paris 1790), pl. opposite p. 40
C. Wilson

can most readily be understood 'with reference to a series of texts coinciding persistently in content' to that of the paintings in that they make use of biblical examples to illustrate the horrors of tyrannical rule.[105] For Binski,

dating the Bible pictures to the mid-1260s obliges us to believe that Henry III, whose extensively documented artistic inclinations seem to have been conservative and irenic, was capable, during and after a catastrophic rebellion, of surrounding his own bed with an astonishing experiment: narratives with much thoroughly nasty content, some of which had been used against him by men [that is, the baronial opposition] who had challenged him openly and successfully.[106]

By the 1290s, Binski argues, 'the association of the Bible stories [depicted in the chamber] with the older baronial cause will have loosened to the point where Edward, a more confident man than his father, could take them over'.[107] In Binski's estimation a further indication that Edward I was the patron of the Old Testament scenes is the circumstance that their most prominent component, the very long sequence of scenes from I Maccabees filling the two uppermost, deepest and most continuous of the chamber's six bands, had a real-life counterpart in the person of Edward I, whose martial attainments earned him a reputation as a Maccabee, a hammerer of his foes.[108] Binski sees the extended narration in the uppermost bands of the deeds of Judas, the most celebrated of the Maccabees, as 'an uncompromising statement of heroic and virtuous action', a deliberately contrived contrast with 'all the bands beneath [which] concerned wicked, not good, kings'.[109]

Very little of this is cogent. Henry III's adoption of St Edward as his 'yardstick of kingly conduct'[110] in the early 1230s will surely have equipped him with a well-nigh unshakeable conviction that he was a virtuous king, one whose rule had nothing in common with that of the tyrants portrayed on the walls of his chamber. Moreover, Henry is likely to have been far more capable than Binski thinks of viewing with equanimity images of impious rulers suffering God's punishment. He will inevitably have encountered Last Judgement imagery where kings are included amongst the damned, and he himself had commissioned for St Edward's shrine a precious metalwork figure of St Peter trampling the emperor Nero.[111] St Edward, Henry's kingly exemplar, had even allowed himself to smirk during mass when it was revealed to him that God had just caused the king of Denmark to drown as he was on the point of setting off to invade England.[112] Binski's observation that the morally positive thread running through the history of the Maccabees differentiated the uppermost bands from the bands beneath is indisputable, although it should be said that we have no grounds for supposing that the downfall of the tyrants vanquished by the Maccabees in the unrecorded majority of scenes was underplayed. In Edward Crocker's copy of one of the two groups of scenes from I Maccabees that had survived until 1819, that in which Judas Maccabeus battles against Nicanor, the impious Seleucid governor of Judea, the latter's death at Judas's hands is very prominent, and there is a badly damaged area that almost certainly showed the Jews cutting off Nicanor's head and right hand in order to display them at Jerusalem (I Maccabees 7, 47).[113] The suggestion made by Binski that the special prominence accorded to I Maccabees was in some way connected to Edward I's military prowess is at odds not only with the clear documentary evidence that his work in the chamber from 1292 was confined to repair and refurbishing, but also with the near-certainty that the rhetorical flourish which made a Maccabee of him (posthumously) reflected his relentless pursuit of Scotland's subjugation starting in 1296. Immensely self-confident though he undoubtedly was, Edward was also a realist, and it is hard to believe that the military successes he had achieved by 1292 would have qualified him in his own estimation as a hero in the Maccabean mould. He had certainly shown excellent generalship in the campaign that culminated in the defeat of the baronial rebels at Evesham in 1265, but his deeds of derring-do in the Holy Land in 1270–72 had hardly matched the Maccabees in terms of tenacity or military impact, and they can have meant little once Crusader power had been crushed in 1291. His conquest of Wales in the early 1280s was impressive, but Edward will have realized that this was essentially a triumph of superior resources.[114] It is important to note that the privileging of the two topmost painted bands containing scenes from I Maccabees was even greater than Binski supposed, for, in common with all earlier writers on the chamber, he wrongly assumed that a further two bands extended along most of the north wall.[115] In fact any bands at that level would have had to be confined to the east and west extremities of the north wall, as most of the elevation was taken up by three large windows towards the west end, by the fireplace and its projecting hood, which will have been decorated with some iconographically self-contained subject matter,[116] and by the walling that formed a backing to the king's bed and its high canopy (Fig. 4).

Not the least extraordinary aspect of the historiography of the paintings in the king's chamber at Westminster is the failure of all those who have written on the topic to mention the contexts in which many medieval people would have encountered the Maccabees narrative on a regular basis. From the 8th century onwards, the daily Office had incorporated readings drawn from sections of the Bible that were specified in accordance with the divisions of the liturgical year.[117] In the prologue to Jacobus de Voragine's *Legenda Aurea*, a work of the 1260s or 1270s, where the lections of the Office are explained in terms of the symbolism of the year's fourfold division, the last of the divisions, the part of the year extending from the octave of Pentecost to Advent, is characterized as 'the period of pilgrimage [which] is that of our present life, in which we wander as pilgrims amidst a thousand obstacles [and in which] the Books of Kings and Maccabees are recited, wherein are set forth many wars, to symbolize the spiritual struggle which we must undertake'.[118] In fact Jacobus was oversimplifying, as I Maccabees provided the lections for October and Kings those for the period from the first Sunday after the octave of Trinity to the first Sunday of the calends of August, but it is interesting that for him the outstanding readings were drawn from those books, the very ones that predominated in the king's great chamber at Westminster. As Jacobus further explains, the Maccabees are the only saints of the Old Testament whose feasts are celebrated by the Latin Church, their festival being 1 August. For any devout Christian, therefore, I Maccabees will have been an integral part of his or her mental furniture and not, as Paul Binski stated in 1986, 'towards the periphery of sacred history'.[119] For Henry III, and no doubt for Edward I and Edward II also, the Maccabees lections in October will have had a powerful association with St Edward, whose principal feast, that of his Translation, occurred on 13 October, almost in the middle of the month. As one would expect of the great promoter of the Confessor's cult, Henry is known to have celebrated the October feast most earnestly,[120] and he and his court would have heard the Maccabees lections on the feast itself and also during the octave. As if to reinforce the Confessor's place within the last division of the liturgical year, the curtains and other textile accoutrements of the bed occupying the site of his death were green, the correct colour for church furnishings and vestments between the octave of Pentecost and Advent.

Once the link between the Confessor and I Maccabees is understood, it becomes possible to recognize the Westminster paintings as an iconographic entity rather than as an ad hoc assemblage formed of two campaigns of work carried out at widely separated dates and for two kings with radically different preoccupations and ambitions. It is true that the chamber was not coherent in purely visual terms, for the imagery relating directly to St Edward — the coronation on the north wall and the two figures representing St Edward and the Pilgrim on the embrasures of the window directly opposite — defined a discrete zone centred on the king's bed that will have seemed unrelated to the Old Testament scenes that occupied far more of the wall surfaces. But this discreteness was a most effective way of asserting the special and privileged status of the bed-centred zone, and it invites comparison with other revered sites that gave rise to works of art that are related to their settings in unconventional or even anomalous ways. A major surviving example of the phenomenon is the Lady Chapel of Glastonbury Abbey, an exceptionally highly wrought structure that replaced the legend-laden *Vetusta Ecclesia* burnt in 1184 and resembled its primitive wattle-built predecessor in being a free-standing building that obstructed any clear view of the main abbey church's west front.[121]

Of course, the Maccabees scenes and other biblical narratives at Westminster amounted to more than a way of associating the commemoration of St Edward with the correct liturgical season — the chamber's large areas of green fictive drapery would have sufficed to achieve that, at least in theory. For those attending the banquets held annually on the principal feast of St Edward the many dozens of lively and densely packed scenes, rendered in brilliant colours and glittering with many gilded metal embellishments,[122] will have formed an appropriately festive backdrop, and for the likes of Symon Semeonis they will have made a spectacular visitor attraction, but in Henry III's eyes their main value will surely have been that they provided a foil for the beneficent and peaceful nature of the Confessor's rule. There could hardly be a greater contrast than that between the serene frontal image of St Edward undergoing crowning and the furious struggles raging in many of the Old Testament scenes. In what reads like an extended aside in his 2011 article, Paul Binski concedes that such a moral antithesis could have been envisaged by Henry III were it not for what he sees as the political impossibility of commissioning the Bible scenes during the 1260s, and in making that point he offers the valuable observation that the scene of St Edward's coronation was confronted on the opposite wall by images of two exceptionally wicked kings who fulfilled the role of foil to perfection: Abimelech, whose life ends after he is 'crowned' by a millstone dropped by a woman, and Antiochus, who is shown seated under a canopy strikingly reminiscent of that which surmounts the coronation image.[123] It was tentatively proposed earlier that the lower bands to which these two scenes belonged were afterthoughts added before 1272 to the post-1263 scheme, and if that was the case it would suggest that an attempt was being made to point up further the foil function of the Old Testament scenes.[124]

CONCLUSION

HENRY III's decision to sleep in a bed occupying the same site as the bed slept in by St Edward two centuries before was, it has been argued here, a means of attaining a measure of spiritual proximity to the Confessor and also a way of advertising the placing of his kingship under the aegis of his holy mentor. This interpretation, when viewed in conjunction with the near-certainty that Henry's main aim in remodelling his great chamber in the early 1230s was to provide for a very extensive display of wall-painting, and with the record that in 1236 the upper parts of the walls were occupied by paintings in the form of a 'great history', constitutes a case for thinking that there already existed a scheme of painting essentially similar in form and meaning to that installed after the fire of 1263.[125] The evidence is assuredly fragmentary, but all of it points towards the same conclusion: Henry III's reworking of his chamber in Westminster Palace in the 1230s was the earliest artistic expression of his devotion to the saint who was to be a lodestar to him throughout his long and often stormy reign.

The murals painted in the chamber by Walter of Durham after the 1263 fire resembled the other major works of painting commissioned by Henry III in the 1260s in being fully abreast of contemporary French developments, and it is probable that they were more lavishly decorated and more extensive than the pre-fire paintings. The other principal component of the post-1263 chamber, the lofty timber canopy over the king's bed, was certainly more French and more elaborate than its predecessor could have been. Its appearance can be reconstructed in outline, and it is evident that its only contemporary parallel was an object known to Henry III, the canopy that his brother-in-law Louis IX had recently installed in the Sainte-Chapelle above the shrine housing the relics of Christ's Passion. The decision to make use of such an exemplar was a notably ambitious assertion of the sacrality of England's monarchy at a time when political power had been wrested from Henry III by his barons, and it seems likely that the exceptional splendour of the restored chamber as a whole was meant to demonstrate the enduring virtue[126] of the Henrician vision of English kingship under the patronage of St Edward.

ACKNOWLEDGEMENTS

I am much indebted to the following for clarification of points relating to their several fields of expertise: Paul Crossley, Maureen Jurkowski, Philip Lankester, David Park, Lucy Sandler and Charles Tracy.

NOTES

1. My translation of Latin text printed in *Itinerarium Symonis Semeonis ab Hybernia ad Terram Sanctam*, ed. M. Esposito, Scriptores Latini Hiberniae IV (Dublin 1960), 26. The term 'Painted Chamber' is eschewed in this paper on the grounds that applying it to Henry III's chamber would be an anachronism; see also n. 25 below. In Henry III's reign the terms used were *camera regis* or *magna camera regis*, hence 'king's chamber' and 'king's great chamber' here.

2. By far the most detailed account is P. Binski, *The Painted Chamber at Westminster*, Society of Antiquaries of London, Occasional Papers, n.s., 9 (London 1986), where the early-19th-century rediscovery, recording and discussion of the paintings are discussed at 24–31. The most important items in the earlier literature are those in the abbreviated references given at ibid., xi. Binski returned to the topic in his article 'The Painted Chamber at Westminster, the Fall of Tyrants and the English Literary Model of Governance', *Journal of the Warburg and Courtauld Institutes*, LXXIV (2011), 121–54. Publications touching on the paintings that had appeared since 1986 are listed ibid., 121 n. 2. To these may be added: C. M. Kaufmann, *Biblical Imagery in Medieval England 700–1550* (London/Turnhout 2003), 197–205; M. P. Lillich, *The Gothic Stained Glass of Reims Cathedral* (University Park PA 2011), 251–62; P. Binski, 'Function, Date, Imagery, Style and Context of the Westminster Retable', in *The Westminster Retable: History, Technique, Conservation*, ed. P. Binski and A. Massing with M. L. Sauerberg (Cambridge/London/Turnhout 2009), 16–44, at 30–35; P. Binski, *Gothic Wonder: Art, Artifice and the Decorated Style 1290–1350* (New Haven CT/London 2014), 65, 132–33, 315–16, 350.

3. C. Given-Wilson, *The Royal Household and the King's Affinity: Service, Politics and Finance in England 1360–1413* (New Haven CT/London 1986), 5.

4. J. Ashbee, 'The Function of the White Tower under the Normans', in *The White Tower*, ed. E. Impey (New Haven CT/London 2008), 125–39, at 134–36; P. Dixon, 'The Influence of the White Tower on the Great Towers of the Twelfth Century', ibid., 243–75, at 243–45.

5. So far as I am aware, this point has not been made before, but for the suggestion that the hall 'may very well have stood on the site of the Confessor's hall', see W. R. Lethaby, 'The Palace of Westminster in the Eleventh and Twelfth Centuries', *Archaeologia*, LX (1907), 131–48, at 142. For late-18th- and early-19th-century antiquarian opinion, which favoured attributing the fabric of the household hall to the Confessor, see J. Crook and R. B. Harris, 'Reconstructing the Lesser Hall: An Interim Report from the Medieval Palace of Westminster Research Project', *Parliamentary History*, 21 (2002), 22–61, at 24–27.

6. For a plan showing the relationship of the 11th-century Abbey church to the core buildings of the Palace, see C. Thomas, R. Cowie and J. Sidell, *The royal palace, abbey and town of Westminster on Thorney Island: Archaeological Excavations (1991–8) for the London Underground Limited Jubilee Line Extension Project*, MoLAS Monograph 22 (London 2006), 57 (fig. 34). Numerous details of this and the other general plans of the above-ground structures of Westminster Palace included in this volume (figs 45, 65) are not explained or justified in the text and should be treated with the greatest caution.

7. Its single-storey structure is evident from references contained in an order issued by the king in February 1245 for new paintings in the chapel; *CR 1242–47*, 287.

8. For the door, see n. 20 below. The timber floor must have survived the 1298 fire as its restoration was part of the comprehensive repairs undertaken at the start of Edward II's reign; R. A. Brown, H. M. Colvin and A. J. Taylor, *The History of the King's Works: The Middle Ages*, 2 vols (London 1963), I, 507 and n. 6. It has been suggested recently that this hall was always a first-floor hall; Crook and Harris, 'Lesser Hall' (as n. 5), 54–57. This is unlikely, as the window sills would have come very close to the floor, as they do in the so-called 'Constable's Hall' of *c*. 1160 in Durham Castle because of the insertion of a later floor. High plain dados would seem to have been the norm in both halls and monastic refectories in the 12th century. An instruction issued by Henry III in December 1244 makes clear that a new porch leading into what would later be called the Privy Palace, a structure that was certainly at ground-floor level, stood alongside the door into the household hall; *CR 1247–51*, 311; *King's Works* (as above), I, 503–04. Recognizing the household hall as a single-storey hall removes any objection to accepting as a fireplace the wide recess recorded in the centre of the south wall at ground-floor level, *pace* Crook and Harris, 'Lesser Hall' (as n. 5), 40.

9. On the strength of a reference to a 'new hall' in 1167, this expenditure is associated with the household hall in *King's Works* (as n. 8), I, 493. On stylistic grounds this interpretation can be rejected. In the Middle Ages the application of the epithet 'new' to buildings often signified newness relative to some other structure, and in this case Westminster Hall, completed in 1099, will have been meant.

10. The best record of the exterior elevation of the east wall is the drawing of 1819 by John Buckler in BL, Add. MS 36370, fol. 206r. The other most important records of the architecture of the chamber are: the interior views of 1799 looking east and west by William Capon in the library of the SAL; the plan and interior elevations by Edward Crocker in the Ashmolean Museum, Oxford (here reproduced as Fig. 3), and

the details drawn by Frederick Mackenzie, reproduced in J. G. Rokewode, 'A Memoir on the Painted Chamber in the Palace at Westminster ... [Read 12th May 1842.]', SAL, *Vetusta Monumenta*, VI (London 1885), 1–37, pls XXVI–XXXIX, at pl. XXVII (reproduced as Fig. 2).

11. Rokewode, 'Painted Chamber' (as n. 10), 8, pl. XXXIX, 22; Binski, *Painted Chamber* (as n. 2), pl. XXVb.

12. The simplicity was somewhat offset by their painted treatment. Some of the original imposts were recarved with foliage in the 1260s and possibly also in the 1230s; P. Tudor-Craig, 'The Painted Chamber at Westminster', *Archaeol. J.*, 114 (1957), 90–105, at 99; Binski, *Painted Chamber* (as n. 2), col. pl. IIa, pls Va, VII.

13. The retention of this door explains the king's order for the building of a new lobby (*oriolum*), which faced the Thames and lay between his new chamber (that is, the Great Chamber) and the Receipt of the Exchequer (cf. Fig. 1E); *CR 1234–37*, 245. For other examples of *oriola* in Henry III's time, see below and n. 19.

14. Geoffrey Gaimar, *L'Estoire des Engleis*, ed. A. Bell (Oxford 1960), lxxii–lxxiii, 190.

15. A short account of this topic is included in the section on St Stephen's Chapel in a work on the beginnings of Perpendicular architecture that I have in preparation.

16. T. Craib, 'Itinerary of King Henry III', 1923, TS in Map Room, TNA, Kew, which I have consulted in the privately circulated text produced under the auspices of English Heritage and edited by S. Brindle and S. Priestley. The years when some residence other than Westminster saw most of Henry III are 1216, 1217, 1236, 1251, 1264, 1266 and 1267. For the panels forming frontals and retables to the altars in the chapels of St Stephen and St John the Evangelist at Westminster, see *CR 1231–34*, 9.

17. For the reconstruction of the chamber in the 1230s, see *King's Works* (as n. 8), I, 494–500.

18. In point of richness the remodelling of the king's chamber at Westminster does not begin to compare with William Marshal II's remodelling *c*. 1234–35 of the hall and chamber in the Great Tower of Chepstow Castle, for which see N. Coldstream and R. K. Morris, 'The Architecture and Decoration of the Marshals' Great Tower', in R. Turner and A. Johnson ed., *Chepstow Castle: Its History and Buildings* (Logaston 2006), 101–12, at 112.

19. The other examples of covered stairs leading to king's chambers in Henry III's time include those at Clarendon (1239) and Feckenham (1251); *CLR 1226–40*, 251, 402; *CLR 1245–51*, 301. See also C. Wilson, 'The Royal Lodgings of Edward III at Windsor Castle: Form, Function, Representation', in *Windsor: Medieval Archaeology, Art and Architecture of the Thames Valley*, ed. L. Keen and E. Scarff, BAA Trans., xxv (Leeds 2002), 15–94, at 44, 87 n. 112. A good idea of the appearance of such structures can be gained from the well-known early-15th-century cut-away view of the Sainte-Chapelle in Paris contained in a breviary in the municipal library at Châteauroux (Indre); for a reproduction, see J.-M. Leniaud and F. Perrot, *La Sainte-Chapelle* (Paris 1991), 84. The only known reference to the pentice connecting the king's chamber at Westminster to the south transept of the Abbey is in *CR 1261–64*, 29.

20. *King's Works* (as n. 8), I, 498; H. M. Colvin ed., *Building Accounts of King Henry III* (Oxford 1971), 418. For the ceiling, see M. Liversidge, P. Binski and J. Lynn, 'Two Ceiling Fragments from the Painted Chamber at Westminster Palace', *The Burlington Magazine*, 137 (June–December 1995), 491–501. For the ceiling of 1819, which replicated in plaster the form of its predecessor, see J. M. Crook and H. M. Port ed., *The History of the King's Works*, VI: *1782–1852* (London 1973), 519. The introduction of the floor into the hall after the 1263 fire suggests strongly that the door was cut through the centre of the west wall to create a direct connection between the chamber and the hall. For this door see, Crook and Harris, 'Lesser Hall' (as n. 5), 49.

21. The west wall had a single window placed high up for which 7 ft of glass were purchased in January 1340; TNA, E 101/470/7. The window in the upper part of the east wall is not closely datable, but the horizontal internal head shown in all the 18th- and early-19th-century interior views of the chamber suggests a post-medieval date. For the queen's chamber and the Exchequer chamber, see *King's Works* (as n. 8), I, 50, 540; H. Colvin, 'Views of the Old Palace of Westminster', *Architectural History*, 9 (1966), figs 54–84, 122–23, 126, 128.

22. What was almost certainly the 12th-century wall head is clearly visible in the drawing above the two large windows in the east wall. The older wall head was not preserved on the other elevations, but its retention on the east wall will have been due to the wall walk it carried, the only means of access to the turret rising from the north-east corner. It is not impossible that the windowless upper walls were created by blocking the windows of a late-12th-century upper storey taken up by a private bedchamber. This would imply that Henry II had been willing to build a chamber block whose walls overtopped those of the hall in a non-traditional way. See also Mark Collins's paper in this volume, Fig. 1.

23. The description of this feature as 'bestiary paintings' in W. R. Lethaby, 'Medieval Paintings at Westminster', *Proceedings of the British Academy*, 13 (1927), 123–51, at 136, and in *King's Works* (as n. 8),

I, 497, is misleading. It can be assumed that *panellus* relates to *pannus*, a cloth (cf. R. E. Latham, D. R. Howlett and R. K. Ashdowne ed., *Dictionary of Medieval Latin from British Sources* (Oxford 1975–2013), which has an early-13th-century example meaning 'cloth strip'), and that the lions, beasts and birds were based on the affronted beasts and birds that decorated many luxury textiles of Byzantine or Islamic origin. The imitations of banner-like hangings painted in the blind arcades on the clearstorey walls of the early-13th-century parish church at West Walton, Norfolk, probably give a good idea of the *panelli* being imitated in the short-lived scheme at Westminster, although their patterns are simpler.

24. The 'good and strong boards' ordered for the chamber in 1244 are not unreasonably interpreted as wainscoting in *King's Works* (as n. 8), I, 122, although the verb *lambruscare* can equally well refer to the underdrawing of roofs to form flat or canted ceilings, as in the hall at Woodstock in 1244; *CLR 1240–45*, 224. The sense of the word must be 'to line with wood' either roofs or walls. The chamber's painted imitation of a curtain is paralleled in the only major painted interior commissioned by Henry III to have left substantial remains; D. Park and R. Pender, 'Henry III's Wall Paintings of the Zodiac in the Lower Ward of Windsor Castle', in *Windsor: Medieval Archaeology, Art and Architecture of the Thames Valley* (as n. 19), 125–31, at 126–27. The fictive curtain at Westminster is described, for no obvious reason, as a dado in *King's Works* (as n. 8), I, 497. A parallel for the high zone of fictive drapery proposed here occurs in the late-12th-century painting at the east end of the central aisle of the Galilee Chapel in Durham Cathedral. Visualizing Westminster's faux drapery in this way makes it much easier to understand how further subjects (including four figures of the Evangelists, one to each wall) could have been added to the chamber's paintings later on. The only extant English medieval wall-paintings known to this writer that evoke the concept of the superimposition of self-contained figural scenes on to a field formed of fictive drapery are those in the Lady Chapel (south choir aisle) of the parish church of St Thomas of Canterbury in Salisbury. However, the Salisbury paintings, which appear to date from *c*. 1475–81, were executed in a single campaign of work. Perhaps the images painted over part of the fictive curtain at Westminster included the 'map of the world of the king which is in his chamber at Westminster' ('Mappa Mundi Regis quod [*sic*] est in camera sua apud Westmonasterium'); *Matthæi Parisiensis Monachi Sancti Albani: Historia Anglorum*, ed. F. Madden (Rolls Series, XLIV, 3 vols, London 1866–69), III, li n. 1. The map might have been in another room altogether, for in 1318–19 mention is made of a Mappa Mundi Chamber whose location in the Palace is not given; TNA, E 101/468/20, mem. 19 dorse, a reference that seems not to have been made use of in the literature on Mappae Mundi.

25. TNA, E 101/468/2, roll 9 (mem. 15). As virtually all writers on the chamber have noted, the term *camera depicta* first occurs in 1307, but the 1290 reference is important, as it invalidates Paul Binski's use of the 1307 reference to buttress his claim that the chamber became 'comprehensively painted' only as a result of the 1292–97 campaign of work; Binski, 'English Literary Model of Governance' (as n. 2), 153. Curiously, other parts of E 101/468/2 are cited by Binski in Liversidge, Binski and Lynn, 'Two Ceiling Fragments' (as n. 20), 496 n. 24.

26. The second floor, the royal floor, of the gigantic keep of Colchester Castle, begun in 1075, was never completed, but the floor below, evidently intended for Eudo, William the Conqueror's steward, has a chamber whose unparalleled length relative to its width, together with its possession of two fireplaces and a garderobe with two entrances, strongly suggests longitudinal division by a timber partition into an inner and outer chamber; G. T. Clark, 'Some Account of the Keep of Colchester Castle', *Archaeol. J.*, 39 (1882), 239–56, at 250. The accounts given in the Lives of Thomas Becket of the saint's stormy visit to the royal castle of Northampton in October 1164 vary in detail, but virtually all mention the existence of two chambers, one reached by Becket and another beyond the first, where Henry II and his council were debating how to punish the archbishop. Not surprisingly, the issue of the king's other uses of those rooms does not arise in any of the narratives. It has been stated that the inner chamber was at a higher level (D. Knowles, *The Episcopal Colleagues of Archbishop Thomas Becket* (Cambridge 1951), 169–70), but it is not clear in any of the texts that a vertical as against a hierarchical distinction is meant. Of Henry III's residences that in the Upper Ward of Windsor Castle is the one most likely to have had a sequence of two chambers the inner of which was an actual bedchamber; Wilson, 'Royal Lodgings of Edward III' (as n. 17), 64 (fig. 21). By the early years of his reign, Henry III had at Havering, Essex, a 'great stone chamber' and an 'old chamber' (*King's Works* (as n. 8), II, 956), but their physical relationship is not known. At Clarendon, a favourite house, Henry almost certainly had just a single first-floor chamber. That Edward I had a bedchamber other than the great chamber at Westminster by 1276 is proved by a payment for 'four beams for the foot of the bed of the lord King in the small chamber' (*iiii tignis ad pedem lecti domini Regis in camera parva*); TNA, E 101/467/6-2, mem. 9. This chamber might or might not be that whose demolition was ordered by Edward I shortly before his departure for a long period of absence from the kingdom (13 May 1286–12 August 1289); TNA, E 372/131, rotulus 26. Materials for the new chamber, which was of stone, were being bought in 1286 (ibid.). It was structurally complete by 1289, when materials for its painting were paid for; TNA, E 101/467/19,

mem. 3. Between 1290 and 1292, it was decorated with figural paintings by Master Walter of Durham, and in the latter year it was first referred to as the Green Chamber on account of the green paint covering much of its walls; TNA, E 101/468/2, roll 3 (mem. 4); E 101/468/4, mem. 1. A new stone-built bedchamber for the king that faced on to the small garden was built from 1289, and in 1292 twelve iron hooks for hanging its curtains were bought and installed: TNA, E 101/467/19, mem. 1; E 101/468/4, mem. 1. If these hooks were to support iron bars for curtain rings they imply the existence of six windows, one fewer than in the king's great chamber. Perhaps curtains were needed in the small chamber because the bed itself, unlike that in the great chamber, was not curtained. The Green Chamber of 1286–89 and the new bedchamber of 1289–92 are confused in *King's Works* (as n. 8), I, 504–05. By 1290, the existence of two chambers for the king's use, both lying beyond his great chamber, was evidently starting to cause problems for the clerk of his Westminster works, who in 1290 resorted to describing the great chamber by means of the cumbrous formula 'the king's great outer chamber where the king's chamberlains lie' (*magna camera forinseca regis ubi camerarii regis jacent*); TNA, E 101/468/2, mem. 16. It cannot be a coincidence that the first use of the descriptor 'painted' occurs at this time (see preceding note).

27. *CR 1232–47*, 169.
28. *King's Works* (as n. 8), II, 407.
29. The chamber below the great chamber appears to have occupied the western half of the ground floor. For the Antioch Chamber, described in 1251 as a low chamber in the king's garden, see *King's Works* (as n. 8), I, 502. The Marculf Chamber is placed below the great chamber ibid., but the 15th-century document indicating that the chamber stood below (*infra*) the Painted Chamber must mean that it stood below the walls of the latter chamber rather than directly underneath it. It was certainly close to the river, because one of its walls was reinforced by a flying buttress that stood directly in the Thames and on that account needed frequent repairing. The mending of the lead roof of the Marculf Chamber in 1289 proves conclusively that it was a self-contained structure; TNA, E 101/467/19, mem. 2. A parallel for the rare phenomenon of a single-storey chamber in a residence of Henry III is that ordered to be built at King's Cliffe, Northamptonshire, in September 1244; *CLR 1240–45*, 262.
30. *Matthæi Parisiensis Monachi Sancti Albani: Chronica Majora*, ed. H. R. Luard (Rolls Series, LVII, 7 vols, London 1872–83), III (1876), 497–98. No doubt a direct response to this failure of security, despite being dated 6 September, three days before the date given by Paris for the Woodstock incident, was the king's order that the windows of the vaulted room below his privy near the Thames at Westminster be barred with good strong bars of iron so that no-one could enter; *CR 1237–42*, 99.
31. For this *privatam cameram* (a standard euphemism in Henry III's building records), see preceding note. Wardrobes in Henry III's reign were generally on the ground floor. For references of 1241 and 1249 to the king's Westminster wardrobe, see *CR 1237–42*, 178; *CR 1247–51*, 203. The first of those references qualifies the word 'wardrobe' with the clause 'where the king's clothes hang', presumably because the term was starting to be applied to privies.
32. Wilson, 'Royal Lodgings of Edward III' (as n. 17), 65–67.
33. *CR 1247–51*, 464.
34. The likeness will have been enhanced by the presence at the ends of the passageway defined by the spere of a pair of doors, for which see p. 154 and n. 13 above. The presence of two doors here explains the reference to the painting of the chamber's oriels in January 1265; *CLR 1260–67*, 156. The disparity in the widths of the two doors means that the spere could not have abutted against the north and south walls of the chamber and that it must have been free-standing; cf. M. Wood, *The English Mediaeval House* (London 1965), 141 (fig. 51), pl. XXVD. For documentary references to speres, see L. F. Salzman, *Building in England down to 1540: A Documentary History* (Oxford 1952), 260. Salzman's reference to speres as 'spurs' is etymological nonsense, for the word is obviously a cognate of Middle High German and modern German *Sperre*, a barrier.
35. TNA, E 352/82, rotulus 19; E 372/134, rotulus 2; E 101/467/20. A spere of some kind would have been needed in the late-11th-century royal lodging in the White Tower of the Tower of London. Without it, the king's chamber would have been open to the gaze of all those approaching the hall via the main stair in the keep's north-east turret; Wilson, 'Royal Lodgings of Edward III' (as n. 19), 87 n. 102; Ashbee, 'Function of the White Tower' (as n. 4), 134, 135 (fig. 100).
36. TNA, E 372/123, rotulus 21 (Easter 1278–Easter 1279). The most interesting items are two seats (*cathedre*), one square and one round with columns, but the only pieces specifically stated to be for the king's chamber(s) are a table beside his bed and a 14-ft-long form; TNA, E 101/467/6-2, mems 4, 5, 10 (14 March 1274–9 May 1277).
37. The *Rules* drawn up 1240–42 by Robert Grosseteste, bishop of Lincoln, for the running of the household of the young countess of Lincoln advised strongly that whenever possible she should take meals in hall 'before your people', avoiding eating in private; D. Oschinsky, *Walter of Henley and other Treatises on*

Estate Management and Accounting (Oxford 1971), 192–94, 406. The clear implication of those comments is that good old ways were being abandoned, at least by some lords for some of the time. The earliest direct reference to England's kings eating in their great chamber at Westminster appears to date from *c*. 1311; *King's Works* (as n. 8), II, 1042.

38. There appear to be no references to the king's seat here that are earlier than the late 14th century, but the presence of such a piece of furniture, at least on a temporary basis, can probably be inferred from the use of the chamber for the opening sessions of parliament, for which see p. 161 above and nn. 41–42 below. The *tabernaculum* mentioned as being above the king's seat in the hall at Woodstock in 1252 (*CLR 1251–60*, 24) will probably have been a cloth of honour, and the reference is valuable on account of its early date; compare the representation of the pope's throne in the manuscript of Matthew Paris's Life of St Edward commissioned by Henry III *c*. 1255–60 (Cambridge University Library, MS Ee.3.59); M. R. James ed., *La Estoire de Seint Aedward le Rei* (Roxburghe Club, 1920), fol. 14v. In 1244, a boarded ceiling had been added to part of the roof of the same hall (see n. 24 above), and it can probably be assumed that this was over the royal seat and that it was the equivalent of a celure in an ecclesiastical context.

39. For Henry's presence at Westminster on the feast-days of St Edward, see D. Carpenter, 'King Henry III and Saint Edward the Confessor: The Origins of the Cult', *English Historical Review*, 122 (2007), 865–91, at 868–69. There are several references to the victuals provided for the banquets held on October 13, including an order for 100 mutton carcasses issued on 16 July 1269; *CLR 1267–72*, 186. For Henry III's expenditure on feeding his household and also paupers on the feasts of St Edward, see D. A. Carpenter, 'The Household Rolls of King Henry III of England (1216–72)', *Historical Research*, 80 (2007), 22–46, passim; S. Dixon-Smith, 'The Image and Reality of Alms-Giving in the Great Halls of Henry III', *JBAA*, CLII (1999), 79–96.

40. I. M. Cooper, 'The Meeting-Places of Parliament in the Ancient Palace of Westminster', *JBAA*, 3rd series, III (1938), 97–138, at 112.

41. Ibid., 113. On 20 March 1310, while parliament was in session, the magnates met in the Painted Chamber to appoint 'Ordainers' to reform the kingdom and the king's household; J. E. Powell and K. Wallis, *The House of Lords in the Middle Ages* (London 1968), 275. For meetings of the Commons there in 1343 and later, see A. Hawkyard, 'From Painted Chamber to St Stephen's Chapel: The Meeting Places of the House of Commons at Westminster until 1603', *Parliamentary History*, 21 (2002), 62–84, at 62. From 1376 onwards, the name Parliament Chamber was being applied to it; Powell and Wallis, *House of Lords*, 399.

42. J. R. Maddicott, *The Origins of the English Parliament 924–1327* (Oxford 2010), 164; Carpenter, 'Henry III and Saint Edward' (as n. 39), 888 n. 124.

43. It is possible to see symbolism in the choice of meeting place for the parliament of January–March 1265, the first not summoned under royal authority, for this was Westminster Hall, the most publicly accessible room in Westminster Palace and not part of the residential complex occupied by the king. Other factors in the choice of venue might have been the incompleteness of the restoration of the king's great chamber after the February 1263 fire and the large size of the parliament, which included knights of the shire and representatives of the boroughs; Maddicott, *Origins of the English Parliament* (as n. 42), 204, 234.

44. See n. 24 above. Unreferenced statements in this and the following two paragraphs may be verified in: *King's Works* (as n. 8), I, 493–500 (covering Henry III's but not Edward I's work); *Building Accounts* (as n. 20), passim; and Binski, *Painted Chamber* (as n. 2), 16–22.

45. *Building Accounts*, 422–23; *CLR 1267–72*, 10.

46. Binski, *Painted Chamber* (as n. 2), 36.

47. For comments on the imitation enamels and gems used in the framing elements of the Coronation scene and one of the triumphant Virtues (Fortitude?), see H. Howard and M. L. Sauerberg, 'Polychrome Techniques at Westminster 1250–1350', in *The Westminster Retable* (as n. 2), 290–318, at 301, 303 (fig. 23), 304. For gilded tin-relief decoration, see n. 122 below. For Charles Stothard's observation regarding the short-lived scheme of decoration applied to half of the chamber's ceiling (unfortunately not specifying which half), see Liversidge, Binski and Lynn, 'Two Ceiling Fragments' (as n. 20), 493. The fact that the painted heads on the ceiling were not of saints does not reduce the value of the observation.

48. Painting of, inter alia, the roods in the chapels of the king and queen in the Tower of London (during the year Easter 1278–Easter 1279, TNA, E 101/467/7-2) and divers reparations to paintings in Westminster Palace and the painting of a small engine made for Prince Alphonso (TNA, E 101/467/7-7, 20 November 1278–19 November 1279).

49. Painting of the chamber green in 1289; TNA, E 101/467/19, mem. 3. Painting of the Majesty and Evangelists in 1290; TNA, E 101/468/2, roll 3 (mem. 4), roll 9 (mem. 19); E 372/147, rotulus 27 dorse.

50. TNA, E 101/468/2, mems 3, 7, 10, 15 (20 February 1290–Easter 1291).

51. TNA, E 101/468/21, fol. 31r.

52. *King's Works* (as n. 8), I, 519.

53. Binski, *Painted Chamber* (as n. 2), 24–29.

54. N. Morgan, *The Douce Apocalypse: Picturing the End of the World in the Middle Ages* (Oxford 2006), 21, 24, 29; P. Binski, 'Function, Date, Imagery, Style and Context' (as n. 2), 35–40. Morgan and Binski regard the Westminster Retable as English work, but for detailed arguments favouring a French origin, see C. Wilson, 'The Architecture and Ornament of the Westminster Retable as Evidence of Dating and Origin', in *The Westminster Retable* (as n. 2), 79–96; M. A. Michael, 'The *Bible Moralisée*, the *Golden Legend* and the *Salvator Mundi*: Observations on the Iconography of the Westminster Retable', *Antiq. J.*, 94 (2014), 93–125, especially 120–22.

55. 'Notes and Remarks, by the late Mr. William Capon, to accompany his Plan of the ancient Palace of Westminster [Read 23d December, 1824.]', SAL, *Vetusta Monumenta*, V (London 1835), 1–7, pl. XLVII, at 7. Capon made a scale drawing of these remains, but it seems not to have survived. Curiously, there is no mention of Capon's record of the fictive drapery in Binski, *Painted Chamber* (as n. 2), and in idem, 'English Literary Model of Governance' (as n. 2), 154, the west wall of the chamber is even said to have been 'blank' in the 13th century. See also n. 74 below.

56. Binski, *Painted Chamber* (as n. 2), 96, 98, 102. Binski has also suggested that Henry III's financial difficulties in the 1260s made that an unlikely time for the commissioning of major wall-painting; Binski, 'English Literary Model of Governance' (as n. 2), 144–5. However, the amounts of money needed to pay for wall-paintings would have been small compared with those involved in the completion of the precious metalwork and building work needed in advance of the planned 1269 dedication of Westminster Abbey. For indications that Henry III's household was enhanced rather than reduced after the defeat at Lewes, perhaps because de Montfort wished to give the impression that the king remained in control, see B. J. Wild, 'A Captive King: Henry III between the Battles of Lewes and Evesham, 1264-5', *Thirteenth Century England*, 13 (2011), 41–56, at 48–49. For the role of de Montfort's regime in continuing with the building of Westminster Abbey, see D. Carpenter, 'Westminster Abbey in Politics, 1258-1269', *Thirteenth Century England*, 8 (2001), 49–58, at 51.

57. Binski, 'English Literary Model of Governance' (as n. 2), 122.

58. CR 1254–56, 157; TNA, E 101/467/7-7; E 101/467/19, mem. 3; Binski, *Painted Chamber* (as n. 2), 17–18.

59. On these terms, see *Dictionary of Medieval Latin from British Sources* (as n. 23), where, however, there is no acknowledgement that *reparare* can quite often mean 'to make' rather than 'to repair'. For examples of the term used in Westminster building accounts that have been mistranslated as 'to repair', see *Building Accounts* (as n. 20), 196–97; *King's Works* (as n. 8), I, 528–29. Among a good many examples of the use of 'repair' to mean 'make' in English texts is that in the will of John Wadeluff, 1530: 'To the reparacion of a new Rode loft in Darfeld church x markes, yff it be begune w'in thre yeres [...]'; *Testamenta Eboracensia*, V, Surtees Society 79 (London/Durham 1884), 299. For binomials, see the discussion of 'lexical doublets' in D. Crystal, *The Stories of English* (London 2004), 151–52. The binomial *renovari et emendari* is used in connection with painting work Brother William was to do in 1260 in Henry III's chapel and chamber at Windsor Castle; W. H. St. J. Hope, *Windsor Castle*, 2 vols (London 1913), I, 78 n. 107.

60. Some of the label stops in the aisle wall arcades of the Angel Choir of Lincoln Cathedral (1256–80) indicate the three-dimensional form of this kind of headgear.

61. Binski, 'English Literary Model of Governance' (as n. 2), 126 (fig. 5). Other examples of using headgear to indicate cultural distance are the nasals to the bascinets worn by many soldiers.

62. C. Wilson, *The Gothic Cathedral: The Architecture of the Great Church 1130–1530* (London 1992, rev. edn), 192–94.

63. J. Bony, *The English Decorated Style: Gothic Architecture Transformed 1250–1350* (Oxford 1979), 22.

64. The patron, or at least the recipient, of the book was Henry III's eldest son, the future Edward I, and the making of the book will have predated his going on Crusade in 1270; Morgan, *Douce Apocalypse* (as n. 54), 9. The architectural settings in the Douce Apocalypse include many novel French details drawn from the Westminster Retable and from the relic platform and canopy in the Sainte-Chapelle, yet the overall character of the architecture is very different from any in contemporary French painting.

65. The stylistic diversity of the architectural settings has been ascribed to Master Walter's desire for variety; Binski, 'English Literary Model of Governance' (as n. 2), 149. This cannot be ruled out altogether, yet there is a striking lack of parallels in late-13th-century Northern European painting for the use of very modern architectural forms alongside forms that were out-of-date by about a generation. That architectural settings were being used in the Old Testament scenes to generate cultural distance is obvious from the ogee-profiled domes used in two depictions of the Jerusalem Temple; ibid., 130 (fig. 11), 131 (fig. 12). Michael of Canterbury was capable of incorporating limited numbers of elements based on much earlier designs such as would not have been considered to have utility as sources by other late-13th-century architects (see, for example, R. Willis, *The Architectural History of Canterbury Cathedral* (London 1845), 99), and while it is tempting to imagine him explaining this penchant of his to Walter of Durham, the reality is that Michael's

'archaisms', unlike the 1260s-style features shown in the copies of the paintings in the king's great chamber, were seamlessly worked into designs of ultra-modern character in such a way that non-architects would have been unable to isolate them.

66. *CR 1234-37*, 26; *CR 1253-54*, 165.

67. For the Green Chamber paintings, see n. 49 above. For the Langley paintings, see *King's Works* (as n. 8), II, 972. Edward II appears to have been more inclined to commission new wall-paintings than Edward I: in 1315-16 the very large sum of £176 3s. 4d. was spent on paintings of unknown form and iconography by Master Thomas of Westminster at La Neyt (TNA, E 101/468/17, mem. 2 dorse), a manor house of the abbots of Westminster whose site lay about one mile (1.6 km) south-west of the Abbey and which had been appropriated by the king during a vacancy; and in 1324 40s. were paid to John of St Albans, who had contracted to paint the life of Edward I in the household hall at Westminster; *King's Works* (as n. 8), I, 508 n. 7. See Plan B, p. x.

68. The homage of 1278 is explicitly stated to have taken place in the king's chamber; *CR 1272-79*, 565.

69. As witness Edward I's comment, made to a surprised Charles of Anjou early in 1273, after he had learned of the deaths of his father and his son John, that it was easy to beget more sons, but losing a father was irredeemable; *Chronica Monasterii Sancti Albani: Willelmi Rishanger, Chronica et Annales*, ed. H. T. Riley (Rolls Series, XXVIII.2, London 1865), 78. Edward's commissioning in the 1280s of a tomb for his father that was of unprecedented magnificence, and his ordering of the superlatively fine bronze effigy that was added to the tomb in the early 1290s, both show a level of effort in the commemoration of a predecessor that was not to be matched by any later English king.

70. Purchase of oil in 1289 for painting green the walls of the Green Chamber and for repairs to the king's great chamber; TNA, E 101/467/19, mem. 3. Purchase of oil in 1290 or 1291 for the paintings of the Evangelists in the Green Chamber; TNA, E 101/468/2, roll 9 (mem. 19).

71. For example, Cooper, 'Meeting-places of Parliament' (as n. 40), pl. X, and Colvin, 'Views of the Palace of Westminster' (as n. 21), figs 108, 114.

72. *King's Works* (as n. 8), I, 505.

73. S. M. Newton, *Fashion in the Age of the Black Prince: A Study of the Years 1340-1365* (Woodbridge 1980), 1-5 and passim.

74. Paul Binski has asserted that there were no Old Testament scenes on the west wall, a view that appears to be based on assumptions about the scope and pace of the Maccabees narrative in the two uppermost bands that are insecure, because the content of most scenes is unknown and because the order of even the few episodes known to have been depicted did not follow strictly the biblical sequence; idem, *Painted Chamber* (as n. 2), 82, 118-19; 'English Literary Model of Governance' (as n. 2), 154. Edward Crocker's elevation of the south wall (here reproduced as Fig. 3) includes an inexplicable anomaly: the overlapping of one of the late medieval windows in the south wall with the scene of the ambush of the Jambrites' wedding (Binski, *Painted Chamber* (as n. 2), cat. no. 15, pl. XI). The presence of the north walk of the late medieval cloister south of the chamber probably explains why most of the paintings that survived to be recorded in 1819 were on the lower parts of the south wall. The cloister was discussed in the paper on the Privy Palace that I gave to the 2013 Westminster conference of the BAA and which I hope to publish in due course. Probably of 15th-century date were the two sculptured corbels in the east wall, which appear in all the late-18th- and early-19th-century views of the interior. It is tempting to think that they bore statues of St Edward holding the ring and St John the Evangelist in the guise of a pilgrim, imagery which would have continued the commemoration of St Edward after the 13th-century paintings had disappeared from view.

75. The Lives of St Edward and the Bayeux Tapestry all strongly imply what everyone would have taken for granted, namely that the saint's death took place in his chamber in Westminster Palace.

76. Cooper, 'Meeting-places of Parliament' (as n. 40), 120-21, where the suggestion is made that the name might have had to do with the presence of Henry III's painting of St Edward's coronation and where other examples of the usage of this name are given. See also Powell and Wallis, *House of Lords* (as n. 41), 521, where the suggestion is made that the frequent use of the name 'St Edward's Chamber' in the 1470s and early 1480s was a compliment to Edward IV. The switch to the never-explained name Chamber of the Holy Cross under Henry VII (ibid., 530) does indeed suggest that the previous name had a Yorkist taint in the eyes of the first Tudor.

77. Carpenter, 'Henry III and St Edward the Confessor' (as n. 39).

78. P. Binski, *Westminster Abbey and the Plantagenets: Kingship and the Representation of Power, 1200-1400* (New Haven CT/London 1995), 99.

79. *Annales Monastici*, ed. H. R. Luard (Rolls Series, XXXVI, 5 vols, London 1864-69), IV (1869), 252. In 1290, Henry III was translated into his present tomb. Without mentioning that Henry III's bed and chamber were the successors to those of the Confessor, Binski notes that the bed and the coronation image behind it 'would have been as cogent an assertion of Henry's immediate, physical identification with the saint-king as

was his later occupation of the Confessor's old grave in Westminster Abbey'; idem, *Painted Chamber* (as n. 2), 36.

80. P. Binski, 'Reflections on *La Estoire de Seint Aedward le Rei*: Hagiography and Kingship in Thirteenth-century England', *Journal of Medieval History*, 16 (1990), 333–50, at 344. For the illustrations see *La Estoire* (as n. 38 above); http://cudl.lib.cam.ac.uk/view/MS-EE-00003-00059/34 (accessed 16 August 2014).

81. *La Estoire de Seint Aedward le Rei*, ed. K. Y. Wallace, Anglo-Norman Text Society 41 (London 1983), I, lines 9–14; *The History of Saint Edward the King*, trans. T. S. Fenster and J. Wogan-Browne, Medieval and Renaissance Texts and Studies 341 (Tempe AR 2008), 53.

82. The chronicler Roger of Wendover recounts how when Henry III seized Hubert de Burgh's treasure in October 1232 the enemies of the former justiciar urged the king to have him put to death. In refusing Henry is said to have observed that he would rather be reputed a foolish and negligent king than a cruel and tyrannical one; *The Flowers of History by Roger of Wendover*, ed. H. G. Hewlett (Rolls Series, LXXXIV, 3 vols, London 1886–89), III, 42. The nearest that Paul Binski has come to explaining the presence of the image of Edward the Confessor's coronation in the king's chamber are the statement cited in n. 79 above and his assertions that the bed was 'the iconic centrepiece of the chamber' and 'the centrepiece of a sacral conception of kingship'; Binski, 'Function, Date, Imagery and Style' (as n. 2), 34.

83. The possibility of such a picture in the pre-1263 chamber is mooted in Binski, *Painted Chamber* (as n. 2), 40. For the *Flores Historiarum* images of St Edward's and other English kings' coronations, see N. Morgan, *Early Gothic Manuscripts (II) 1250–1285* (London 1988), 50–52.

84. *CR 1234–37*, 270.

85. Wallace ed., *La Estoire* (as n. 81), 29, lines 980–1040; *The History of Saint Edward* (as n. 81), 66–67.

86. In 1251, Henry III visited the site of the miracle, the Chapel of St John the Evangelist in the churchyard of Clavering parish church, and gave orders for various benefactions, including a wall-painting apparently following the standard iconography; *CLR 1245–51*, 342; V. H. Galbraith, 'Edward the Confessor and the Church of Clavering', *Transactions of the Essex Archaeological Society*, n.s., 16 (1923), 187–90; 17 (1926), 48–49, at 49.

87. S. Dixon-Smith, 'Alms-Giving in the Great Halls of Henry III' (as n. 39), 87–88.

88. Binski, *Painted Chamber* (as n. 2), 42–43.

89. *CLR 1245–51*, 325.

90. Binski, *Painted Chamber* (as n. 2), 40; cf. Lillich, *Gothic Stained Glass of Reims* (as n. 2), 255. On the conflation of the *lectulus* and the *ferculum*, see the latter, 262.

91. *CLR 1240–45*, 205; *CR 1242–47*, 169. A green 'double cloth' for the king's bed (almost certainly, but not explicitly, for that at Westminster) is mentioned in April 1239; *CLR 1226–40*, 376.

92. Binski, *Painted Chamber* (as n. 2), 14, 30. The panelling made for the bed in 1253 (*Building Accounts* (as n. 20), 248) might well have formed a low enclosure between the corner columns, one that will have further enhanced the king's privacy.

93. *King's Works* (as n. 8), I, 129.

94. This undated payment occurs in an account rendered by the king's goldsmith, William of Gloucester, for the period c. 1257–72 (G. G. Scott, *Gleanings from Westminster Abbey* (Oxford/London 1863), 113), where it is preceded and succeeded by payments for two other of Henry III's artistic commissions that are known from other sources to have been finished in 1258. The last reference to work at Windsor Castle by Brother William the king's painter dates from 1271; *CLR 1267–72*, 191.

95. For a possibly early-13th-century instance of the use of the word *tabernaculum* to mean a cloth of honour, see *The Use of Sarum*, ed. W. H. Frere, 2 vols (Cambridge 1898, 1901), I, 202, 204. An early example of *tabernaculum* used to mean an architecturally treated canopy is the reference to that over an image of the Virgin installed in 1250 in the Chapel of St Mary in the Jewry, London: *CR 1247–51*, 380–81.

96. *King's Works* (as n. 8), II, 868.

97. Cf. Binski's reconstruction (Binski, *Painted Chamber* (as n. 2), 14 (fig. 2)), which is rendered in line and therefore conveys no hint of the darkening that would have resulted from its horizontal tester set level with the top of the coronation painting.

98. Binski has suggested that the canopy existing before 1263 was reinstalled after the fire; Binski, 'Function, Date, Imagery' (as n. 2), 34. This is extremely unlikely, as the seat of the fire was the chimney next to the bed and the roof of the chamber was either destroyed or damaged so badly that it had to be replaced.

99. TNA, E 372/132, rotulus 26. The same account contains a payment of £13 10s. 11d. for 'painting round the King's bed' (*pictura circa lectum Regis*). Late in 1277 or early the following year, a payment was made for 'painting the enclosure next to the King's bed' (*interclausuram juxta lectum Regis*); TNA, E 372/121, rotulus 21 dorse.

100. Payment for materials for various works 'with a wooden buttress for the canopy of the King's bed' (*cum uno boteras lingne [sic] ad tabernaculum lecti Regis*); TNA, E 372/134, rotulus 2. It is not impossible

that the columns of the 1244 reference cited above denoted buttresses, for this usage was not uncommon; cf. *King's Works* (as n. 8), I, 858 n. 5.

101. 'To Master J, glazier, for the repair (or making) of one boss for the canopy of the King's bed in his great chamber' (*Magistro J vitrario pro reparacione unius Bose ad tabernaclum lecti Regis in sua magna camera. Summa xiijs iiijd*); TNA, E 101/467/17, mem. 8; L. F. Salzman, 'Medieval Glazing Accounts', *Journal of the British Society of Master Glass-Painters*, 2 (1927/28), 116–20, 188–92, and 3 (1929/30), 25–30, at 117. Misdated by Salzman to 1287, the reference occurs in an account that runs from early May to early November and is dated in the heading 17 Edward I (20 November 1288 – 19 November 1289), although two notes on the dorse give the date as 16 Edward I. In 1296, the team working on the paintings of the chamber included Vincent '*le verrer*'; TNA, E 101/547/18, mem. 4. Unfortunately, there is no indication in the accounts of what Vincent was doing, but there would have been plenty of repair work for him other than on the bed canopy if W. R. Lethaby was correct in his suggestion that the numerous paterae on the ceiling resembled their counterparts on the Westminster Retable in being inlaid with glass; Lethaby, 'Medieval Paintings at Westminster' (as n. 23), 136. Since Vincent would have been a very rare name for an Englishman, the entry raises the possibility that a French specialist in glass-inlay work had been recruited. Against that is his relatively low rate of pay, 5d. per day. Master John, the glazier who had repaired the boss of the bed canopy in 1287 was a regular glazier involved in the making of stained-glass windows. For an invaluable survey of glass-inlay work on paintings and sculptures, see R. Page, 'Glass Inlay in Europe in the Thirteenth and Fourteenth Centuries', in *The Westminster Retable* (as n. 2), 107–23.

102. A dating of 1254 is proposed in F. Gebelin, *La Sainte-Chapelle* (Paris 1943, 3rd edn), 52–57. The relic platform is certainly secondary to the construction of the chapel itself; R. Branner, 'The Grande-Châsse of the Sainte-Chapelle', *Gazette des Beaux-Arts*, 6th period, 77 (1971), 5–18, at 14. The biographer of St Louis, Jean de Joinville, mentions that his subject ascended to the relic platform (*l'eschaffaut*) in order to bring down the relic of the True Cross before going on Crusade for the second time in 1267; E. Bozoky, 'Saint Louis, ordonnateur et acteur des rituels autour des reliques de la Passion', in *La Sainte-Chapelle de Paris: Royaume de France ou Jérusalem céleste?*, Actes du Colloque, Paris, Collège de France, 2001, ed. C. Hediger (Turnhout 2007), 19–34, at 22. The dating evidence is summarized as 'constructed around 1254 and completed by 1270 at the latest' in M. Cohen, *The Sainte-Chapelle and the Construction of Sacral Monarchy: Royal Architecture in Thirteenth-Century Paris* (Cambridge 2015), 159. For the mid-19th-century reconstruction of the relic platform and canopy, see J.-M. Leniaud, *Jean-Baptiste Lassus (1807-1857) ou le temps retrouvé des cathédrales* (Paris 1980), 59–61.

103. The segmental arch of the recess in the east face of the reliquary shown in the 18th-century engravings that record the reliquary before its total destruction in the French Revolution (here reproduced as Fig. 11) is said to be an error, on grounds that amount to nothing more than an unwillingness to accept such an arch form as mid-13th century, in Branner, 'Grande-Châsse' (as n. 102), 7. The cupboard function of the recess gave the segmental arch rather obvious practical advantages over a pointed arch.

104. The heavenly connotations of the cloth of honour are evident from the term 'celure' commonly applied to it in the Middle Ages. For dome symbolism, see E. B. Smith, *The Dome: A Study in the History of Ideas* (Princeton NJ 1950). A possible influence on the bed canopy at Westminster is the type of vaulted stone canopy found in a small number of major mid-13th-century English church monuments, most notably those of Archbishop Walter de Grey (d. 1255) at York Minster and Bishop Giles Bridport (d. 1262) at Salisbury Cathedral.

105. Binski, 'English Literary Model of Governance' (as n. 2), 121. For Henry III's desire to be a virtuous king, see n. 82.

106. Ibid., 145. Binski has asserted that the paucity of extant documentation and Henry III's known financial difficulties in the 1260s make it highly unlikely that he undertook a redecoration of the chamber on the scale of that partly recorded in 1819, but this view takes no account of the fact that the extant documentary evidence for the structural repairs after the 1263 fire gives a very incomplete picture of the works that must have been needed. Perhaps Henry was able to make use of 'privy purse' funds that have left behind no documentary traces.

107. Ibid., 152.

108. Ibid., 147; M. Prestwich, *Edward I* (London 1988), 119 and n. 40, 558.

109. Binski, 'English Literary Model of Governance' (as n. 2), 127, 131, 140.

110. The 'yardstick' image comes from Binski, 'Reflections on *La Estoire*' (as n. 80), 333.

111. The inclusion of kings among the damned in representations of the Last Judgement was not new, but for a possible indication of the sort of image that Henry III knew, see that signed by W. de Brailes in Cambridge, Fitzwilliam Museum, MS 330; N. Morgan, *Early Gothic Manuscripts (I) 1190–1250* (London 1982), 118, ill. 238. For discussion of the (possibly invented) story in the *Magna Vita* of St Hugh of Lincoln, in which the saint attempts to teach King John using as a visual aid an otherwise unrecorded sculptured

portal at Fontevrault showing kings in heaven and hell, see L. Grant, 'Naming of Parts. Describing Architecture in the Middle Ages', in *Architecture and Language: Constructing Identity in European Architecture c. 1000-c. 1650*, ed. G. Clarke and P. Crossley (Cambridge 2000), 46–57, at 46–47. For the image of St Peter trampling Nero, see *CPR 1266–72*, 139.

112. Wallace ed., *La Estoire* (as n. 81), 37–39, lines 1279–1350; *The History of Saint Edward* (as n. 81), 70–71; Binski, *Westminster Abbey* (as n. 78), 56 (fig. 71), 144 (fig. 191). Oddly, in a publication not concerned with the Painted Chamber, Binski admits the affinity between the *Estoire*'s account of the downfalls of Godwin and his son and of Harold, and 'the relish for royal downfalls exhibited' in the paintings of the king's great chamber; Binski, 'Reflections on *La Estoire*' (as n. 80), 341.

113. Binski, *Painted Chamber* (as n. 2), pl. Xb.

114. J. R. Maddicott, *Simon de Montfort* (Cambridge 1994), 334–45; Prestwich, *Edward I* (as n. 108), 66–85, 170–201.

115. This error has been disseminated by the rendering of the north elevation in Edward Crocker's drawing (here reproduced as Fig. 3), which is not a record but a reconstruction of what he assumed once existed, on the basis of what he had observed on the other elevations.

116. The hoods of 13th-century fireplaces in important rooms seem always to have projected from the main wall plane, a feature exploited by Henry III, who often ordered them to be decorated with iconographically self-contained schemes of painting. Charles Stothard attributed to the fireplace hood of Henry III's great chamber a series of paintings of the Labours of the Months on blocks used to fill up some of the windows; Rokewode, 'Painted Chamber' (as n. 10), 2.

117. P. Guéranger, *The Liturgical Year* (London/New York n. d.), 6–7. The selection of readings from the specified books was never totally standardized; G. W. H. Lampe and P. R. Ackroyd, *The Cambridge History of the Bible: Volume 2, The West from the Fathers to the Reformation* (Cambridge 1975), 232–33. The readings for October in the late-13th-century manuscripts of the Hyde Abbey Breviary start at the beginning of I Maccabees and extend less than one-third of the way through the book; *The Monastic Breviary of Hyde Abbey, Winchester: Temporale*, ed. J. B. L. Tolhurst, 2 vols, Henry Bradshaw Society 69–70 (London 1931, 1933), II, fols 146r–49v. Perhaps other parts of I Maccabees were read in the refectory at Hyde during October. For references to Bible readings in both choir and refectory, see D. J. Reilly, 'French Romanesque giant Bibles and their English relatives: Blood relatives or adopted children?', *Scriptorium*, 56 (2002), 294–311, at 300.

118. *Jacobi a Voragine Legenda Aurea vulgo Historia Lombardica dicta*, ed. T. Graesse (Leipzig 1850), 1; *The Golden Legend of Jacobus de Voragine*, ed. and trans. G. Ryan and H. Ripperger (New York/London/Toronto 1941), 1.

119. *Golden Legend* (as n. 118), 1, 400–01; Binski, *Painted Chamber* (as n. 2), 95. St Augustine had determined that the Maccabees were martyrs of Christ; R. Ziddé, *Les martyrs Maccabées : de l'histoire juive au culte chrétien. Les homélies de Grégoire de Nazianze et de Jean Chrystostome* (Leiden 2007), 166.

120. Matthew Paris says that it was his custom on the eve of the feasts of the Confessor to fast on bread and water and wear woollen clothes; *Chronica Majora* (as n. 30), V, 47–48.

121. Further examples are the monument raised in the late 13th century over St Elisabeth's burial site at Marburg, whose orientation relates not to the existing church but to its demolished predecessor built in 1231–32, and the Wenceslas Chapel in Prague Cathedral, whose planting over the saint's original burial place made it impossible to lay out the east and south arms of the cathedral in a regular way; A. Köstler, *Die Ausstattung der Marburger Elisabethkirche* (Berlin 1995), 14–20; P. Crossley and Z. Opačić, 'Prague as a New Capital', in *Prague: The Crown of Bohemia 1347-1437*, ed. B. D. Boehm and J. Fajt (New Haven CT/London 2005), 59–73, at 69.

122. Considerable quantities of tin were bought in connection with painting work in the king's chamber in 1265 and 1289 (*Building Accounts* (as n. 20), 398; TNA, E 101/467/19, mem. 3), as well as at later dates. Tin will have appeared prominently in other parts of the chamber, for it was routinely used in the royal residences on the ironwork of windows and doors; for example in 1277–78 (TNA, E 372/121, rotulus 21, dorse) and 1278–79 (TNA, E 101/467/7-7). The brilliant whiteness of refined tin, which was such that its application to ironwork could be described as 'whitening' (*dealbacio*), was presumably in evidence even after it had been gilded. The single mention of 'coloured' tin in 1265 that puzzled Howard Colvin (*Building Accounts*, 398) was probably a reference to the less refined 'blue' tin, and since that material was evidently being used for painting work, there is the possibility that it had been purposely chosen in order to achieve a different effect from that of 'white' tin. For discussions of the use of tin relief decoration in the great chamber of Westminster Palace, see J. M. Nadolny, 'The Techniques and Use of Gilded Relief Decoration by Northern European Painters, c. 1200-1500' (unpublished Ph.D. thesis, Courtauld Institute of Art, University of London, 2000), 219; Howard and Sauerberg, 'Polychrome Techniques' (as n. 47), 303 (fig. 24), 304–05, 307; H. Howard, 'Edmund Crouchback: Technique of the Tomb of a Crusader', in *Westminster Retable* (as n. 101), 319–40, at 334–36, 349 n. 76, 340 nn. 77, 78, 81.

123. Binski, 'English Literary Model of Governance' (as n. 2), 145–46.

124. If we had fuller records than we do of the Old Testament paintings facing the scene of St Edward's coronation, it is likely that they would have shown a rather concerted pattern of balancing the imagery to either side of the window whose embrasures bore images of St Edward with the ring and St John the Evangelist in the guise of a pilgrim. The imagery from IV Kings was all confined to the area to the right of the window, but whatever was their counterweight on the left had vanished by 1819, when the surviving paintings were recorded.

125. A possible indication that the Maccabees scenes in the chamber were conceived before the 1263 fire is that they are iconographically unrelated to the Maccabees illustrations in the *Bibles moralisées* produced for Louis IX in the 1230s, one of which (that known as 'Oxford-Paris-London'), it has been suggested by John Lowden, probably came into Henry III's possession during one of his three visits to Louis in Paris during the period 1254–62; J. Lowden, *The Making of the Bibles Moralisées*, 2 vols (University Park PA 2000), I, 185–86. Lowden's suggestion becomes a virtual certainty when account is taken of the so-far unnoticed imitation in one of the scenes of *La Estoire de Seint Aedward le Rei* of one of the strange asymmetrical two-part canopy types peculiar to the *Bibles moralisées*; *La Estoire* (as n. 38), fol. 8r (http://cudl.lib.cam.ac.uk/view/MS-EE-00003-00059/21 [accessed 16 August 2014]), and A. de Laborde, *Étude sur la Bible moralisée illustrée conservée à Oxford, Paris et Londres*, 5 vols (Paris 1911–27), II, pt 2, pl. 350 (Paris, Bibliothèque nationale de France, MS 11560, fol. 126r). There appear to be no other examples of imitations of the architectural settings in the *Bibles moralisées* by mid-13th-century English artists, but see Wilson, 'Architecture and Ornament' (as n. 54), 87–89.

126. That is virtue not just in the modern sense of the word but also in the medieval sense of supernatural or miraculous power.

'The New Tower at the End of the King's Garden': The Jewel Tower and the Royal Treasure

JEREMY ASHBEE
with an appendix by PAUL EVERSON

In the short time that the building has been open to public view, there has been general acceptance that the Jewel Tower was built in the mid-1360s specifically to store jewels and plate of Edward III's treasure. Documentary and archaeological evidence have concurred that it stood on land seized from Westminster Abbey. This paper contains a review of the immediate setting of the new tower, a revision of its place in medieval administrative history, and a debate around its interpretation as a specially designed treasury.

INTRODUCTION

THE building now called the Jewel Tower is one of four surviving structures of the medieval Palace of Westminster, and is the only part of the Privy Palace to stand above the ground (Fig. 1). These facts alone make the tower nationally and internationally important, reflected by its designation as a Grade I listed building and scheduled ancient monument, and by its inclusion within a World Heritage Site.[1]

This significance does not rest on a long tradition of scholarly study; for most of its existence, the Jewel Tower has been largely unknown to specialists and lay people alike. Built in the most secluded area of the medieval royal palace and seen only by a privileged few, the tower was later absorbed into a sequence of post-medieval building complexes that cocooned the medieval structure and entirely hid it from view. Only in the mid-1950s was the tower finally revealed by the demolition of the adjacent buildings, including the substantial rear ranges of 6 and 7 Old Palace Yard, a stable on the tower's western side, and a cottage and garage for the Prime Minister's chauffeur.[2] The tower, in the guardianship of the Ministry of Works, Public Buildings and Ancient Monuments, was opened to the public in 1956 and interpreted by an official guidebook, written by Arnold J. Taylor (1911–2002), then Assistant Chief Inspector of Ancient Monuments.[3] A few antiquarian and topographical publications had preserved the idea that the stone tower originated as Edward III's jewel-house,[4] but Taylor's guidebook represented the first dedicated treatment in print of the Jewel Tower's history and architecture.

Taylor's interpretation of the tower, particularly the function for which it was built, has been universally accepted. He followed Thomas Frederick Tout, the greatest authority on the medieval royal Wardrobe, in stating that a branch of the organization

Fig. 1. Modern photograph of the Jewel Tower, facing west
English Heritage

called the Privy Wardrobe operated in the Palace of Westminster,[5] and inferred that it was based in the Jewel Tower. Using the evidence of Exchequer accounts and indentures, Taylor evoked the sophistication and richness of the collection, overwhelmingly silver plate, held by the keepers of the king's jewels in the Privy Palace, following this with an unqualified statement that 'the Jewel Tower was the repository from which these items were distributed and into which accessions were received'.[6]

The 1956 guidebook and its 2013 successor contained detailed descriptions of the building, but were by their nature not intended to provide full historical discussion, something that the Jewel Tower has never enjoyed.[7] However, statements about the tower's early history, the individuals and organizations that used it, the circumstances of its construction, and the notion of the building as a specially designed 'strongroom' contain substantial gaps, and rest on assumptions that should not be accepted uncritically. This article sets out a number of issues, some of them still unresolved, that surround the tower's origins, setting and function in the Middle Ages.

THE CONSTRUCTION OF THE JEWEL TOWER

THE Jewel Tower was largely built between the summers of 1365 and 1366. Its construction is well documented in a roll of particulars submitted by the 'clerk and surveyor of the king's works in his palace of Westminster', William Sleaford, and a summary in the Pipe Roll.[8] Sleaford's particulars run from 28 September 1365 to 27 September 1366 and describe work to several buildings of the Palace, including repairs to the shingled roofs of Westminster Hall and the Exchequer, and the construction from scratch of a clock tower at the north end of the complex. The Jewel Tower was another new building, identified as 'the new tower at the end of [or "beside"] the king's garden' ('nova turris ad finem gardini regis'). The account does not describe the start of the tower's construction, which may have taken place slightly earlier, but the building seems to have been largely complete by September 1366. None of the details in the document is irreconcilable with the present structure, although several features are not mentioned, notably the fine tierceron vault over the main room on the ground floor (Fig. 2). The account provides invaluable details about the craftsmen who built the Jewel Tower, and some of the architectural features that have now been lost. The masonry works were directed by Henry Yevele, with Thomas Hardegrey taking an important subsidiary role. (The idea that Yevele designed as well as built the Jewel Tower is certainly plausible, but cannot be confirmed.) William Herland was nominally the leading carpenter and was paid the same wages as Yevele (12d. per day), but his son Hugh was described as 'warden' (*apparillator*), directing the carpentry work. Other figures prominent in the works included Stephen Smith, the carpenter Richard Burnham (who manufactured wooden doors, windows and internal partitions), the glazier John Brampton, and Thomas Bolton (who contracted for the excavation of the moat around three sides of the tower and its connection to an existing ditch running to the Thames). During this year, gardeners under Robert Gardyner made additions to the Palace garden, laying turves and building fences and hedges.

Lost details mentioned in the account include one or more floors of red 'Flanders tiles', 97 square feet of glass windows 'worked with flowers and borders of the king's arms', Reigate stone doors and windows (the largest presumably traceried), and gargoyles in Beer stone. The interiors were relatively plain and were plastered white rather than painted in colours.[9] Master Stephen Smith manufactured iron grilles to protect three large and ten small windows, the ironwork being set in place by the mason Thomas Hardegrey. Among the items carved by the masons during the winter were parapets (*creste*); a sketch of *c.* 1530, the only known depiction of the Jewel Tower before its alteration in the 18th century, shows the Jewel Tower with crenellations.[10]

Fig. 2. Tierceron vault over the main room on the ground floor
English Heritage

THE SETTING OF THE JEWEL TOWER

THE tower's immediate environs were investigated archaeologically by the Ancient Monuments branch of the Ministry of Works in the mid-1950s during the clearance of buildings, when the west and south-east parts of the tower's medieval moat were discovered, and in 1962–63, before construction of the Abingdon Street underground car-park, when the moat excavations were extended.[11] Watching briefs by the Museum of London Archaeology Service, connected with the refurbishment of 6 and 7 Old Palace Yard, followed in 1994 and 1995;[12] other smaller watching briefs have since taken place in and around the building.[13]

The 1963 excavations, directed by Michael Green, revealed a battered ashlar-faced wall running east–west, less than 5 m (16 ft 5 in.) south of the outer edge of the Jewel Tower moat, interpreted as the remains of a south-facing waterfront. This discovery has led to the idea that in the late Middle Ages, the Westminster bank of the Thames contained a broad inlet south of the Privy Palace, with the Abbey precinct wall standing on the foreshore. Green had dated the waterfront's construction to the 13th century, and believed that in the mid-14th century it was reduced in height to form a quay in front of the Jewel Tower moat, but was still washed by the river on its south side.[14] The idea that there was at some stage a waterfront in this position is not in dispute, but there is frustratingly little information about the sequence by which the land to the south was reclaimed from the river.

Excavations have also produced the stone footings of other late medieval buildings close to the tower, including large masonry structures to the north and east.[15] Within the Jewel Tower moat was found a raft of timber piles, interpreted as the supports for a landing stage: this could be reached from within the Jewel Tower garden by a flight of steps running down through the palace's south curtain wall.[16]

Further details of the tower's setting and the circumstances in which it was constructed are provided in the *Liber Niger Quaternus* of Westminster Abbey. The book was only compiled in its present form in the mid-15th century, and its version of events is highly partisan as well as late: some of the details are not to be accepted at face value. However, other sources confirm that it describes a genuine event, a dispute in the 1360s between the keepers of the Privy Palace and the monks of Westminster over a royal encroachment into the Abbey precinct.

The *Liber Niger* includes two consecutive anecdotes about William Usshborne/Husseborne, keeper of the Privy Palace from March 1349 until his death in or before August 1368.[17] The first tells the story of how Usshborne forcibly took from the monks a certain close (*clausum*) and created for the king a garden with a fish-pond. Some time later, around the feast of St Peter ad Vincula (1 August), during a feast with his neighbours, he choked on a portion of a pike from this very fish-pond and immediately died. The chronicler ended the anecdote by interpreting Usshborne's death as divine retribution for his sacrilege in seizing the meadow and garden of the infirmary and the prior of Westminster's garden ('pratum et gardinum infirmarie et similiter gardinum prioris Westmonasterii'). The second tale seemingly refers to the same dispute, and relates how judgement also overtook one of Usshborne's accomplices, a leadworker of Westminster Abbey. While building the garden and a new tower, labourers had disturbed the remains of an ancient chapel containing the lead coffin of a hermit. Usshborne and the leadworker plotted to lift the coffin using its iron rings, dispose of the hermit's bones in the monks' cemetery, and reuse the lead, but as soon as the coffin was delivered into his workshop, the leadworker lost all bodily strength, and forthwith died. This text contains two topographical points of particular interest. Where now stood the king's tower and the small garden adjoining, there had been a path to the convent's water-mill, used by the monks for processions at Rogation and other times. The rubric for this section names the intrusive building as 'Jewel House' ('turri vocato le Jewellhous').[18]

The *Liber Niger* also contains a transcript of Edward III's confirmation of the grant made to the monks in reparation for the loss of their land, with further details about the changes in the 1360s. The confiscated land was now occupied by

a large part of a certain tower in the southern corner of the Privy Palace, together with a small close to the west beside the said tower, within the precinct of the abbey on the soil of Saint Peter [...] Between the said tower and the wall of the infirmary, where now lies the said close, there used to be a footpath and cart-track running as far as the corner of the tower *et cetera*.[19]

Combination of documentary and surviving topographical evidence suggests that around 1365, royal officials seized from the Abbey a rectangular area, around 15 m (49 ft 3 in.) deep and 45 m (147 ft 8 in.) long, mostly carved out of the infirmary precinct. (After 1364, the infirmary was itself being rebuilt and enlarged, and possibly the royal annexation of land was opportunistic, exploiting disruption caused by building works in progress.)[20] Taylor plausibly inferred that the keepers of the Privy Palace needed this land in order to build the new tower without impinging on the existing royal garden.[21] Within the confiscated plot, royal workmen excavated a moat around the north, west and south sides of the tower, extending an existing ditch 9 perches long (45 m) that already delineated the southern boundary of the Privy Palace. The northern limit of the confiscated land was an earlier wall running east–west, originally dividing the monastic cemetery from the infirmary to the south; a stretch of this wall still survives, and is abutted by the later precinct wall that was probably built in the 1370s after the monks and the king had grudgingly settled their dispute (Fig. 3). A thin strip of land around the counter-scarp, and a rectangular area north of the tower constituted 'no-man's land', outside both the Abbey and Palace precincts.[22] The documentary reference to the Abbey's former path and cart-track, probably running south or south-east towards the mill, must describe the approximate line the path had taken before the tower and moat were created. In this context, the excavated footings of a medieval building in the re-entrant angle of the 1370s Abbey precinct wall are of some interest. Clearly added after the tower and moat and provisionally interpreted as a minor gateway in the precinct wall, it perhaps allowed the monks some measure of continued access to their water-mill, skirting the new boundary of the royal Palace, as they had enjoyed before the construction of the Jewel Tower.[23]

THE KING'S JEWELS AND PLATE

THE received interpretation of the Jewel Tower's original function is derived from the work of T. F. Tout, and is most clearly set out in Arnold Taylor's 1956 guidebook

FIG. 3. Reconstruction showing the Jewel Tower and its environs, c. 1500, by Terry Ball, amended by Richard Lea
English Heritage

to the building. In summary, it holds that in the mid-14th century, through the demands of the Hundred Years' War and new requirements for storing gunpowder weapons, the Privy Wardrobe, dealing with the most sensitive royal property, became increasingly specialized as an arms repository and manufactory, and in a process of rationalization, oversaw the removal of other classes of object from its principal base at the Tower of London.[24] One of the new out-stations of the Privy Wardrobe was inside the Palace of Westminster, presumably located there to keep the king's personal jewels and other precious goods close at hand for him to use in the Palace.

Tout gave a brief account of the establishment of the Westminster Wardrobe (without mentioning the Jewel Tower by name) and identified the clerk John Sleaford, keeper of the Privy Wardrobe in the Tower of London, as responsible also for Westminster in 1368.[25] This reading has given rise to the interpretation, followed by Taylor, that jewel-storage at Westminster was administered by the Privy Wardrobe. But the present writer has not been able to substantiate this point, and at the moment it appears that responsibility at Westminster fell not to John Sleaford but to his brother William, who has already been mentioned as clerk and surveyor of the king's works at Westminster (and also at the Tower of London), and who accounted for the construction of the Jewel Tower in 1365–66.[26] Accounts, writs and indentures show that William Sleaford held several other titles in the 1360s and 1370s, including Dean of St Stephen's Chapel, 'keeper of the Wardrobe in the Privy Palace', and most evocatively 'keeper of the jewels and gold and silver vessels in the Palace of Westminster/Privy Palace', but no document identifies him as an official of the Privy Wardrobe.[27] Moreover, while accounts show that there certainly was a building at Westminster called 'Privy Wardrobe', this appears to have been different to the 'tower called the Jewelhouse'.[28]

Identifying the places at Westminster in which William Sleaford kept the jewels and plate (and also textiles and books) is made hazardous by the conventions of jewel accounts. Contemporary and slightly later documents provide much descriptive detail about the objects themselves, usually including their weight and sometimes monetary value, and for obvious reasons they are generally clear in identifying the individuals who were charged with keeping the objects. By contrast, many of these documents are silent about where the items were kept, and even those that do speak of named repositories, such as the 'High Tower' in the Tower of London (White Tower), or the treasury in the cloister of Westminster Abbey (Pyx Chamber), sometimes also list items that were kept in other un-named places. Several highly detailed lists of the objects in William Sleaford's care have survived, and in none of these is a location indicated;[29] Taylor's assumption that many or all were kept in the Jewel Tower is supported by (later) circumstantial evidence, but it must remain an assumption.

What the accounts provide is an evocative description of the objects themselves, and indirectly of activities that the keeper undertook, wherever the items were held. They demonstrate above all that this was by no means a static collection. Items of plate were delivered to William Sleaford from a number of sources, including keepers of the Wardrobe of the Household, and indeed the Privy Wardrobe at the Tower of London (although later documents show that various 'jewels' remained there or were returned to the fortress).[30] Other items were tracked moving out of store, either to be used by the royal household at feasts, or dispensed as royal gifts. On such occasions, men-at-arms might escort these precious consignments to their destinations.[31] One account from the 1400s gives useful details about transport of 'jewels' from 'the tower in the Palace of Westminster assigned for them' by cart to Eltham for Easter, by barge to Windsor for St George's Day, and by cart to Berkhamstead for Whitsun, and receiving them back after use; the account includes payments to porters at Westminster for carrying the goods short distances between the tower and their transport.[32]

The primary duties of the keeper are also made abundantly clear in these accounts: to check the objects for signs of wear and breakage, and, with appropriate warrant, to arrange for goldsmiths to repair them, and to make sure that items were adequately documented, with accurate weights and descriptions of the items, their decoration, and identifying marks of manufacture and ownership.[33]

AN INTERPRETATION OF THE BUILDING

ALL published discussions of the Jewel Tower have accepted, usually implicitly, that the tower was designed and built for the administration and security of precious goods, and that in the Middle Ages these were the only uses to which it was put. However, it has recently been proposed that a dispassionate appraisal of the tower's setting and architectural form might lead to a completely different interpretation.[34]

The Jewel Tower can alternatively be understood as a building designed and built for the king's pleasure and relaxation. Its secluded location at the far end of a walled palace garden, away from the main royal apartments, would be ideal for a banqueting house or summer-house. The fact that it took the form of a *tower*, with a spiral stair rising into a turret standing proud above the leads, would give it additional appeal as a 'prospect tower', with views from the battlements over the palace garden and the garden beside the abbot's mill, south along the River Thames, and west into the Abbey precinct next door. For periods of inclement weather, when access to the roof would be too uncomfortable or dangerous, the tower contained three large glazed windows overlooking the garden; that on the middle floor at least incorporated stone window-seats from which the king and his intimates might contemplate their surroundings in comfort. Association with the garden may also lie behind the iconography of flowers, foliage and birds in the bosses of the ground-floor vault, or the lost stained-glass 'windows worked with flowers'. At times the ground and first floors might be used for informal dining and recreation, the vault and originally moulded fireplaces providing a fittingly sophisticated setting. The top floor, now spartan in its bare stonework but potentially softened with hangings and other furnishings, might even serve as an occasional bed-chamber for the king, his security maintained by iron bars over the windows and two successive wooden doors closing off the room from the stair-well.

The location and general form of the Jewel Tower have close analogues in Tudor garden buildings, such as the brick corner towers at Ashby de la Zouch Castle (Leicestershire), probably built in the 1530s,[35] and similar structures shown by Wyngaerde in the Privy Garden of Hampton Court Palace, from around the same date.[36] There is no doubt that such buildings had medieval antecedents, although standing examples are lacking;[37] documented buildings, several in timber, called 'Pleasance' and 'Spyhouse' existed in the 15th century,[38] and presumably the tall stone tower in a corner of a walled garden illustrating 'April' in the *Très Riches Heures du Duc de Berry* accorded with the same general concept.[39] So too do references such as that for a stair at the Tower of London *c.* 1500, leading up from the garden to a 'round tower where the king was accustomed to take his rest'.[40]

'The New Tower at the End of the King's Garden'

The documentary record allows the possibility that the storage of jewels at Westminster expanded or was transferred into a building conceived and built for a different purpose. Jewels and plate had certainly been kept in the Privy Palace before the tower's construction; William Sleaford himself had been keeper of gold and silver vessels there since November 1361, and must initially have used other buildings, possibly continuing in this manner after the Jewel Tower was built.[41] His building accounts for the tower say nothing about its function, calling it 'the new tower beside/ at the end of the king's garden';[42] letters patent of the 1370s likewise merely speak of the 'tower in the south corner of the Privy Palace'.[43] Only from the 1400s is there a suggestion that the Jewel Tower held the king's valuables, in the account for transporting jewels; even this is not conclusive, since it only states that a tower in the palace, not necessarily this one, was 'assigned' for them.[44] References to the 'tower called Jewelhouse' appear in 1442,[45] and by 1451 one of the palace gardens was named after the 'Jewel House', presumably because it lay close to the building then used for this purpose.[46] Finally, in the second half of the 15th century, the *Liber Niger* mentions the 'tower named *le Jewellhouse*' while chronicling the seizure of land from the monastic infirmary, unquestionably the present Jewel Tower.[47] While the tower may have been used from its earliest days as a strong-room, this cannot be confirmed before the mid-15th century.

That said, features of the building's design favour the traditional interpretation as a treasury. Apart from the large east windows facing toward the Palace, the tower's medieval fenestration was extremely ungenerous; the main room on the ground floor was lit by a single window, that on the first floor by two, and only on the second floor was there a reasonable provision of five windows.[48] Internally the main rooms on the ground and first floors were uncomfortably dark and confined, rather than open to the garden and surroundings, while externally the tower presented to the south and west largely plain slabs of masonry, allowing little encouragement to thieves. The substantial iron grilles that originally covered every window in the tower also suggest a high concern for security,[49] and the water-filled moat was a feature more useful than beautiful, being hidden behind high walls.[50] The duplicated doors of the second floor are credible as protection against a serious risk of theft, similar in intent, if not in thickness, to the portcullis-framed double doors fitted at the Pyx Chamber after the 1303 burglary of the royal treasury (Fig. 4).[51] Admittedly all of these security devices could protect the king against assassins as well as his goods against thieves, but they sit badly with thoughts of the pleasures of the garden. Moreover, as Lesley Milner's researches have demonstrated, the grotesque human and humanoid figures of the two main bosses of the ground floor accord well with sculptural programmes in other medieval treasury buildings, notably those in secular cathedrals such as Lincoln and Exeter. This does not explain all of the motifs in the vault of the Jewel Tower, but it does appear as a distinctive trope in buildings designed for this function.[52]

The interpretation preferred in this paper is that the Jewel Tower was built as a store for the jewels and plate, and as an office for the keeper. Ascription of functions to individual rooms is necessarily an entirely speculative matter, but the character of the ground-floor room, with a large stained-glass window, fireplace, and rib-vault would seem a fittingly impressive setting in which the keeper (an important royal clerk) or his deputies might transact business with other royal officials and with the London goldsmiths who manufactured and repaired the objects. The middle floor, another high room, though ceiled in timber, contained further architectural pretension in its fireplace and window-seats, and probably also served as an office for clerks as

FIG. 4. The main room on the second floor, facing north. The double door made this the most secure space in the tower, suitable for keeping the most valuable items
English Heritage

well as a store. The second floor, with much plainer detailing, and secured by double doors, would be effective as a store, its floor filled with large wooden chests in which the items were secured. Each storey contained a small retiring room with a latrine for the needs of the staff, some of whom may have been lodged in the tower at night. The final point of awkwardness about the interpretation of the Jewel Tower as a treasury is its sole access through the garden of the Privy Palace, where a measure of seclusion might be expected. The comings and goings of the jewel-keeper and his grooms, the porters, men-at-arms, and the goldsmiths delivering goods or taking them away for repair, must have brought considerable activity to wherever the Jewel House was located. But if the royal garden at Westminster was routinely invaded by outsiders, this was hardly unique among royal gardens in the Middle Ages; certainly the documentary evidence from the 15th century suggests that disturbance became institutionalized, with the construction of substantial buildings close to the Jewel House.[53] The provision of stone steps leading down through the south wall of the garden to a landing stage, conceivably an original feature of the 1360s, can be understood as allowing the 'jewels' to be transported away by barge, as much as a facility for the king's pleasure boats (Fig. 5).[54] And finally, the reconstruction of Edward III's itinerary, necessarily a very conjectural matter, suggests that around 1360 the king dramatically reduced the frequency and duration of his stays at Westminster, in

'The New Tower at the End of the King's Garden'

FIG. 5. Reconstruction by Terry Ball, showing the Jewel Tower in the corner of the Privy Palace garden, c. 1400
English Heritage

favour of other local residences such as Windsor and Sheen, a pattern that continued for the rest of the reign, and through much of his grandson's.[55] If this phenomenon was deliberate, the tower's construction around 1365 would make more sense in connection with the king's absences than with his stays, and a centrally located base for the distribution of objects, accessible by barge as well as by cart, is convincing as an interpretation for the tower's original purpose.

CONCLUSION

MUCH of the early story of the Jewel Tower is uncontroversial. Its identification as the only survivor of the Privy Palace, the date of construction and the identification of the craftsmen are not in dispute, and these alone would single it out as a structure of enormous historical significance. Its architecture, apart from the flourish of the ground-floor vault, is less remarkable: the tower is well built but stylistically simple and even utilitarian, and as such would cause problems for Pevsner's famous dichotomy between 'architecture' as embodied by Lincoln Cathedral, and 'building' exemplified by a bicycle shed.[56]

Uncertainty remains over what the tower was designed to do, a problem exacerbated by the (not unappealing) fact that as either a medieval garden building or a treasury, such a survival would be rare, with few or no buildings for comparison. Either it was a sturdily built pleasure pavilion, pressed into a different service when the court's absences from Westminster became too obvious to overlook and the king's gold and silver plate exceeded the capacity of existing stores; or, in the interpretation favoured here, the tower was something altogether stranger, a secure but heavily over-designed garden shed. To accept this would be akin to imagining that 'a star architect, a Richard Rogers or Zaha Hadid, was commissioned to build a strong-room for the national gold reserves, at the bottom of the Chancellor of the Exchequer's garden' (Fig. 6).[57] Strange though this is, the architectural history of medieval England and Europe contains many such oddities, often 'vanity projects' of magnates and ecclesiastics, and when investigating why structures came to be built and what was done with them afterwards, the lens of modern common sense can distort as often as it clarifies.

FIG. 6. Reconstruction by Chris Jones-Jenkins, showing the Jewel Tower from the south-west in the time of William Sleaford
English Heritage

ACKNOWLEDGEMENTS

In researching the Jewel Tower for the 2013 guidebook and re-presentation, I received generous assistance from a number of scholars, notably Jenny Stratford, Marian Campbell, Mark Collins, Lesley Milner, Andrew Thrush and Jane Spooner. At the Westminster conference, I benefitted from hearing the presentation of Christopher Wilson, as a result of which several points of detail were amended, while throughout, Tim Tatton-Brown provided invaluable suggestions and responses. I owe a particular debt for this paper to Paul Everson, who responded to my conference presentation with an intriguing alternative interpretation. This appears beside the 'traditional' version that I continue to favour, but I hope I have left open the possibility of exploring this hypothesis to the greater depth that it undoubtedly deserves.

APPENDIX

'The New Tower at the End of the King's Garden': A Suggestion about the Jewel Tower at Westminster

THIS note reports the main elements of a discussion about the Jewel Tower at and after the British Archaeological Association's 2013 conference at Westminster, in the sort of exchange such conferences seek to provoke but perhaps less commonly do.[58]

Building work on the tower took place in 1365–66, and the structure is identified in contemporary building accounts as 'the new tower beside [or on the edge of] the king's garden' or 'in the angle of the king's Privy Palace'. Received understanding of the building's function was developed by Arnold Taylor and has been restated, following new research, by Jeremy Ashbee.[59] Briefly, it is that the tower was purpose-built as the accommodation for the Privy Wardrobe or treasury of plate and other valuables at Westminster and was occupied through the latter part of the Middle Ages in that role. Subsequent, well-documented uses — to store records of parliament in the 16th to 18th centuries, and as the office of the Board of Trade Standards in the 19th — reflect that original function and continue our understanding of its established character as a building.

The suggestion made here does not question this well-documented and richly textured sequence of use from the mid-15th century onwards. It does, rather, propose — *additionally* to the accepted storyline — that the tower was in fact originally constructed for a different function, namely as a garden building, a sort of pavilion or banqueting house, as indeed its brief characterization at the time of its construction might be thought to imply. That it was converted to other, practical uses in the 15th century is unsurprising, since this was the fate of many royal apartments over time, and such change frequently brought with it a change of nomenclature and new perceptions about appropriate use.

No single fact or reference proves this counter-proposition. Considerations relevant to this view may perhaps helpfully be assembled in several groupings: circumstances surrounding the tower's construction; details of the tower's architecture; and, probably most significantly, its location and context.

Construction

THE circumstances surrounding the acquisition of the site to allow the tower to be built were evidently exceptional. They speak, on one side, of the determination of royal officials to acquire the particular small plot, on the other, of the answering the vehement resentment of the Westminster Abbey community. The latter's record of the death of William Usshborne — the royal official responsible — is cast as divine retribution (or rather more specifically retribution of their patron Peter) for a sacrilegious act. The transaction had multiple consequences. There was a bite taken out of the Abbey precinct, and a re-entrant created that impinged uncomfortably closely on the east end of the Church of St Katherine, the community's infirmary church.[60] The community lost access to a revered hermit's cell, and just possibly, in the context of a royal garden's development, this locale itself may have been a symbolically desirable acquisition. The outflow of the community's main drain was rerouted, evidently to empty into the new stone-lined channel or inlet alongside the Jewel Tower.[61] The Thames foreshore plot next to the south was also acquired as an extension of the Privy Palace, and developed as gardens, whose design required the Westminster Abbey community to move their mill, which stood at the outflow of the Mill Ditch branch of the Tyburn stream. It may be this pleasure ground, called in the royal building accounts 'the king's new garden by the Abbey water-mill', that featured the pond and orchards mentioned in documents.

The Jewel Tower was the most substantial and focal feature in these developments of the amenities of the Privy Palace in the latter part of Edward III's reign, and its siting was at the nub of the antagonism with the monks of Westminster. These circumstances of effort and ill will may be understandable for a building for the direct use and pleasure of the king, but perhaps appear implausible for a building of practical use and accommodating royal officials and servants. Since the monks were compensated for the straightforward loss of land and amenity, it might be thought that the persistent ill feeling had other, non-financial grounds.

Architecture

As built in 1365–36, the Jewel Tower was a stylish and well-appointed structure, and unusual in its L-shaped footprint. The chambers on all three floors were equipped with fireplaces and had access to garderobes, whose facilities were located in the generous secondary spaces of the short arm of the L. The main windows on at least the ground and first floors were originally equipped with window seats, of which only traces now survive, but from which the view was similarly into the king's adjacent privy garden. No doubt these lost windows, on which the lighting of the chambers relied, were quite large and elaborately treated: part of the glazing, at least, featured royal arms and floral patterns. Whereas the lower two chambers had only the one and two windows respectively, concentrating (like many later garden buildings) on inward views to the privy garden, the five windows of the second-floor chamber afforded more light and greater outlook. Great significance has been attached to the double doorway of this second-floor chamber. Evidently an original feature, this arrangement is taken, on the analogy of the double doorway fitted to the Pyx Chapel in the Abbey, as demonstrating that this room was a secure room for storing especially valuable jewels and plate. Its main window also has fittings for internal wooden shutters. Perhaps in the building's suggested alternative function what the room secured was something more valuable than mere plate or jewels, namely the king's person, rest and privacy. The latter-day 'oaks' of Oxbridge colleges — presuming them to be bowdlerized derivates of earlier elite arrangements — offer some sort of analogy for securing privacy through doubled doors.[62] But more significantly the second, outer door at the

Jewel Tower had only two effective positions: one was closed on the room; the alternative was closed on the rising staircase, yoking together the upper room with the roof space and turning the top-most part of the tower into an exclusive suite.[63] As a suite for the king, this arrangement offered the ultimate in seclusion: perhaps the only place the king might be alone. Furthermore, the roof might allow the king to be *seen* to be alone; or in company and intimate conversation with privileged favourites. The two-bay tierceron vault with its suite of sculpted bosses gives the ground-floor chamber a distinct grandeur. Its direct and close analogy (by Yevele's brother Robert in 1361), indeed, is found in work for Edward III in the gateway through the Bloody Tower at the Tower of London, which in turn resembles the vault of the Inner (so-called 'Norman') Gate at Windsor.[64] The vice was generous in scale and formed a distinct northern element of the building. It gave access not only to the three-storey stack of chambers but also to the roof, which afforded privileged views in all directions (see below). This aspect of the tower — irrelevant, even counterproductive, to its supposed function as a secure store — is wholly in keeping with a primary original function as a garden building, affording a unique facility to the king.

The tower was the work of no less skilled a combination than Henry Yevele, master mason, and Hugh Herland, master carpenter. Though this job fell relatively early in his distinguished career, Yevele had been in overall charge of works at both the London royal palaces of Westminster and the Tower since 1360. So we may expect every aspect of the building to fulfil a specific original brief. The question about the tower's architectural form and details is whether they are actually appropriate for a storage and service building or, in their generous scale, stylish detailing, and royal associations, were more probably intended for direct royal use as an adjunct to the privy garden. In particular, the ground-floor chamber might easily have served for the banqueting that in the later Middle Ages was closely associated with gardens.[65] Perhaps the deployment of vaulting was itself thought appropriate, or suitably exotic, in that context.[66] The roof-top vantage recalls the earlier Outlook Tower on the eastern, riverside frontage of the palace, which had given previous monarchs not only a magnificent down-river outlook but also a view over an earlier privy garden there.

Location and context

THE Jewel Tower's location within the contemporary layout of the Privy Palace is not in question. It was situated at the outer, south-west corner of the king's privy garden, whose rectangular plot was defined by a high wall, at least on its south and west sides, with the new 14th-century royal apartments lying to its east. Just that topographical context alone urges that the tower was in its original construction related to the privy garden. The character of the garden itself was an intimate, reserved space, in its nature the most remote space in the Privy Palace, access to which was strictly restricted to the king and his intimates. The tower at its south-west corner afforded the ultimate sanctuary, perhaps for study or as part of the metaphorical construct of the garden as an image of paradise or of the Virgin, or anyway 'for relaxation, contemplation, private discourse, and for enjoyment of the sensuous delights of the garden'.[67] Contrariwise, to envisage routine access to this space by a royal official and his servants may seem implausible. The roof-top viewpoint afforded pleasurable views in a garden context: down into the enclosed privy garden and back east to the royal apartments beyond it, and down over the garden extension or pleasure ground to the south and the upstream reach of the Thames beyond. It offered a locale for the most private conversations, but it also afforded a close, almost intrusive, view into the Abbey complex, with the ancient Church of St Katherine in the near foreground and the sanctuary of the Abbey church — burial place of English kings and shrine of the country's royal saint — bulking large behind.[68] It overlooked, and symbolically oversaw, the Westminster Abbey community, which no doubt contributed to the keen resentment the monks felt about its creation. Such views may have been suitable for royal contemplation and privileged enjoyment; looked at differently, they seem improbable facilities to provide for a royal official and his servants. The L-shaped footprint of the building and the arrangement of its fenestration emphasize, architecturally, its intimate connection with the enclosed privy garden.[69] Even one of the tower's puzzling features — namely the way its outward-facing walls are ashlar-faced, in contrast to the rubble of the faces of the elevations into the privy garden — may indicate that these façades were plastered and decorated with imagery reinforcing the garden context, in the way illuminations show,[70] or just had a refined masonry finish.

Where are the parallels or analogies for this suggested building type in the 14th century? Towers of various forms on the bounds of walled medieval privy gardens can be found in manuscript illumination: in a leaf from the Hours of Louis XII that depicts Bathsheba bathing, in the garden of Gaston Phébus, count of Foix, and in an image of 'Ladies and Gentlemen in a Garden' in the British Library — all late-15th-century works[71] — or in the 15th-century illumination reproduced in the new site guide.[72] Candidate surviving English parallels one might point to are smaller and/or later: the pair of fancy garden towers at Ashby de la Zouch, for example, are thought likely to date to the 1530s — the era when Henry VIII disposed towers prolifically around his gardens at Hampton Court[73] — rather than originating with the 15th-century work that transformed that residence.[74] Was this a new building type of the 16th century? Perhaps the suggestion that the Jewel Tower represents an essentially similar building type, well preserved from the later 14th century, is so novel that parallels and analogies will only emerge in the wake of its recognition. There are hints in the 'overlooking chamber' at Everswell alongside the famous waterworks, cloister and walled orchards there; or in the 'queen's tower' at Clarendon — as yet not surely identified archaeologically, but which clearly stood on the garden side of the royal apartments; or in other instances of apartments of leisure and pleasure, where royal privacy and garden spaces were linked together in a variety of architectural configurations often featuring or evoking a tower.[75] A fuller study might extend, *inter alia*, to towers featuring a stack of chambers and a location adjacent to gardens, with the question whether they might have been other than the routine residential or lodging accommodation they are conventionally taken for.

NOTES

1. List Entry no. 1003580, Old County Number LO55. The Westminster World Heritage Site was inscribed by UNESCO in 1987.
2. TNA, Work 14/2169 and 2170.
3. A. J. Taylor, *The Jewel Tower, Westminster* (London 1956).
4. For example, R. Widmore, *An History of the Church of St. Peter, Westminster, Commonly Called Westminster Abbey* (London 1751), 174; J. T. Smith, *Antiquities of Westminster: The Old Palace; St. Stephen's Chapel ... &c.* (London 1807), 33.

5. T. F. Tout, *Chapters in the Administrative History of England*, 6 vols (Manchester 1930–33), IV (1928), 483.
6. Taylor, *The Jewel Tower* (as n. 3), 9.
7. J. Ashbee, *The Jewel Tower* (London 2013).
8. TNA, E101/472/14; E372/211 rot. 50.
9. Examination of the ground-floor vault in January 2013 revealed no evidence for polychromy, but only white ground over both bosses and ribs. The pupils of the principal northern boss had been painted black. Jane Spooner, personal communication.
10. London, Victoria & Albert Museum, Prints and Drawings, E128-1924. See also Mark Collins's paper in this volume, Fig. 1, 206.
11. H. J. M. Green, 'Excavations of the Palace Defences and Abbey Precinct Wall at Abingdon Street, Westminster, 1963', *JBAA*, 129 (1976), 59–76.
12. C. Thomas, R. Cowie and J. Sidell, *The royal palace, abbey and town of Westminster on Thorney Island: Archaeological Excavations (1991–8) for the London Underground Limited Jubilee Line Extension Project*, MoLAS Monograph 22 (London 2006).
13. MoLAS, 'Proposed Ticket Office, 6–7 Old Palace Yard and the Jewel Tower Garden: Archaeological Impact Assessment and Archaeological Watching Brief Report' (unpublished reports, 2006).
14. Green, 'Excavations of the Palace Defences' (as n. 11), 64.
15. Green, 'Excavations of the Palace Defences' (as n. 11), 67; Thomas, Cowie and Sidell, *The royal palace* (as n. 12), 85, fig. 70. Also prelim Plan B, p. x.
16. Green, 'Excavations of the Palace Defences' (as n. 11), 64. Note that Green interpreted the steps as later than the initial construction of the moat, although alteration in this area is more readily explicable as a development of 1365–66, when an existing curtain wall was extended westwards with the expansion of the garden.
17. *CPR 1348–50* (London 1905), 270; *CPR 1367–70* (London 1913), 326.
18. Westminster Abbey Muniments Book 1, *Liber Niger Quaternus*, fol. 80v.
19. Ibid., fol. 79r. See also *CPR 1370–74* (London 1914), 193, and *CPR 1374–77* (London 1916), 478–79.
20. B. Harvey, *Living and Dying in Medieval England 1100–1540: The Monastic Experience* (Oxford 1993), 88–89, summarizing Westminster Abbey Muniments 19344–75, 19419.
21. Taylor, *The Jewel Tower* (as n. 3), 5.
22. Michael Green reported in 1976 that the curtain wall running north from the Jewel Tower had been observed under the west wall of 6 and 7 Old Palace Yard; Green, 'Excavations of the Palace Defences' (as n. 11), 64, 67 and figs 3 and 4. This is the interpretation followed here, but an alternative reconstruction is to see this stretch as part of the pre-1360s precinct wall, demolished during the confiscation. A strict reading of the *Liber Niger* would place the offending garden and fish-pond in this general area, immediately north of the Jewel Tower.
23. Thomas, Cowie and Sidell, *The royal palace* (as n. 12), 105; photograph of September 1955 in English Heritage Archives, AL1114/140/01 PA.
24. Tout, *Chapters*, 469–72, etc. The argument that arms storage at the Tower of London exceeded capacity has since been refuted; R. Storey, 'The Tower of London and the *Garderobae Armorum*', *Royal Armouries Yearbook*, 3 (1998), 176–83.
25. Tout, *Chapters* (as n. 5), 483.
26. Ibid., 384, 458 n. 2.
27. For example, TNA, E101/400/2 *passim* and E101/401/11.
28. See for example TNA, E101/473/18, fols 3r and 3v, in which both terms appear, presumably denoting different buildings.
29. Ibid., TNA, E364/25 rot. 47A, 48.
30. TNA, E364/25 rot. 48. F. Palgrave ed., *The Antient Kalendars and Inventories of the Treasury of His Majesty's Exchequer*, 3 vols (London 1836), II, 86, gives details of jewels, including coronation regalia, kept at the Tower of London in the early 15th century.
31. For example, TNA, E403/556 m17, containing a reference to five 'personas defensabiles' riding between London and Woodstock while taking jewels to the king there.
32. TNA, E101/404/18 m14.
33. See TNA, E101/401/11 for a writ requiring William Sleaford to account for discrepancies in his record-keeping, resulting from changes to the weights of objects through repairs and reclassification within different parcels.
34. The following paragraph derives entirely from suggestions made by Paul Everson, personal communication, and see below Appendix (p. 199).
35. J. Goodall, *Ashby de la Zouch Castle and Kirby Muxloe Castle* (London 2007), 13–14.

36. S. Thurley, *Hampton Court: A Social and Architectural History* (New Haven CT/London 2003), 92–95. See also the 1570s adaptation of the Swan Tower at Kenilworth, overlooking the castle garden and the mere outside; R. K. Morris, 'The Architectural Setting of the Earl of Leicester's Garden', in *The Elizabethan Garden at Kenilworth Castle*, ed. A. Keay and J. Watkins (London 2013), 21–32, esp. 28–29.

37. H. M. Colvin, 'Royal Gardens in Medieval England', in *Medieval Gardens*, ed. E. B. Macdougall (Washington DC 1986), 7–22, esp. 16–20; O. H. Creighton, *Designs upon the Land* (Woodbridge 2009), 45–99.

38. J. Harvey, *Mediaeval Gardens* (London 1981), 105–06.

39. P. Henderson, *The Tudor House and Garden: Architecture and Landscape in the Sixteenth and Early Seventeenth Centuries* (New Haven CT/London 2005), fig. 198.

40. BL, Egerton MS 2358, fol. 16r.

41. TNA, E364/25 rot. 48.

42. TNA, E372/211 rot. 50; E101/472/14.

43. For example, *CPR 1370–74*, 193.

44. For other towers in the Privy Palace, see for example 'an other towre' in TNA, E310/19/95, no. 68, c. 1560; 'certeyne towres standinge, adioyninge unto the Colledge wall' in John Norden's description of 1592, reproduced in R. B. Rye ed., *England as Seen by Foreigners in the Days of Elizabeth and James the First* (London 1865), 98; Green, 'Excavations of the Palace Defences' (as n. 11), 67. I am indebted to Andrew Thrush for these references, personal communication.

45. TNA, E101/473/18, fol. 3v.

46. TNA, E364/89 rot. Ed.

47. Westminster Abbey, *Liber Niger Quaternus*, fol. 80v, etc.

48. TNA, E101/472/14; see payment for 'iii grossis ferramentis et x ferramentis minoribus pro fenestris camerarum predicte turris iuxta gardinum Regis', confirming the number of medieval windows.

49. Ibid., also including payment to the mason Thomas Hardegrey for fitting the ferramenta over the windows.

50. It is notable that the earlier ditch running along the south side of the Privy Palace had not been maintained, and needed to be cleared out in 1366: it had not previously been a garden feature of any interest. See TNA, E101/472/14. Was it also the (or related to the) abbey's main drain to the Thames from the reredorter?

51. J. Ashbee, 'The Royal Wardrobe and the Chapter House', in *Westminster Abbey Chapter House: the history, art and architecture of 'a chapter house beyond compare*, ed. W. Rodwell and R. Mortimer (London 2010), 112–23, esp. 121; D. W. H. Miles and M. C. Bridge, *The Tree-Ring Dating of the Early Medieval Doors at Westminster Abbey, London,* English Heritage Research Report, 38/2005 (2005).

52. Lecture given at Courtauld Institute of Art colloquium on 6 February 2012, 'Inhabited Spaces: Treasure Rooms in the Cathedrals of Lincoln and Exeter, Westminster Abbey and the Jewel Tower, Westminster Palace', given as part of Lesley Milner's Ph.D. thesis at the Courtauld Institute of Art ('Behind Closed Doors: A Contribution to the Medieval Treasure House (*Domus Thesaurus*) of an English Cathedral').

53. For example, TNA, E364/89 rot. Ed; E364/100 rot. B; Green, 'Excavations of the Palace Defences' (as n. 11), 67. I am indebted to Christopher Wilson, personal communication, for the intriguing reference to the construction in the 1440s of three sheds ('shuddorum') in the 'privy garden of the Privy Palace of Westminster for Eleanor, lately duchess of Gloucester, confined there for various reasons'; TNA, E101/473/18, fol. 2v. The same document (fol. 10r) describes a similarly intrusive stable with solar built within the 'king's garden beside the abbot of Westminster's water-mill'.

54. Green, 'Excavations of the Palace Defences' (as n. 11), 64.

55. S. Priestley, 'The Personal Itinerary of Edward III, 1327–77', unpublished report for English Heritage, (2000); N. Saul, *Richard II* (New Haven CT/London 1997), 468–74. Note however that on occasions the king might still keep 'secret household' at Westminster, though presumably this imposed less demand for jewels and plate than a full court; see for example TNA, E372/210 rot. 48.

56. N. Pevsner, *An Outline of European Architecture* (Harmondsworth 1942), 23.

57. Description provided by Simon Thurley, personal communication.

58. The participants in this exchange have been, to different degrees, Jeremy Ashbee, Christopher Wilson, John McNeill and Tim Tatton-Brown, but it was instigated by Paul Everson, who contributes this note recording a proposition where his is the minority view. The Jewel Tower at Westminster featured in the conference programme in various ways: as a visited building; as the subject of Jeremy Ashbee's paper (published in these transactions); tangentially in Christopher Wilson's account of the elaborate extension of the palace of Westminster southwards, as the 'privatum palatium', in the later 13th and 14th century (similarly published here); and also in a tour of Westminster Abbey's precinct and its walled definition on the east, led by Tim Tatton-Brown, and in his account of the abbey's water supply and its outflow.

59. Taylor, *The Jewel Tower* (as n. 3), 5; Ashbee, *The Jewel Tower* (as n. 7); Ashbee, above. In what follows, the documentation ably set out by Jeremy Ashbee is taken as common ground and not further referenced.

60. See Stuart Harrison and John McNeill in this volume, Part I, 69–103.

61. See Tim Tatton-Brown, this volume, Part I, 1–22 and Fig. 2.

62. *OED*, 'oak', meaning 4c.

63. I owe this observation to conversation with David Stocker.

64. R. A. Brown, H. M. Colvin and A. J. Taylor, *The History of the King's Works: The Middle Ages*, 2 vols (London 1963), II, 726, esp. nn. 6 and 8; TNA, E101/472/9 m3, and E101/472/10 m2 (references supplied by J. Ashbee); J. Goodall, *The English Castle* (London 2011), 286.

65. For example, L. Impelluso, *Gardens in Art* (Los Angeles 2007), 43–44. There was a banqueting house amid gardens in the royal 'Pleasance en Marys' at Kenilworth; see J. Harris, *Medieval Gardens* (London 1981), 106.

66. Christopher Wilson (in discussion) notes that the English secular elite did not favour vaulted spaces in this era. There seem to have been none in the new work at the Palace of Westminster, and Edward III's royal lodging at Windsor contained only one room that was vaulted and which subsequently had a wooden ceiling introduced to make it conform to the norm; see C. Wilson, 'The Royal Lodgings of Edward III at Windsor Castle', in *Windsor: Medieval Archaeology, Art and Architecture of the Thames Valley*, ed. L. Keen and E. Scarff, *BAA Trans.*, XXV (Leeds 2002), 15–94.

67. P. Henderson, *The Tudor House and Garden* (New Haven CT/London 2005), 73.

68. As Terry Ball's reconstruction painting elegantly conveys; Taylor, *Jewel Tower* (as n. 3), back cover.

69. See, similarly, Terry Ball's effective reconstruction painting; Taylor, *Jewel Tower* (as n. 3), 6.

70. For example, Impelluso, *Gardens in Art* (as n. 66), 126.

71. Jean Bourdichon, Leaf from the Hours of Louis XII, Tours, 1498–99 (J. P. Getty Museum Los Angeles, MS 79, recto); Master of the Soane Josephus, *Jean Froissart's Chronicles*, Bruges, *c.* 1480–83 (ibid., MS Ludwig XIII 7, fol. 9): illustrated in B. C. Keene, *Gardens of the Renaissance* (Los Angeles 2013), 50–51, 60–61; Impelluso, *Gardens in Art* (as n. 66), 26.

72. Ashbee, *The Jewel Tower* (as n 7), 9–11; Impelluso, *Gardens in Art* (as n. 66), 28–29.

73. Henderson, *The Tudor House and Garden* (as n. 69), 76–79 (for Hampton Court), and 167–77 (more generally for the established tradition of towers, lodges and secret houses, of which many 16th- and 17th-century examples can be documented).

74. Goodall, *Ashby de la Zouch Castle and Kirby Muxloe Castle* (as n. 36); S. Newsome, M. Canti, J. Leary, L. Martin and P. Pattison, *Ashby-de-la-Zouch Castle, Leicestershire: A Multi-Disciplinary Investigation of the Castle Garden*, English Heritage Research Department Report Series 52-2008, 38–43.

75. *King's Works* (as n. 65), II, 1015–16; T. B. James and A. M. Robinson, *Clarendon Palace*, Society of Antiquaries Research Report XLV (London 1988), 21–22 (documentary), 99–104 (archaeology); T. B. James and C. Gerrard, *Clarendon: Landscape of Kings* (Macclesfield 2007), 70–73; J. Ashbee, '"The Chamber called Gloriette": living at leisure in thirteenth- and fourteenth-century castles', *JBAA*, 157 (2004), 17–40.

The Topography of the Old Palace of Westminster, 1510–1834

MARK COLLINS

The medieval Palace of Westminster existed on the same site from at least the 11th century and developed to become the principal residence of the English monarchs until c. 1531, after which the Palace became the home of the legislature. The site was occupied by the Exchequer and the Law Courts as well as by both Houses of Parliament. The buildings underwent numerous transformations from the Reformation onwards before fire destroyed many of them in 1834.

INTRODUCTION

THE arrival of the Tudors at the Palace of Westminster marked its zenith in terms of size and magnificence. Something of its splendour may be appreciated in an image of about 1530 (Fig. 1, a composite of two halves of a drawing that at some time was cut in half and is now separated between two museums). This shows the clock tower to the right, with the long roof ridge (and louvre) of Westminster Hall to the left of the clock; then St Stephen's Chapel in the centre, projecting to the front of the view, with the Lesser or Household Hall to the left; and next, the dog-leg of the Painted Chamber, Queen's Chamber, and what was probably the Queen's Chapel (later known as the Prince's Chamber). The cloister of the College of St Stephen is hidden from view to the north of the chapel, but the top of the bell tower is visible at its north-west corner.[1]

The 14th-century buildings that still stood at the Dissolution appear in the foreground near the river, namely, the two White Chambers, the Green Chamber, the chapel of Edward III, and, on the far left, tall crenellated towers.[2] No information has survived for the substantial towers on the left of the drawing, which stood between the landing stage and the moat that led east from the Jewel Tower into the Thames. The length of the river front was about 900 ft, similar to the length of the present, Victorian, Palace, and altogether the Palace used to cover six acres. Two engravings by Wenceslaus Hollar (1607–77) also provide an overview of the main features of what later became known as New Palace Yard (Figs 2 and 3): the king's entrance or High Gate is seen top right, and in front of it the tall, canopied, octagonal 15th-century fountain known as the Great Conduit.[3] Westminster Hall was still host to the four courts: the King's Bench and Chancery on the dais at the southern end, the Common Pleas by the west wall, and the Exchequer through a doorway in the north-west corner. The Exchequer offices remained in their accommodation to the north-east of Westminster Hall.

Although in the early 16th century Westminster was still the centre of court ceremony and administration and was the most significant royal residence adjacent to

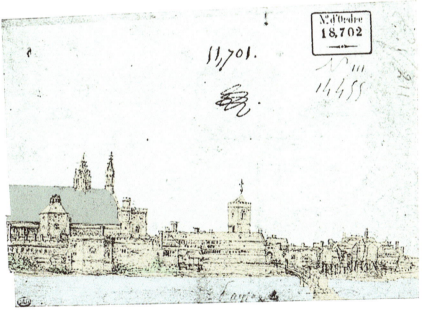

Fig. 1. Two sections of a single drawing now entitled *Westminster Abbey and Parliament House, from the Thames*, c. 1515–32 (Victoria & Albert Museum, acc. no. E 128-1924) and *Vue de Londres avec Westminster Hall et les édifices environnants* (Musée du Louvre, INV 18702, verso). The drawing, perhaps by Lucas Cornelis de Kock (1495–1552), was split at some time prior to 1750; the two pieces are now in different institutions. The colour is a recent addition by Jeremy Ashbee and Richard Lea.

Fig. 2. *Sala Regalis cum Curia West-monasterij, vulgo Westminster hadl*, 1647, engraving by Wenceslaus Hollar
Palace of Westminster Collection, WOA 681

The Topography of the Old Palace of Westminster, 1510–1834

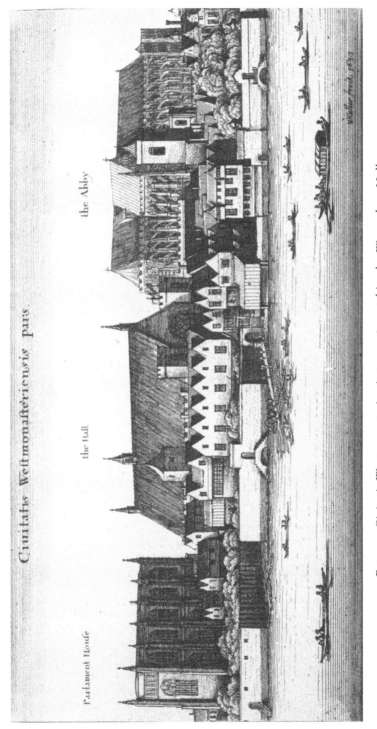

FIG. 3. *Civitatis Westmonasteriensis pars*, 1647, etching by Wenceslaus Hollar
Palace of Westminster Collection, WOA 845

the capital at that time, some of the most important events of Henry VII's and Henry VIII's reigns took place not at Westminster, but at the new Tudor palaces of Richmond and Greenwich. Nevertheless, lavish celebrations continued to be staged at Westminster. In February 1511, a tournament was held to celebrate the birth at Richmond of Henry, son and heir of Henry VIII. The elaborate pageantry took place in New Palace Yard and cost nearly £4,400 — the most expensive celebration of Henry VIII's reign with the exception of the Field of Cloth of Gold. On the second day, after evensong and a banquet, entertainment was provided in the White or Lesser Hall, with songs, dancing, and a pageant.[4]

THE FIRE OF 1512/13

IN 1512, Parliament sat at Westminster, and in June an allegorical tournament was held, with the king taking part in the jousting. (Such allegorical pageantry was abandoned after this occasion.) Then, in late 1512 or early 1513, 'a great part of this Palace of Westminster was once againe burnt [...]' as Stow put it, 'Since which time it hath not been reedified; onely the great Hall, with the offices near adioyning, are kept in good reparations, and serveth as afore'.[5] This fire effectively brought to an end the 500-year long association of the monarchy as a domestic entity with the Palace of Westminster. Although the main chambers survived, some of the privy buildings appear to have been too badly damaged for the court to continue on the site. Henry VIII moved out, and the royal family never returned, except for occasional ceremonial events.

What exactly was lost in this fire? We have no record, but certainly Westminster Hall and St Stephen's Chapel were not seriously affected, nor it would seem was the Painted Chamber, for the 14th-century wooden roofs of the former, and the 13th-century wooden roof of the latter survived. Maybe the Lesser Hall, the Queen's Hall, or the Great Kitchen to the west were damaged, but in any case the fire acted as the catalyst for the departure of the king.

Henry built accommodation in the Tower of London for court officials who had lost their premises in the fire, whilst he himself spent a good proportion of his time at Greenwich Palace. The site at Westminster was given over to Parliament, to the Law Courts, and the Exchequer, and here the legislature operated in increasingly inconvenient, albeit picturesque buildings for a further 320 years. The Palace was developed for administrative purposes; for example, the royal court no longer required the household hall, so the Court of Requests began to sit in the Lesser Hall in 1516.[6] In the following year, work took place 'lengthening and making of the Sterre Chamber', with further work undertaken to this range soon afterwards.[7]

The principal 16th-century contribution at the Palace was undoubtedly a rebuilding of a 14th-century structure belonging to the College of St Stephen — an institution that had continued with a separate life of its own, even after the fire and the departure of the royal family — that is, the two-storey cloister, built around 1520. The earlier cloister had been constructed by Edward III to the north of the chapel and to the east of Westminster Hall; immediately to the east of the cloister stood the vicars' houses. This new cloister was similar in its high quality and architectural importance to its later 14th-century brother cloister at Windsor Castle (where Thomas Wolsey [1475?–1530] was a canon 1511–14), and also that to be found at Old St Paul's Cathedral (until it was destroyed by the Great Fire of 1666). The St Paul's structure was double-height in form, built in the 1330s by William de Ramsey III, with a chapter-house and chapel projecting into the courtyard.[8] The layout appears to have been repeated at Westminster and leads one to speculate that this cloister also was by William de Ramsey.

In early 1514, Wolsey became dean of St Stephen's College; he then stepped down from this role and became archbishop of York later in the same year. The replacement cloister was built in the late Perpendicular style soon after 1514, during the early years of the last dean of the college, Dr John Chambre (1470–1549), physician to Henry VIII (Fig. 4).[9] The master mason was almost certainly William Vertue (d. 1527), assisted by Henry Redman.[10] Vertue was also probably responsible for both the high vault of Henry VII's Chapel at Westminster Abbey (1506–09), and the high nave and chancel vaults of St George's Chapel, Windsor Castle. The ground-storey south walkway was originally an open colonnade, each of the archways onto the inner courtyard being about 10 ft wide. The lower fan-vaulted walkways were provided with bosses that

FIG. 4. *View of the Speaker's Cloister and Oratory*, 1834, G. Hawkins, lithograph (after the fire of October 1834)
Palace of Westminster Collection, WOA 34c

featured emblems of the Passion, fleurs-de-lis, and portcullises for the Beaufort family (Henry VII's mother), together with the arms of Edward the Confessor, Edward III, England ancient, Henry VIII and his first queen (Catherine of Aragon), and Thomas Wolsey. The projecting bay at Westminster houses a lower chapel with a delicate vault and an upper chapel with small canopied niches between the windows (Fig. 5). On becoming archbishop of York, Wolsey developed the accommodation at his official Westminster residence by the Thames known as York Place (later Whitehall Palace). Then, in January 1515, Wolsey began Hampton Court, and it was he who became the principal patron of significant secular architectural projects rather than the king; he was made cardinal in September of the same year and, in December, Lord High Chancellor. So Wolsey prospered until his fall from grace in 1529, when he gave up the Great Seal after failing to obtain Henry's divorce from Catherine.

After the fire, when Henry required a residence near Westminster and London, he stayed at Lambeth Palace with William Warham (c. 1450–1532), the archbishop of Canterbury.[11] This arrangement stood for ten years until his new palace of Bridewell was complete in 1522; Cardinal Wolsey's fall from favour in 1529 then released magnificent accommodation of a scale and quality worthy of Henry and his court. York Place, which Wolsey had greatly extended and rebuilt, became free for appropriation by the king, even though it belonged to the archdiocese. Between 1530 and 1532, the king began to make ambitious improvements to York Place: he spent over £8,000 in the first year, spurred on by a desire to provide accommodation for Anne Boleyn. Henry's chief surveyors, Thomas Heritage and Thomas Alvard, were ordered to demolish 'some porcions' of the Old Palace of Westminster, and the materials were carted away to help to form the new buildings at York Place. In addition, the royal mews at Charing Cross and the old manor at Kennington were to be 'pulled down, overthrown and made prostrate' for the same purpose. A record was made to show that Ralf Williams was paid 'for devising and making of engijnes for the overthrowing of the walls of the king's olde Palace of Westminster'. He was paid £4 to demolish 'a Toure of stone and bricke at the king's place within his paleis'. Over 3,000 cartloads of 'olde stone, bricks, & chaulke' were taken away north along King Street to provide rubble for the walls at the New Palace.[12] In 1532, Henry acquired a further property nearby, this time from Eton College, namely the hospital and convent of St James the Less, which he rebuilt. He then took land from Westminster Abbey to make a park between this new Palace of St James and York Place, the latter renamed his New Palace of Westminster. Henry also acquired Hampton Court from Wolsey in this year; he spent more money on Hampton Court and Greenwich than on any other of his palaces.

In 1536, after reconstruction of the two new palaces was complete, the king passed an Act of Parliament to annexe both York Place and St James's Palace and the acreage between them to the Old Palace of Westminster: 'the said parke, shall be from hensforth the Kynge's hole Paleys at Westminster'. The Old Palace, the Act states, had long been 'in utter ruine and decaye', and it was declared to be 'only as a member and parcel' of York Place.[13] Although theoretically part of the same complex, the Old and the New Palace of Westminster were physically separated by the west–east wall of the Wool Staple (replaced by Bridge Street in the mid-18th century, which adjoined the north–south run of Cannon Row), and further north by Lamb Alley.[14] Along Lamb Alley Henry VIII built a boundary wall, south of the large new orchard of York Place, approximately where Richmond Terrace, originally a row of houses built in the

FIG. 5. *Lower Chapel of Cloister of the College of St Stephen*, 1795, engraving by James Basire, from Topham and Englefield, *Some Account of the Collegiate Chapel of St Stephen* (as n. 69), pl. XIV
Palace of Westminster Collection, WOA 1847

early 19th century, stands to this day. The dean's and canons' houses belonging to St Stephen's College remained on the south-east side of Cannon Row, which itself could be entered from King Street by way of St Stephen's Alley. Soon, the name 'Whitehall' was given to Henry's new property, and, as the legislature began to take it over, the Old Palace alone maintained the title 'Westminster'.

Demolitions continued at Westminster throughout the 1530s and 1540s: the Privy Palace with chambers for the king's squires, the queen's ladies in waiting, the keeper of the Privy Seal, and some noblemen all disappeared; removed by 1550 were the Antioch Chamber (built by Henry III, its precise site unknown) and the Marculf Chamber (near the Painted Chamber and next to the river, also built by Henry III and used for the touching for the king's evil);[15] and the two chambers of Edward III south of the southern landing stage (the 'Queen's Bridge') along with the Chapel of St John the Evangelist (whereabouts uncertain) all disappeared. Also demolished was the whole of the Prince of Wales's palace, which probably stood to the west of the Lesser Hall, near the wall of the Abbey, a part of the complex that seems never to have been recorded. The walls of the Green Chamber of Edward I, and the most easterly of the two White Chambers of Edward II apparently survived into the early 19th century, albeit within later buildings (Prelim Plan B, p. x).[16] The southern extent of the Palace was marked by a lane later known as Parliament Place, which led down to the 'Queen's Bridge', later known as the Parliament Stairs. Much further south was a channel from the Tyburn that must have been used to power the Abbey mill and to clear offal from the Palace slaughterhouse built adjacent to it, visible in Norden's 1593 bird's-eye view.[17] Notwithstanding the destruction of so much of the fabric, the upkeep of the surviving sections of the Palace was taken in hand. Structures were repaired in 1535 with the 'ripping, lathing and new tiling not only the Star Chamber, the Council Chamber of examination, the Duchy Chamber, the Dining Chamber, but also the gallery going to the said Duchy Chamber and over the Receipt'; all these buildings were in the vicinity of the north-east corner of Westminster Hall.[18]

When meeting at Westminster before the fire of 1512, usually in the Painted Chamber, Parliament opened with the king in residence. After the fire, however, with the king now at his new Palace of Whitehall or elsewhere, the connection between the monarch's place of residence and Parliament was severed. Henceforth, the king would journey from Whitehall to the Palace of Westminster, where his presence would be limited to the opening and closing of Parliament. In 1536 occurred the first opening of Parliament in what became known as the 'Parliament Chamber', formerly the Queen's Chamber.[19]

THE DISSOLUTION

THE year 1536 saw the Act of Parliament to suppress the lesser monasteries, and in order to process the considerable changes in ownership of lands and property engendered by the first stages of the Dissolution new courts of law were built near Westminster Hall: the courts of Augmentations (1536), First Fruits and Tenths (1540), Wards and Liveries (1540), and Surveyors (1542).[20] The Court of Augmentations was built on the site of the offices of the auditors of foreign accounts, which once stood between the Exchequer, north-west of Westminster Hall, and the Inner Gateway; this new court fronted New Palace Yard with a narrow, full-height bay and an octagonal stair turret (Fig. 6).[21]

Fig. 6. *View of the South Side of the Augmentation Office*, 1793, watercolour by W. Capon
Palace of Westminster Collection, WOA 6923

Henry VIII died on 29 January 1547. Further major legislation in 1547–48 would lead the church closer to the Reformation. The collegiate foundation of St Stephen was vested in the Crown following the suppression of free colleges and chapels (the Dissolution of the Colleges Act).[22] The site and other buildings of the college were mostly granted to Sir Ralph Fane (or Vane, d. 1552), but Edward VI gave permission for St Stephen's Chapel to be especially reserved for use as the debating chamber for the House of Commons when it assembled in Parliament. Prior to that date, the Commons had met for its Westminster sittings in either the refectory (demolished 1544) or the chapter-house at the Abbey nearby.[23] Parliament gradually thereby assumed more control of the Westminster Palace site, and for the first time the Commons had a fixed meeting place.[24] The first such meetings took place in St Stephen's in 1548, 1549 or 1550. The extraordinary change of use for and secularization of the chapel,[25] perhaps the finest royal chapel in the country, emphasized not only the ascendancy of State over Church, but also the increasingly aloof position of the monarch with regard to Parliament.

The two rows of choir stalls facing one another were at once used by the opposing sides of Parliament without alteration to the ecclesiastical layout, thus instituting the traditional plan of the Commons' Chamber down to the present time (Fig. 18). The medieval wall-paintings were covered by wooden panelling behind the seating, and whitewash might have covered some of the stonework of the walls above. The stained

FIG. 7. Court of Exchequer, interior: *Representation of the Ceremony of Presenting the Sheriffs of London*, M. Whichello, 1811
Palace of Westminster Collection, WOA 923

glass was replaced with plain leaded lights, whilst a lower tier of the east window was fitted with opening casements for ventilation. Small, apparently original statues were left in place on the east wall however, and if a false ceiling was not installed, some of the old coloured decoration may well have remained visible at high level.[26] The later Tudors either rebuilt or modified the old institutions on the site. Under Elizabeth, expensive new buildings for the Exchequer were constructed. A new Exchequer Chamber was built in 1565–67, the name corrupted over time to become 'Queen Elizabeth's Chamber', or 'Bedchamber'. It stood between the Court of Augmentations of 1537–38 and the north-west corner of Westminster Hall. The Court of Exchequer (Fig. 7) was rebuilt in 1569–70 with walls of diapered brickwork, but leaving much of its 13th-century stone origins intact (Jansen, Fig. 9, 101).[27] At about this time, the buildings once occupied by the College of St Stephen on the east side of Westminster Hall were also taken over by the Exchequer. The cloister and the adjoining former vicars' houses were taken over as the residences of the auditor and tellers of the Exchequer.[28] In 1599–1602, the Star Chamber range overlooking the river to the east and dating from the time of Henry VIII and earlier was partially reconstructed in brick to form the five-gabled range that served as the eastern boundary of New Palace Yard (Fig. 8).[29] The range was connected at its northern extremity to the Water Gate,

The Topography of the Old Palace of Westminster, 1510–1834

FIG. 8. *Buildings on the Eastern side of New Palace Yard*, W. M. Fellows after J. T. Smith, 1808, from *Sixty-two additional plates to Smith's Antiquities of Westminster* (as n. 73)
Palace of Westminster Collection, WOA 2983

which led to the King's Bridge, or paved and boarded landing stage for the king's boat. As though to emphasize the increasingly public nature of the buildings, in 1551 the moat at the southern boundary of the site (that once extended from the Jewel Tower to the River Thames frontage) was filled in.[30] It was perhaps dammed off from the river, like the moat at the Tower of London. 'The College Sewer' from the Abbey flowed into the river further south.[31]

THE GUNPOWDER PLOT

ALL the principal medieval buildings that survived at the southern end of the Palace were double height with undercrofts below (Fig. 1), but with no cellars, that is, St Stephen's Chapel, the Lesser Hall, the Painted Chamber, the Queen's Chamber, and the Prince's Chamber (Figs 9 and 10). The most low-lying building appears to have been the vaulted late-13th-century undercroft of St Stephen's. The lack of security at the undercroft beneath the House of Lords' Chamber (in the former Queen's Chamber)

Fig. 9. *The Painted Chamber, Westminster*, T. Whichillo, 1804, from *Select Views of London and its Environs* (London 1804)
Palace of Westminster Collection, WOA 6276

led to the Gunpowder Plot's almost successful attempt on the life of the king and those in Parliament. Robert Catesby (1573–1605) and fellow conspirators decided to blow up the House of Lords at the State Opening of Parliament in 1605. At first, they tried secretly to break through the lower walls of the chamber, but they were too thick, so they rented the undercroft beneath it, and placed here, at ground level, thirty-six barrels of gunpowder disguised by piles of wood (Fig. 11). Guy Fawkes (bap. 1570, d. 1606) was captured in the early hours of 5 November, and he and three other conspirators were sentenced to hanging, drawing and quartering in Old Palace Yard nearby; the others met a similar end in St Paul's Churchyard.[32]

Hidden away next to these packed undercrofts were 'Heaven' and 'Purgatory', two taverns popular in the 16th, 17th and early 18th centuries, situated west of the Lesser Hall, whose origins were connected with two other ale houses, called 'Hell' and 'Paradise', to the north, near the Court of Exchequer. 'Hell' and 'Purgatory' were once debtors' prisons.[33]

FIG. 10. *North-East views of the old House of Lords, the Prince's Chamber, 1807*, and *South East views of the Princes Chamber and the old House of Lords, 1809*, J. T. Smith, etchings, from *Sixty-two additional plates to Smith's Antiquities of Westminster* (as n. 73)
Palace of Westminster Collection, WOA 4796

FIG. 11. *Views of the four sides of a Cellar under the old House of Lords . . .* , etching by J. T. Smith, 1804, from *Antiquities of Westminster* (as n. 73)
Palace of Westminster Collection, WOA 1905

In 1621, the architect Inigo Jones became an MP, and he was asked to help with increasing the seating in St Stephen's. In the summer recess of that year, his design for a new gallery at the lower end of the chamber was implemented to help ease congestion in the main body of the House.[34] Then, in 1623–24, immediately following his design for the Banqueting House at Whitehall, Jones was asked to provide a barrel-vaulted ceiling of wood and plaster in the Lords' Chamber. The ceiling was based on a segment of the 4th-century *trompe l'œil* mosaic vault in the north ambulatory at S. Costanza in Rome, a design that had already been used for the ceiling of the chapel of St James's Palace in 1540.[35] The early 17th century also saw the establishment of the great library of the antiquary and MP Sir Robert Bruce Cotton, Baronet (1571–1631) at his private house;[36] the collection contained two original copies of Magna Carta. Cotton House stood between the south side of the House of Commons, or 'Parliament House' as it became known, and the Painted Chamber. Its private garden stretched eastwards down to the river, and access was provided by a passage running at ground level from Old Palace Yard and under the Lesser Hall.[37]

PARLIAMENT AND COMMONWEALTH

IN January 1649, the High Court met in the Painted Chamber to try and convict King Charles I of treason and his death warrant was signed, probably also in the Painted Chamber.[38] The court then proceeded a few days later to Westminster Hall, which had been fitted up for the king's trial (Fig. 12). (Charles I stayed at Sir Robert Cotton's house during the trial.) On 27 January he was sentenced to death, and executed outside the Banqueting House in Whitehall three days later. The monarchy and the House of Lords were abolished, and the Commonwealth was declared. Little actual damage was done to the Palace during the Civil War; Oliver Cromwell himself moved into Whitehall Palace, not Westminster,[39] but he undertook his second installation, as Lord Protector, in June 1657 in Westminster Hall using the Coronation Chair, removed from Westminster Abbey for the purpose and put on a dais at the southern end of the hall 'under a prince-like canopy of state'.[40] The Palace of Westminster was neglected, and sometime between 1658–60 — just before the Restoration — the Great Conduit in New Palace Yard was demolished; fortunately, it had been depicted by Hollar a few years prior to this in his engraving of New Palace Yard.[41] Coffee houses began to be built around the north door of Westminster Hall, and from 1659, political meetings were held by the Rota Club at the Turk's Head, sometimes called Mile's Coffee House, adjacent to the King's Stairs in New Palace Yard (Fig. 13).[42]

THE RESTORATION

FOR the coronation of Charles II in 1661, following the Restoration, a substantial new dais with a front wall was built in Westminster Hall, and the destruction of Henry III's mid-13th-century Purbeck marble table, which still apparently stood on the old dais, was carried out unceremoniously (Figs 14 and 15).[43] By now, the table was no longer revered as a stone symbol of the permanence of kingly power and the development of the English law: it was smashed, and broken pieces of it were used as rubble in the new wall. Fragments of the gently Gothic-arched trestles were discovered in the remaining footings of this wall and retrieved from it during repair works in 1960, and more fragments were excavated in 2006, after which they were reassembled for display (Fig. 16).[44] In either 1661 or 1680, a door had been cut in the centre of the

FIG. 12. *Trial of Charles I, Westminster Hall*, from J. Nalson, *A True Copy of the Journal of the High Court of Justice for the Trial of K. Charles I* (London 1684)
Palace of Westminster Collection, WOA 7166

The Topography of the Old Palace of Westminster, 1510–1834

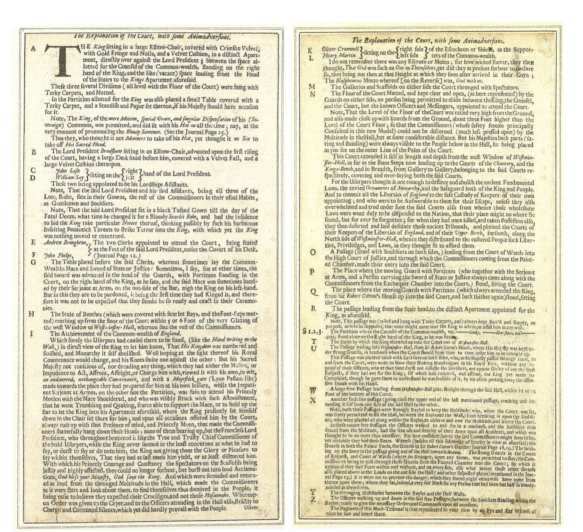

FIG. 12. (Continued)

south wall of Westminster Hall leading into the Court of Wards, meaning that by this time the 13th-century marble throne had also been removed, its whereabouts now unknown.[45] This central doorway then became one of two entrances to Wren's staircase to the House of Commons, the other being from the north-east corner of Old Palace Yard (Fig. 17). The courts of King's Bench and Chancery continued to sit on the dais on either side of the doorway and the steps leading to it. The old doorway to the Commons' Chamber, situated in the east wall immediately in front of this dais, then fell into disuse and was blocked up around 1800. In order to facilitate the passage of the Commons to meetings between both houses, which were held in the Painted Chamber, the Long Gallery was built in 1678, running to the Painted Chamber from the Commons' Chamber, parallel with and to the east of the Lesser Hall.[46]

During the Commonwealth, the Commons' Chamber in St Stephen's Chapel had been used rarely and had not been maintained. By January 1692, urgent repairs were required, and the Surveyor General, Sir Christopher Wren (1632–1723), who was concerned about the safety of the roof of the old chapel, removed the roof and also took away the early-14th-century wooden vault and clerestory together with the exterior flying buttresses. In the body of the chapel below, Wren created a Classical debating chamber with a new, lower false ceiling, wainscoting, and bench seating (Fig. 18).[47] The three eastern bays contained the debating chamber and the two western bays housed the lobby of the House. Three small round-headed arched windows in the east wall, and six small windows on each of the north and south walls replaced the Gothic traceried windows. A narrow passage was constructed below these windows on the exterior to provide north–south access without crossing the chamber itself. Inside, galleries provided extra seating on the long sides and, across the west wall, a place for 'Strangers', or visitors. Two iron columns, probably the first ever manufactured in Europe, supported the west gallery.[48] The medieval wall-paintings remained hidden, covered now by the new wainscoting. In order to accommodate the additional MPs occasioned by the Acts of Union of Scotland with England in 1707, the side galleries were widened. The lack of decent ventilation in the chamber following Wren's alterations was to annoy members throughout the rest of the life of the building.[49]

Elsewhere, more of the medieval fabric began to be eroded or neglected. In 1698 William III gave Edward III a clock tower in New Palace Yard to the parish of St Margaret, and on their order Wren demolished it in the same year.[50] The great gateway in the north-west corner of New Palace Yard (known as the King's Gate, or 'High Gate' of Richard II) was removed in 1706.[51] Also in 1706, 'by the Queen's order', Wren demolished Edward III's clock tower in New Palace Yard. The Cotton Library was removed first to Essex House on the Strand in 1712, because of the dilapidated state of Cotton House, and then in 1730 to Ashburnham House at Westminster Abbey, where it was partially damaged by fire the following year.[52] Cotton House was partially taken down in 1724 and then ordered to be demolished in 1737; the house for the Clerk of the House of Commons was built on its site.[53] The Small Gate across St Margaret's Lane was demolished in 1728 to allow passage of the king. In 1734, attention was drawn to the 'slovenly' appearance of the courts of law in Westminster Hall, and, as a final indignity perpetrated on the medieval buildings, in 1740 the hall roof was examined and found to be in such a bad state that the hammer-beams had to be supported by substantial wooden props.[54] One development of the earlier buildings took place in contrast to this destruction: in 1722–25, a clerestory of Diocletian windows was added to heighten the walls of the Court of Requests, formerly the Lesser Hall (Fig. 19).

The Topography of the Old Palace of Westminster, 1510–1834

FIG. 13. *New Palace Yard*, J. Boydell, c. 1770
Palace of Westminster Collection, WOA 323

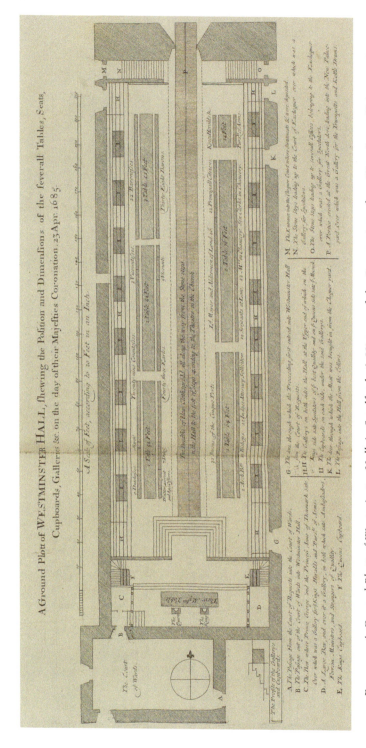

FIG. 14.   *A Ground Plott of Westminster Hall*, in Sandford, *A History of the Coronation of … King James II* (as n. 43)
Parliamentary Archives

FIG. 15. A Prospect of the inside of Westminster Hall, James II's coronation banquet, S. Moore, in Sandford, *A History of the Coronation of ... King James II* (as n. 43)
Palace of Westminster Collection, WOA

DESIGNS FOR A NEW PARLIAMENT

ALL this dilapidation must have been seen as a tempting call to action by the architects in charge at the Board of Works; Christopher Wren was the first to take a fresh look at the whole site of the Palace when he produced designs for a new Parliament building. Whitehall Palace burnt down in January 1698, and William III commissioned a new building. Wren's Parliament was to have been little more than an adjunct to a large new Whitehall Palace and would have been joined to it on the south-west by a long gallery. The Old Palace of Westminster would have been pulled down, except for Westminster Hall, and the Abbey would have been denuded of all its surrounding ancient buildings, including the cloisters, chapter-house, and St Margaret's Church. Parliament would have formed a square block directly opposite the north door of Westminster Hall, on the site of Cannon Row, but the completion of Hampton Court and Kensington Palace at this time prevented the work from being undertaken.[55]

Subsequently, it was announced that Richard Boyle, 3rd earl of Burlington (1694–1753) would design a new Parliament, but no plans were forthcoming, and in the end

Fig. 16. The King's High Table reassembled, *c.* 1250, with a replica trestle and conjectured top section in the background made in 2007

Photograph by Nick White (2012) © Parliamentary Estates Directorate Archive

it was William Kent (1685–1748) — albeit evidently in alliance with Burlington — who produced a scheme in 1732, the final plans for which were submitted to the Lords of Treasury in 1739 (Fig. 20). St Stephen's Chapel was to have been retained, but the bulk of the new buildings would have been Palladian. The new Parliament would have cost £167,067, but nothing was done, probably because of the war with Spain. All Kent managed to do in his lifetime was to create the 'Strawberry Gothick' enclosures to house the courts of the King's Bench and Chancery in 1739.[56] A year later, the Court of Common Pleas was moved outside the hall to the west. Following his death, Kent's designs for a new Parliament were realized in part by his disciples who still carried the flame of Kentian Palladianism. Under the supervision of the architects John Vardy (1718–65) and Kenton Couse (1721–90), the 'New Stone Building', as it was called, was built in two phases between 1755 and 1770 to the west of Westminster Hall, first on Exchequer Yard and then to the south on Fish Yard (Fig. 21). The crowded accommodation contained the King's Bench Record Office together with the Exchequer, Remembrances, Pipe, Augmentations and Tally offices, and committee rooms for the Commons. During the second half of the 17th century, the Exchequer offices were gradually removed from the Palace to the west side of Whitehall and renamed the Treasury, and in 1733, Kent produced designs for a new Treasury building overlooking Horse Guards Parade.

Limits were placed on the siting of any new palace when, in 1736, the Westminster Bridge Commissioners were created under an Act for building a bridge across the Thames immediately to the north of the medieval site of the King's Bridge, which had

The Topography of the Old Palace of Westminster, 1510–1834

FIG. 17. *The First Day of Term*: Westminster Hall, 1758, coloured line engraving by H.-F. Gravelot
Palace of Westminster Collection, WOA 673

by the 18th century become known as Westminster Stairs, and after the bridge was built in 1750, was known as Westminster Bridge Stairs.[57] The approaches to New Palace Yard were transformed; Bridge Street, Parliament Street, and Union Street were constructed on the old Wool Staple and site of its Weigh House; and large new terraces of houses were built. In 1786, the Treasury established His Majesty's Stationery Office in the north-east corner of New Palace Yard overlooking the river and bridge. Around Cannon Row, new streets were laid out where the canons' houses had stood; Bridge Court, Manchester Buildings, Derby Street and, farther north, timber yards occupied the river bank. The Transport Office was built in Cannon Row in 1816,

FIG. 18. *The House of Commons in Session*, 1709, P. Tillemans, oil on canvas
Palace of Westminster Collection, WOA 2737

afterwards taken over by the Board of Control for Indian Affairs.[58] To the south, in Old Palace Yard, houses may either have been refaced in the 18th century (for example, numbers 1–5 on the west side) or built anew (such as the terraces in Abingdon Street).[59] The demolition of the Clerk of the Parliament's house and the construction of 6 and 7 Old Palace Yard in 1754–56 (which still stand) was designed to provide

The Topography of the Old Palace of Westminster, 1510–1834

FIG. 19. *The House of Lords as the Court of Requests*, W. Heath
Palace of Westminster Collection, WOA 2542

FIG. 20. *Front to the Old Palace Yard*, Kent's design of c. 1739 for the new Houses of Parliament, from a drawing dated c. 1830
Palace of Westminster Collection, WOA 51

two houses behind a single Palladian front, one for the Clerk of the Parliaments, the other for the Clerk Assistant.[60] The designer was almost certainly Isaac Ware (1704–66), one of a group of architects attached to the Office of Works, who were followers of Lord Burlington and William Kent.[61] Adjoining the rear of the building stood the Parliament Office, which was connected by a single-storey block to the adjacent 14th-century Jewel Tower, which was used to contain the records, including Acts of Parliament.[62]

The next architect to make a speculative design for a new Houses of Parliament was James Adam (1732–94) in 1760–62, followed by the civil engineer and architect John Gwynn (1713–86), who in 1766 also suggested a great Classical structure.[63] Around the time of the American Declaration of Independence, both an anonymous writer as well as the architect John Soane (1753–1837) proposed constructing a British Senate House to replace the old buildings.[64]

In 1780, the Gordon Riots broke out, and the mob tried to enter both houses of Parliament while they were sitting. Anti-war protests and food riots took place in Westminster, and the king's carriage was attacked at the State Opening of Parliament in 1795. William Pitt banned mass meetings around the Palace, and calls were made for improvements to security and to the Palace, firstly with a report by a committee and fourteen architects on the poor accommodation for Parliament. They wrote: 'The Danger from Fire [...] surpasses any Language of which they are Masters'.[65]

FIG. 21. *View of Westminster Hall, Law Courts etc. from the North West*, 1835, C. Burton after S. Russell
Palace of Westminster Collection, WOA 1420

JAMES WYATT

COMMITTEES were set up to improve the approaches to the site of the Palace, whilst the Lords demanded fresher air in their chamber. As one of three 'attached architects' at the reorganized Board of Works, with personal responsibility for Whitehall, Westminster, and so on, John Soane also entered the fray in 1794, when he was asked to provide plans for a new House of Lords.[66] Soane in fact made Classical designs for both houses, and these were presented to George III, but the state of the country at the time prevented their execution. The king preferred the architecture of James Wyatt (1746–1813), who became Surveyor General and Comptroller of the Office of Works on the death of Sir William Chambers in 1796.[67] Soane's buildings were deferred when Wyatt replaced him at Westminster.

By now, the Gothic idiom was becoming more acceptable and began to appear alongside the prevailing Neoclassicism. Wyatt stated that he wanted 'the whole [palace] [...] to assume the appearance of a large Gothic edifice'.[68] From the 1790s, the first serious attempts were made to record the medieval architectural remains of the Palace, firstly by the antiquary John Carter (1748–1817), who made his survey plan in 1791–92, and then by Carter and John Topham (1746–1803), in *Some account of the Collegiate Chapel of St Stephen*.[69] In 1828, the architect and draughtsman William Capon (1757–1827) produced an invaluable coloured plan of the ground floor of the buildings drawn from surveys made between 1793 and 1823.[70] The appointment of James Wyatt as Surveyor General, however, marked the beginning of an unhappy phase in the fate of the medieval fabric, which caused an unfortunate spat between the antiquaries and the architect. In 1799, Wyatt undertook new buildings for

Commons' offices overlooking Old Palace Yard, and in August 1800, the enlargement of the Commons' Chamber in St Stephen's Chapel ready to accommodate the increased number of MPs because of the forthcoming Acts of Union with Ireland. Wyatt decided to narrow the walls by cutting them back on the inside, thus destroying the remaining 14th-century wall-paintings.[71] This activity caused the altercation with the antiquaries, and most vociferous of these was John Carter, who had attacked Wyatt's work in several articles printed in *The Gentleman's Magazine* after 1789. In 1796, following the criticism by Carter and others, Wyatt failed to be elected to the Society of Antiquaries; out of spite, Wyatt hindered Carter whilst he and his friend William Capon tried to record the paintings discovered in St Stephen's in 1800;[72] similarly, Wyatt denied full access to J. T. Smith (1766–1833), another antiquary working at Westminster at this time. Nevertheless, the wall-paintings found so unexpectedly were much admired, and gave rise to Smith's invaluable book *Antiquities of Westminster*.[73] Smith's book provided more details of the painted surfaces than the record made by Richard Smirke (1778–1815), the official artist for the Society of Antiquaries, arriving as he did too late to make a fuller set of drawings.[74]

Wyatt had planned new buildings for the whole of Parliament in the Gothic style, but not all were carried out; only Speaker's House (1802–08) (Figs 22 and 23) and the Old Palace Yard offices (1805–07) were constructed, at a cost of over £200,000. Speaker's House was on the site that before 1794 housed the auditor of the Exchequer; it was entered from New Palace Yard via St Stephen's Court, later known as Speaker's Court.[75] On the east of this courtyard stood the Receipt of the Exchequer, which from the early 19th century was used as the site for the house of the Clerk Assistant. The residence of the Speaker was built to the north and east of the 16th-century cloister, whilst the cloister itself was occupied by his servants' rooms, which were partitioned from one another by lath and plaster walls. The courtyard lost the dignity of its status, and was filled with a large shed-like kitchen. Part of the ground storey of the projecting bay was converted into a scullery, whilst chimneys, sinks and cupboards were cut into its windows and walls.[76] The Speaker's new staircase replaced the 14th-century bell-tower of St Stephen, which was demolished in 1802 (Fig. 24).[77] Wyatt built a long façade for the house onto the garden and the river and 'Gothicized' the mutilated east window of the former St Stephen's Chapel to match the style of this new domestic range. The Speaker's state dining room occupied the two eastern bays of the undercroft chapel and was known as the 'Grotto Room'.[78] The buildings for Commons' offices added by Wyatt in Old Palace Yard were in such a debased 'Carpenter's Gothic' style that, during debate in the House of Commons they were compared with a prison and even with a gentlemen's lavatory (Fig. 25).[79] The wine merchant John Bellamy owned premises on the northern part of the site of Wyatt's range. From 1773, Bellamy, as deputy housekeeper, provided simple food and drink for Members as a private business; his son continued the venture into the 19th century. Nearby were taverns and coffee houses, such as Alice's Coffee House and Waghorn's Coffee House.

Wyatt's work both here and at the Office of Works was judged to be so poor that he had to abandon further projects; he did, however, undertake two small repairs and alterations in the Palace. Firstly, in 1801 when more room was needed with the arrival of 100 Irish peers, Wyatt moved the House of Lords to the Court of Requests, or Lesser Hall. Secondly, in 1805, the decision was made to remove the 18th-century buildings from the north end of Westminster Hall. Carter had written: 'Away with these usurping excrescences, of sheds, hovels, taverns, and alehouses that blot out and

The Topography of the Old Palace of Westminster, 1510–1834

FIG. 22. *The Speaker's House from the river*, after Wyatt, c. 1802
Palace of Westminster Collection, WOA 1980-1-M

disfigure the walls of old English splendour and old English hospitality!'.[80] Wyatt removed the later buildings in 1807 — two coffee houses known as the Exchequer and Oliver's — and carried out minor repairs to the north front. Eight of Richard II's 14th-century statues, depicting kings and queens, remained in the lower tier of niches, although some were in a badly mutilated state.[81] To the east, the northern end of the Exchequer Office range — marked by three gables — was demolished in 1808, along with the Water Gate leading to the King's Bridge.

Meanwhile, the Westminster Improvements Commission spent over £250,000 on the surrounding area.[82] Slums to the north of the Abbey and the Sanctuary were cleared; St Margaret's Street was widened; and buildings on the latter's west side, such as the old Ordnance Office, were removed to form a new enclosed garden, which was later developed by E. M. Barry (1830–80) to form Parliament Square. The demolitions were so extensive that the area was called the 'Great Desert of Westminster' (Fig. 26).[83]

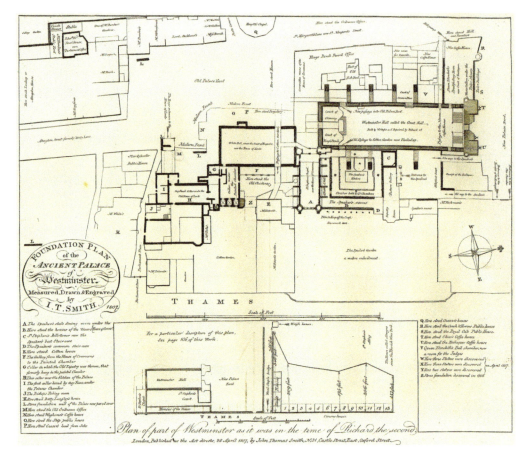

FIG. 23. *Foundation Plan of the Ancient Palace of Westminster. Measured, Drawn and Engraved by J. T. Smith*, published 25 April 1807, from *Antiquities of Westminster* (as n. 73)
Parliamentary Estates Directorate Archive

JOHN SOANE

THE Office of Works was reorganized on the death of Wyatt in 1813. John Soane took over as one of three attached architects for Whitehall and Westminster; the others were Robert Smirke and John Nash. Soane's first annual survey for the Office of Works in 1816 reported on the poor and dangerous conditions of the structures and the likelihood of fire at any time, and stated that the north front of Westminster Hall was in 'a most dangerous state of dilapidation'. He also recommended that the Royal Entrance should be remodelled.[84]

In 1819, Soane restored the Painted Chamber by providing a new roof and plaster ceiling to match the 13th-century original, which had become unsafe, and he exposed the medieval wall-paintings that had been discovered in the window reveals in 1799.[85] Edward Crocker II (*c.* 1757–1836), clerk of the works at the Palace 1818–29, was in

The Topography of the Old Palace of Westminster, 1510–1834

FIG. 24. *Painted Chamber and Bell Tower of Cloister*, 1805, J. T. Smith, from *Antiquities of Westminster* (as n. 73)
Palace of Westminster Collection, WOA 199

Fig. 25. *View of the House of Lords and Commons from Old Palace Yard*, c. 1820, Robert Havell (the Elder) and Robert Havell (the Younger)
Palace of Westminster Collection, WOA 1085

charge of the restoration and converted the room into the Court of Claims (Fig. 27). Crocker made watercolours of the wall-paintings that had been uncovered, including those of the coronation of St Edward and the Virtues and Vices.[86] Furthermore, Charles Alfred Stothard (1786–1821) was asked by the Society of Antiquaries to make watercolours depicting these paintings before they were plastered over later in the same year.[87] Soane rebuilt in Bath Stone the north front of Westminster Hall to the 14th-century design, and, in an early instance of conservation-standard repair, he promised to 'strictly adhere to the original style of architecture, wherever the same is practicable'.[88] Soane replaced the vault over the porch, which had long been missing, and could not resist providing more elaboration to the carving of the canopies above the statue niches. The master-mason was Thomas Gayfere (1775–1827), who had carried out a careful repair of Henry VII's Chapel at the Abbey 1807–22 — surprisingly careful, considering that it was carried out under the supervision of Wyatt.[89] Soane's work on the hall began in 1819 and was completed in 1823; the cost was nearly £27,000.[90] The eight remaining mutilated 14th-century statues depicting kings and queens were removed from the lower tier of niches and disappeared.[91] Soane also undertook repairs to the hammer-beam roof: the truss at the northernmost end — left

The Topography of the Old Palace of Westminster, 1510–1834

FIG. 26. *Westminster Hall, St Margaret's, Westminster Abbey*, 1826, watercolour by A. C. Pugin
Palace of Westminster Collection, WOA 6373

FIG. 27. *The Court of Claims in the Painted Chamber*, 1821, S. W. Reynolds
Palace of Westminster Collection, WOA 922

unfinished during the medieval construction — finally was completed, and ships' timbers were used to repair others.[92] Windows were made along the lower part of each of the two slopes of the roof, and the decayed medieval louvre was replaced with a near replica made from cast iron. The cost of all these roof repairs was about £4,000.[93]

GEORGE IV AND SOANE

IN January 1820, George IV (1762–1830) acceded to the throne, heralding a new phase of substantial change at the Old Palace.[94] Custom dictated that the Court of King's Bench and the Court of Chancery be removed from the southern dais of Westminster Hall in preparation for the coronation banquet.[95] Following the banquet, these courts were banished at the command of the Prime Minister, Lord Liverpool, because he 'was so struck with the grand effect of that unique edifice'. In 1821, Soane designed seven new law courts to replace those removed, and they were built to fit between the west face of the hall and the New Stone Building, following removal of the Court of Exchequer.[96] Soane created a Palladian façade adjacent to the north front of the hall, but members of a Commons' select committee did not like it — it was said to present the 'Bad taste of the present age' — and it was demolished in 1824.[97] It was immediately rebuilt to a new Soane design in the Gothic style to harmonize with the late-14th-century entrance to Westminster Hall (Fig. 21).[98] Inside the hall, four new doors were cut through the west wall to serve the long single passage leading to the new courts. The elegant Greco-Gothic interiors survived until 1883, when the courts were demolished and their function was transferred to the newly opened Royal Courts of Justice on the Strand.[99]

After the departure of the king from the Palace of Westminster in the 16th century, the monarch was required to travel there from one of the newer palaces, such as St James or Whitehall; the royal progress to open Parliament was consequently neither very ceremonial, nor even particularly convenient or salubrious. New Palace Yard was no longer used as the king's entrance, because the northern end of the complex was taken over by the Commons and the law courts. An entrance for the king had been constructed at the south-east end of Old Palace Yard, near to where the House of Lords' Chamber stood, but the yard was never able to accommodate the full sweep of a coach and four, so an ignominious exit had to be made down the narrow route to the south called Dirty Lane, today the much wider Abingdon Street (Fig. 28). The royal entrance, ingloriously located next to a public house called the Star and Garter, had been a modest and unassuming affair, little more than a wooden lych-gate of the kind to be found at a country churchyard.[100] The gate led to a simple covered staircase, and the king walked up one flight to the robing room housed in the Prince's Chamber. Once robed and wearing the Imperial State Crown, the king then walked directly through a door to the throne in the House of Lords. The accepted route for the monarch lasted for 250 years in this form, until arrangements were devised to be more fitting for a newly influential nation, and to satisfy George IV's taste for show.

George IV commissioned a new Royal Entrance in February 1822.[101] Substantial reforms to the layout of the old entrance were carried out by Soane, who prepared designs to make it, as he said, 'more commodious'.[102] A 'Scala Regia' or king's staircase would replace the insignificant gateway, and a Royal Gallery would provide a dignified route to the Lords' Chamber (Fig. 29). The Scala Regia was similar to the principal entrance stair at the Vatican known by the same name, designed by Bernini

The Topography of the Old Palace of Westminster, 1510–1834

FIG. 28. *View of Old Palace Yard*, c. 1700, anon.
Palace of Westminster Collection, WOA 6263

FIG. 29. *The Arrival of Her Gracious Majesty Queen Victoria*: the Royal Gallery at the State Opening of Parliament in 1837, G. Baxter
Palace of Westminster Collection, WOA 1850

and built 1663–66. To carry out his scheme, Soane demolished in 1823 both the old House of Lords, formerly the Queen's Chamber, and the Prince's Chamber.[103] The new Royal Entrance was completed on 1 February 1824 after work continued night and day.[104]

Soane's new route included places in the Royal Gallery for invited guests, who were given both raised seating and standing room in front — the first time this had occurred at a State Opening or Closing (Prorogation). None of the spectacle inside had been seen by the general public before this time. The Scala Regia niches were to have contained statues of medieval kings and the Royal Gallery was to have contained large paintings of the battles of Trafalgar and Waterloo, although they were never executed.[105] In 1826–27, Soane provided libraries for both Houses — Gothic outside, but with some Soanian classicizing inside — together with five new Commons' committee rooms. Again Soane warned of the danger of fire, and in 1831 and 1833 parliamentary select committees chaired by the MP Joseph Hume (1777–1855) examined whether a new Parliament should be built on a different site.[106] J. W. Croker, MP 1780–1857, said that the current accommodation was 'a series of narrow dark, tortuous passages'.[107] In 1831, James Wyatt's eldest son, Benjamin Dean Wyatt (1775–1855) was instructed to replan the House of Commons completely.[108] Jeffry Wyattville (1766–1840), James Wyatt's nephew and one of fourteen architects who contributed to the final report, also supplied lithographed designs. One chamber was on a semicircular plan based on the Continental model.[109] The committees suggested that as none of the proposed alterations could improve the situation, a new House of Commons should be built. The Treasury was unwilling to foot the bill, and no new Parliament building was forthcoming.

ROBERT SMIRKE

IN 1834, Robert Smirke reported on the condition of the interior of Westminster Hall, and in 1834–36 he and carried out repairs to the stonework; the roof had been repaired only a few years previously, so there was no need for further work there. Smirke replaced the floor, at the same time lowering it to return it to approximately the level established by Richard II.[110] The new paving consisted of over 500 massive York stone slabs; he renewed all the interior wall-facings with 6 in.-deep ashlar of Huddlestone stone, a pale magnesian limestone from Yorkshire and similar to the Marr stone used in the original corbels, and so on. Much tracery from the windows, about 95% of the original Reigate stone cornice below them displaying Richard II's white harts and helms, and the corbels depicting the royal arms and those of the Confessor were replaced 'in exact correspondence with the original work'.[111]

THE FIRE OF 1834

THE work had only just begun when it was interrupted in a most spectacular fashion. On 16 October 1834, the long-anticipated disaster struck, when the Old Palace was badly damaged by an accidental fire that continued throughout the night.[112] Almost two-thirds of the buildings were burnt out, and it was said that Hume's motion had been passed without a division (Figs 30 and 31).[113] By remarkable chance, the two architects who came to be inextricably linked with the site, Charles Barry (1795–1860) and Augustus Welby Pugin (1812–52), both began their association with the rebuilding of the Palace of Westminster on the night of the fire. Each man stood by — albeit in separate locations and unaware of the other's presence — to watch the flames engulf the buildings both old and new. With undisguised pleasure, Pugin noted to a friend the destruction of the recent Classical work, and the feeble 'Gothick' additions:

There is nothing much to regret, and a great deal to rejoice in. A vast quantity of Soane's mixtures and Wyatt's heresies have been effectually consigned to oblivion. Oh it was a glorious sight to see his composition mullions and cement pinnacles and battlements flying and cracking [...] The old walls stood triumphantly amidst this scene of ruin while brick walls and framed sashes, slate roofs etc. fell faster than a pack of cards.[114]

Happily, important structures remained unharmed, including Westminster Hall; the fan-vaulting of the cloister (although parts of the upper galleries were gutted); the lower chapel of St Stephen's (Fig. 32); and John Soane's royal processional rooms. Nor were the latter demolished immediately to make way for the new building, because they continued to be used by Queen Victoria for the first few years whilst the New Palace was under construction.[115] The outer walls of some of the buildings were left intact, such as those of the House of Lords (or Lesser Hall) and the Painted

MARK COLLINS

Chamber, and these two rooms were roofed in by Robert Smirke to provide temporary accommodation for the House of Commons and House of Lords respectively. The work was completed in February 1835 ready for the State Opening of Parliament.[116] In the same month, Smirke provided the designs for a New Palace that had been requested of him, and they were even approved by the king before an outcry forced a competition to be held instead.

The old site itself was reused, because the ancient *genius loci*, including Westminster Hall and St Stephen's, excited such feelings of national pride in the continuity of Parliament's long history. The other ruined medieval and later buildings were then removed piecemeal with that overflowing confidence and *sang froid* of the early Victorians, but not without protests from the antiquaries. On the east side of New Palace Yard, the Exchequer Office and Star Chamber, undamaged by the fire, were pulled down early in 1836; the apparently unstable walls of St Stephen's Chapel were taken down in the summer of 1837,[117] and the remaining Exchequer offices on the east side of St Stephen's Court were removed at the same time. A long new granite river wall was constructed some 60 ft out into the river to the east of, and parallel with the old wall of the gardens, and the site was then gradually prepared for the construction in stages of Charles Barry's immense New Palace. To provide a solid foundation, a 9 ft-thick raft of concrete was laid, except in the courtyards of the new building, thereby destroying much of the surviving below-ground archaeology. The first stone was laid in April 1840, and the old Speaker's House was demolished in 1842 as the new building rose in front of it.[118] Once the New Palace interiors were sufficiently prepared for business, the Painted Chamber could be demolished — in about 1847 — then the Lesser Hall in September and October 1851. Later in the same year, Soane's Royal Entrance, Royal Gallery, Library and Parliament Office also disappeared.

Both Westminster Hall, which had come through the fire unscathed, together with the site of the upper St Stephen's Chapel, became entrance halls to the New Palace; the lower chapel of St Stephen's was restored to form once again a place of worship — the Chapel of St Mary Undercroft — and the repaired cloister housed an MPs' cloakroom on the ground floor with offices above.[119]

Then, following the fire, the topographers Edward Brayley (1773–1854) and John Britton (1771–1857) wrote the book that became the swan-song of the medieval buildings: *The History of the Ancient Palace and Late Houses of Parliament at Westminster*, published in 1836.[120] Thomas Chawner and Henry Rhodes's pre-fire plan — made immediately before the destruction — informed the topographical detail. The book was given added poignancy by the draughtsman and architect R. W. Billings (1813–1874), who illustrated it with drawings showing the damaged buildings.[121]

APPENDIX

Surviving Fragments from the Medieval
Palace of Westminster, Now Dispersed

CHESHIRE

Leasowe Castle, near Wallasey, Wirral

Star Chamber encadrement and possibly other fragments from the Palace removed to his country house by General the Hon. Sir Edward Cust, 1st Baronet (1794–1878), MP 1818–32, military historian, and later Comptroller of the Household to Queen Victoria. The Star Chamber range

The Topography of the Old Palace of Westminster, 1510–1834

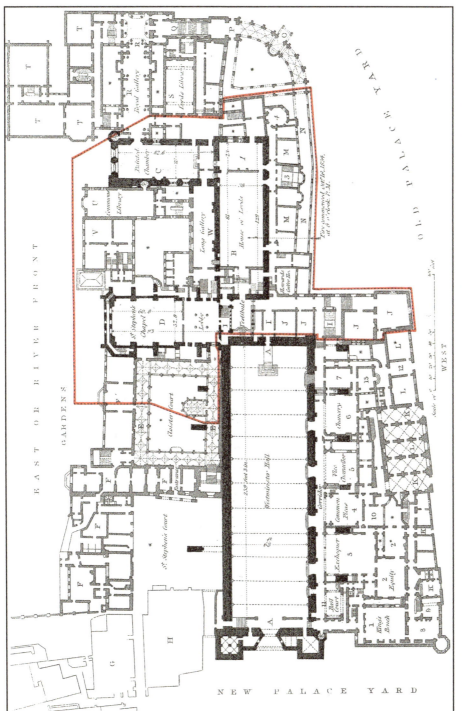

Fig. 30. *Parliamentary & Other Offices, Courts, &c. Westminster.* Drawn by R. W. Billings, from materials in the office of Woods and Forests. Plate II (principal floor plan) from Brayley and Britton, *History of the Ancient Palace and Late Houses of Parliament* (as n. 45). The area within the red line shows the extent of the fire of 16 October 1834, which effectively destroyed the historic centre of the Palace of Westminster

Parliamentary Estates Directorate Archive

MARK COLLINS

Brayley and Britton key
A.A.   The Great Hall [Westminster Hall].
B   The Old Court of Requests [1801–34: House of Lords; 1835–51: House of Commons] (1 The King's Robing Room; 2 Lobby; 3 Stairs; 4 Lord Chancellor's Room).
C   The Painted Chamber, fitted up for the House of Lords in 1834–5. [1835–47: House of Lords].
D   St Stephen's Chapel, late the House of Commons. [House of Commons: 1547–1834]
E.E.   The Cloister, attached to the same.
F.F.F.   The Speaker's House.
G   Part of the offices of the Exchequer.
H   Houses of John Rickman, Esq. Clerk Assistant of the House of Commons and Wm. Godwin, Esq. Author of the "Life of Chaucer", &c. [an honorary official of the Exchequer].
I.I.   Stairs to the House of Commons.
J.J.   Committee Rooms.
K.K.   The Judges' Entrances to the respective Law Courts which are numbered on the Plan in the following order: [see below].
L.L.   Grand Inquest Jury Rooms.
L.*   Library of the Masters in Chancery
M.M.   Committee Rooms to the House of Lords.
N.N.   Arcade to the House of Lords.
O   The King's Entrance Porch.
P   Entrance to the King's Staircase, which is at Q.
[Q   King's Staircase]
R.R.   The Royal Gallery.
S   Library of the House of Lords.
T.T.T.   Parliament Offices.
U   Library of the House of Commons.
V   House of the Clerk of the House of Commons [Mr. Ley].
W   Long Gallery.
**   Open courts.

Law Courts:
1   Court of King's Bench
2   Court of Equity
3   Court of Exchequer
4   Court of Common Pleas
5   Vice Chancellor's Court
6   High Court of Chancery
7   Lord Chancellor's retiring room
8   Judges' retiring room
9   Attendants' waiting room
10   Barons' retiring room
11   Bail Court
12   The Lord Chancellor's entrance
13   Attendants [an explanation of 13 was omitted from original key]

FIG. 31.   *Panorama of the Old Palace of Westminster*, 1834, G. Scharf
Palace of Westminster Collection, WOA 3793

was demolished early in 1836, and Cust bought the stone fireplace and wooden over-mantel, and perhaps the plaster ceiling depicting portcullises, fleur-de-lis, roses and pomegranates, together with panelling. The over-mantel and panelling were later transferred to Windsor Castle, where they remain in room no. 280, formerly called the Equerries' Writing Room (given to George V in 1913 by Cust's grandson, Commander Sir Charles Leopold Cust, 3rd Baronet (1864–1931)).[122] The stone fireplace and ceiling remain at Leasowe. Also in this house is a column or newel-post that appears to be that which until *c.* 1835 stood at the foot of the staircase in the north-east corner of Westminster Hall leading up to the offices of the Receipt of the Exchequer. The column seems to have been reused as the newel on the ground floor of the staircase at Leasowe.

KENT

Ingress Abbey, Greenhithe

A celebrated 19th-century lawyer, James Harmer (1777–1853), acquired some unidentified stone remnants of the Old Palace, and, in a letter of 25 June 1841, he proposed their use in the alteration of his Elizabethan revival house, which he had built in 1833: 'I have many fragments of stone architecture from the old House of parliament [*sic*] that will come in very appropriately'. Although this house still exists, the alteration was either never built, or it has been removed. A folly of 1833 known as 'The Grange' in the grounds of the Abbey might incorporate Tudor window tracery from the Old Palace.

LONDON AND WESTMINSTER

Museum of London, City of London

Human bones from about nine separate burials discovered beneath floor of the Chapel of St Mary Undercroft in 1992.

Fig. 32. *Lower chapel after the fire of October 1834 showing fragments of stonework from the upper chapel (House of Commons Chamber)*, G. Moore
Palace of Westminster Collection, WOA 5195

Two small fragments of the oak roof from Westminster Hall, late 14th century, removed during repairs *c.* 1920. A phile containing the preserved remains of deathwatch beetle from the same source.

Leather key belt holding two keys for the Star Chamber, *c.* 1500, ID no. 27.131/1.

Museum of London Archaeology store, Hackney

Tas-de-charge of an oak truss from Westminster Hall, late 14th century, removed during repairs *c.* 1920.

Floor tile depicting a lion, from St Stephen's Chapel, 13th century.

Fragments of stone trestles from subsidiary table(s) on dais in Westminster Hall, 15th or 16th century.

British Museum, Holborn

Fragments of stone displaying wall-painting from St Stephen's Chapel, *c.* 1349–63 presented to the museum by the Society of Antiquaries of London in 1814. Fragments of mouldings from the chapel that were in the collection of Sir Gilbert Scott (1811–78) were presented to the museum by the architect and antiquary C. R. Baker King in 1883. MLA 83, 3-10, 1-2.

Two painted wooden panels depicting figures, from the ceiling of the Painted Chamber, c. 1263–66. Adam Lee, Labourer in Trust, removed panels from this room in 1816 and it is presumably these panels that were rediscovered in 1993 and then entered the museum. MLA 1995, 4-1.1 and MLA 1995, 4-1.2.[123]

Crozier made from oak and deal, once belonging to William Lyndewode (c. 1375–1446), bishop of St David's; found with the remains of the bishop in January 1852 during Barry's repairs to the Undercroft Chapel. Lyndewode's mummified remains were re-buried in the north cloister of Westminster Abbey in March of the same year.[124]

Sir John Soane's Museum, Lincoln's Inn Fields, Holborn

Entrance Front: four statue pedestals from north front of Westminster Hall (late 14th century), inserted into façade of Soane's house in 1825.[125]

The Monk's Parlour: square wooden patera from the ceiling of the Painted Chamber (after 1263), M 363. Boss of oak in form of rosette, said to come from Painted Chamber (15–16th century), M 118.[126] Wooden model of louvre on Westminster Hall designed by J. W. Hiort for repairs in 1819–20. Hiort's louvre was replaced by F. Baines in 1916, and the latter version was itself replaced in 1947 following war damage (still extant).

The Monk's Yard: 'Cloister' made from two arches of window openings in the old House of Lords (13th century), demolished 1823 to make way for Soane's Royal Gallery. Between these arches, a statue canopy (late 14th century) from the north front of Westminster Hall, removed 1819–20. An arch from the Prince's Chamber, also demolished 1823, stands nearby. Several fragments from St Stephen's Chapel (14th century), removed about 1800.[127]

The West Chamber: stone canopy from the east front of St Stephen's Chapel (1325–34). Below are fragments of cresting from St Stephen's Chapel (14th century).[128] Cast of an Elizabethan chimney-piece from the Exchequer Chamber, the original now in the Tapestry Room of St James's Palace.[129]

Whetstone Park: above door in basement: royal arms once in the Court of King's Bench, rebuilt by Soane 1820–24; papier mâché.[130]

Sir John Soane's Museum also contains drawings and models of the Old Palace.

Victoria & Albert Museum, South Kensington/Hammersmith

Plaster cast of angel termination from a hammer-beam, Westminster Hall roof, c. 1922 (REPRO.A.1922-14).

Plaster casts taken from St Stephen's Chapel and formerly held in the Royal Architectural Museum; transferred to the V&A in 1916 (coupled capital: REPRO.A.1916-1129).

Formerly in Lambeth, whereabouts no longer known

A statue of a king discovered in a garden in Meadow Road, Stockwell in 1928, possibly from the north front of Westminster Hall; restored. It may have been set up somewhere in the borough by Charles Tennyson D'Eyncourt, who was MP for Lambeth in the 1830s and 1840s.[131]

Trinity Church Square, Southwark

A statue of a king possibly from the north front of Westminster Hall, perhaps from one of the higher niches; much restored. It was set up here c. 1825, when the square was first laid out.

Jewel Tower, Westminster

Eight carved capitals, 12th century. Ten capitals and an entablature were discovered by Robert Smirke during his repairs to the walls of Westminster Hall in the 1830s. Two of the capitals and the entablature are now missing.[132]

MARK COLLINS

Palace of Westminster, Westminster

Several large 14th-century statues of kings from the higher niches and gable pinnacle on the north front of Westminster Hall were removed sometime around 1700, but disappeared. Two more 14th-century statues were removed from the south gable pinnacle about 1825–30, and these might be the two statues acquired in 1836 by the MP, Charles Tennyson D'Eyncourt (1784–1861) for use on the exterior of his house, Bayons Manor, at Tealby (Lincolnshire), which he built in the style of a medieval castle during the early 1840s. A new south pinnacle was built by Robert Smirke in 1836, and three copies of the old statues were installed within its niches; these three replacements were given to the Royal Architectural Museum by Sir Charles Barry between 1855 and 1877.[133] On closure of the museum in 1916, the three statues went to the Victoria & Albert Museum; they were then returned to Westminster Hall in 1923 following repairs to its roof, and were placed in window reveals inside. The two original 14th-century statues at Bayons Manor were bought by the Ministry of Works before the demolition of the house and placed next to the others inside the hall in 1963 (these statues were vandalized whilst still at Bayons). All the statues were removed in 2014 for conservation and with the intention of better displaying them at the Palace in the near future.

Fragments forming parts of three Purbeck marble trestles belonging to the king's high table from Westminster Hall, *c.* 1250 (now in storage).

Fragments of Purbeck marble from the 12th-century conduit, and Caen and Huddlestone limestone from the 15th-century conduit; excavated from New Palace Yard (now in storage).

Two (plaster?) roundels of about 1822 by Thomas Banks (1735–1805), one depicting 'Dawn' and the other 'Dusk' were saved when Soane's Scala Regia was demolished in 1851. The roundels were placed in the entrance lobby leading to the house once allocated to the Librarian of the House of Lords, where they remain today.

St James's Palace, Westminster

Tapestry Room: contains an Elizabethan chimney-piece from the Exchequer Chamber. A cast of this fireplace is in the West Chamber (north wall) at Sir John Soane's Museum.[134]

Society of Antiquaries of London, Westminster

Plaster medal of the face of Bishop Lyndewode; made after this mummified body was found in the Chapel of St Mary Undercroft in 1852.

Two fired clay tiles and a Saxon urn found during construction of the Victorian Palace.

Westminster School, Westminster

A wooden door from the Star Chamber in a classroom to the right of the 'Shell', located above the Abbey Museum.

OXFORDSHIRE

St James the Great, Radley

Wooden tester of pulpit. The 16th-century carved oak panelling and tester are said to have once formed the canopy of the Speaker's Chair in the House of Commons' Chamber and were given in 1653 to the church by William Lenthall (1591–1662) of Besselsleigh Manor, Berkshire (now Oxfordshire), Speaker from 1640 to 1653.

SOUVENIRS

Many small trinkets were made from remnants of wood and lead found in the ruins after the fire in 1834 and sold as souvenirs.

The Topography of the Old Palace of Westminster, 1510–1834

NOTES

1. Composite of *Westminster Abbey and Parliament House, from the Thames*, c. 1515–32 (Victoria & Albert Museum, acc. no. E 128-1924) and *Vue de Londres avec Westminster Hall et les édifices environnants* (Musée du Louvre, INV 18702, verso). The drawing, perhaps by Lucas Cornelis de Kock (1495–1552) was split at some time prior to 1750, and the two pieces are now in two different institutions. See A. Saunders 'Westminster Hall: a Sixteenth Century Drawing?', *The London Journal*, 12/1 (June 1986), 29–35. For the development of the Palace site as a whole, see R. A. Brown, H. M. Colvin and A. J. Taylor, *The History of the King's Works: The Middle Ages*, 2 vols (London 1963), I, 491–52; John Crook in this volume, 1–21; and C. Thomas, R. Cowie and J. Sidell, *The royal palace, abbey and town of Westminster on Thorney Island: Archaeological investigations (1991–8) for the London Underground Limited Jubilee Line Extension Project*, MoLAS Monograph 22 (London 2006). For St Stephen's Chapel, the cloister, Painted Chamber, and Westminster Hall, see J. Cherry and N. Stratford ed., *Westminster Kings and the Medieval Palace of Westminster*, British Museum Occasional Paper 115 (London 1995); RCHME, *An Inventory of the Historical Monuments in London*, II: *West London* (London 1925); D. Gerhold, *Westminster Hall: Nine Hundred Years of History* (London 1999); and H. St George Saunders, *Westminster Hall* (London 1951). Also see John Goodall's paper in this volume, 111–19.
2. C. Wilson, 'The Royal Lodgings of Edward III at Windsor Castle: Form, Function, Representation', in *Windsor: Mediaeval Archaeology, Art and Architecture of the Thames Valley*, ed. Laurence Keen and Eileen Scarff, BAA Trans., xxv (Leeds 2002), 15–94, especially figs 12 and 23. See also the drawing illustrated in Fig. 1.
3. For another early view of the Palace, by Antonis van der Wyngaerde (c. 1525–71), c. 1544, see Oxford, Ashmolean Museum, Oxford, WA1950.206.1.
4. N. Williams, *Henry VIII and his Court* (London 1971), 47–48.
5. J. Stow, *Survey of London*, ed. C. L. Kingsford, 2 vols (Oxford 1908), II, 117.
6. J. Crook and R. B. Harris, 'Reconstructing the Lesser Hall: An Interim Report from the Medieval Palace of Westminster Research Project', in *Housing Parliament: Dublin, Edinburgh and Westminster*, ed. C. Jones and S. Kelsey, Parliamentary History 21/1 (Edinburgh 2002), 22–61.
7. H. M. Colvin, D. R. Ransome and J. Summerson, *History of the King's Works*, IV: *1485–1660 (Part II)* (London 1982), 288.
8. Harvey, *English Mediaeval Architects: A Biographical Dictionary Down to 1550*, 2nd edn (London 1987), 215.
9. http://www.british-history.ac.uk/vch/london/vol1/pp566-571 (accessed 23 February 2015).
10. Harvey, *English Mediaeval Architects* (as n. 8), 220, 273.
11. N. Samman, 'The progresses of Henry VIII', in *The Reign of Henry VIII: Politics, Policy and Piety*, ed. D. MacCulloch (Basingstoke 1995), 59–73, at 70.
12. *King's Works* (as n. 7), 287.
13. 28th Henry VIII, Chapter XII, 1536: 'An Act declaring the Limits of the King's Palace of Westminster'.
14. Cannon Row was changed to 'Canon' Row at the instigation of the Parliamentary Works Directorate in 1992 to better reflect the probable origin of the name.
15. See the papers in this volume by Virginia Jansen (89–110) and Christopher Wilson (152–86).
16. Marked as 'Very ancient walls' on the plan of William Capon, engraved by James Basire in 1828 and published by the SAL in 1828, a year after Capon's death: *Plan of the ancient Palace of Westminster, by the late Mr William Capon measured and drawn between 1793 and 1823*; see 'Notes and Remarks, by the late Mr. William Capon, to accompany his Plan of the ancient Palace of Westminster [Read 23d December, 1824.]', SAL, *Vetusta Monumenta*, V (London 1835), 1–7, pl. XLVII. The chambers were demolished in 1823.
17. See *Londinium Feracissimi Angliae Regni Metropolis*, by G. Braun and F. Hogenberg, from *Civitates Orbis Terrarum*, I (first published 1572); the late-16th-century map *Civitas Londinium* attributed to Ralph Agas; and best of all John Norden's 1593 map of Westminster from *Speculum Britanniæ*. On the mill, see also Tim Tatton-Brown, this volume, Part I, 7–8.
18. *King's Works* (as n. 7), 288.
19. I. M. Cooper, 'The Meeting-Places of Parliament in the Ancient Palace of Westminster', *JBAA*, 3rd series, 3 (1938), 97–138, at 127–28.
20. The position of the Court of Surveyors to the south-west of the hall was established during archaeological investigations in 2005–06: B. Barber, N. Holder, C. Philipotts, J. Pearce and B. Richardson, 'Excavations at Cromwell Green and Westminster Hall, 2005–6: further evidence for the development of the medieval and post-medieval Palace of Westminster', *TLMAS*, 64 (2013), 109–41.
21. The court managed lands confiscated by the Crown. The front was later partially covered by two taverns, the Royal Oak and the Coach and Horses; both were taken away in 1808 as part of a move by

Parliament to clear space for the public in New Palace Yard. This court building survived until most of it was demolished in 1793.

22. 'An Acte whereby certaine Chauntries Colleges, Free Chapelles and the Possessions of the same be given to the Kinges Majestie' (1547), 1 Edw.6 CAP. XIV, which came into force in December 1547.

23. See David Harrison in this volume, 133–51.

24. *King's Works* (as n. 7), 291–92.

25. By contrast, its only rival, St George's Windsor, was to remain a royal chapel, and these were the only chantries not abolished.

26. An engraving of the chamber showing the Commons assembled in 1640 shows two statues, one on each side of the window and panelling at low level; British Museum, Prints and Drawings, 1885, 1114.124, 1–3. The panelling appears to have been covered in *trompe l'oeil* barley-sugar twist columns and tall fronds of foliage depicted on the Second Seal of the Commonwealth dated 1651; British Museum, Prints and Drawings, 1880, 0911.1240. Coloured decoration remained into the 19th century on the window mouldings at high level, as may be clearly seen in three watercolours made after the fire of 1834; Palace of Westminster Collection, WOA 260, WOA 1254 and WOA 6925.

27. The Court of Exchequer survived until 1823, when it was demolished and replaced by Soane's new law courts. Seven octagonal wooden columns were removed and names and dates were revealed beneath; see H. M. Colvin ed., 'Views of the Old Palace of Westminster', *Architectural History*, 9 (1966), 21–184, here fig. 68.

28. Ground-plan of St Stephen's Cloister, c. 1593: Hatfield House, Cecil Papers, 24/62; first-floor plan: ibid., 24/61.

29. *King's Works* (as n. 7), 297. The medieval court of law known as the *Sterred Chambre* or *Camera Stellata* was given a more independent status by Henry VII in 1487 and was so named because the ceiling was, as Stow wrote, 'decked with the likeness of Stars guilt'. Stow, *Survey of London* (as n. 5), II, 119–20. Notes appear in the accounts over the years for regilding the stars. The court was abolished during the Long Parliament, beginning in 1641.

30. *King's Works* (as n. 7), 288.

31. See the plans of c. 1664 in TNA, MPE 486.

32. *House of Commons Journal*, I (1547–1629) (London 1802), 256, marginal note, 5 November 1605. Thirteen years later, Old Palace Yard was also the scene of the execution of Sir Walter Raleigh (1552–1618), also on the charge of treason; F. Barker and P. Jackson, *London: 2000 Years of a City and its People* (London 1974), 110–11.

33. H. B. Wheatley and P. Cunningham, *London Past and Present: Its History, Associations and Traditions* (London 1891), 201–02. The origin of these names is not known; they may refer to paintings they possibly once held.

34. See the research for 1604–29 undertaken by the History of Parliament Trust (http://www.historyofparliamentonline.org/volume/1604-1629/member/jones-inigo-1573-1652 [accessed 23 March 2015]), and A. Hawkyard, 'Inigo Jones, the Surveyors of the Works and the "Parliament House"', *Parliamentary History*, 32/1 (2013), 16–59, at 18.

35. *King's Works* (as n. 7), 300.

36. C. G. C. Tite, *The Manuscript Library of Sir Robert Cotton*, Panizzi Lectures 1993 (London 1994), 79–85.

37. For the site of the famous library (in the former Chapel of St Laurence), see John Crook in this volume, 11.

38. A. W. McIntosh, *The Death Warrant of King Charles I*, House of Lords Record Office Memorandum no. 66 (London 1981), 6–15.

39. S. Thurley, *Whitehall Palace: An Architectural History of the Royal Apartments, 1240–1690* (London 1999), 98. Cromwell moved into Whitehall in 1654 and died there four years later.

40. J. Towill Rutt ed., *Diary of Thomas Burton, Esq.*, 4 vols (London 1828), II, 511. See also W. Rodwell, 'The Coronation Chair from the later Middle Ages to the seventeenth century', in idem ed., *The Coronation Chair and Stone of Scone: History, Archaeology and Conservation* (Oxford 2013), 119–32, here 130.

41. V. Horsman and B. Davison, 'The New Palace Yard and Its Fountains: Excavations in the Palace of Westminster 1972–4', *The Antiquaries Journal*, 69/2 (1989), 279–97.

42. The club was founded by the republican James Harrington (1611–77) and it attracted the likes of Milton and Marvell; J. Timbs, *Club Life of London*, 2 vols (London 1866), II, 15.

43. The dais and wall may be seen still *in situ* on *A Ground Plott of Westminster Hall* in F. Sandford, *A History of the Coronation of ... King James II ... and of his royal consort Queen Mary ... on Thursday the 23 April 1685* (London 1687).

44. M. Collins, P. A. Emery, C. Phillpotts, M. Samuel and C. Thomas, 'The King's High Table at the Palace of Westminster', *The Antiquaries Journal*, 92 (2012), 197–243. The table is now kept in storage as part of the Parliamentary Estates Directorate's Architectural Fabric Collection.

45. The doorway may have been cut through for Charles II's coronation banquet, then blocked up and reopened for Viscount Stafford's trial in November 1680, then blocked again, because it no longer appears on the 1685 plan for James II's coronation (as n. 43); see Collins et al., 'The King's High Table' (as n. 44), 229–30, and E. W. Brayley and J. Britton, *The History of the Ancient Palace and Late Houses of Parliament at Westminster* (London 1836), 440.

46. O. C. Williams, 'The Topography of the Old House of Commons: A monograph, with reproductions of relevant plans and drawings' (unpublished typescript, 1953), 3. Three photographic copies of this work were made by the Ministry of Works: one copy for the BL, one for the Ministry of Works' Library, and one for the House of Commons Library.

47. H. M. Colvin, J. Mordaunt Crook, K. Downes and J. Newman, *The History of the King's Works*, V: *1660–1782* (London 1976), 385–418. A makeshift ladies' gallery was provided above the ceiling when women were banished from the Strangers' Gallery in 1778. The view to the floor of the House could only be made through a ventilation shaft above the chandelier, and listening to speeches was difficult.

48. The columns were probably of wrought iron; they were provided by the French designer and contractor for decorative ironwork, Jean Tijou (fl. 1689–1712) shortly after his work for Wren at Hampton Court Palace. See A. W. Skempton ed., *A Biographical Dictionary of Civil Engineers in Great Britain and Ireland*, I: *1500 to 1830* (London 2002), 801–02.

49. J. M. Crook and M. H. Port, *The History of the King's Works*, VI: *1782–1851* (London 1973), 603.

50. *King's Works* (as n. 47), 385–86; the single bell in the clock tower had been the hour bell ('Edward of Westminster', later 'Great Tom of Westminster'), which had been removed in 1698; it was sold to the Dean and Chapter of St Paul's Cathedral, carried by road but broken en route, melted down, recast on two separate occasions - lastly in 1716 - to form new bell ('Great Tom') and hung in the south-west tower, from where it still strikes the hours.

51. During demolition of some remaining lower parts of the gate in June 1807, William Capon found an 11th-century carved capital showing William Rufus and Gislebertus, the abbot of Westminster. The inscription appears to refer to the building of the cloister at the Abbey. Capon sold it to Sir Gregory Osborne Page-Turner, 4th Baronet (1785–1843) for 100 guineas; it is now lost. See 'Antiquarian Researches', *The Gentleman's Magazine*, CI/1 (1831), 545–47, here 545; Brayley and Britton, *History of the Ancient Palace and Late Houses of Parliament* (as n. 45), 416, 444–46 and pl. XXXV; also John McNeill and Stuart Harrison, this volume, Part I, 69–103.

52. TNA, WORK 6/15 and 4/7; *King's Works* (as n. 47), 417–18. The library could well have been completely destroyed in the Palace fire of 1834 had it stayed put; it had been transferred to the nation by Sir Robert Bruce Cotton's grandson through an Act of Parliament in 1701 (12 and 13 William III, chapter 7), and in 1753 it formed one of the three founding collections of books and manuscripts making up the British Museum. See also Eddie Smith, this volume, Part I, 372–415.

53. TNA, WORK 11/363.

54. Lead from the roof was sold to defray the cost of repairing the roof, and the lead was replaced with Westmoreland Slate, 1749–50; TNA, WORK 6/17, 46.

55. The plans are at All Souls College, Oxford: V.4–6 and V.2.

56. Raised to form a two-storey screen in 1755; *King's Works* (as n. 47), 389–90.

57. The 'Act for Building a Bridge across the River Thames, from the New Palace Yard, in the City of Westminster, to the opposite Shore in the County of Surrey' (9 Geo. 2 C. 29) received royal assent in 1736. It was designed by the Swiss engineer Charles Labelye (bap. 1705, d. 1762), and built 1738–50; C. Labelye, *The Present State of Westminster Bridge* (London 1743). It was replaced by the present structure in 1854–62. The last section of the Bridge Street terrace was demolished in September 1864 in preparation for Charles Barry's northern range to New Palace Yard which never materialized because of the cost.

58. See *A Plan of Part of the Ancient City of Westminster*, published by C. Fourdrinier & Co. in 1761; LMA, k126550x.

59. Abingdon Street, leading onto Millbank was once called Lindsay Lane, after Lindsay House nearby, which was later acquired by the earl of Abingdon; before this the road was known as Dirty Lane. The streets to the west around Smith Square were laid out in the first quarter of the 18th century on the former Tothill Fields. These streets were the first to break the former southern boundaries of the Abbey and Palace, although wharves and workshops had been already constructed along the river bank in the 16th century.

60. Almost all the 18th-century houses in the vicinity have gone; a few survive in Great College Street and Canon Row, and only one in Great George Street.

61. For a front elevation drawing, see New York, Columbia University, Avery Architectural Library, IE/5. John Soane carried out alterations to no. 7 and perhaps also to no. 6 in 1792–93, inserting a new staircase

and enclosing a through corridor between the houses to form a hallway. The lion-head masks and the Medusa's head roundel are part of this work. TNA, WORK 5/82, vol. 17.

62. J. Ashbee, *The Jewel Tower* (London 2013), containing earlier pictures of 6 and 7, Old Palace Yard.

63. J. Gwynn, *London and Westminster Improved, Illustrated by Plans. To which is prefixed a Discourse on Publick Magnificence* (London 1766).

64. It was a youthful dream: 'without regard to expense or limits as to space'. Like Wren, Soane wanted tidy vistas and wrote that 'the obstructions which disfigure and hide so much of Westminster Abbey Church — the Chapter House and other ancient structures adjacent, should be removed'; J. Soane, *Designs for Public and Private Buildings* (London 1828), 23, pls XXXII and XXXIII.

65. *Journals of the House of Commons*, 43 (3 June 1788), 531.

66. S. Sawyer, 'Delusions of National Grandeur: Reflections of the Intersection of Architecture and History at the Palace of Westminster, 1789–1834', *Transactions of the Royal Historical Society*, 6/13 (2003), 237–50.

67. H. Colvin, *A Biographical Dictionary of British Architects 1600–1840* (New Haven CT/London 1995, 3rd edn), 1107–08.

68. *The Times*, 23 October 1806, 3, col. 3.

69. J. Topham and H. Englefield, *Some Account of the Collegiate Chapel of St Stephen, Westminster ... from drawings by J. Carter*, issued with fourteen additional plates by J. Dixon, R. Smirke and G. Naylor, commentary by H. C. Englefield, Society of Antiquaries (London 1795–1811).

70. Capon, *Plan of the ancient Palace of Westminster* (as n. 16).

71. A few segments of the wall displaying paintings are now in the British Museum, a gift of the Society of Antiquaries of London. See also Christopher Wilson in this volume, 152–86.

72. John Carter made 'many restorations' on his drawings to help give an understanding of the original appearance; *Description of the Additional Plates of St Stephen's Chapel*, Society of Antiquaries of London (London 1811), notes to pl. XV.

73. J. T. Smith, *Antiquities of Westminster* (London 1807). There followed *Sixty-two additional plates to Smith's Antiquities of Westminster* (London 1807–09).

74. The brother of the architect, Robert Smirke. Richard Smirke's drawings were copied on a large scale in the 1920s by E. W. Tristram (1882–1952), painter and art historian. Tristram's paintings hang in the lobby below the MPs' staircase to the terrace at the Palace of Westminster.

75. The post of auditor of the Exchequer was held by the 2nd duke of Newcastle from 1751, and when he died in 1794, the king appropriated the house to the Speaker. The house was found to be damp, and Charles Abbot, on election to the office of Speaker in 1802, ordered its replacement; Williams, *The Topography of the Old House of Commons* (as n. 46), 19 n. 8.

76. Brayley and Britton, *History of the Ancient Palace and Late Houses of Parliament* (as n. 45), 455–56. In 1826, the kitchen was removed, thereby re-establishing much of the original appearance of the open courtyard of the cloister, although the parapet and pinnacles, which had disappeared many years before, were not replaced at this time, and neither was the tower rebuilt next to its north-west corner. TNA, WORK 1/14, 409, and 5/109.

77. Capon, *Plan of the ancient Palace of Westminster* (as n. 16). According to Ivy Cooper, it was Sir Robert Walpole as auditor of the Exchequer (1739–51) who made the state dining room in the chapel; I. M. Cooper, 'The Meeting-places of Parliament' (as n. 19), 133.

78. A 'picture gallery' and a 'tapestry room' are located in Speaker's House on the plan of the Palace in J. T. Smith's *Antiquities of Westminster* (as n. 73). On the same plan, Smith mentions piles to 'keep off the Craft' discovered in 1803 close by the river wall of the former vicars' houses; this wall was then used as the east wall of the new house for the Speaker.

79. 'Westminster Improvements', *Hansard's Parliamentary Debates*, XI (1808), 863–65.

80. J. Carter, 'The Pursuits of Architectural Innovation. No. XIX. The Antient Palace of the Kings of England at Westminster', *The Gentleman's Magazine*, LXX/1 (1800), 33–36, at 36.

81. *Foundation Plan of the Ancient Palace of Westminster. Measured, Drawn and Engraved by J. T. Smith*, published 25 April 1807. Carter noted on a pencil drawing of 1780 that one statue was destroyed during a previous restoration undertaken in that year; WCA, box 58, no. 37.

82. *King's Works* (as n. 49), 516. The commissioners began in 1800; 41 George III c.13.

83. *The European Magazine and London Review*, 51 (January–June 1807), 178–82.

84. TNA, WORK 1/8, 463; and 1/9, 283, 304–20, 419–21.

85. The Painted Chamber had long held a mythical status, because it was thought to have been the place in which Edward the Confessor died. The earl of Chatham and his son, William Pitt, had both been given the honour of a lying-in-state in the room, in 1778 and 1806 respectively; E. Holt, *The Public and Domestic Life of His Late and Most Gracious Majesty, George the Third*, 2 vols (London 1820), II, 149–51.

86. Crocker's drawings are now at the Ashmolean Museum, Oxford. He was encouraged to paint them by Sir Gregory Osborne Page-Turner, 4th Baronet; J. Alexander and P. Binski ed., *Age of Chivalry: Art in Plantagenet England 1200–1400* (New Haven CT/London 1987), 344.

87. J. G. Rokewode, 'A memoir on the Painted Chamber in the Palace at Westminster (Read 12th May, 1842)', SAL, *Vetusta Monumenta*, VI (London 1885), 1–37, pls XXVI–XXXIX (designs by C. A. Stothard). See also P. Binski, *The Painted Chamber at Westminster*, Society of Antiquaries of London, Occasional Papers, n.s., 9 (London 1986), and Christopher Wilson in this volume, 153–86.

88. TNA, WORK 1/8 and 1/9.

89. See T. Tatton-Brown and R. Mortimer ed., *Westminster Abbey: The Lady Chapel of Henry VII* (Woodbridge 2003).

90. *King's Works* (as n. 49), 503. For the appearance of the hall immediately following Soane's work, see L. N. Cottingham, *Plans, Elevations, Sections and Details at large of Westminster Hall* (London 1822).

91. J. T. Smith plan, published April 1807.

92. Brayley and Britton, *History of the Ancient Palace and Late Houses of Parliament* (as n. 45), 441. TNA, WORK 4/24, 242.

93. For a reconstruction drawing of the original louvre by Jill Atherton, see Julian Munby in this volume, Fig. 3, 128.

94. S. Sawyer, 'Sir John Soane's Symbolic Westminster: The Apotheosis of George IV', *Architectural History*, 39 (1996), 54–76.

95. Following a tradition, George IV stayed in the Speaker's House on the night before the coronation. After the ceremony in the Abbey came the lavish coronation banquet in Westminster Hall, at a cost of £25,184. Subsequent monarchs shied away from holding such banquets. See J. Richardson, *George IV: A Portrait* (London 1966), 221; R. Strong, *Coronation* (London 2005), 374.

96. On the site of the Court of Common Pleas, the Court of Exchequer and Inner Court of Exchequer, and the 'Judges Chambers'; Capon, *Plan of the ancient Palace of Westminster* (as n. 16). Soane's new courts opened in 1826; A. Wedgwood, 'Soane's Law Courts at Westminster', *AA Files*, 24 (1992), 21–40, here 40. See also Soane, *Designs for Public and Private Buildings* (as n. 64), 8–17.

97. M. H. Port ed., *The Houses of Parliament* (New Haven CT/London 1976), 8. Wedgwood, 'Soane's Law Courts' (as n. 96), 36.

98. It cost £9,000 to replace the façade; ibid., 36.

99. For an archaeological assessment of the west side of the hall and a description of the annexe by J. L. Pearson that replaced Soane's courts, see House of Commons, *Report from the Select Committee on Westminster Hall restoration, together with the proceedings of the Committee, minutes of evidence, and appendix* (London 1885).

100. Beside this was the passage down to the landing at Parliament Stairs; see the 1685 plan for James II's coronation (as n. 43).

101. S. Sawyer, 'Sir John Soane and the Late Georgian Origins of the Royal Entrance', in C. and J. Riding ed., *The Houses of Parliament: History, Art, Architecture* (London 2000), 137–47.

102. J. Soane, *A Statement of Facts Respecting the Designs of a New House of Lords, as Ordered by the Lords Commissioners and Humbly Submitted to the Consideration of their Lordships, by John Soane, F.A.S. Architect to the Bank of England, and Member of the Royal Academies of London, Parma and Florence* (1799), 11 (footnote); idem, *Designs for Public and Private Buildings* (as n. 64), 17–19.

103. Together with William Capon, Soane carefully recorded the Prince's Chamber and the old House of Lords, and their demolition. Soane took parts of the Queen's Chamber windows for his collection at his home in Lincoln's Inn Fields. See P. M. Rogers, 'Medieval fragments from the old Palace of Westminster in the Sir John Soane Museum', in *Parliamentary History, Libraries and Records: Essays Presented to Maurice Bond*, ed. H. Cobb (London 1981), 1–8.

104. Soane, *Designs for Public and Private Buildings* (as n. 64), 18.

105. A scheme of paintings depicting eighteen battle scenes was devised for Charles Barry's Royal Gallery in the New Palace of Westminster. In the event only those depicting Trafalgar and Waterloo were executed; London, House of Lords and House of Commons, 'Seventh Report of the Commissioners on the Fine Arts: with Appendix', *Parliamentary Papers, House of Commons 1847 (862)*, XXXIII, Appendix 1, 13. See also T. S. R. Boase, 'The Decoration of the New Palace of Westminster, 1841–1863', *Journal of the Warburg and Courtauld Institutes*, XVII (1954), 319–58, here 342.

106. Soane, *Designs for Public and Private Buildings* (as n. 64); Parliamentary Papers IV, 'Reports from the Select Committee on the possibility of making the House of Commons more commodious and less unwholesome', *House of Commons Sessional Papers no. 308* (1831), 655, and Parliamentary Papers XII, 'Report from the Select Committee on House of Commons' Buildings', *House of Commons Sessional Papers no. 269* (1833), 487.

107. Parliamentary Papers XII, 'Report from the Select Committee on House of Commons' Buildings', *House of Commons Sessional Papers no. 269* (1833), q.929.

108. Parliamentary Papers XI, 'Report from the Select Committee on House of Commons' Buildings', *House of Commons Sessional Papers no. 269*, plans printed 13 May 1833.

109. The Palais de Luxembourg, Paris, which was remodeled 1799–1805 to form a legislature by Jean Chalgrin (1739–1811).

110. Smirke's brother, Sydney, wrote careful archaeological reports on the project in three papers: S. Smirke, 'Remarks on the Architectural History of Westminster Hall: in a Letter from Sydney Smirke, Esq. F.S.A. to Sir Henry Ellis, K.H., F.R.S. Secretary (Read 28th May, 1835)', *Archaeologia*, XXVI (1836), 406–14; idem, 'Second Letter from Sydney Smirke, Esq. F.S.A. to Sir Henry Ellis, K.H., F.R.S. Secretary, on the Architectural History of Westminster Hall (Read 4th February, 1836)', *Archaeologia*, XXVI (1836), 415–21; idem, 'A further Account of the original Architecture of Westminster Hall. In a letter from Sydney Smirke, Esq. F.S.A. to Sir Henry Ellis, K.H., F.R.S. Secretary (Read 2nd February, 1837)', *Archaeologia*, XXVII (1838), 135–39. Robert Smirke's masonry repairs, wall linings, recarved sculpture, cornice and floor remain substantially unaltered today.

111. Brayley and Britton, *History of the Ancient Palace and Late Houses of Parliament* (as n. 45), 441.

112. For a full account of the fire, see C. Shenton, *The Day Parliament Burned Down* (Oxford 2012). See also letter by Frances Rickman to her sister dated 20 October 1834 in the Parliamentary Archives, RIC/3. Frances was the daughter of John Rickman (1771–1840), Clerk Assistant in the Commons, who lived in a house in the south-east corner of New Palace Yard; the letter describes the fire which was still burning at the time.

113. *The Times*, 18 October 1834, 5.

114. A. W. Pugin, letter to E. J. Wilson, 6 November 1834; M. Belcher, *The Collected Letters of A.W.N. Pugin*, 4 vols (Oxford 2001–12), I: *1830 to 1842*, 42.

115. See also the fine sketches (now in the British Museum) by George Scharf Sr; some are published in Peter Jackson, *George Scharf's London: Sketches and Watercolours of a Changing City 1820–50* (London 1987), 130–33. The originals are in vol. III of Scharf's drawings in the Prints and Drawings Department of the British Museum.

116. Brayley and Britton, *History of the Ancient Palace and Late Houses of Parliament* (as n. 45), 464.

117. See Museum of London, watercolours 46.41/1–3.

118. *King's Works* (as n. 49), 534.

119. See Steven Brindle in this volume, 257–69.

120. Brayley and Britton, *History of the Ancient Palace and Late Houses of Parliament* (as n. 45).

121. C. J. Richardson published separately his *Plan of the Parliamentary and other Public Buildings adjacent to Westminster Hall etc.*, in August 1835. The government commissioned Frederick Mackenzie to produce measured drawings of St Stephen's Chapel, but Mackenzie imagined what some portions might have looked like. F. Mackenzie, *The Architectural Antiquities of the Collegiate Chapel of St Stephen, Westminster, the Late House of Commons: Drawn from Actual Survey and Admeasurements Made by Direction of the Commissioners of Her Majesty's Woods and Works etc.* (London 1844).

122. J. Harris, *Moving Rooms: The Trade in Architectural Salvages* (New Haven CT/London 2007), 44.

123. M. Liversidge and P. Binski, 'Two ceiling fragments from the Painted Chamber at Westminster Palace', *The Burlington Magazine*, CXXXVII/1109 (August 1995), 491–501. Lee was later to produce reconstruction drawings and perspectives of St Stephen's Chapel; A. Lee, *Description of the Cosmoramic and Dioramic Delineations of the Ancient Palace of Westminster and St Stephen's Chapel* (London 1831); M. Galinou, 'Adam Lee's drawings of St Stephen's Chapel, Westminster, Antiquarianism and Showmanship in Early 19th Century London', *TLMAS*, XXXIV (1983), 231–44.

124. J. Prior, T. J. Pettigrew, W. J. Thoms, J. Bruce and J. Y. Akerman, 'Report of the Committee appointed by the Council of the Society of Antiquaries to investigate the circumstances attending the recent Discovery of a Body in St Stephen's Chapel, Westminster', *Archaeologia*, XXXIV/2 (1852), 406–30.

125. *A New Description of Sir John Soane's Museum* (London 2001, 10th rev. edn), 3.

126. Ibid., 39–40.

127. Ibid., 39.

128. Ibid., 46.

129. Ibid., 45.

130. Ibid., 34.

131. *Morning Post*, 23 March 1928; WCA, E33.5.

132. Smirke, 'Second Letter' (as n. 11), 419–20.

133. *Architectural Museum, Cannon Row, Parliament Street, Westminster, 1855: Catalogue* (London 1855); *Royal Architectural Museum: Catalogue of Collection, 1877, with a guide to the museum by Sir G. Gilbert Scott* (London 1877).

134. *A New Description of Sir John Soane's Museum* (as n. 125), 45.

The New Palace of Westminster

STEVEN BRINDLE

Much of the Palace of Westminster was destroyed in the great fire of October 1834. The New Palace, built to designs by Sir Charles Barry between 1841 and 1861, is one of the greatest 19th-century buildings in Britain, arguably in the world, and one of the great icons of British culture. This short article summarizes its complex building history, and briefly describes the remarkable partnership between Barry and Augustus Welby Pugin, the extraordinarily talented designer who was responsible for much of the detail of the interiors.

> None the less amazing: Barry's and Pugin's grand
> Dark-lantern above the incumbent Thames.
> (Geoffrey Hill, *To the High Court of Parliament*)

WESTMINSTER has been the heart of the English and British state since the mid-12th century, arguably earlier. Whether one dates its pre-eminence to Edward the Confessor's decision to rebuild Westminster Abbey, to the Conqueror's coronation, to William Rufus's decision to build the Great Hall, or the moment when the annual courts of the Exchequer began to be held there, is a matter of academic interest, but the pre-eminence is an established fact of British culture. Nowhere else in the country has quite so many layers of cultural significance and meaning — historic, political and symbolic — though Windsor runs a close second. The architectural expression of this meaning and the accommodation of the myriad functions that sustain it are shared between two great complexes, the Abbey and the Palace: Church and State. Westminster is unique in Britain, although there are places that seem comparable. Durham's great cathedral, monastery and castle, long the seat of its prince-bishops, is a domestic parallel. The Kremlin in Moscow is perhaps the most directly comparable, in uniting the weight of history with continuing political importance. Hradčany Hill in Prague, still the seat of the Czech president, is a good parallel, as is the Vatican. The Île de la Cité in Paris, an excellent historic parallel to Westminster, today retains only a selection of its functions, chiefly ecclesiastical and judicial. Wawel Hill in Cracow, beautiful as it is, today has historic rather than political significance. Such places are heavy with symbolic importance, and their images have become a visual shorthand for big ideas: the Church, the Crown, the State, the law, government, a whole nation.

The famous fire of October 1834 and the consequent need to replace the medieval Palace with new buildings to house Britain's legislature was therefore an important moment (Fig. 1). The Old Palace had lost the royal private apartments in the fire of 1513 and its function as a royal residence partly as a result, but even this had not been so devastating a break with the past.[1] The massive medieval buildings were clad, inside and out, in an 18th- and 19th-century carapace: by 1800 modest houses, coffee shops and taverns clung, barnacle-like, to the ancient walls. Successive attempts

Fig. 1. After J. M. W. Turner, *The Palace of Westminster on Fire, October 1834*
Palace of Westminster Collection, WOA 273

in the 19th century by official architects — of the likes of James Wyatt (1746–1813), Sir Robert Smirke (1780–1867), and Sir John Soane (1753–1837) — to tidy it up and render it more presentable had largely replaced these accretions with a variety of claddings: the medieval core remained, but its surfaces were now mostly hidden by a series of pragmatically applied layers, some Classical in style, some Gothic and Christian, together constituting an architectural representation of Georgian culture. The discovery of some of the buried layers of the medieval Palace, notably in St Stephen's Chapel and the Painted Chamber, generated antiquarian excitement, but official indifference; this juxtaposition of intense interest and casual destruction, too, was characteristic of the age.[2]

After the fire, there was an urgent need for temporary accommodation. Smirke, one of the former official architects to the Office of Works, repaired and reroofed the Painted Chamber for the House of Lords and the old Lords' Chamber for the House of Commons with remarkable speed: they were ready in February 1835.[3] Smirke hoped to receive the commission for the major rebuilding as well: he prepared designs that Sir Robert Peel's government might have accepted but for the opposition of several members. Parliament appointed a select committee to consider the matter in March 1835; it drew up a brief for the work, requiring that 'the style of the buildings be either Gothic or Elizabethan'.[4] This was a measure of the advance of the Gothic Revival: ten years earlier, it would probably have been neo-Classical. Commissioners were appointed to oversee the resulting competition, for which ninety-seven entries were received. Number 64, by Charles Barry (1795–1860, Fig. 2), was generally felt to be outstanding. The commissioners unanimously agreed that his design bore 'throughout such evidence marks of genius and superiority of talent, as fully to entitle it to the preference we have given it'.[5]

Barry was forty-one when he was declared the winner in May 1836. The works of this self-made man from a modest middle-class background, raised in London, already embraced country houses, churches, schools, and the Travellers' Club in Pall Mall. Most of Barry's works were in varieties of the Classical style, but he was building the new King Edward's School in Birmingham in a richly decorated Perpendicular Gothic manner, close to the style of his competition entry.[6] For his designs for the school and his competition drawings, Barry solicited the help of a remarkable man, Augustus Welby Northmore Pugin (1812–52, Fig. 3), son of a French émigré artist and designer. Pugin had already acquired a remarkable understanding of the Gothic style, assisting his father as a designer and illustrator.[7]

The brief for the competition acknowledged that the New Palace could and should expand onto the Thames foreshore. Barry's revised design of 1836 took full advantage of this, setting the eastward line of his design just inside the allowable limits. The brief also specified that Westminster Hall, saved from the fire by extraordinary efforts, be retained. Barry's design went further, retaining St Stephen's Cloister and the adjacent crypt of St Stephen's Chapel. The brilliance of Barry's planning was a major factor in

FIG. 2. Henry William Pickersgill, *Sir Charles Barry*
Palace of Westminster Collection, WOA 2729

FIG. 3. John Rogers Herbert, *Augustus Welby Northmore Pugin*, 1845
Palace of Westminster Collection, WOA 2586

his success: his competition entry envisaged two main axes, both running north–south. The main one would incorporate the Lords' and Commons' chambers separated by a public lobby, with the royal entrance at the south end, as it had been in the Old Palace. Committee rooms, dining rooms, and libraries would constitute a secondary axis, along the river front. A series of internal courtyards separated them. Barry set his river front at 90° to Westminster Bridge, which placed it at an acute angle to the main axis, giving the building something of a wedge shape. This was criticized; Barry acknowledged the criticisms, and a revised design of 1836 sets out the essentials of the plan as built, with the two main axes running in parallel. A third axis was introduced at ground-floor level, running through a series of enlarged courtyards, to provide for services of all kinds. At the northern and southern ends of the Palace there were now two large courtyards, giving access to a series of official residences, for the Speaker, the librarians, and the clerks to the two houses. The main parts of the building shared a common principal floor level and an upper floor level housing further committee rooms and subsidiary spaces, but the residences at the outer extremities of the building were kept separate, with different floor levels and their own entrances and staircases. Functionally, the plan could be described as a greatly expanded, rationalized and regularized version of the Old Palace, which was natural enough.[8]

Barry's designs for the exterior were equally assured. He adopted a late Perpendicular style, taking his cue from the neighbouring Henry VII Chapel and St Stephen's Cloister, and he devised a regular grid of ornament for his mainly symmetrical façades, balancing this with a carefully controlled asymmetry in the massing and skyline of the huge building (Fig. 4). Late Georgian England had already created numerous large-scale buildings in the Gothic style: a simplified Perpendicular manner was what came most naturally to architects of the previous generation, like Wyatt, the style's basic rectilinearity and capacity for being reduced to formulae rendering it peculiarly comprehensible to the Georgian mind.[9] Pugin recognized this quality in Barry's designs, characterizing them as 'All Grecian, Sir: Tudor details on classic body'.[10] This was not the negative criticism it might seem: Pugin certainly appreciated the outstanding qualities of Barry's design. Pugin's role in the design of the Palace has been a matter of much discussion, but it seems clear that the overall responsibility for the plan, the massing, and the regular organization of the façades was all Barry's. Pugin helped with the competition designs, and helped again with the preparation of detailed drawings in 1836–37, after Barry had won the job: he added much of the building's decorative richness, lifting it to a level far above the mechanical 'Wyatt Gothic' of the previous generation. It may be doubted whether Barry could have done this for himself. Barry was a great architect and a superb manager; Pugin was not, strictly speaking, a great architect, but he was a designer of genius. It was, in many ways, an ideal collaboration.[11]

In April 1837, the official estimates came in at £642,822 for building, though it was acknowledged that there would be numerous additional costs, for purchase of land, embankment, carriage ways, warming and ventilation, furniture, artworks and so on; the total cost was expected to reach £1,000,000.[12] The estimates were approved, and work began that summer, rather sadly, with the demolition of the shell of St Stephen's Chapel above crypt level, as Barry had reported it to be unsafe.[13] In September of that year, the first contract, for the coffer dam, river wall, and part of the foundations, was let to Messrs Lee of Lambeth. Behind the new river wall, a massive bed of mass concrete was to be laid over the whole site. Messrs Lee took a second contract, for more of the foundations. Progress was difficult and slow, but by June 1839 it was far

The New Palace of Westminster

FIG. 4. E. Walker, *The Palace of Westminster from the River*, 1851
Palace of Westminster Collection, WOA 1637

enough advanced for Barry to recommend letting the third contract, for the greater part of the river front.[14] Messrs Lee had performed satisfactorily but slowly, and the next contract was won by a remarkable firm, Grissell & Peto. The company had risen to prominence in the 1830s,[15] carrying out a variety of large engineering jobs, including some of the early contracts for the Great Western Railway.[16] The superstructure of the third contract was begun on 27 April 1840, with Mrs Barry laying the first stone. Grissell & Peto employed about 500 men on the site and were outstandingly good organizers, an ability sustained by imposing a strict discipline on the workforce. This generated discontent, and the work was dogged by strikes in 1841–43, but nevertheless the range was ready to receive its roofs in the spring of 1844.

Progress was being made on the fourth contract, for the 'return' wings towards New Palace Yard and Abingdon Street, by December 1841. The fifth contract, for the huge spinal range of buildings and the Victoria Tower at the south-east corner, was let to Grissell & Peto in August 1842: Barry thought it would cost about £212,249. For the first four years, then, Barry and his contractors had made good progress with their colossal task. Through the mid-1840s, however, the work slowed down, dogged by complexities, some of which were inherent to the project, but more of which were generated for Barry by his clients. First of all, the two houses of parliament had been considering the question of ventilation, a perennial problem in the Old Palace. To contemporary culture, which enjoys high standards of public health and sanitation and is able to take proper drains for granted, this can seem like just another odd Victorian obsession. In London of the 1840s — rife with cholera (with scientific opinion divided as to whether it was transmitted by air or not), and with no proper sewerage system (with the streets and the Thames periodically choked by refuse and raw sewage) — this was a matter of pressing concern.

A Scots chemist, Dr David Boswell Reid, was chosen to design the ventilation of the two temporary chambers. His scheme for the Commons' Chamber was generally a success, while his scheme for the Lords was not. In January 1840, Reid was appointed as the official consultant for the warming and ventilation of the New Palace at a salary of £500. By and large he had the confidence of the Commons, but not of the Lords. Barry was instructed to accommodate Reid's ideas, and Reid was instructed to defer to Barry 'on all points affecting either the Solidity or the Architectural character of the building'. Thus a situation ripe with potential for confusion was created. Reid's scheme turned out to be of megalomaniac extent and complexity. Broadly speaking, it involved taking fresh air from vents at high level, drawing it down through ducts into the basement, warming it to the required temperature, dispersing it by convection through the building through another series of ducts in the wall and floor voids, then drawing it out via ceiling vents through yet another series of riser ducts, back up to roof level, where a final series of ducts would come together in a central tower, not envisaged in Barry's plans, through which the 'vitiated air' would be vented. All this was to be fitted into a building whose plan, outlines and cost were already fixed. As Barry noted, it would take up the entire basement, the entire roof void, and innumerable voids and cavities in the intervening structure, incidentally compromising the building's intended fireproof character.[17]

Dr Reid kept changing his mind as to the details of his scheme, and Barry was driven to distraction trying to obtain clear designs or specifications from him. Thus began a complex series of wrangles that absorbed huge amounts of Barry's time. The tension between Barry and Reid burst into the open in 1845: the architect complained that for lack of information from Reid, all work on the river front had stopped, and fourteen carpenters been laid off. The dispute went through various stages of arbitration (which came down firmly for Barry) and examination by committees of both houses. After over a year of this, the Lords restored Barry's responsibility for completing their house in June 1846, but the Commons stood by Dr Reid. In December 1847, after another year and a half of wrangling, the Treasury was presented with three different estimates for warming and ventilating the Commons' side of the Palace: one each from Barry and Reid, and Barry's calculation of Reid's plan.[18] Reid continued to be responsible for the ventilation and lighting on the Commons side of the building until his dismissal in 1852, immensely complicating Barry's task: Reid's systems never worked properly and had to be drastically simplified.

Dr Reid was probably the greatest of Barry's problems, but he was far from being the only one. There was a protracted dispute over the design and construction of the clock, too complex to summarize here, which ran through most of the 1850s.[19] There were the periodic visitations from the Royal Commission, appointed to oversee work in 1848. There were the independent activities of the separate Fine Art Commission, set up under the chairmanship of the Prince Consort in 1841 to commission works of art for the New Palace; needless to say, Barry was not made a member of it. Then there was the matter of Barry's own remuneration. Barry had assumed at the outset that he would receive the customary 5 per cent fee, to cover the vast amounts of work generated by the project. The Treasury and the Office of Works, nervous of appearing extravagant against a background of economic difficulties, did not make any decision until March 1839, almost three years after Barry had won the competition, when they said that he would receive a lump sum of £25,000, preposterously low in relation to the scale of the project. Barry, undermined by his good faith and reluctance to give up the job, was in a weak negotiating position. For years he protested in vain. By 1849, he pointed out, 'between 8000 and 9000 original drawings and models have been made, a large proportion from my own hand and the remainder under my immediate supervision [...]'.[20] Some years later, after Barry had put the matter in the hands of his solicitor, the Treasury grudgingly conceded a 3 per cent fee for the last few years of work.[21]

There were problems of the usual kind in a project of this scale: problems with the ground, over the supply of Anston magnesian limestone from south Yorkshire, and with the design of the drains. There were more unusual problems relating to Barry's choice of iron as the main roofing material. Complex frames of cast and wrought iron were to carry massively heavy plates of cast iron covered in a layer of zinc: this primitive form of galvanizing failed, the plates began to rust, and eventually had to be painted. Most of the roof-frames and much of Barry's cast-iron plate system remains in place today. All of these, though, were overshadowed by Barry's problems with Dr Reid, with the Treasury and the Office of Works, and with the committees of both houses, which looked over his shoulder and regularly called him in for examination. He was vehemently and publicly criticized by members of both houses throughout the whole protracted story. It was as well that Barry had a strong personality and a forceful character — a weaker man might have crumbled under the strain. Caught between the Treasury, the Works, Dr Reid, the commissions and the committees, the architect's patience wore thin; in his evidence, deference tended to die out, and a truculent asperity set in.[22]

Faced with problems on this scale, and probably the worst clients in Britain, Barry could rely on three great supports. One was his excellent contractors, Grissell & Peto, who took the contract for 'finishings' in December 1844. Another was the team of superb craftsmen working for them and their various subcontractors. The third was

Pugin, who now returned to assist with the decoration of the interior. Pugin had left the scene after helping Barry detail the exterior in 1836–37. In the meantime, he had established his own career as an architect and designer, and had become famous through his extraordinary books championing the Gothic style, among the most remarkable architectural polemics ever written: *Contrasts* (1837), *True Principles of Pointed or Christian Architecture* (1841) and *An Apology for the Revival of Christian Architecture in England* (1843). There is no evidence that Barry and Pugin had met since 1837, but on 3 September 1844, with large parts of the building approaching completion, Barry wrote a remarkable letter:

Dear Pugin, I am in a regular fix respecting the working drawings for the fittings and decorations of the House of Lords [...] Although I have now made up my mind as to the principles and, generally, as to the details for them, including a new design for the throne [...] I am unfortunately unable to get the general drawings into such a definite shape as is requisite for preparing the working details, owing to a lameness in one of my legs [...] Now as I know of no one who can render me such valuable and efficient assistance, I am induced to write to you [...][23]

For £200 a year plus expenses, Pugin agreed to provide drawings and instructions for all the ornamental work in wood, with expenses payable for designs in other materials. One of the most successful design collaborations in British history was thereby relaunched. Pugin had a genius for design. He produced hundreds of original drawings for the detail of the Palace, of which many survive, marvels of vividness and originality, often produced at near-incredible speed.[24] Grissell & Peto had set up their Thames Bank Workshops over the river in Lambeth, where over 200 craftsmen were at work on the fittings for the Palace.[25] Pugin's first great work was detailing the interior of the House of Lords, which was completed in April 1847 (Fig. 5). His charismatic personality, which springs from the pages of his correspondence, became a factor in the project, as he drew in a number of remarkable contractors to realize his designs. Foremost among them was John Hardman Jr of Birmingham, the metalfounder who produced the ornamental brasswork for the Palace. Dissatisfied with the glass-makers chosen by the Fine Art Commission, Pugin persuaded Hardman to turn his hand to stained glass as well.[26] The cabinet-maker John Webb made some of the more elaborate pieces of furniture. Wallpapers, furniture, textiles and carpets, all designed by Pugin, were supplied by the decorators J. G. Crace & Company. The potter Herbert Minton of Stoke on Trent turned his hand to the encaustic tiles which, as Pugin persuaded Barry, were the best surface for the floors of the main circulation spaces.[27]

By March 1848, the main body the building was roofed, and both the great towers were nearing 100 ft in height. The Commons' Chamber was in experimental use from May 1850. The members complained bitterly about its acoustics. The room's proportions were originally similar to those of the Lords' Chamber, but they demanded a lower, canted ceiling, similar to that of their temporary chamber, the installation of which involved halving the surface area of the windows. The alterations were completed by April 1851, marring the proportions of the room and giving it a dark and claustrophobic atmosphere (Fig. 6).[28] The completion of the chamber allowed Barry to order the demolition of the Commons' temporary chamber (the old House of Lords or Court of Requests) in June 1851, and start work on the new façade to Old Palace Yard.[29] It was a sad moment for medievalists, for this was William Rufus's Lesser Hall, and it may have been part of the Confessor's Palace. It was destroyed without record, though much of its foundations must survive under Old Palace Yard, as it was largely outside the footprint of the new building.

The New Palace of Westminster

FIG. 5. Joseph Nash, *The State Opening of Parliament in the House of Lords' Chamber in 1857*, painted 1858
Palace of Westminster Collection, WOA 2941

The top of the clock tower was Pugin's last contribution to the Palace before his tragically premature death, aged forty, in 1852.[30] Barry worked on the Palace until his own death on 12 May 1860, by which time the building had been substantially completed, at a total cost of £2,400,000.[31] The design for the flagstaff atop the magnificent Victoria Tower was on his drawing board. Queen Victoria had used the new Sovereign's Entrance below it for the first time in February 1852, and knighted its architect a few days later. The two houses, however, had never really appreciated Barry. His colleagues in the architectural profession subscribed generously to a memorial for him. Its promoters hoped for a prominent site near St Stephen's Entrance: it was eventually accorded a more modest home on the stairs leading up from the Lower Waiting Hall. Only six MPs out of 658 subscribed to it.[32]

Barry was succeeded as architect to the Palace by his eldest son, Edward Middleton Barry. A fair amount remained to be done, and Barry Jr's work is marked outside by his use of Portland Stone on the arcades and piers around New Palace Yard. His masterpiece at the Palace of Westminster was his redecoration of the Crypt Chapel, the lower storey of Edward I's St Stephen's Chapel, in a rich High Victorian style that

STEVEN BRINDLE

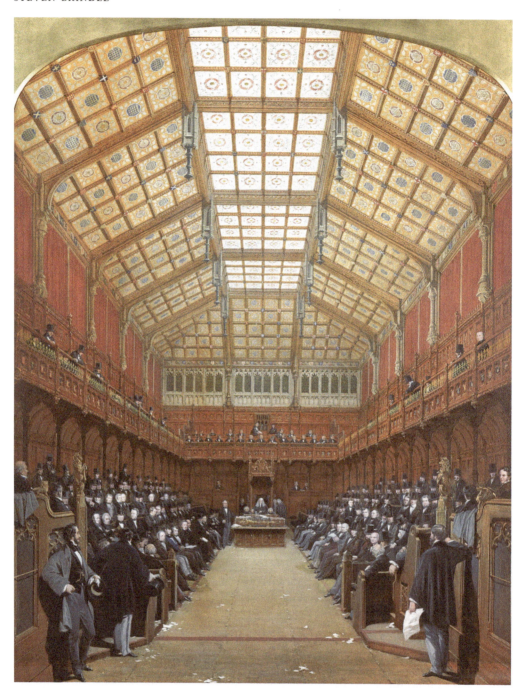

FIG. 6. Joseph Nash, *The House of Commons' Chamber in 1858*
Palace of Westminster Collection, WOA 2934

The New Palace of Westminster

is quite distinct from Pugin Sr's work.[33] E. M. Barry's work there was overshadowed by a sad and very public dispute between him and Pugin's family who felt, with some reason, that their father's tremendous achievements there had not been properly acknowleged.[34] In 1870, E. M. Barry was dismissed as architect to the New Palace by a new First Commissioner of Works, with insulting bluntness.[35]

Barry and Pugin's Palace changed remarkably little between 1870 and the Second World War. The prestige of the 'Mother of Parliaments' was at its peak, and the great building became its great symbol. Further artworks were commissioned, murals from themes in English history that have been derided, but which can now be appreciated as enjoyable works of narrative art. The mosaics in St Stephen's Hall and the Central Lobby designed by Sir Edward Poynter and Robert Anning Bell are at a higher artistic level.[36]

On 11 May 1941, the Commons' Chamber received a direct hit from a German incendiary bomb and was completely destroyed (Fig. 7). Until October 1950, the Commons sat in the Lords' Chamber, while the lords sat in the adjacent Royal Gallery. For Churchill and his government, who had been engaged in the most desperate struggle in Britain's history, the rebuilding had to emphasize tradition and continuity over radicalism and a break with the past: the new chamber was built to follow

FIG. 7. A marked-up photograph of an engraving by William Washington of the House of Commons' Chamber after it was gutted by an incendiary bomb on 11 May 1941
Palace of Westminster, WOA 2386

the form and plan of the old closely. A Gothic design was similarly inevitable, and the architect, Sir Giles Gilbert Scott (1880–1960), was chosen largely on the strength of his responsibility for the astonishing new Anglican Cathedral in Liverpool. Scott achieved remarkable things in his new Commons' Chamber, built 1946–50, fulfilling his brief perfectly, while reinterpreting Barry and Pugin's architecture in a way that is wholly complementary and wholly original.[37] Not even his skill, though, could improve the proportions of the room he was required to recreate.

Since then, the Palace has coped with waves of change. The need for members of both houses to have offices with space for secretaries and assistants, the increasing complexity of legislation, and the huge expansion in the work of the committees have placed new pressures on the building, vastly greater than anything Barry could have envisaged. The old residences, other than the Speaker's house, have mainly been converted into offices: the drawing room of the clerk of the House of Commons, for example, is now the Prime Minister's office. Further office-blocks have been created within courtyards and on the roofs. This has not sufficed, of course: the two houses have spread into other buildings, down Millbank, in Richard Norman Shaw's former Metropolitan Police headquarters on Canon Row, and in the new Portcullis House across Bridge Street. A dedicated organization, the Parliamentary Works Directorate, has run the estate since 1992: during each summer recess it oversees the great annual labours that are needed to maintain the Palace and adapt it for the modern world. In recent years, it has received a new data and video network, fire compartmentation, reinforced secondary glazing, and new catering facilities, among other things. At the same time, Barry and Pugin's fabric has been treated with exemplary care based on thorough research. Barry's Anston stone has fared badly in London's polluted atmosphere. It failed very quickly, with experiments on stone preservation techniques beginning in the 1860s. The Proceedings of the Royal Institute of British Architects report the discussions and results from about 1861. Charles Barry was dead, but his son took a lot of the blame — partly because he used Portland, so knew of the failure. The row clearly affected MPs' views of the Barrys. All the façades have now been cleaned, and large areas have been refaced using the harder-wearing Clipsham stone. Much of the carved work had to be renewed, and this has been done superbly well. Inside, all the works listed above, and many more, have been carried out with the greatest care for Pugin's decoration. In many places, where his work had been obliterated or covered up, it has been restored: ceilings have been repainted, wallpapers restored, furniture repaired, and stonework cleaned. A long programme of work to replicate the worn areas of the Minton tile floors is now in progress.[38] Nevertheless, these alterations have inevitably been piecemeal in nature. Many of the building's services still require complete replacement, and recent reports have suggested that the only way to achieve this would be to empty the building, either half of it at a time, or the whole of it. If this happens, it will be the first time that Parliament has ever left the Palace of Westminster.

Each year, the Queen visits Parliament for the state opening, and the New Palace comes into its own on these occasions. The building, like the ceremony, does so much to impart a uniquely British flavour to our legislature, adding dignity and a sense of continuity to our democracy. It keeps the Gothic style alive as part of the setting of our public life, endlessly recycled in television images, newspaper photographs, and cartoons. Barry and Pugin's Palace have become an indelible part of British identity at home and abroad: their clock tower and the sound of its bells are our symbol of symbols.

The New Palace of Westminster

NOTES

1. H. Colvin ed., D. R. Ransome and J. Summerson, *The History of the King's Work*, IV: *1485–1660 Part II* (London 1982); S. Bradley and N. Pevsner, *The Buildings of England, London 6: Westminster* (Yale/London/New Haven CT 2003), 212–14.
2. J. Mordaunt Crook and M. H. Port, *The History of the King's Works*, VI: *1782–1851* (London 1973), 496–532.
3. Ibid., 573–76.
4. Ibid., 575–78; B. Cocks, *Mid-Victorian Masterpiece* (London 1977), 28–29.
5. *King's Works* (as n. 2), 577–79.
6. Cocks, *Mid-Victorian Masterpiece* (as n. 4), 22–28; H. M. Colvin, *Biographical Dictionary of British Architects, 1600-1840* (London/New Haven CT 1996, 3rd edn), 101–05. The main published biography is still that by his son the Reverend Alfred Barry, *The Life and Works of Sir Charles Barry, R.A., F.R.S.* (London 1867).
7. A. Wedgwood, 'The Early Years', in *Pugin: A Gothic Passion*, ed. P. Atterbury and C. Wainwright (London/New Haven CT 1994), 23–33; R. Hill, *God's Architect: Pugin & the Building of Romantic Britain* (London 2007), chapters 1–4.
8. *King's Works* (as n. 2), 580–85. Bradley and Pevsner, *Westminster* (as n. 1), 214–16.
9. A. Wedgwood, 'The New Palace of Westminster', in *Pugin: A Gothic Passion* (as n. 7), 219–36.
10. Ibid., 221.
11. *King's Works* (as n. 2), 588–94; Wedgwood, 'New Palace' (as n. 9), 224–25, 236; Bradley and Pevsner, *Westminster* (as n. 1), 216–18.
12. *King's Works* (as n. 2), 601.
13. Ibid., 601 and n. 7.
14. Ibid., 601–03.
15. Ibid., 602–04.
16. J. Cox, *Samuel Morton Peto (1809–1889): The Achievements and Failings of a Great Railway Developer* (Oxford 2008), 13–19.
17. *King's Works* (as n. 2), 603–20; Cocks, *Mid-Victorian Masterpiece* (as n. 4), 42–47, 56–60.
18. *King's Works* (as n. 2), 616–19.
19. Cocks, *Mid-Victorian Masterpiece* (as n. 4), 68–73; *King's Works* (as n. 2), 621.
20. Cocks, *Mid-Victorian Masterpiece* (as n. 4), 37.
21. Ibid., 34–41.
22. Ibid., 52–55.
23. Quoted in Wedgwood, 'New Palace' (as n. 9), 223.
24. Several of the designs are illustrated in *Pugin: A Gothic Passion* (as n. 7).
25. Wedgwood, 'New Palace' (as n. 9), 224–27.
26. Ibid., 228–33; A. Eatwell and A. North, 'Metalwork', in *Pugin: A Gothic Passion* (as n. 7), 172–84.
27. Wedgwood, 'New Palace' (as n. 9), 231–33; P. Atterbury, 'Ceramics', in *Pugin: A Gothic Passion* (as n. 7), 143–52, esp. 146–49.
28. *King's Works* (as n. 2), 621–24.
29. Ibid., 625.
30. Hill, *God's Architect* (as n. 7), 480–82.
31. *King's Works* (as n. 2), 625–26.
32. Cocks, *Mid-Victorian Masterpiece* (as n. 4), 85–87.
33. Wedgwood, 'New Palace' (as n. 24, 2000), 133–34.
34. *King's Works* (as n. 2), 588–95; Cocks, *Mid-Victorian Masterpiece* (as n. 4), 91–92
35. Cocks, *Mid-Victorian Masterpiece* (as n. 4), 88–107.
36. W. Vaughan, '"God Help the Minister who Meddles in Art": History Painting in the New Palace of Westminster', in *The Houses of Parliament* (as n. 24), 225–40.
37. G. Stamp, '"We Shape Our Buildings and Afterwards Our Buildings Shape Us": Sir Giles Gilbert Scott and the Rebuilding of the House of Commons', in *The Houses of Parliament* (as n. 24), 149–61.
38. This paragraph is written from the author's own experience as English Heritage's Inspector of Ancient Monuments and Historic Buildings, responsible for advice relating to the Palace and for liaising with the Parliamentary Works Directorate, 1993–2001.

Previous Volumes in the Series

I. *Medieval Art and Architecture at Worcester Cathedral* (1978), ed. G. Popper
II. *Medieval Art and Architecture at Ely Cathedral* (1979), ed. N. Coldstream and P. Draper
III. *Medieval Art and Architecture at Durham Cathedral* (1980), ed. N. Coldstream and P. Draper
IV. *Medieval Art and Architecture at Wells and Glastonbury* (1981), ed. N. Coldstream and P. Draper
V. *Medieval Art and Architecture at Canterbury before 1220* (1982), ed. N. Coldstream and P. Draper
VI. *Medieval Art and Architecture at Winchester Cathedral* (1983), ed. T. A. Heslop and V. Sekules
VII. *Medieval Art and Architecture at Gloucester and Tewkesbury* (1985), ed. T. A. Heslop and V. Sekules
VIII. *Medieval Art and Architecture at Lincoln Cathedral* (1986), ed. T. A. Heslop and V. Sekules
IX. *Medieval Art and Architecture in the East Riding of Yorkshire* (1989), ed. C. Wilson
X. *Medieval Art, Architecture and Archaeology in London* (1990), ed. L. Grant
XI. *Medieval Art and Architecture at Exeter Cathedral* (1991), ed. F. Kelly
XII. *Medieval Art, Architecture and Archaeology at Rouen* (1993), ed. J. Stratford
XIII. *Medieval Art and Architecture at Lichfield* (1993), ed. J. Maddison
XIV. *Medieval Art and Architecture in the Diocese of St Andrews* (1994), ed. J. Higgitt
XV. *Medieval Art, Architecture and Archaeology at Hereford* (1995), ed. D. Whitehead
XVI. *Yorkshire Monasticism: Archaeology, Art and Architecture* (1995), ed. L. R. Hoey
XVII. *Medieval Art and Architecture at Salisbury Cathedral* (1996), ed. L. Keen and T. Cocke
XVIII. *Utrecht, Britain and the Continent: Archaeology, Art and Architecture* (1996), ed. E. de Bièvre
XIX. *'Almost the Richest City': Bristol in the Middle Ages* (1997), ed. L. Keen
XX. *Medieval Art, Architecture, Archaeology and Economy at Bury St Edmunds* (1998), ed. A. Gransden
XXI. *Southwell and Nottinghamshire: Medieval Art, Architecture, and Industry* (1998), ed. J. S. Alexander
XXII. *Medieval Archaeology, Art and Architecture at Chester* (2000), ed. A. Thacker
XXIII. *Medieval Art and Architecture in the Diocese of Glasgow* (1999), ed. R. Fawcett
XXIV. *Alban and St Albans: Roman and Medieval Architecture, Art and Archaeology* (2001), ed. M. Henig and P. Lindley
XXV. *Windsor: Medieval Archaeology, Art and Architecture of the Thames Valley* (2002), ed. L. Keen and E. Scarff
XXVI. *Anjou: Medieval Art, Architecture and Archaeology* (2003), ed. J. McNeill and D. Prigent
XXVII. *Carlisle and Cumbria: Roman and Medieval Architecture, Art and Archaeology* (2004), ed. M. McCarthy and D. Weston
XXVIII. *Medieval Art, Architecture and Archaeology at Rochester* (2006), ed. T. Ayers and T. Tatton-Brown
XXIX. *Cardiff: Architecture and Archaeology in the Medieval Diocese of Llandaff* (2006), ed. J. R. Kenyon and D. M. Williams
XXX. *Mainz and the Middle Rhine Valley: Medieval Art, Architecture and Archaeology* (2007), ed. U. Engel and A. Gajewski
XXXI. *King's Lynn and the Fens: Medieval Art, Architecture and Archaeology* (2008), ed. J. McNeill
XXXII. *Prague and Bohemia: Medieval Art, Architecture and Cultural Exchange in Central Europe* (2009), ed. Z. Opacic
XXXIII. *Coventry: Medieval Art, Architecture and Archaeology in the City and its Vicinity* (2011), ed. L. Monckton and R. K. Morris
XXXIV. *Limerick and South-West Ireland: Medieval Art and Architecture* (2011), ed. R. Stalley
XXXV. *Medieval Art, Architecture and Archaeology at Canterbury* (2013), ed. A. Bovey
XXXVI. *Newcastle and Northumberland: Roman and Medieval Architecture and Art* (2013), ed. J. Ashbee and J. Luxford
XXXVII. *Medieval Art, Architecture and Archaeology in Cracow and Lesser Poland* (2014), ed. A. Rożnowska-Sadraei and T. Węcławowicz
XXXVIII. *Norwich: Medieval and Early Modern Art, Architecture and Archaeology* (2015), ed. T. A. Heslop and Helen E. Lunnon